Minority Literatures and Modernism:
Scots, Breton, and Occitan, 1920–1990

A lively renascence of literature written in minority languages has been taking place in Europe. In this study, William Calin offers a comparative analysis of three twentieth-century minority-language literatures flourishing today in the United Kingdom and France – literatures written in Scots, Breton, and Occitan.

For each of the three literatures, Calin examines the major writers and their masterpieces in poetry, the novel, and theatre. His thesis is that all three literatures have evolved in a like manner, repudiating their sentimental, romantic folk heritage and undertaking to create in terms of European modernism and postmodernism. Combining a variety of modern critical approaches with theoretical and cultural considerations, Calin demonstrates the intrinsic importance of these literatures and their contribution to culture in both aesthetic and broadly human terms. His conclusion raises a number of questions: Is there a common form of narrative prevalent in minority cultures that is neither realism nor metafiction? Is the minority-language theatre limited to plots treating past history and the rural present? How can high modernist poetry express regional concerns yet attain universality? What constraints are imposed on writers working in minority languages, and what traits will be shared by minority literatures?

Calin's pioneering study is the first comparative examination of the Scots, Breton, and Occitan achievements as parts of an international, European totality, underscoring in comparative terms their contribution to Europe as a whole.

WILLIAM CALIN is Graduate Research Professor of Romance Languages, University of Florida, and author of *A Muse for Heroes: Nine Centuries of the Epic in France* and *The French Tradition* and *The Literature of Medieval England.*

MINORITY LITERATURES AND MODERNISM

Scots, Breton, and Occitan, 1920–1990

William Calin

UNIVERSITY OF TORONTO PRESS
Toronto Buffalo London

ISBN 0-8020-4836-6 (cloth)
ISBN 0-8020-8365-X (paper)

Printed on acid-free paper

University of Toronto Romance Series

Canadian Cataloguing in Publication Data

Calin, William
Minority literatures and modernism : Scots, Breton, and Occitan, 1920–1990

(University of Toronto romance series)
Includes bibliographical references and index.
ISBN 0-8020-4836-6 (bound)   ISBN 0-8020-8365-X (pbk.)

1. Breton literature – 20th century – History and criticism.   2. Occitan
literature – 20th century – History and criticism.   3. Scottish literature –
20th century – History and criticism.   4. Modernism (Literature).
5. Literature, Comparative.   I. Title.   II. Series.

PN56M54C34 2000   809′.9112   C00-931241-2

University of Toronto Press acknowledges the financial assistance to its
publishing program of the Canada Council for the Arts and the Ontario
Arts Council.

University of Toronto Press acknowledges the financial support for its
publishing activities of the Government of Canada through the Book
Publishing Industry Development Program (BPIDP).

To Roparz Hemon

In memoriam

CONTENTS

ACKNOWLEDGMENTS

I am beholden to colleagues who have given unstintingly of their time, counsel, expertise, and good wishes. Especially with this kind of project, for me people will ever be associated with place – in Montpellier, Philippe Gardy, Gérard Gouiran, Danielle Julien, Robert Lafont, Philippe Martel, François Pic, and Yves Toti; in Rennes, Per Denez, Francis Favereau, Yann-Ber Piriou, and André Ropars; in Paris and North Carolina, Paol Keineg; in Edinburgh, Philip Bennett, Ian Campbell, Cairns Craig, Peter Jones, and John Renwick; in Massachusetts, Patrick Ford and René Galand / Reun ar C'halan; in California, Marc Bertrand; and in Florida, Andrés Avellaneda, Edward Baker, and Geraldine Nichols.

Much of the academic year 1996–7 I spent in France on a fellowship from the American Council of Learned Societies, and the spring and summer of 1997 as Visiting Research Fellow at the Institute for Advanced Studies in the Humanities, University of Edinburgh. Without subvention from the American Council of Learned Societies and from the University of Florida Research Foundation, this book would never have been completed nor published.

I wish to express gratitude to the anonymous readers for the University of Toronto Press; to superb senior editors at the Press, Ron Schoeffel and Anne Forte; to my copy-editor, Theresa Griffin; and to Ruth Pincoe, who read proof and made the index. And special thanks to my graduate student research assistants Elizabeth Droppleman, Traci Browning, and Jeannine Arias.

MINORITY LITERATURES AND MODERNISM

INTRODUCTION

Europe today contains between seventy and seventy-five autoctonal languages, ranging from the tongue with the most native speakers, Russian, to the one with the least, Manx. These include, therefore, both languages of wider currency ('langues de grande diffusion') and lesser-used languages ('langues moins répandues'). Some thirty-five of the autoctonal languages can be designated 'minority languages.'[1] This means that, within a particular nation-state, they are spoken by a minority of the inhabitants and, in most cases, do not enjoy the benefits and privileges accorded to a national language. The status of the minority languages, their cultural development, how they are considered both by their own speakers and by the majority language users, will vary enormously from country to country and from tradition to tradition. The kind of literature produced, how it reflects linguistic and national sentiment, how it copes with the history of the minority culture and with the presence of the dominant culture, will also vary from country to country. Within the nations of Western Europe, with their long and brilliant traditions of national culture, we often ignore the minority or regional languages and literatures. Yet their existence and their contribution to civilization both past and present are as great as those of minority languages and literatures anywhere on the face of the globe. They become particularly worthy of scrutiny at this moment, when the European community is ready to promote minority languages as part of a European cultural model.

This book offers a comparative analysis of three twentieth-century minority-language literatures which flourish today inside the borders of the United Kingdom and France – literatures written in Scots, Breton, and Occitan.

Occitan, or, as it is sometimes still called, Provençal, is an independent romance language spoken in the South of France. Occitan, like French, evolved from the Latin spoken in Gaul. Eight centuries ago it was the lan-

guage of the troubadours, poets who created courtly love and the medieval courtly lyric, one of the high points of Western civilization. Over the
centuries Occitan never died out, though it did evolve (decline) from a
literary koine and high court speech to the level of local patois. Over the
centuries the literature fell into decline, yet the periods of decline alternated with a number of renascences: during the Baroque age, in the
nineteenth century, and, above all, over the last forty to forty-five years,
which have witnessed a most exciting literary revival.

Scots, or, as it is sometimes called, Lallans, is an independent Anglic
or Anglo-Saxon language (some would say a variety of English; I believe
they are in error) spoken in the Scottish lowlands. Scots, like English,
evolved from the Anglo-Saxon speech introduced into Britain at the
time of the Germanic invasions. Its history is remarkably, phenomenally
similar to that of Occitan. In the late Middle Ages and early Renaissance
the King's Scots in Edinburgh was comparable in dignity and prestige to
the King's English in London. Scots was the language of the Scottish
court and the medium for a rich literary production (with Henryson,
Dunbar, Douglas, Lindsay, and others) which far surpassed in quality
what was written during the same period in English. Over the centuries
Scots, like Occitan, never died out, though it too evolved (declined)
from a literary koine and high court speech to the level of local patois.
Here too, over the centuries the literature fell into decline, yet the periods of decline alternated with periods of renascence: during the age of
Fergusson, Ramsay, and Burns; and, above all, since the 1920s, the age
of the modern Scottish Renaissance.

Breton is the Celtic language spoken in Brittany. Related directly to
Welsh and Cornish (the latter now extinct as a grass-roots language),
Breton was introduced on the Continent, primarily during the period
from the fifth to the seventh centuries, by settlers (invaders, refugees,
missionaries) from Cornwall, Devon, and Wales who were fleeing the
Anglo-Saxon, Irish, and Pictish incursions into their lands. Influenced
by the surviving Gaulish substratum, Breton evolved from the British or
Brittonic speech of these settlers. It is, then, a sister language to Cornish
and a sister or close cousin to modern Welsh, related to Welsh much as
Scots is to English and Occitan to French. From the early tenth century
the Breton nobility began to adopt French (Gallo-Romance) as its court
speech, and the capitals – Rennes and Nantes – were situated in a non-
Breton speaking area. Thus, in contrast to Irish and Welsh, Breton produced no major written literature prior to the nineteenth century and,
some would say, none prior to the twentieth century. The nineteenth-

century revival – the equivalent of Burns and Mistral – is centred on the collection-adaptation of folk-songs, Villemarqué's *Barzaz Breiz*.[2] The oral tradition – including folk-songs and narrative, in prose and in verse – was magnificent. However, the language itself was treated as an inferior idiom, as it had been treated for centuries. In this context, the superb modern literary Renaissance in Breton begins in the 1920s yet really bears fruit, in major artistic production, from the 1940s to the present.

Whatever their linguistic differences (they are not all of a kind), the three languages are the determining factor in the culture of political minorities that can be identified by the way they speak; and they partake of a similar cultural history. Whatever their differences in terms of literature, by 1900 or 1920 all three languages – Scots, Breton, and Occitan – had fallen to the level of local patois, lacking prestige and dignity. It was assumed, by native speakers at home and by cultural elites in London and Paris, that these languages were mere regional dialects, socially unacceptable, practised by low-class and uneducated people, unfit for modern uses, and of interest only to extremists and antiquarians. In sociolinguistic terms they were restricted codes, from every point of view. The preceding tradition, against which today's intellectuals react so strongly, is this linguistic context and also the nineteenth-century cultural context. Whatever the merits of Burns and Scott, the *Barzaz Breiz*, and Mistral and Aubanel, by 1900 or 1920 all three regions had given rise to an 'official' local culture derived in part from these classics of the earlier revival. Kailyard novels and Whistle-Binkie poems; Celtic folk-songs, folk-tales, and religious propaganda; Provençal reworking of the old 'empire of the sun' and 'Latin race' – this tradition was remarkably similar in all three language regions. It was, *grosso modo*, a sentimental, romantic, folk heritage. The writers and publicists of the time declared themselves to be rural, poetic, traditionalist, and Christian (Presbyterian in Scotland, Catholic in Brittany and Provence) as opposed to central English and French modernity assimilated to the city, progress, industrialization, reason, parliamentary democracy or the Republic, and free thought. Provincial identity was grounded in a vision of the past: exaltation of authentic Scottish, Breton, and Provençal life of the soil, idealized whether it was the immediate rural past, the Middle Ages, or some in-between realm presumed to be a Golden Age of nobility and adventure.

One explanation for this phenomenon is that, in Scotland, Brittany, and Provence, as in Russia, Hungary, and Romania, the nineteenth-century renascence and the culture to which it gave rise are a school and movement of romanticism, given that romanticism was intimately bound to the cult of the native language and to the cultivation of a national poetic consciousness. Therefore, the renascence was saturated with all the elements that characterize European romanticism: relative formal traditionalism, the exaltation of nature and the individual, a certain rustic primitivism, nostalgia for the national past, cultivation of personal sentiment and sentimentality, and, in a number of major figures though not all, what would appear later to have been a political stance on the Right or, at the least, a resolutely apolitical stance oriented toward art for art's sake.

A second explanation, in line with postcolonial theory, would state that the minority culture accepts the dominant Self's vision of itself and willingly becomes Other vis-à-vis that Self. Hence the myths of rural primitivism, the myths of nostalgia. Hence also the fact that the dominant culture (London, Paris) adopted without a struggle the Scottish, Breton, and Occitan myths which had become a culture of cliché: Scotch whisky, Breton cider, and Rhône wine; charming, eccentric ministers and curés; dashing youths who become soldiers or sailors; sweet young maidens at home; sacrifice and backwardness; lost causes and shallow hygiene; country dances and festivities; 'typical' emotional extremes of choler and melancholy; and candour, simplicity, and naïvety. All this was adopted, indeed welcomed in London and Paris as a charming eccentric Other that offered no threat and no promise of a serious movement for political autonomy or cultural renewal. Indeed, the dominant culture to some extent itself invented the dichotomy and the parameters of a cultural discourse that called for the dichotomy.

It is the thesis of this book that in the twentieth century the three literatures – Scots, Breton, and Occitan – each independent of the others, evolved in a like manner. In all three, writers – independently – repudiated the sentimental, romantic folk heritage. In all three, they undertook to engage totally in European modernity by creating in terms of European modernism. From the 1920s to the 1940s and 1950s forward-looking intellectuals in all three regions sensed that the forms assumed by their culture had to be renewed. The renewal meant replacing nostalgia for the rural, traditional past by literature grounded in the present – in modern, urban life. In Scotland and Brittany, in the regions of Oc, and in Eastern Europe modernism was to take the form of anti-romanticism and to adopt as its generic traits formal innovation; social realism; an urban as well as a rural décor; the cultivation of a wider range of language and of genre including prose fiction; the refusal of sentimental nostalgia for the past; the refusal of what the French call, with distaste, *du folklore*; and, in many, a political stance resolutely on the Left or, at least, to the left of their predecessors.

In Eastern Europe intellectuals are so conscious of culture and of the need to extol the national past that they have had a tendency to consider, rightly or wrongly, Mayakovsky and Brodsky as the natural inheritors of Pushkin and Lermontov, and Blaga and Arghezi as the natural inheritors of Alecsandri and Eminescu. Perhaps the best they could do, under the Red Terror, was to think of the national patrimony as harmonious and one, and to defend it with passion.

Also, by the time of Mayakovsky and Blaga their lands had achieved independence from native and foreign autocracy. They were no longer living the colonial condition. Whereas, on the contrary, in Scotland, Brittany, and Southern France, lands containing a minority (and still colonized) culture, the situation was different. It was necessary to wrest free from what was perceived as the ideological fetters of the romantic heritage become a culture of cliché. For this reason the moderns in Scotland and Occitania proclaimed their modernity by thrusting away Burns and Mistral – fathers whose weight threatened to be mortal – and by rehabilitating an older, more authentic cultural past, closer to the totality of life and to the language in its vital totality. Hence the structures of repudiation which, elsewhere, I claim to be inherent in literary history since the Middle Ages, hence the strong sons of modernism throwing off the fathers and reclaiming worthy grandfathers from the Middle Ages.[3] Hugh MacDiarmid's cry in Scotland was 'Dunbar! not Burns.' Since the 1940s, in the South of France, where writers have turned to the troubadours for inspiration, their cry was or could have been 'Guilhem, Bernat, Arnaut, Guiraut, Peire! et non Mistral.' In Brittany, where there was no comparable medieval heritage, writers invented or appropriated one. They claimed as their own medieval literature in Welsh, and Arthurian romance, called in French *roman breton,* which, they believed, was of Breton origin.

In terms of language, intellectuals in all three regions called for the creation of a high-culture tongue that would be capable of functioning in all ways that English and French are wont to do. It would be more learned and, at the same time, more all-embracing. On the agenda were the following: lexical enrichment of the vernacular (spoken and written) to be obtained by consulting scholarly lexicons and by returning to earlier stages in the culture, again the Middle Ages, or, in the case of Breton, by borrowing from other Celtic languages; a bridging of the dialects and the attainment of a form of linguistic unity by adopting a uniform, unified, 'rational' orthography and/or by writing in a central literary koine intelligible to all educated readers in the language; the creation of scholarly, standardized dictionaries and grammars; the translation of classics from foreign tongues; and use of the language as an arm in the struggle for cultural and, if possible, political autonomy.

The writers and intellectuals called for a literature open to the modern world to replace provincial and village narrowness, a literature modern in all respects, and insisted that this literature of modernity alone would make Scots or Breton or Occitan worthy of being a truly European language and part and parcel of European culture. It alone would be capable of rising to the same heights as the ancient classics in the culture, would renew the presumed ancient dignity of the culture and language, and thus would provide historical continuity with that past. It would then become, as French literature is for speakers of French throughout the world, the most precious heritage of the people and the mark of their identity. To do this, the Scottish, Breton, and Occitan writers prescribed and often practised difficult, modern poetry exploiting the entire historical range of verse, metre, and diction in the language; fiction – brief and extended – set in an urban as well as rural locus and treating complex modern social and ideological themes in narratologically innovative forms; and a serious theatre, both comic and tragic, both historical and contemporary, that would again be comparable to and capable of rivalling the dominant theatre of London and Paris.

The modernist rebellion, in Occitania as in Brittany, and in Scotland also, did not occur without opposition, fierce and righteous opposition. The opposition came first of all, as was to be expected, from disciples of the old Romantics who considered the new literature and the new ideology to be at best an aberration, at worst an act of treachery. This meant, in Scotland, numbers of people in or associated with the Burns Society; in the South of France, the Felibrige, who deemed themselves the direct heirs of Mistral and the standard-bearers of Provençal legitimacy. The opposition came from any number of people actively writing in the old, folksy manner and for all those who believed that the local literature had to remain grounded in the local dialect and the village and must not try to do and say the things that English and French do. They considered the dialect (Aberdeenshire Doric or Provençal or Gascon) more significant and more clearly defined than the language taken as a whole; they disliked or ignored literature written in the literary language taken as a whole. A striking example, also a tragic anomaly, concerns Per Jakez Helias, a great modernist writer in Breton, who, because of a commitment to his native Bigouden region and a commitment to folklore, refused to recognize the great modernist writers of the Skol Walarn (Gwalarn School) who preceded him and/or were his direct contemporaries.[4] To be fair to Helias, his aesthetic blindness was also grounded in questions of politics and ideology going back to the Second World War. The contentiousness of the giants of modernism, their political and ideological struggles, and their internal quarrels led, in all three language regions, to schisms and excommunications. The excommunicated and the schismatic could evolve into ferocious naysayers and often did. Finally, in all three regions the majority of the writers of modernism and postmodernism were cultural nationalists and, often, political nationalists; they were natural rebels, associated with left-wing causes or, in Brittany during the Occupation, accused of collaborationist causes. Modern Breton literature is all but identified with the Emsav (Movement/Awakening), which has become also the term for Breton nationalism. Those who did not share the cause and were not committed to the militancy often could not accept either the literature or its aesthetic program. The story of these controversies, these Picrocholine Wars, is a fascinating one, although, for obvious reasons, it does not enter directly into the fabric of this book.

In spite of dissension from within, in spite of indifference or outright hostility from without, the result, I am convinced, was highly successful, leading to a major literary renascence in all three language areas. The quality and the relative quantity of texts of the first rank (masterpieces) are striking and a tribute to artistic creation in our era. The three areas do, of course, reveal an inevitable chronological disparity. Scotland came to the fore in the 1920s, with the great personal achievement of Hugh MacDiarmid; MacDiarmid's friends and disciples have continued the Renaissance from the 1930s up to the present. Although in Brittany Roparz Hemon called for the same sort of renewal from the 1920s on, major works justifying the call appeared in significant number from the late 1930s and the 1940s and have not diminished since then. Again, in Occitania the literary consciousness was rife in the 1930s, but the masterpieces date almost entirely from since the war and, some would say, since the 1960s.

A second range of disparity occurs with regard to literary genre. Scots or Lallans is the most restricted code of the three and, prior to 1990, did not enjoy a continuous tradition in extended prose fiction. Occitan has had difficulty maintaining a continuous tradition in the theatre. Breton, with perhaps the most expanded code of the three, has produced a continuity of major works in all the genres, nonetheless privileging brief fiction over the long novel.

The three principal sections of this book will explore the twentieth-century renascence in the three language areas. I begin with Scotland, chronologically the first of the three to attain a modernist conscious-ness. I set forth briefly the cultural theory of Hugh MacDiarmid, the founder of the Scottish Renaissance, then examine representative poetry of his in Scots, primarily his masterpiece, *A Drunk Man Looks at the Thistle*, followed by *To Circumjack Cencrastus* (Squaring the Circular Scottish Snake). This is followed by a reading of poetry from some of MacDiarmid's leading inheritors: Robert Garioch, Sydney Goodsir Smith, and Tom Scott. I shall include criticism of Lewis Grassic Gibbon's *A Scots Quair* (A Scots Book), the great novel sequence of the Renais-sance, and of the historical drama in Scots or in English and Scots by Robert McLellan and Donald Campbell.

The Breton section begins with a brief discussion of the cultural pro-gram espoused by Roparz Hemon, the Breton MacDiarmid, as stated in the journals *Gwalarn* and *Arvor*. I begin with the great Breton genre, poetry: Hemon's own *Barzhonegoù* (Poems) and collections by the lead-ing Christian poet, Maodez Glanndour, and by Anjela Duval; then treat the flowering of the novel, with Youenn Drezen's *Itron Varia Garmez* (Our Lady of Carmel) and *Skol-louarn Veig Trebern* (Little Hervé Trébern Plays Hookey), Hemon's *Mari Vorgan* (The Mermaid) and *Tangi Kerviler*, and long *nouvelles* by Per Denez. This essay will conclude with a discussion of the extraordinarily powerful theatre from the pen of Per Jakez Helias.

For the Occitan regions I explore the cultural theory of the Institut d'Estudis Occitans group, stated especially in the periodical *Oc* and, later, in the polemical writings of Robert Lafont, then continue with a reading of the best poetry from the tradition, by René Nelli and Ber-nard Manciet, and also Max-Philippe Delavouët's *Pouèmo* (Poem), a modernist text from the rival Mistralian camp. This section will also look at the creation of the modern novel, works of fiction in the realism and 'magical realism' modes by Jean Boudou, *La Grava sul camin* (The Gravel on the Roadbed), *La Santa Estèla del centenari* (The Felibrige Cen-tennial), and *Lo Libre dels grands jorns* (The Book of the Last Days), and Robert Lafont, *L'Icòna dins l'iscla* (The Icon on the Island), concluding with the first Occitan *nouveaux romans*, Lafont's *La Festa* (The Festival) and Jean-Claude Forêt's *La Pèira d'asard* (The Stone of Chance). Last of all, I critique historical plays, first in Occitan and subsequently in French and Occitan, by Lafont.

A chapter will treat a number of developments from the late 1960s and 1970s that can be designated 'postmodern.' In the regional languages they occur partly in reaction to yet also flourish alongside the culture of high modernism which preceded them by decades. This postmodernism implies a turning away from high art toward a more popular register – speech grounded in popular, sometimes local usage – and a literature overtly committed to the politics of revolt. Under this heading are (1) the Glasgow Theatre of Bill Bryden, Roddy McMillan, and Tom McGrath; (2) the Breton 'Sixties Poets,' especially Paol Keineg; and (3) the Occitan 'Poets of Decolonization,' especially Jean Larzac.

In the conclusion I raise comparative questions that cut across the three cultures such as: Is there a common form of narrative (magical realism? allegorical romance?) prevalent in minority cultures, which is neither realism nor metafiction? Is the minority-language theatre limited to plots treating past history and the rural present? How can high modernist poetry express and be grounded in regional concerns yet also attain the universality of a Valéry or a Rilke? In general, what constraints are imposed on writers working in the lesser used languages? What traits – ideological or formal – will be shared by minority literatures congruent in time yet separated in space?

The conclusion also addresses directly critical and theoretical concerns that have been broached throughout this volume. Like my other books, this one will combine the close reading of texts from a variety of critical perspectives – Freudian, Jungian, Marxist, phenomenological, narratological, intertextual, and gender-related – with theoretical and cultural considerations that, I hope, transcend the format of a scholarly monograph. The employing of modern critical approaches, now the norm in university circles for literatures of wider circulation, is equally valid and no less important in the case of the minority literatures. It is perhaps to be regretted yet is nonetheless a fact that only by and through a tradition of high-level criticism and a corpus of modern critical texts will a national or regional literature attract the attention of the international scholarly community. Modern approaches and the books to which they give rise can help surmount the indifference or condescension with which London and Paris normally hold their minority cultures. Because of more than a dozen books devoted to his work, Hugh MacDiarmid cannot be considered an eccentric anomaly in dialect; he has to be taken seriously. Modern criticism – as distinguished from regional paeans of praise or regional declarations of ideology – can help to decipher the minority text, to reveal its inner workings, and to indicate how and why these Scots, Breton, and Occitan works are indeed of the first class, deserving to be an inherent and recognized part of *Weltliteratur*.[5] The central focus of my reading of Scots, Breton, and Occitan works will therefore be critical analysis. By means of criticism and by means of the comparative method (widely applied to the more widely diffused languages), I hope to demonstrate the importance of these minority literatures in their twentieth-century renewal, and their contribution to our culture, both in aesthetic and in broadly human terms.

I address directly, without weighing the book down, modernism and postmodernism, colonialism and postcolonialism. A far from negligible corpus has accumulated in recent years in these areas – the one of periodization, the other of ideology.[6] Although, as with all approaches, they can give rise to reductionism, they have much to contribute. This book will engage the validity of modernism, postmodernism, and postcolonialism for the comprehension of European minority literatures; more important, it will demonstrate what an awareness of these literatures can bring to the theory of modernism, postmodernism, and postcolonialism.

A note on the scholarly tradition: nothing quite comparable to this study exists in the secondary literature. There are excellent histories of literature in modern Scots and of Scottish literature generally, over a dozen books on MacDiarmid, and fine work on Gibbon. However, the other writers in Scots – the poets and the dramatists – have been relatively neglected. And nothing comparable exists in Breton and Occitan. Although we have, written in French and, for Breton, also in Breton, introductions to the field, general literary history, surveys, and article collections, there are no full-length critical studies or the kind of modern-critical and theoretical readings prevalent in writing on French and English. *Minority Literatures and Modernism* is the first book in English on modern Breton and Occitan and the first, or one of the first, to treat these traditions from a modern-critical perspective. It is the first comparative scrutiny of the Scots, Breton, and Occitan achievements as parts of an international, European totality, underscoring in comparative terms their contribution to Europe as a whole.

The English translations of texts in Breton and Occitan are my own except when otherwise indicated. For the material in Scots, I offer, relying upon the standard dictionaries and the poets' own word lists, a brief glossary, pages 347–8. Given the disparity in orthography among writers and schools, I respect the *graphie d'origine* of all texts, citations, and references.

SCOTLAND

INTRODUCTION

The great writer Hugh MacDiarmid / Christopher Murray Grieve devoted a lifetime to calling for and helping build the renewal of Scottish literature in the twentieth century. He was one of the most prodigiously energetic activists of his time – as a speaker, lecturer, and campaigner, as a founding member of the National Party of Scotland and the Scottish Pen Club, and as a contentious member – in and out – of the Communist Party UK. In *The Scottish Chapbook*, the review he founded in 1922, in dozens of other reviews, some of which he founded and/or edited himself, in dozens of books, and in thousands of articles, letters, speeches, and occasional pieces, under his own name and a dozen pseudonyms, MacDiarmid spread the word, from the 1920s to his death in 1978. Following in his wake, especially from the 1940s on, a second wave of writers contributed to elaborating the doctrine of modernism in Scots. They and the third wave continue today.

In the February 1923 issue of the *Chapbook* MacDiarmid calls for 'a great Scottish Literary Renaissance' (p. 182). Here, and in subsequent articles, the most important of which he collected in *Albyn*[1] and *At the Sign of the Thistle*,[2] he makes it clear that his linguistic and literary ideas on Scots form part of a larger program – the renewal of Scottish cultural life in its totality, including education and forming one element in a national regeneration that should lead to, and will be impossible to attain without, full political independence.

MacDiarmid attacks many things, including the stereotypes of Scotland and the Scot: 'Scotland connotes to the world "religious" bigotry, a genius for materialism, "thrift," and, on the social and cultural side, Harry Lauderism and an exaggerated sentimental nationalism, which is obviously a form of compensation for the lack of a realistic nationalism' (*Albyn*, pp. 76–7). He objects equally to stereotypes concerning the

Scots language – that it is a low-class patois for low-class people, useful for 'couthy' speech in bad novels, cartoons, and the music hall, and that, since it is allegedly only slang and a dialect of English, it has to give way to progress.

He also denounces the current state of Scottish culture, a culture so insignificant that it all but justifies the stereotypes: 'Scotland has ceased to hold any distinctive place in the political or cultural map of Europe. [...] Scottish arts and letters [have been reduced] to shadows of their former or potential selves, qualitatively beneath contempt in comparison with the distinctive arts and letters of any other country in Europe. There is no Scottish writer today of the slightest international standing' (*Albyn*, p. 76). As he sees it, Scotland is ignored by the London establishment, the church is involved in sectarian bigotry, the press has been bought heart and soul, and nothing genuine remains. That this has occurred is the fault of history and, more particularly, the fault of the English ascendancy in Scottish life. Three traumatic occurrences – the Protestant Reformation, the Union with England, and the industrial revolution – contributed to the subjection of Scotland and the Scots to London, with the result that all that is not English is occulted, and the Scottish people are alienated from their own traditions. Most important from a literary perspective, the conquerors' speech – English – was imposed on the conquered peoples, who actually converse in Scots or Gaelic. This imposition works hand in hand with and contributes to the process of social, political, and economic subjugation. The imposition of English is particularly nefarious given that, according to MacDiarmid, the tradition of poetry in English since Wordsworth, indeed since Milton, is stilted, confining, and in decline, and, as a vital language for vital poetry, English is exhausted.

MacDiarmid bemoans the specifically Scottish tradition in prose, the Kailyard novel, which recounts vignettes of life in rural villages, peopled with picturesque, pawky, nippy, crafty, and otherwise droll characters, in stories redolent with cosy domesticity and warm, nostalgic sentimentality. However, given that MacDiarmid is, first and foremost, a poet obsessed with the state of poetry, it is to be expected that his rage focuses, above all, on the wretched condition of Scottish poetry, the verse equivalent of Kailyard, due to the nefarious influence of Robert Burns and his successors. In a speech delivered on 21 January 1928 and published in *At the Sign of the Thistle* and in innumerable other writings culminating in *Burns Today and Tomorrow*,[3] MacDiarmid attacks the beloved national poet and the tradition he left in his wake. As Mac-

Diarmid sees it, Burns is a far-from-major figure in his own right, inferior to his contemporary Fergusson and to the medieval Makars, to be
critiqued for a narrow range, limited, for the most part, to amorous and
comic songs, that is, to a folk-oriented, non-intellectual lyricism. Furthermore, whatever Burns's virtues, it is his defects which have been
consecrated and perpetuated by generations of successors who themselves build upon the master's provincialism, insularity, and practice of
the local dialect. One can imagine the rage of the Establishment, all
those who lived for Rabbie and the annual Burns Suppers, when they
read a passage such as this:

> The effect of Burns' work on Scots poetry is well-known. It has reduced it
> to a level that is beneath contempt. Little or no poetry that has been pro-
> duced in Scots since Burns' day has been of a quality to support compari-
> son for a moment with the average of contemporary poetry in any other
> European country. It is all of the kailyard kind; sentimental, moralizing,
> flatfooted, and with little or no relation to reality. (*Albyn*, p. 37)

In reaction to this state of affairs and to renew cultural life in Scotland, MacDiarmid proclaims first of all the qualities inherent in the
Scots language. In contrast to English, which he believes to be in a state
of decline, Scots offers directness of utterance and intensity of feeling.
The vernacular contains a vast lexicon not to be found in English and
thus a reservoir of symbol and metaphor, not to speak of elements
unique to the Scottish experience and the Scottish unconscious.

MacDiarmid's program is to revitalize and to reintegrate the Scottish
dialects in order that they become again, as they once were, the natural,
accepted medium of cultural intercourse. To do so, he proposes 'Synthetic
Scots,' a literary koine grounded in the dialects yet independent from
and overreaching them. To justify this, he invokes the example of Dante:

> Dante's conclusion was that the corruption common to all the dialects
> made it impossible to select one rather than another as an adequate liter-
> ary form, and that he who would write in the vulgar must assemble the pur-
> est elements from each dialect and construct a synthetic language that
> would at least possess more than a circumscribed local interest: which is
> precisely what he did. [...] He wrote a vulgar that could have been spoken
> by an ideal Italian who had assimilated what was best in all the dialects of
> his country, but which, in fact, was certainly not spoken, nor ever had been.
> (*At the Sign of the Thistle*, p. 184)

In order to create and to enhance Synthetic Scots, MacDiarmid envisages borrowing from all the dialects, consulting the old dictionaries,
especially for lexical items, and (re)turning to writers from the Middle
Ages. Hence the oft-cited battle cry 'Not Burns – Dunbar!' (*Albyn*,
p. 35). Because the Makars provide richer, more comprehensive discourse than is to be found in Burns and his successors, but also for more
general, all-encompassing reasons of culture,

> it is necessary to go back behind Burns to Dunbar and the Old Makars –
> great Catholic poets using the Vernacular, not for the pedestrian things to
> which it has latterly been confined, but for all 'the brave translunary things
> of great art.' The younger Scottish poets are repossessing themselves of
> noble media and high traditions; and a splendid mystical and imaginative
> spirit is reuniting them over a period of five centuries with their mighty
> predecessors. (*Albyn*, pp. 12–13)

Enriched by the linguistic maturity and the aesthetic and intertextual
complexity of the old classics, the modern writer in Scots will be able to
create a modern, adult literature capable of treating all features of modern, adult life. And, once this is brought about, the new literature in
Scots will be worthy of contributing, on a footing of equality, to the literature of Europe and be open to all European literary currents, giving
and taking freely in a process which will no longer be mediated by the
English. That first August 1922 manifesto includes, as one of its planks,
'To bring Scottish Literature into closer touch with current European
tendencies in technique and ideation.' Elsewhere MacDiarmid writes,
'No revival of Scots can be of consequence to a literary aspirant worthy
of his salt unless it is so aligned with contemporary tendencies in European thought and expression that it has with it the possibility of eventually carrying Scots work once more into the mainstream of European
literature' (*Albyn*, p. 42). It is, therefore, by repudiating romantic, folkloric, stereotypical Scottishness and by imitating the latest formal and
doctrinal innovations from abroad that literature in Scots can be
authentically modern and authentically Scottish and can, in turn, have
an impact on the great literatures abroad.

One inevitable result of such modernism – in language and in form –
will be to make writing in Scots more difficult than it was in the past
and, inevitably, less accessible to the traditional reading public. Perhaps
the chief objection to MacDiarmid's ideas and to his poetry, in the
1920s, the 1930s, and still today, states that part of the lexicon is not in

current spoken usage and the integrity of no single dialect is respected, and therefore that the literature is artificial and, consequently, difficult to read. MacDiarmid responds to such critiques in a number of ways. First of all, he observes that the goal is a literary language, a koine which will serve as the medium for artistic written discourse. His purpose is not to displace the tongue spoken in the street or on the farm. More important, however, is the argument that hard poetry is the norm in all modern languages, including English, and that only a minority of people are capable of appreciating poetry in any language, including English. Mac-Diarmid and his successors have stated again and again that the Shakespeare and the Keats we read were never spoken by anyone on the planet, including Shakespeare and Keats. Since poetic speech is never the equivalent of spoken discourse, the modern writer in Scots ought not to be constrained any more than poets in French and English are. MacDiarmid felt so strongly on this point that, in the name of the cause, he went to extremes: 'Most people do not think; and all the significant thinking of the day is probably being done by a dozen or two people' (*At the Sign of the Thistle*, p. 195). As late as 1964, he denied, to the revival of folk-songs and folklore in general, validity as a cultural, artistic endeavour.[4]

Hugh MacDiarmid's ideal of a Synthetic Scots persisted throughout his lifetime and after his death, and has lasted up to today. In the 1940s and 1950s the term Lallans (Lowlands) came into fashion as the designation for high literary Scots. In 1946 the unfortunate neologism 'Plastic Scots' was proposed and then quickly withdrawn.[5] From the 1970s on, with the greatness of MacDiarmid's own corpus recognized and the master welcomed into the Scottish canon, the argument shifted to other issues. Defenders of Scots had now to counter the accusation that Mac-Diarmid himself was a uniquely brilliant phenomenon yet that his example could not and did not lead to a sequential, living tradition. It was necessary to defend and illustrate Scots, first of all by stating and restating that the language is not merely a dialect of English and, second, by demonstrating the continuing vitality of poetry in Scots and the list of major figures who cultivated and continue to cultivate the vernacular. Then, the New Makars of the second wave and their successors strove to expand the range of Scots, especially in the domain of prose, so that, like modern French and English, it could serve as the medium for all literary uses. The journal *Lallans* was founded in 1973 to publish Scots prose in a variety of genres – fiction but also literary criticism, theory, history, linguistics, general social commentary, and light or heavy jour-

nalism: 'Nou Lallans'll ne'er regain the stature o a rale language till we
hae a hantle-sicht mair prose-writin nor we hae the day, and sae we sall
gie the gree til prose.'[6] That over one hundred writers have appeared in
Lallans, a number of whom write prose of a high order, testifies to the
success of the venture. Of equal importance is the effort to further the
use of Scots, both as a subject of study and, where possible, as a medium
of instruction, in the schools.

In the domain of language planning, the chief call has been for the
creation of a unified, standard tongue, a normalized Scots that can be
taught in the schools and that would form the basis for all serious literary production. Since 1977 a Language Planning Committee has been
working on the problem. Here the foremost need is to find and impose
a unified orthography and, also, a unified grammar. On 11 April 1947
the Makars Club, which included the leading writers of the time, met
and approved a 'Style Sheet' on grammar and spelling. It was published
in the *New Alliance and Scots Review* in 1947 and has been reproduced a
number of times since then.[7] It proposes a modicum of standardization
on the line of Middle Scots. Although it has never been followed slav-
ishly, the great majority of writers have conformed, more or less, to the
thrust of the Style Sheet. The Style Sheet has been supplemented by the
'Scots Language Society, Recommendations for Writers in Scots,'[8] and a
number of authorities, including Purves and McClure, have proposed
their own systems.[9] It has to be admitted, however, that MacDiarmid's
original program and the projects of the more recent writers have been
realized only partially. The unification and standardization of the language, its use for all literary registers and modes, and its being taught in
the schools have progressed less rapidly than is the case for Breton and
Occitan. These aspects of language planning implementation – and
even of codification and elaboration – are being negotiated now, in
our time.[10]

POETRY

HUGH MacDIARMID

Not only did Hugh MacDiarmid stake out a claim for a Scottish literary
Renaissance and the cultural and literary renewal of the Scots language.
On top of this, he wrote a mass of poetry in Scots and in English, his
Scots poetry of the 1920s and early 1930s making him by general con-

sent the greatest poet of modern Scotland and helping to create the twentieth-century Scottish Renaissance as a fact of history. By being one of the first, in poetry, to break away from the Romantic clichés that had dominated the idea of Scotland for a century and a half and by his commitment to relate his work to contemporary life, the contemporary mind, and the broader European civilization, MacDiarmid sought to destroy one tradition and to replace it with another, his own. His tradition was Scottish modernism, which inevitably parallels the English modernism of Pound and Eliot a decade earlier and French modernism, which goes back to Baudelaire and Rimbaud. As extreme as such formulations may appear, in retrospect scholars are largely agreed that the man from Langholm embodies his age as no one else, and that much of the subsequent literary scene, up to us, comes from him and could not exist were it not for his example. Also, he is the only writer discussed in this book, in addition to the Breton Per Jakez Helias, to have attained (admittedly in his old age and posthumously) a degree of genuine acclaim in international academic circles.

Following in the wake of Swinburne and the early Yeats, and for that matter the French Symbolists, MacDiarmid began by writing poems in the Symbolist mode and in English. Then, starting in September 1922, he published a series of lyrics in his own, newly conceived Synthetic Scots. The best of these, which include 'The Watergaw' (The Rainbow), 'The Eemis Stane' (The Teetering Stone), 'The Bonnie Broukit Bairn' (The Pretty Tear-Stained Child), and 'Empty Vessel,' are considered to be masterpieces, lyrics equal to the best of Dunbar and Burns. These texts, with their resemblance to Eliot and Donne, are especially prized, for they are grounded in the concrete reality of rural life and given expression in vital, living Braid Scots yet, at the same time, reveal an objective correlative and, beyond the senses, mystical or metaphysical meditation and a concern for ideas, the intellectual realm absent from the pseudo-popular verse of the predecessors.

The two collections of lyrics from these years – *Sangschaw* (Song Festival) from 1925, and *Penny Wheep* (Small Ale) from 1926 – are considered by a number of specialists to be MacDiarmid's finest achievement. Others, and I support their opinion, deem the high point to be the long poem, made up of a number of lyrics with lyrico-narrative connections, entitled *A Drunk Man Looks at the Thistle*, published also in 1926.[11] It contains lyricism, satire, translation, intertextual allusion, and philosophical meditation, in the authentically modernist mode of distortion, fragmentation, and the arcane. This astounding text is written in Scots, hitherto a tongue for the condescending evocation of rustics and eccentrics; the new Synthetic Scots becomes the medium for poetry of high intellect, comparable to the verse of Valéry, Rilke, and Eliot, and is thus exploited for MacDiarmid's own ideal, the full range of literary purpose.

More than *Le Cimetière marin* or *The Waste Land*, *A Drunk Man* is grounded in, and its structure determined by, a narrative. The implied reader discovers or pieces together this narrative from the poem as it is purported to be delivered orally by the Speaker. The Speaker has drunk too much with his cronies at the pub. Staggering home in a stupor, late at night, he falls down. Raising his head, the Speaker gazes at the moon and at a giant-seeming thistle close to his head which partially blocks his vision. In his drunken state, the Speaker beholds the moon through the thistle and the thistle highlighted by the moon, and he begins to talk (whisper, shout, sing) about moons, thistles, himself, and life. This 'talk' is the text of *A Drunk Man*.

The narratological given – that the poem consists in the purportedly uncomposed, unstructured, and irrational ramblings of a drunkard – allows for, indeed requires, structural fragmentation and distortion, the juxtaposition of the sublime and the ridiculous, of high philosophical inquiry and of low physical obscenity. Similarly, the alleged drunken state of the Speaker allows for all that is violent, exuberant, and orgiastic in his discourse, his joy in words and in verbal creation. Ultimately, the Speaker proves to be an unreliable narrator as a logical, credible, and coherent witness. Yet, at the same time, he is a very reliable narrator in modernist terms. His irrationality is more genuine, profound, and true than another man's discursive prose, and his stream of consciousness more authentic, as structure and as reality, than another's ordered discourse.

The exhilaration and the disorder have a direct cause – whisky, imbibed by the Speaker at the pub. The Speaker commences his monologue by alluding self-consciously to the whisky, which is Scotch and recognized by everyone to partake of the stereotype of all things Scottish. He begins with the stereotype of the blabbering, humorous, incoherent Scotsman high on spirits. Yet, immediately, irony and a quality of intellectualism are introduced as he bewails – as a poet and intellectual in the throes of melancholia – the decline in the quality of Scotch, associating it with his insights into the decline of Scottish culture. On a more personal level, this implies recognition of his own temporary decline – since he is inebriated, it is difficult for him to think and speak – associated with and metaphorically due to the decadence of Scotland. Whisky can be a source of inspiration; it can also bring pain. And it will always be a source of humour. The Speaker laments that part of the decline is due to his drink being watered down and that he will be in hot water with Jean, his wife, when he returns home:

Water! Water! There was owre muckle o't
In yonder whisky, sae I'm in deep water
(And gin I could wun hame I'd be in het,
For even Jean maun natter, natter, natter) ... (p. 88)

The whisky also reminds him of being forced out of his mother's womb against his will. As a result, he endures the drink but not the chaser. And what is the result? The wrong alchemical formula – he takes in whisky and pisses out water.

This whisky-water discussion occurs at night, in a nightmare world, in which the Speaker undertakes a quest into and through the night. In an especially significant statement he declares that God created light but only a little. As a result we humans are left with darkness, which is our only reality. We are cats gazing in the night. Yet darkness has its compensations. True poetry is associated with the dark, as is mantic inspiration. The dark is Dostoevsky's element, he who saw farther than others. In the chaos of night will be found a place for all, even Scotland.

Also, the night is associated with the world of dreams. At one point the Speaker himself, having lost his rational faculties, speculates whether he is lying on the ground, as it appears, or perhaps only dreaming the experience while sleeping beside Jean in his bed at home. He also wonders whether he is the drinker or the drink, that is, himself contained in a bottle of spirits, and whether reality exists in the world or in his head. Here the implied reader recognizes, as does the Speaker, the extent to which his disjointed, stream-of-consciousness version of reality conforms to the world of dreams as much as to the state of drunkenness. He also recognizes, as the Speaker does not, that the experience recalls a tradition in Scottish, English, and ultimately French medieval allegory, where the dream vision convention allows for a narrative structure and for visionary insights comparable to those of the twentieth-century Scotsman. The Speaker's text communes with the best of the national character and the national tradition in art.

On one level, the Speaker appears to blame the moon for his predicament. He blames her for the fact that he is drunk and lost, wandering about following her instead of sleeping at home. In a superb collage

taken from Alexander Blok, the Narrator invokes the 'silken leddy,' a
strange, entrancing woman whom he perceives mirrored in his glass
while he sits in the tavern. In another passage the Speaker compares his
brains to seaweed, left withered and sucked dry when the tide (*sub luna*)
recedes. It is clear, however, that these versions of the Fatal Woman are
ultimately conceived in positive terms. In the Speaker's imaginary, the
moon and the lady embody something akin to Goethe's *Ewig-weibliche.*
The moon stirs up in him conscience, thought, and discontent. Like the
whisky (also a spirit), she brings him inspiration and knowledge of the
self through the irrational and the artistic, which are her traits, for, in
the traditional gendered view of Western civilization, the feminine is
characterized by darkness, the flesh, the physical, the sexual, transgression, imagination, the irrational, and madness, all attributes of the
moon, as opposed to man's solar light, the spirit, the wind, law, reason,
and sanity. The female moon will be the Speaker's muse. She is or will
be a mother-figure for him and for Scotland. Therefore, the Speaker's
quest, in the dark night of the soul, is also for this female presence in
himself, the *anima* – woman, inspiration – without which neither he nor
Scotland can be made whole. Only by coming to terms with her, by integrating her, will he arrive at Jungian maturation.

A Freudian reading would perhaps be more congruent than a Jungian one, however, given the blatantly phallic imagery produced by the
Speaker's imagination, including the structures of desire evoked by
thoughts of his wife, Jean. Jean proves to be an earthly rival to the moon
as well as the Speaker's objective correlative of it (her). More than once
the Speaker's train of thought is broken into by the visual presence of
Jean and his memory of sex with her in the past or his desire for the
same in the present. To the extent that the implied reader is expected
to imagine a narrative around the Speaker's discourse, at this point the
Speaker might be having an erection. The Speaker seemingly himself
alludes to this phenomenon when he ponders on woman's amazing
powers, all of which come from man's testicles. In an oft-discussed passage, the Speaker claims woman (Jean) is both goddess and whore, she
who carries thistles not a rose. Has she not been a whore for milleni-
ums? Woman then replies that although all men have known her,
because all men have known her she will be a loving, nurturing help-
mate to him – he should forget her past:

But I can gi'e ye kindness, lad,
And a pair o' willin' hands,

And you sall ha'e my breists like stars,
My limbs like willow wands,

And on my lips ye'll heed nae mair,
And in my hair forget,
The seed o' a' the men that in
My virgin womb ha'e met ... (p. 103)

Thus the Speaker meditates on the nature of womankind, all the daughters of Eve. Redemption, to the extent it is possible, will come not from the Virgin Mary (Ave) but from the Primal Woman (Eva), who offers the thistle as a renewed Tree of Life and of Knowledge. He also, in my opinion, seeks to come to terms with his own wife, who perhaps was not a virgin when they wed. Later, he declares that woman (Jean), descended from Eden, can bring us either good or ill. Love is good, he declares, and need not be joined to matrimony. Fulfil ourselves, he bursts out, and forget about having children.[12]

Opposite the moon, in antithesis to it, yet seized by the Speaker's gaze in conjunction with the moon and piercing it visually, stands the thistle. In the Speaker's mind, the thistle is as magnificently phallic as the moon is vaginal. On the one hand, embodying the Speaker's intellect or his virility or the Scottish identity, it does or can or will rise to the stars and grasp the infinite. It bursts forth in flowers, which the Speaker calls roses. On one occasion it is transformed into Yggdrasil, the world-tree in Scandinavian mythology, and to the Holy Rood in Scripture. However, the Speaker plays continually on the perceived negative aspects of the Scottish thistle, a weed in contrast to the cultivated English rose. Therefore, in the Speaker's inebriated (poetic) imagination, the thistle becomes, literally, an alligator, a bellows, a gargoyle, a skeleton, the bagpipes, a dragon, and an octopus.[13] As the thistle rises to the sky, the Speaker perceives it to wither away and fall, metamorphosed into a weed. An image of his wasted sexual power, it used to lie in his heart yet now is uprooted. The thistle's ugliness and its thorns shape the Speaker's thoughts; *it* is the Speaker, his shadow, his dark Other. The Speaker bears this giant thistle inside him as a cross, which tears apart his flesh. His body, alive yet also rigid in death, reflects, in his bones and nerves, the twitching of the thistle in a breeze.

We see to what extent this phallic image is incommensurable with the moon. As a metaphor for the Speaker, for Scotland, for the human intellect, and for humankind, it cannot measure up. Its other qualities –

spiny, thorny, sterile – make of it a testimony to impotence, the Speaker's sexual and intellectual lack, and mankind's in face of the infinite. We are nothing in God's eyes – we are just a spider web or a snail's trace on the wall or a twig on Yggdrasil or coral insects atop the reef. Yet it is the conjunction of the thistle and the moon or the thistle and the rose or himself and Jean that elicits the Speaker's cry of wonder. His nighttime quest is an intellectual search and a dream voyage (as he lies more or less prone). We can imagine it to be something like Rimbaud's Season in Hell, assimilated to a *bateau ivre*. Unlike Rimbaud, however, in this quest he can make extremes meet, he is fascinated when and where they meet, for this *conjunctio oppositorum* is the means by which he attains truth and is the truth of his land, the oft-cited 'Caledonian Antisyzygy.'[14] Yet, because of the clash of opposites, there will never be an answer to the Speaker's question or a resolution to his problem. He struggles with his consciousness and the nature of reality, he is desperate to know. Yet he discovers the only knowledge to be that of the quest itself. So, obsessed with paradox and antithesis, with reality and the infinite, the Speaker grapples, questioning again and again, wrestling with the pricks and thorns and burrowing into the roots. In the end he can only express the unknowable and the clash of opposites as the texture of his discourse and our poem: the sublime and the ridiculous, the meditative and the bawdy, the high and the low, as the thistle itself rises up yet also digs itself into the mire.

We have seen that levels of symbolism emanate from the thistle, and that, on one of these levels, it is recognized to be the traditional emblem for Scotland. A *Drunk Man* contains a sequence of discontinuous yet congruent meditations on the land and the people, as important as the philosophical questioning and the personal confession. As we saw, the Speaker begins with a comment on Scotch whisky, an entity everyone recognizes to be Scottish, and notes its decline – it is watered down in his pub – relating this phenomenon to the decline in Scottish culture. Culture has declined since the Golden Age of Dunbar. Burns himself is not personally at fault, observes the Speaker; it is the liars and hypocrites who exploit the Burns myth. These include pompous bourgeois of the St Andrew's societies who sleep away while the Speaker wakes. These include also the hierarchy of the Church of Scotland. Later the Speaker compares the expanding thistle, now conceived as a weed, to empty human intellect, which stifles life in his land, a Presbyterian thistle that crucifies its own roses. In this line he beholds the plant's whirls and swirls like the coils of a snake and its flowers like hanged men. Finally, in a vision of mankind throughout history, the Speaker singles out the Scots, the great ones and the frauds. They differ from the others in that they never change, eternally steadfast in their ignorance.

The collapse of the Speaker's people is total – social, political, intellectual, cultural, and spiritual. There is, or there could be, hope for betterment in the present. Scholars have noted the importance of a passage at the midpoint.[15] In this passage, the rose of the thistle rises proudly to heaven, red like fire, but then shrivels and withers, falling back to earth to die:

> A rose loupt oot and grew, until
> It was ten times the size
> O' ony rose the thistle afore
> Hed heistit to the skies. [...]

> And still it grew until it seemed
> The haill braid earth had turned
> A reid reid rose that in the lift
> Like a ball o' fire burned. [...]

> Syne the rose shrivelled suddenly
> As a balloon is burst;
> The thistle was a ghaistly stick,
> As gin it had been curst. (pp. 120–1)

This alludes to the most important immediate 'event' of the time when Hugh MacDiarmid was completing *A Drunk Man* – the General Strike of 1926, to which he and so many in the Scottish (and English) working classes gave their all, only to be betrayed by the Labour party leadership in London. Christ himself is nailed to this cross, and at his crucifixion the devils laugh.

The Speaker then displaces his hopes for a better world and a better Scotland onto the future. For a man of his political persuasion and who later would compose three 'Hymns to Lenin,' the future means the Soviet Union. The Speaker is convinced that the Russians and the Scots are alike, both of them people of extremes, people of misery, madness, and disease, and people of the night. That MacDiarmid's is the communism of a poet and not a political man becomes apparent when the implied reader is made aware that the Russian figure invoked to show him and the thistle the right path is Dostoevsky. The thistle's leaves shake like snow. The Speaker and Dostoevsky have trouble communicating, they speak different languages; yet they are alike. The Speaker welcomes Dostoevsky's patriotism and his mysticism. He even welcomes Dostoevskian madness in the hopes that he can be a Scottish Dostoevsky and prophesy for the Scots as the great Russian did for his people.

Toward the end Dostoevsky gives way to Dante. Quoting Dante, the Speaker claims to write from love ... or from hatred. Whereas Dante evokes the mystical rose, the Speaker returns ever to his thistle. Then, developing a version of *terza rima* (2395–646), the Speaker has a vision of the great cosmic circle or wheel. This image he takes from the astrological Great Year of the Zodiac (via Yeats), one turn of the wheel equaling 26,000 years, and, also, I believe, from the medieval notion of the Wheel of Fortune, going back to Boethius. It also resembles and is derived from Dante's cosmic rose in *Paradiso*. I have no power over the wheel, cries the Speaker; I, God, the devil, and Scotland are all fixed on it. Our songs cannot rise to it. Yet we endure and think and write. It is ablaze in fire, and its light is our authentic human consciousness.

These passages indicate that, in spite of the appeals to Dostoevsky and Dante, and in spite of the Speaker's commitment to a kind of mysticism and his mastery of Christian culture, *A Drunk Man* is, in no sense of the term, a Christian poem. Dante illustrated his vernacular as MacDiarmid hopes to illustrate Braid Scots. Dante underwent a dream pilgrimage of the soul much as MacDiarmid's Speaker does. However, the Speaker's pilgrimage is resolutely secular, even anti-Christian, his humanism a response to the Christian faith of Dante and Dostoevsky. We have seen how the Speaker envisages God as indifferent to man's fate, one for whom human beings are at best the trace of a spider or a snail; and how God created only a little light, so that people live in the night and must see and walk alone. In addition, MacDiarmid exploits traditional Christian imagery, reshaping it for his own purposes. On the one hand, Jean is portrayed negatively as the daughter of Eve, fallen from Eden. Yet it is as such, as a woman of sin and of virtue, a whore from the ages unredeemed by any Virgin Mary, that she and her sisters, in their female sexuality, offer man his only light and his only taste of paradise. The Holy Rood itself is, in the Speaker's mind, transmuted into the thistle. Since Christ or, rather, the Speaker is crucified on the thistle, the history of Scotland and of humanity displaces in importance orthodox *Heilsgeschichte*. It will be the fate of a Scottish poet to take on the sins of his people and to break open their tomb, yet, as always, this new, secular Christ-figure remains impaled on the thistle, a saviour, a martyr, and a failure.

A Drunk Man Looks at the Thistle concerns not just any Scottish drunkard. Hugh MacDiarmid is concerned with the future of poetry in his
land. The assimilation between the Scottish poet and Christ and the fact
that the Narrator himself is a would-be Scottish poet underscore this
fact. The heightened presence of Burns, Dostoevsky, and Dante in the
Speaker's imagination, and therefore in his text, as well as the shift from
Burns (the abandoned past) to Dostoevsky and Dante (the possible
future) also contribute to the Speaker's argument and, ultimately, to his
program. *A Drunk Man* itself embodies and fulfils the program, in part
because of its aesthetic and intellectual quality, in part because of its
overt intertextuality. Burns, Dostoevsky, and Dante are not isolated figures in the poem. The Speaker consistently alludes to famous writers
and books. He also intersperses in the text his own translations from the
corpus of European modernism. These include poems by Blok, Hip-
pius, Lasker-Schüler, and a number of others. The tradition of 'collage,'
as Aragon labelled it to define surrealist practice (and his own), as
much as anything else defines the texture of *A Drunk Man* and its
modernity. For it stands thus as a focus in Scotland for European
modernity. Nothing could be more foreign to the post-Burns tradition
of a folksy, intimate, rural Scottishness; nothing could more shock the
1920s Scottish literary public and alter its horizon of expectations. This
MacDiarmid does with brio, while at the same time – in the mocking,
undermining spirit of the Caledonian Antisyzygy – having his Speaker
ask how it is that a village drunkard can be possessed of so much culture, and answering that it can be explained only by the acknowledged
superiority of Scottish education.

In the end, after so much thought and discourse, the Speaker
declares he can say no more, for he doesn't have the answers.[16] He proclaims silence. The narrative frame is then taken up when, now more or
less sober, the Speaker returns home, where his wife will have the last
word:

O I ha'e Silence left
    – 'And weel ye micht,'
Sae Jean 'll say, 'efter sic a nicht!' (p. 167)

She closes the poem. Thus, in the Speaker's mind and in his text,
speech gives way to silence, and Burns, Dostoevsky, and Dante give way
to Jean. Some scholars interpret this passage as a response of mysticism
to the Speaker's questions, the mysticism derived from Tyutchev and his

exaltation of poetic silence. I prefer another reading, which states that after exaltation comes exhaustion, after tragedy comes comedy, and after a masculine scaling the heights of thought and rhetoric the Speaker has to return to the feminine rule of the quotidian in his and Jean's quotidian life.[17] This is a release from tension, in laughter, as, once again, extremes meet, and the Scottish poet, nailed to the thistle, is shown also to be the henpecked husband chastised after a night of binging with his cronies.

In 1930 MacDiarmid published a second long poem, wider in scope than his first venture. This is *To Circumjack Cencrastus* (Squaring the Circular Scottish Snake).[18] Although a number of scholars have endeavoured to rehabilitate *Circumjack*, the general verdict is that it represents a falling off from *A Drunk Man*. According to the majority, *Circumjack* reveals a slack, diffuse structure, repetitiveness, a less fiery imagination, and a less striking texture and diction. One explanation is that the new poem lacks a narrative frame – has no equivalent of the drunk man, the thistle, and Jean – and, therefore, as an expository text, both lyrical and didactic, told by a largely impersonal Speaker, has less immediate appeal to readers.[19] In general, I think this is valid. Yet *To Circumjack Cencrastus* is a powerful and convincing text on its own terms. Were *A Drunk Man* never to have been published, perhaps *Circumjack* would be acclaimed today as a masterpiece of the Scottish Renaissance.

In place of the thistle and the moon in the previous book, here we find, as arch-image and unifying structural element, the 'curly snake.' This is the motif in Celtic iconography – from the Book of Kells to Joyce – of the serpent swallowing its own tail. In the four years since *A Drunk Man*, MacDiarmid has become much more of a Celtic enthusiast. He is now convinced (and his Speaker tells us) that Scotland can develop a meaningful cultural and artistic life only by returning to its Celtic roots. Therefore, the Speaker alludes to Gaelic poets from the past and cites texts in Gaelic. Therefore, he elaborates the Gaelic Idea. And, continuing the Russian motif in *A Drunk Man*, he postulates an East-West Synthesis in which traditional Western civilization will be preserved and enriched by two new forces – the Russians in the East and the Celts in the West. As he sees it, the Celts are necessary to balance the Russians in a supreme, world Antisyzygy.

Although it disappears from the discourse for long patches, the snake dominates the poem. A rich, problematic, and symbolic entity, the icon

stands for many things and evokes many responses. It retains the traditional Celtic mythological attributes of wisdom and of eternity. For Mac-
Diarmid, it inspires and is Celtic thought, his thought. In addition, the
Speaker evokes the snake as a sea-serpent, a monster from the deep. We
hear, then, of people's fear of the snake and of its qualities of movement
and change of colour. Because it is ever-changing and because it comes
from the waters, the snake stands as a symbol of creation. Its coils equal
the ever-renewed cycle of life. It is the source. Therefore, we identify it
as sexual power, as the mother of all or, on other occasions, as an image
of phallic potency. Returning again to myth, the implied reader can
envisage it as a world-serpent, the underlying principle of the cosmos
(and of Scotland), the Celtic equivalent of the Germanic Yggdrasil and
the Celtic Highland answer to the Lowland Scot thistle.

The snake's movements, to and fro, and its ceaseless changes in form,
as it coils and uncoils, from darkness to light, in the ceaselessly changing
waters (female change under the moon) give the Speaker a sense of
evolution in time, that is, of the flow of history, for Scotland and for
mankind as a whole. Because of such universal metamorphosis, there is
hope for Scotland – she will not remain fixed in her current backward
lethargy. The Speaker casts off sentiment, therefore, and old, backward-
looking sea legends. We Scots can have a Renaissance the way the
Germans did, he proclaims. Mary Macleod brought back the tradition
of Gaelic music and changed history. Others can do it also. Maybe we
Scots will find a Celtic Christ, not Jesus and not having to do with Jesus.
We humans, he cries, have risen from the slime. Now it is our duty, no
longer nature's, to evolve:

> Man's in the makin' but henceforth maun mak' himsel.'
> Nature has led him sae faur, up frae the slime
> Gi'en him body and brain – and noo it's for him
> To mak' or mar this maikless torso.
> Let him look to Nature nae mair. (p. 285)

And he exalts, as the finest manifestation of the snake, the restless spirit
of man, human consciousness over the centuries:

> The insatiable thocht, the beautiful violent will,
> The restless spirit of Man, the theme o' my sang. (p. 285)

Matter struggles to fulfil itself as spirit; it and we evolve to higher thought and higher consciousness as a historical process, which is the essence of humanity.

As the essence of humanity we find the Speaker himself, a suffering, thinking, creating human being. Though no longer the drunkard on the roadside, he exists as a flesh-and-blood man and not a disembodied voice. In a series of passages at the centre of the coil (at the midpoint of *To Circumjack Cencrastus*), the Speaker depicts himself, in a cheap office, performing cheap work, daydreaming in front of the window and afraid of being found out by the boss. In the half-light (a reminder of Proust), he imagines Dostoevsky imagining Stavrogin:

> Here in the hauf licht waitin' till the clock
> Chops: while the winnock
> Hauds me as a serpent hauds a rabbit
> Afore it's time to grab it [...]
>
> Here in the daurk, while like a frozen
> Scurl on Life's plumm the lozen
> Skimmers – or goams in upon me
> Wan as Dostoevski
> Glowered through a wudden dream to find
> Stavrogin in the corners o' his mind. (p. 230)

The window grasps him as the snake would grasp a rabbit. He fears death and beholds death peering over his shoulder. The Speaker does this wretched work (MacDiarmid was a badly paid journalist in Montrose) to support his wife and children. He hates the work and the obligation. We see the Speaker as a frustrated artist – one who dreams of the muse beside him in bed, Valéry's Athikte – but wakes up to find her gone. He would like to be a true writer yet, in his job, is forced to speak of Scotland in the language of England. He is only a plasma of ocean, beneath the waters. He cannot rise and cannot think, lying there alongside starfish, bottles, and corks. God doesn't care. We behold the Speaker's alienation, his sense of imprisonment and isolation, in the drudgery of the office and of marriage. And he suffers as a poet, desperately trying to write yet prevented from doing so by the alienation, imprisonment, isolation, and drudgery.

The Speaker is impeded also because he is a Scottish poet trying to write in Scotland. After having evoked the snake, the Speaker immediately alludes to the disunity of Scotland and of Celtic civilization. Later, he observes that the snake feeds on light, and that we Scots are afraid of it and have been so since the time of John Knox. Our universities are dreadfully bad, the students know nothing of Scottish culture. Our country stands in utter dread of ideas, denies the arts and the life of the mind, and exiles its brightest sons. Although the Speaker would like to soar aloft and sing of God, he can't. The Kirk stands in his way. He makes us reflect 'that the Celtic Idea becomes harder and harder to bring about, even to imagine, in a land inherently provincial and anti-intellectual, which has been so for centuries, institutionalized as it were, by the wicked adversary of good snakes, John Knox, and his official, enshrined, Calvinist, English-speaking church.

As in *A Drunk Man*, the Speaker cannot recommend Christianity. He admits that Christianity hasn't failed ... because it has never been tried. It would be nonsense to relaunch it today; you could only reap death. Instead of following long-since discredited creeds, the Speaker espouses a fierce, heroic humanism – existential in a sense – struggling ever in the face of death. The Speaker recites (in collage) a poem of Rilke on death; he composes his own ironic 'Scottish Anthology,' which mocks death and the dead in the spirit of the Greek Anthology. Then he denounces Wordsworth for treachery. Wordsworth betrayed his poetic gift by wallowing in the world's joy, by asking no questions. On the contrary, cries the Speaker, we are here, on this planet, to struggle. Evil is to be defined as the absence of tragedy, as the golden mean and the mass herd in which, because of which, we cease to be ourselves. Yes, I rend the veil, he reasons, and behold (in the window?) myself and death leaning over my shoulder. We must act! If it requires a sword to cut Scotland free, offer me the hilt! He orders the Lion Rampant to descend from the flag and devour politicians, sportsmen, and phoney American tourist pseudo-Scots. In the ocean we find only the thoughts of a few men, fragile and perishable as bits of hair. Yet they and we rise from the slime, an eternal witness to that which resists death and God – the restless human spirit.

This is so because man thinks and also writes. The circular Scottish snake has a heritage. It has a forked tongue which spoke to Eve in the Garden of Eden and gave her the gift of knowledge. Since then, it speaks to and for poets. The poet's home lies in the serpent's mouth, where is to be found the best of all tongues, better than a woman's. Although the mob will never understand, a golden lyric is finer than politics and faith, finer than everything. And the fire and joy of poetry, and of the free mind, are finer than happiness. It is fitting, for so many reasons, that this poem, like *A Drunk Man*, be powerfully intertextual. As with *A Drunk Man*, we find collages – embedded translations of poetic texts and allusion to writers. The Greek Anthology, Burns, Dostoevsky, Proust, and Yeats are evoked, and Rilke is translated. The dream lady, the divine dancer, goddess and muse, is called Athikte – she comes from a text by Valéry. And, because of the Gaelic Idea, Celtic culture takes pride of place. The Speaker sings the praises of Mary Macleod, who restored Gaelic music and, therefore, changed the flow of history. Similarly – here he substitutes bird for snake imagery – the Speaker denounces the foreign parrot telling English lies and come to silence us. In its place he evokes the Mavis of Pabal, who sings alone on a hill. This lovely, singing bird stands as the *imago* for a true Scottish poetry, most likely poetry in Gaelic. Finally, we must never forget that the Circular Scottish Snake is derived from a Celtic tradition which extends from the Book of Kells to *Finnegans Wake*.

For all these reasons, I am convinced that, even more than was the case in *A Drunk Man*, *To Circumjack Cencrastus* is a metatextual work of art, concerned with the conditions of the writer in Scotland and with the nature of language and the poetic process. For MacDiarmid the rise of humanity from the slime and the eternal struggle of the human spirit to be free are ways of accounting for the artist's struggle to create the work of art, to create and to celebrate, in art, the rising, struggling artistic consciousness. Therefore, I agree with those critics who define the poem's subject as its own coming into being.[20] If the structure is less coherent than one might like, this very incoherence reflects the reality of the writer in Scotland – *dixit* MacDiarmid – and of his reality writing it. As the Speaker quests for Athikte and the snake, so MacDiarmid quests for the appropriate form and realization of his idea, to make his subject-matter realize itself in form. This is the poetic process in general and the particular poetic process of this poem on the writing of poetry. Ultimately, the snake is unreachable, unattainable. The poem then recounts the poet's quest for it and celebrates it, whether he succeed or fail. The cosmic serpent swallows its tail. So too the artist returns again and again to his tale, ever striving, ever questing – and, if he fails, he fails as all must, all those who are finite and mortal, tossed about on sea and on land, yet led on by the never-ending vision of the beautiful, magnificent, ever-changing, ever-evolving, coiling, and uncoiling snake.

In the early 1930s Hugh MacDiarmid continued to produce verse in Synthetic Scots. The 'First Hymn to Lenin' (1931) continues the secular, anti-Christian or non-Christian humanism of the earlier sequences. Lenin is praised as the man who engineered the greatest change in history since Christ and who did what Christ's disciples failed to do. Lenin's superiority over Christ lies in the fact that he treats humans as grown-ups, whereas the Christian tradition deems them to be children. No less interesting is the 'Second Hymn to Lenin' (1932), in which the Speaker declares that poetry and art are superior to politics and include (subsume) the latter in themselves. This is a splendidly heterodox position for a poet on the Left, in the 1930s, even when he nuances the statement by proclaiming that, of course, art should spring from genuine human concerns and speak to the people, not uniquely to aesthetes.

My own preference is for 'The Seamless Garment' (1931), a resolutely communist poem and, I am convinced, a most successful one.[21] The Speaker addresses workers in the weaving industry. The work that they do – the garments they produce – are not mere commodities but also contributions to humankind and things of aesthetic value. They should know this, as should society as a whole. In art and politics we have to understand the world, technical production, and art. Just as workers know the reality of their trade, so also Lenin and Rilke, each in his own way, know the reality of the world, knowledge which the workers can share. In this phenomenology of knowing and of knowledge Lenin and Rilke are joined, as also, implicitly, are MacDiarmid's Speaker and the mill workers. This is because life and work, belief and action, are intimately bound together, like the weavers' seamless cloth; and the weavers' skill and understanding of that skill will lead, seamlessly, to constructive action. As they produce fabric, so Hugh MacDiarmid produces his intellectual work and his art, which, he hopes, will resemble theirs in integrity of purpose and result. Once again, the Christian motif is introduced, in that the seamless garment, produced by the *pauperi* of the earth, recalls Christ's cloak, which he gave to *pauperi*. Surely, intimates MacDiarmid, it is better for the masses to live, create, and comprehend on their own, without outside Christian *caritas*. The Speaker helps them, in a comradely manner, by explaining to them what they already surmise. In time, he hopes, work will become less alienating, and machines will serve humanity instead of humans serving machines and the capitalist parasites who own them. Working men will master the means of production so that their labour will cease to be reified. The workers' lives and the Speaker's life, he hopes, will attain the same integrity that we find in the cloth.

From roughly 1934 on, MacDiarmid, without entirely abandoning

Scots, wrote and published mostly in English. He became obsessed with the desire to compose a poetry of facts and ideas and to enrich poetry in English – by creating an aggrandized, scientific, and internationalized or polyglot English comparable to Synthetic Scots. Influenced by Maya-kovsky, among others, he aimed at a poetry of still greater scope, both political and didactic in nature, that would break with traditional English lyricism as *A Drunk Man* broke with the Whistle-Binkie in Scotland.

Striking successes in this line were produced early on. The critics unanimously praise 'On a Raised Beach' (1934) as a masterpiece com-parable, in scope and in nobility, to Eliot at his best – a supremely pow-erful agnostic meditation on a number of the issues also raised in *The Waste Land* and *Four Quartets*. The greater part of MacDiarmid's imagi-nation, however, went into projects for epics – world epics – of science, philosophy, politics, language, and aesthetics all rolled into one. Pub-lished eventually (all of this had been more or less written by 1942) were fragments from the projects – *In Memoriam James Joyce* (1955), *The Battle Continues* (1957), *The Kind of Poetry I Want* (1961), and *Dìreadh* (1974).[22] Of these, differing from most of the specialists, I prefer *The Battle Contin-ues*, a supreme example of Scottish 'flyting,' in which MacDiarmid flays the poet Roy Campbell for having supported Franco during the Spanish civil war. Although the leftist sentiments are excessive, because they are excessive the satire is fierce and magnificent. Only a Dante or a Mac-Diarmid can hate with such power.

Whatever the virtues of these thousands and thousands of lines in English, and even though nothing Hugh MacDiarmid writes is without interest, the vast majority of commentators prefer his poetry in Scots. It made him an icon to the best Scottish writers in his lifetime, and it makes him a uniquely esteemed artistic creator to this day.

ROBERT GARIOCH

Even though Hugh MacDiarmid himself, from 1935 to his death, pub-lished largely in English, he never ceased to encourage writing in Scots. Around him – often in a spiritual rather than a purely physical sense, and inspired by his example, even when disagreeing with his aesthetics or his politics – grew a generation of writers in Scots. The Second Wave of Lallans Makars, also called the MacDiarmid Makars, came to the fore in the 1940s and 1950s, their careers extending through the 1960s and beyond. These writers were, on the whole, more scholarly than Mac-Diarmid. They studied the 'auld leid' (old Scots language). They had a more solid grounding in the medieval Makars,[23] in the century of Fergusson and Burns, and in foreign languages. This generation preferred the term Lallans as the designation of their tongue. They argued with greater rigour for standardization and normalization of the language, devising the famous 'Style Sheet' of 1947 as an important first step toward a unified, rational orthography. They were more urban and urbane than MacDiarmid, creating a social poetry centred on life in the city. Whatever the differences, they produced a highly successful, aesthetically powerful series of works that, like MacDiarmid's, were and are authentically modernist in their treatment of and response to the conditions of modernity.[24]

Robert Garioch / Robert G. Sutherland first began to write in Scots in the 1930s. However, his major production occurred after the Second World War. Because Garioch published widely in the reviews and in newspapers and because he gave a number of public readings, he became known as a comic, indeed a light-comic versifier, the comic being the register most appreciated in those venues. As a public performer, he popularized the persona embodied in this verse – the little man who unmasks the pretensions and the folly of the high and mighty. This is not the only or necessarily the best Garioch, however. The more perceptive scholars have observed, behind the persona and behind Garioch's personal modesty, a wide range of register and mode.[25] He knew well his Dunbar and his Fergusson; he was an intellectual of enormous culture. In the comic and in the serious verse, he proved to be a master craftsman, adept at revitalizing older literary forms, including the sonnet and the familiar epistle. And, behind the good humour, lurk satire of injustice and a sense of pain, dread, and anguish – the modernity that has marked our era.

A good half of Garioch's verse consists of art translations. His most successful achievement in this domain is some 120 sonnets taken from Giuseppe Belli, the nineteenth-century satirist who wrote in the dialect of Rome. It was, so to speak, a perfect fit, for Garioch to transmute to Edinburgh and Braid Scots Belli's Roman wit, composed in urban Romanesco. These translations – which a number of scholars consider to be Garioch's best work – then inspired his own original 'Edinburgh Sonnets.' Here, part of Garioch's success is due to the manipulation of stance and voice, where he adopts the point of view of the mocking outsider or the embarrassed insider. He may don the mask of low or high culture critiquing high or low culture. In all cases he offers satirical demystification and brotherly sympathy – often at the same time.

In what is, after all, occasional verse grounded in the events of the day, the Edinburgh Festival is a privileged target of Garioch's barbs. In one sonnet he recounts a dreadful soirée, a concert of impenetrable contemporary music, in which the music, whatever its intrinsic worth, takes second place to the audience, a flock of trendy culture vultures, twenty-three-year-olds with beards desperate to appear in the swim of things.[26] The Speaker, in disgust, avows he would have preferred listening to a reel of tape at home, where he could also have enjoyed 'serenata sung by randy pussy.' Here the Speaker adopts the voice of 'natural man,' physical in his physicality, unmasking the effete aesthetic pretensions of the concert-goers. To do so, not only does he embody the physical and the (in some sense of the term) anti-intellectual. He also lowers the stylistic register, employing crude vernacular which would shock the aesthetes but which, in context, is congruent with the reality of life, including desire, including the animal, so much more vital than their pretence. This would be a genuine instance of the Bakhtinian 'material bodily lower stratum' indulging in transgression against high clerkish orthodoxy, the clerkish orthodoxy of our time.

The Speaker's persona – as someone who attends the concert or cultural event yet is capable of satirizing the proceedings, one who is both here and there, inside and outside – defines other sonnets in the sequence. One such text is his account of another soirée – a dramatization of Fionn MacColla's *Ane Tryall of Hereticks* on a Saturday night.[27] The performance was followed by an animated discussion which, no doubt, included exchanges between Protestant and Catholic and between Christian and secularist. The discussion was so animated, and people so involved, that it passed the midnight deadline and police had to break it up. The last line expresses the Speaker's mock approval of the police, for how can we dare discuss religion on the Sabbath? ('Wha daur debait religion on a Sunday?'). Here, again, the Speaker undermines artificiality and rigidity, in this case old Scottish 'Blue Laws,' which, in a modern, largely secular society, fail to have relevance. Originally meant to protect the Sabbath from being profaned, they also punish high intellectual theatre and debate. Ironically, of course, as the Speaker hints, this also was their purpose or, at least, their function in a society where a narrow, tyrannical Kirk (the old clerkish orthodoxy) prevented a viable theatrical tradition from ever evolving in Scotland and hoped to prevent viable secular thought as well; but in this it failed, witness the Speaker and his text.

A third of these sonnets revolves around the symbolic clash of culture and of class.[28] Here the Speaker, more genuinely the embodiment of Robert Garioch the poet, recounts a dedication ceremony. He is enjoying the ceremony – it was his idea, he confides – until a group of keelies from the town turn up and point and laugh at the gentlemen, upon which the Speaker becomes embarrassed. The octave is made up of noble French-Latin rhyme-words, to be found in poems by the old Makars; these are formal, linguistic referents to the academic gentlemen, their speeches, and their ceremony: 'occasioun, receptioun, perceptioun, invitatioun, dedicatioun, inceptioun, conceptioun, dissertatioun.' It is also the linguistic equivalent of the visual spectacle, the gentlemen dressed in academic garb. The young men of the people change all that. The stylistic register hops from *genus grande* to something more like the middle range and the normal speech of normal people, and also from the literary past to the concrete present. Significantly, the Narrator feels embarrassed in his academic gown, at which, presumably, the lads are pointing, and embarrassed that, from a presiding Subject, he is transformed into an acted-upon Object, the object of their gaze. Again, as Speaker, the implied author's poetic voice and moral stance are both inside and outside, participating and judging, at the same time. Part of him enjoys the ceremony, part of him is aware of its artificiality and, in the grand scheme of things, its uselessness. As a human being he is torn by his very self-consciousness, which causes embarrassment within the text and also the creation of the text.

Garioch's social voice could adapt to a number of forms. He chose forms congruent with the classical eighteenth century, which was also the golden age of his city. 'The Percipient Swan' (like 'The Canny Hen') redoes La Fontaine in a contemporary setting and manner.[29] The swan pronounces the fable entirely in the first person. It lives a bland, correct, reasonably happy existence in the public park. However, it is aware that humans have clipped its wings. Indeed, it has tried to escape but realizes that, with inadequate wings and inadequate webbed feet, escape is impossible. The swan makes us aware of the drabness of its routine and of the rage and sorrow that smoulder beneath its apparent resignation. The allegory is patent: the swan's life is our life, and the swan is us. Our wings are clipped also, and our freedom denied. Like the best among us (and unlike the mass), not only has the swan no illusions as to its fate; it scorns resignation and acceptance. On the contrary, it says, because it is 'bad' and not 'good' (according to the masters, the humans), it is learning to sing and, when it does sing, will confound them:

Gin I was guid
I wad gae mad,
but my salvation
is that I'm bad.

I'm gaithran virr
to complish ae thing
they never jalouse:
I'm learning to sing. (p. 7)

On one level, this is the exaltation of poetry, of the artistic calling,
whereby the most circumscribed rebels can and do exert freedom and,
by appealing to rebellion, conquer their conquerors. Thus the swan
approaches Robert Garioch, poet, protesting his state. Yet, on another
level, Robert Garioch and the implied reader know something the swan
also is aware of yet denies. The swan's eventual song will be a swansong;
it alludes to and is part of a mythological commonplace. According to
the commonplace, the swan bursts forth in song at the moment of
death. Our poor swan refuses the truth that, if and when it does sing, it
(not the human's 'hale stupid faction') will die, either of natural causes
or, perhaps, dispatched by the masters in their anger.

Among those who may still hold illusions as to their fate, or who are
incapable of reflection on the topic, is the character in Garioch's 'Sisyphus.'[30] In this witty version of the old myth, Sisyphus is a contemporary
Scottish labourer who, once he has pushed the rock successfully up the
hill, takes time off for a break: a bit of cheese and pie. Then, when no
one is looking, he gives the rock a little nudge, and down it rolls, Sisyphus dashing after it to continue his labour. The poet mocks one manifestation of what we can call the trade union mentality, although it is
equally applicable to modern life as a whole – the lack of purpose or of
pride in one's work, the eagerness only to satisfy creature comforts. Sisyphus is assured of monthly pay and of occasional forbidden breaks for
tea. In his stunted, alienated existence, that is all that matters. Yet there
is worse. To ensure the continuance of the paycheck and of the cheese,
he sabotages his own (rather, the boss's) project. Immediate job security
takes precedence over everything, including completion of the work.
The worker connives with the bosses in his bondage; he is as responsible
as they are for his stunted existence and for his avoidance of risk,
change, and imagination.

Garioch was especially successful in what was to be perhaps the most typical genre of the Lallans Makars – the Horatian familiar epistle. In the finest classical tradition, and as a gesture of cultural renewal, these epistles are generally addressed to fellow poets and, as Voltaire did so brilliantly, to poets from the past. Garioch was attracted to the sixteenth-century neo-Latin Scottish poet George Buchanan as much as to Belli. He translated into Scots Buchanan's plays *Jepthes* and *Baptistes*, and also one of Buchanan's poems concerning his misery teaching the humane letters in Paris. Directly following 'The Humanists' Trauchles [Drudgery] in Paris,' Garioch places his own original piece, 'Garioch's Repone [Reply] til George Buchanan.'[31] Garioch institutes a dialogue with the long-dead poet, joining Scot with Scot, the past with the present, and Latin with Lallans. Garioch's Speaker underscores the continuity of culture in a delightfully ironic manner, by insisting upon the fact that he is as wretchedly unhappy a schoolteacher as Buchanan was; in that respect, nothing has changed over the centuries. The Speaker emphasizes how badly he is paid, and that he is too poor (and too old) to learn another calling. The Speaker suffers from material and spiritual penury, the latter because he is always on call, never having time for himself. He recounts an average, representative day. In a magnificently Bergsonian manner, the Speaker portrays for us an endlessly repetitive series of mechanical, useless activities – not just teaching but minding the pupils, policing them really, in their games and their meals. Thus, in the Bergsonian sense, we find 'du mécanique plaqué sur du vivant.'[32] The Speaker's spiritual life is eroded by the repetitively mechanical and physical; and the artificial imposition of the one on the other, plus the repetitiveness, makes us laugh. The loss of time and of the spirit means, for the Speaker, that he can no longer write poetry – the Muse tires of his paying no attention to her and, as a result, she leaves him:

> The Muse, wha doesna share her rule
> wi sordid maisters, leaves the fule,
>   sans merci, til his fate. (p. 37)

Buchanan had, ironically, said farewell to the muses. No less ironically, Garioch still wants his Muse – it is she who, in a huff, drops him. The comedy is rendered all the more effective with the erotic overtones. Garioch plays with the idea that the Muse is a neglected girlfriend who, in any case, knows better than to waste time with academics, and, by implication, that being a schoolteacher also makes a fulfilled love life impossible. The school denies vital humanity in all respects. Yet, behind and beyond the comedy, we realize that Garioch, like Buchanan, is less separated from the Muse than the Speaker will admit, for the very break-up of the relationship is the subject of comic poetry, which is written, and of an intertextual exchange, which does take place.

'To Robert Fergusson' is more subtle and problematic, and also more poignant.[33] The Speaker, as in 'Repone,' compares past and present – in this case the situation of Edinburgh, the subject of Fergusson's own poem 'Auld Reikie.' The sense of place unites the two poets as well as their aesthetic – they share the same classical tradition and the quality of urbanity which goes with it, in part because they are city-dwellers sharing the same spatial *urbs*. The Speaker, like Voltaire's speaker addressing Horace or Boileau, compares past and present in an adult, non-committed manner, so to speak, aware of features of good and ill, a manner which guarantees his urbanity. Garioch's Speaker readily admits progress in terms of filth and stench. The New Town brought benefits, and even the Old Town is more salubrious than in Fergusson's day. With the hygiene, however, came capitalism and the English. Indulging in a bit of pastoral *à la moderne* not uncongenial to Fergusson the author of pastorals, the Speaker contrasts the familiar, democratic, and concrete community life in old Edinburgh with our contemporary Princes Street shops, which would shame the devil. The Speaker, in his Horatian stance, also evokes with nostalgia the more natural sex in Fergusson's day, and his belief that the capital was more fun then. Therefore, he and Fergusson are alike and would be great friends:

> But aye we'd rise wi little hairm
> and cleik ilk ither by the airm,
> singan in unison to chairm
>   awa the skaith,
> syne seek some cantraip, harum-skarum
>   and naething laith. (p. 24)

They would be friends in drinking and wenching but also as artists, quoting Fergusson's predecessor Ramsay and Garioch's predecessor MacDiarmid. A tradition of urban high culture emanates from the Horatian correspondence; Fergusson is recognized as a poet who will live in Edinburgh as long as people drink there. This bit of irony is then rendered tragic as the Speaker states that he has been dreaming (daydreaming?) all night at Fergusson's grave (a time when, in theory, he and the others carouse). Now it is dawn, the spell is broken, and he will go home. On the one hand, we recognize that the bond of poetry did come into being, between these two Horaces and their epochs, because of the poetic epistle 'To Robert Fergusson.' On the other hand, the end of urbanity is solitude, and the modern poet – like Fergusson is his lifetime and now in his grave? – returns alone, to suffer and to create.

Garioch also wrote two long poems in a more serious vein. In my opinion, these are first-rate works which testify to the author's wide range and to the range of uses open to Scots for those who would take a chance and push open the door. In 'The Wire' the Speaker, observing gossamers on a Scottish moor, recalls to mind a landscape of horror.[34] People are imprisoned by barbed wire to which bits of tin are attached so that a clattering noise will occur if anyone touches the wire. When someone does, he is immediately slain by guards in their towers and by marauding watchdogs. Where prisoners have tried to escape, flowers grow, nourished by their blood.

This text is derived from, and alludes to, the author's experience as a prisoner of the Italians during the Second World War. On one level it is biographical. On another, it is allegorical, and successful allegory at that. The Speaker alludes to three kinds of prisoners – those who try to escape, those who tie themselves to stakes so as not to be tempted, and those who wander the camp, working safe areas, careful not to touch the wire. The first group – political idealists? artists? – give their lives madly, yet flowers burst forth from where they trod. The others live their pitiful little lives – middle-class conformists? – for their ground is sterile, without growth. Some are lucid – intellectuals? more serious artists? – yet theirs is the lucidity of despair: 'The truth is clear, and it is wae.'

That woe is the sombre, unbearable truth of human existence is underscored by the locale. The Speaker tells us it is a land without end, where there is no mist and, at the same time, no sun. A locus of hell? A vision of another planet? Garioch makes the implied reader 'feel' his allegory with a nightmare intensity worthy of Kafka or Dante. The nightmare extends to the wire, to the guards – they also are prisoners of hell; they are not allowed to sleep; they shoot because ordered to – and to the dogs. The revelation offered by Garioch is one of discovery and of despair, the discovery of human life or of modernity and the despair of our moral judgment as we respond to it.

Less despairing and, ultimately, more complex is the meditation in Garioch's longest poem, 'The Muir' (The Moor).[35] In this text, among other things, the Speaker meditates on modern nuclear physics, atomic particles, quantum theory, and relativity. Although some critics have denigrated Garioch's capacity to discuss such matters (or the capacity of High Lallans to be the medium for such discussion), I am convinced that the poem succeeds on its own terms and with greater ease than in MacDiarmid's later aggrandized English. The Speaker is torn apart by the problem of knowledge – how can he give credence to such matters? How can he incorporate their truth into his little human frame of reality? Electrons, atoms, quantum particles, pure energy – how can this relate to the Speaker and to the Badenoch Moor in summer on which he is strolling?

The Speaker compares our contemporary scientific vision of reality with the traditional Christian vision from the past. This he portrays as the Christian – Catholic and Calvinist – belief in the reality of a physical hell. On one level, those beliefs were lies; Rabelais helped blow them away. Yet can the Speaker be sure that quantum energy is truer than the devil in hell? Standing before him, will he deny the reality of Satan? Is not Dante's hell alive today, in the heat of Glasgow and the cold of Edinburgh, where real human beings are forced to labour? And when we lost Dante's hell, we lost his world and his certainty in a world.

In the course of the discussion the Speaker evokes his favourite Scottish poet, Robert Fergusson. This time we do not see the witty, percipient drinking companion; we are reminded that Fergusson died young, having been institutionalized in an asylum. Garioch develops the idea that Fergusson went mad in the conviction that he would be damned. The Speaker asks, was Fergusson necessarily wrong to believe in eternal flames of hell burning in a vacuum?

And Fergusson gyte, gyte in Darien,
jummlin his heid wi thochts of Satan's den
and airts invisible whaur deevils prowl [...]
Hou can we say that Fergusson was wud
to skar at an eternity of Hell [...] (pp. 58, 60)

Is that more outlandish than what we are told to believe? Is it not appropriate that poets suffer from melancholia? Why shouldn't Fergusson howl in insanity? Isn't howling a natural act? Don't we all go mad trying to resolve unresolvable questions? And the Speaker avows he cannot tell who is mad and who is sane.

The Speaker recognizes, implicitly, that belief in hell as punishment did not end with Rabelais; indeed he ascribes it to John Knox's Kirk,

ironically the direct inheritor of the Italian Catholic Alighieri. The problem of knowledge – the Auld Kirk versus the New Science – becomes a
problem of history in Scotland with the two Scotlands, the Kirk and
experimental science in their historical dimensions, which both exist
today.

In the last analysis, the Speaker – the voice of Robert Garioch, modern poet and heir of Fergusson – chooses to respond as a humanist,
bringing the problem down to the human dimension. On the Badenoch
Moor, far from an indifferent God yet capable of recalling Eden (*sans*
horse flies), he will accept the reality of his body and of the earth, and
the reality of his consciousness of body and earth. We can follow the
strivings of mad poets and avoid being enslaved to dogma. We can
think, our thought one note in the harmony of the spheres. Thus Garioch and his Speaker attain a relative degree of dignity and freedom,
which is perhaps all that a twentieth-century artist can long for. Thus
ends his powerful and serene meditation on existence.

SYDNEY GOODSIR SMITH

Sydney Goodsir Smith is generally recognized as the finest poet to have
written in Scots since MacDiarmid (Garioch also receives some votes)
and the only one to rival MacDiarmid in range and in intensity.[36] A New
Zealander by birth, Goodsir Smith came to the language in his late
teens or even early twenties. In addition to collections of lyrics and
scholarly work, he composed a number of relatively brief dramatic texts,
some for the BBC, a full-length poetic drama, *The Wallace* (1960), and a
striking piece of experimental prose, *Carotid Cornucopius* (1947, 1964),
in the manner of Rabelais, Urquhart, Sterne, and Joyce.[37] This last piece
testifies to Smith's incomparable command of the language and his
incomparable verbal agility and wit. It also stands as proof that a minority language, in the right hands, is as apt a medium for high-culture creative play and for intellectual high jinks as are the French of Rabelais
and the English of Joyce.

Smith is best known as a poet of love and passion. Throughout his
corpus we find powerful brief lyrics in the metaphysical style or the high
romantic mode of Burns. Smith has also striven to be a political poet.
Although they have found less favour with critics, I find that his poems
of protest – on Prometheus and on John Maclean – and his texts on the
Second World War, especially the Eastern Front, are deeply moving.

These poems are not meant to be intellectually or psychologically problematic. They are rhetorical, in the best sense of the term, and melodramatic in a good sense of the term. 'October 1941' and 'Armageddon in
Albyn' speak to our shared humanity, denouncing the horror of young
men cut down in their prime and the misery of little people caught up
in the holocaust.

The Horatian mode especially appeals to Smith's adopted persona as
a big drinker and prince of pub crawlers. It also appeals to his enormous
literary culture and obsession with what today we call intertextuality.

'To Li Po in the Delectable Mountains of Tien-Mu' is dedicated to the
memory of Robert Fergusson.[38] In it the Speaker recalls a night on the
town. He and his companions drank heavily in one or more Edinburgh
'howfs' and then off they went carousing in the streets, singing, shouting, and pissing against the wind. This band of bards, drunks, and scholars adopts the air of marauders on the prowl for burgesses' daughters
and liquor:

Hola! Hola!
Up and bar the door,
Douce burgesses my dears!
There's reivers on the toun the-nicht!
Guaird weill your liquor
And your dochters pure [...] (p. 102)

In the shouting and singing, Li Po, Fergusson, and Dunbar are evoked,
as if they were present. Then, at the end, the Speaker salutes Li Po and
Fergusson: he thought, for a moment, that all three were on the bash
together, as he hopes they will drink together in the afterlife – on the
other side. The intertextual play establishes a bond among three poets
disparate in space and time – one from the Tang dynasty in China, one
from Enlightenment Edinburgh, and the implied author, Sydney Goodsir Smith, today. The bond exists because of the similarity in lifestyle of
their artistic personae – all three urban and urbane, all three gentlemen
of pleasure, who enjoy a good drink and a good wench. The bond exists
among three Horace-type writers in a Horace-type address, above all
because they are writers, artists, and poets. In the nighttime roistering
and in the dedication, Smith opposes bards and drinkers, including
himself, to the burgesses of Edinburgh, carefully barricaded inside their
comfortable town houses, careful to guard their spirits and their women
from the troublemakers. As with Garioch, and perhaps more than with

Garioch, Smith testifies to alienation from society and to the absence of community except with dead poets.

Communion with a dead poet occurs also in his delightful 'Gowdspink in Reekie' (Goldfinch in Edinburgh), published in 1974, a first, almost identical version having appeared in the *Saltire Review* in 1955.[39] Here the implied author, Sydney Goodsir Smith, addresses his near namesake, the eighteenth-century writer Oliver Goldsmith. They both are poets, they both are outsiders to English centrality (Goldsmith is Irish and Smith a Scot), they both dwelt in Edinburgh for their medical studies, and they both are Smiths. The Speaker indulges in Rabelaisian wordplay, which is also the tradition of Dunbar, as he establishes a bond with Goldsmith. First of all, he insists that gold and a Smith do not really go together any more than silver (money) and a Makar. Poets, genuine poets, cannot become affluent, he jokes, whatever their surnames appear to say. The Speaker then makes the Irishman's gold a central theme in his text. He sets out to refute Goldsmith's economic theories. He alludes, here, not to alleged scholarly writings on the topic but to the well-known lines in 'The Deserted Village': 'Ill fares the land, to hast'ning ills a prey, / Where wealth accumulates and men decay.' Nonsense! cries the Speaker, mocking the nostalgic pastoralism of Goldsmith's lines, it is wrong that as a person grows richer he deteriorates, and vice versa. He asks Goldsmith if, when he lived in Edinburgh, the more money he lost, did he really become a better man? The Speaker insists that, no doubt, capital and currency are bad: yet personally he loves it when he has them, and they can only bring him good.

Along with the theme of currency and exchange, the Speaker develops the traditional Horatian motif of good fellowship. Since Goldsmith studied here in Edinburgh, he must have drunk in the taverns back then just as the Speaker does today, except that (here Smith evokes Villon) Goldsmith's howfs have disappeared like the snows of yesteryear. Be that as it may, the Speaker imagines (dreams, remembers) a night on the town he spent with Goldsmith. Snow feathers fell like pieces of money. The Speaker and 'Ollie' converse together on money and women – Goldsmith in English, the Speaker in Scots. They were together that one time when the Muse burst in through the door. Poor devils they are, insists the Speaker: after a night of drinking, their money is gone and their ideas with it. The only riches are to be found in verse. This said, Goldsmith's ghost stayed with him all evening, if only in his heart. The Speaker drinks a last toast to Ollie, asking – in Villonesque style – for his prayers:

Gowdspink, my maik, my lay is dune –
Pray for this gowdless smith
        What byke ye're in.
I'll see ye syne. Guid nicht! (p. 229)

Thus, good men – poets, rebels, lovers, the poor – are united across the centuries. They stand together in their response to the Muse and in their little community, apart from the burgesses and other decent, right-thinking and night-hating people in John Knox's capital. They, their love, their art, and their drinking are all the Speaker has. He celebrates them in this text and throughout his opus.

The love – a secondary theme in these addresses – is central to many of the best lyrics and to Goodsir Smith's masterpiece, *Under the Eildon Tree* (1948, rev. 1954).[40] This sequence of twenty-four elegies celebrates *fin' amor* – love as passion – in the grand manner of antiquity (Virgil, Ovid, Propertius), the Middle Ages (the troubadours, *Le Roman de Tristan*), and the modern (Ronsard, Shakespeare, Burns). The Speaker's love for his lass (as with the troubadours and trouvères, she bears no name) dominates the text from beginning to end, and the implied narrative is the story of his purported love affair with her.

Other poets will sing of worthier subjects, no doubt – politics or the spirit of the age. They will be the unacknowledged legislators of mankind. The Speaker insists that, unlike them, he lives only for and sings only of love, his love, greater than all others. This is because he is so extreme a person, so totally in the throes of passion that the lass becomes all for him and nothing else exists. This commitment of the loving subject recalls the *joven* of the troubadours, the absolute commitment and gift of self endemic in the young, without which *fin' amor* is impossible. Another courtly trait in the *Eildon Tree* is the notion of love as religion and the Speaker as devotee of the cult, adoring his lass and the goddesses, especially Aphrodite and Hecate, subject to their will and, if necessary, accepting damnation at their hands.

The Speaker is assimilated to Aeneas, Odysseus, Cú Chulainn, and Tristan: spatially, his is a quest and he himself a quest hero in the adventure of love. Yet Eros is not martial heroism, nor does it demand a martial life. The Speaker's first epiphany with his lass occurs at home, on the waterfront, at sunset, as a boat leaves. The intensity of their shared sentiment and their spiritual climax is revealed through tears, trembling, and silence. This precedes immediately the memory of a physical epiphany, making love on the grass beneath the moon, where the lovers partake of earth, sky, and stars, and where the entire world is contained in the narrow space of their embrace.

Magnificent as it is, temporally the Speaker's *fin' amor* cannot endure. Like everything human, it rises and falls, it comes and goes. The lass is blamed, for her cruelty laid him low. Fate is blamed, the downturn determined by the Wheel of Fortune. The gods are blamed, Cupid, the blind loon, or Zeus who laughingly destroyed Orpheus. As a result, Eros brings as much pain as joy and as much misery as happiness. The Speaker suffers in the flesh and in the spirit. Love leads to self-destruction, for he had possessed but now has lost the Grail and the Happy Isles. This destructive passion makes him mad, a fool in the throes of folly. It brings death, as his heart is ripped apart, and Death, the masked blonde surgeon, cuts away at his heart. Later the Speaker again invokes 'Strumpet Daith,' allied with Messalina and Morgan, she whose embrace releases him from love when she grasps him to her breasts dripping poisonous pitch. The end is hell, where the Speaker lies among legions of the erotic damned, having failed to propitiate the goddess and still seeking only a tear. Thus Goodsir Smith renews a tradition of medieval love-death, according to which *fin' amor* attains totality only in death and the couple is united only in the grave, and the tradition of modern psychoanalysis, according to which Eros and Thanatos are irrevocably bound, from birth to death and at every rite of passage.

More than is the case with MacDiarmid, more than will be the case for any poem discussed in this book, *Under the Eildon Tree* sounds and resounds with intertextual allusion. Goodsir Smith evokes the culture of the centuries in as totalizing a manner as Pound or Aragon. Like Louis Aragon, he does so in the name of love, to reinforce the notion of the universality of Eros in our culture and in the human imagination.

The poem's title alludes to the Scottish ballads of the Eildon Tree and the Eildon-Tree Stone in the Eildon Hills, where Thomas the Rhymer, also known as True Thomas, met the fay, was loved by her in the Otherworld for seven years and then allowed to return to our realm with the blessing (or curse) of prophecy and of telling only the truth. Hence the Speaker's great love, his loss, and his declaiming on love in Scots – verse the implied author wants us to believe is true.

True or not, the Speaker is blessed or cursed by the assembly of the gods. His lass is the ward of Artemis, the white goddess, huntress and slayer. The gods play with him and employ Eros to drive him mad.

Cupid, blind and uncaring, tortures him, as does Zeus. Finally, as we have seen, the Speaker is crushed by death, personified as Black Artemis or Aphrodite or the Celtic Bridget or Hecate.

Invoking the panoply of the gods would, perhaps, be perceived as an act of Celtic overreaching were the Speaker the only speaker. As it turns out, he is not; he contains within himself, and speaks in the voice of, the great lovers of history and legend. Therefore, in Elegy X Burns tells of his Highland Mary, insisting that she is real, not an invention according to the scholars. In Elegy XII Orpheus tells of his double loss of Eurydice and of his decision to sing no more but join her in Hades. In Elegy XV we hear of Cú Chulainn's love for both Emer and Fand. In Elegy XVI Dido bewails, in the fire of her death, the loss of Aeneas. In Elegy XX Tristan awaits the coming of death, living only for Isolt and the passion she instils in him. And in Elegy XXII Marc Antony declares, in the high aureate style, his passion for Cleopatra. Since the Speaker himself is a bard, a lover because he is a poet and a poet because he is a lover, all writers who created the books of history and myth are centred in him, and he assumes their voice. He is Catullus and Virgil, Henryson, Douglas, and Burns, Thomas d'Angleterre, Villon, and Ronsard, and Shakespeare. The lass is his love, also his goddess and muse. She can cast him to hell. Yet he can make her immortal through the fame of his verse. Phallic and aesthetic creation are fused, as is the striving for a girl and for a poem. The result is one of the most notable textual exaltations of passion and art in modern literature, comparable to the best of Aragon, Eluard, and Neruda.

This supremely powerful vision of *fin' amor* is then rendered still more powerful by a continuous process of problematization, concretizing, and undermining. The elegies, written in a modern high Lallans which is both vitally contemporary and, in its aureate moments, intertextually medieval, depicts a 'universe' which is, at the same time, universal and local. The Speaker invokes a number of cosmopolitan, international cultural figures, and others which are Scottish, such as Henryson, Dunbar, Douglas, and Burns, or the Celtic Cú Chulainn and Tristan. The action is universal, situated in an interspace of all-encompassing Western civilization, and it is located in today's Edinburgh. The moment of epiphany occurs in the city's own Leith port area, and the lovemaking on the grass, after dark in an Edinburgh public garden. As in Goodsir Smith's other writings, we also hear of the howf; one, in particular ('The Black Bull o Norroway'), is the scene for the Speaker's encounter with the Other Woman, his Dark Lady. It is in this central passage (Elegy

XIII) that the Speaker exalts sensuous life, at table and in bed, and portrays the city itself – staid Edinburgh – after dark as a whore on her back, outstretched and open. The alienated artist attacks bourgeois respectability by comparing life in the capital, all respectable life, to prostitution, which is veiled during the day but explicit in the anonymity of the night, the time of carnival when the bawdy and the body take their revenge, the feminine, 'lunatic' time of the senses, under the reign of Aphrodite and Black Artemis.

The reality of the Dark Lady is crucial. Throughout the poetic sequence, and especially during the first half, the Speaker bewails his fate at having been abandoned by his lass, as a result of her 'flichterie' and 'flegmageerie.' However, slowly but surely in the course of the diegesis, the implied reader discovers that the treachery and guilt belong to him and not to her. First, in *genus grande*, we are told of the tragic love and loss endured by Orpheus, who rightly blames himself along with Zeus for Eurydice's first and second demise. Then, immediately after, occurs the scene in the Black Bull, where the Speaker meets Sandra, a teenage whore. They drink and drink, and copulate and copulate, under the watchful gaze of the girl's mother. Sandra is a land whose ports are open to the sea. She is Venus, Helen, Cynthia, la grosse Margot, Manon Lescaut, Marguerite, and Dumas's Lady of the Camellias. The Speaker will make her immortal. She is a perfect beauty according to the Greek canons, also a pitiful little bitch who serves as an instrument for the Speaker's 'belle nostalgie de la boue' and who, as a bonus, may have given him the pox:

> – Sandra, princess-leman o' a nicht o' lust,
>   That girdelt the fishie seas
>   Frae Leith til Honolulu,
> Maistress o' the white mune Cytherean,
>   Tak this bardic tribute nou!
> Immortalitie shall croun thy heid wi bays,
>   Laurel and rosemarie and rue! [...]
> O, Manon! Marguerite! Camille!
>   And maybe, tae, the pox –
>   Ach, weill! (p. 171)

This delightful bit of undermining and of counter-courtliness à la Jean de Meun or Villon is perceived to be the cause of the break-up with the lass and of the tragedy which is exalted (genuinely and ironically at the same time) as the fate of Orpheus, Aeneas, Cú Chulainn, and Tristan, the fate of a man torn between two loves – the wife and the whore, the light and the dark. For the Speaker's liaison with Sandra is both grotesque and powerfully, humanly erotic. It is a worthy counter-statement to the central *fin' amor* of the *Eildon Tree* as well as its satirical underside.

After Eurydice, Sandra. And after losing Eurydice and, presumably, Sandra also, the Speaker falls into the depths of melancholia, in the Middle Ages and Renaissance the condition of the lover, poet, and clerk, born under the sign of Saturn and subject to the sin of acedia. Smith recasts this convention in Elegy V, where the Speaker portrays himself, in his flat in Edinburgh, sleeping until noon and lolling in bed the rest of the time, amid tea, crumbs, and cigar ash. The 'Slugabed' as artist is derived, in part, from Villon. However, Smith relates him directly to Oblomov, the hero of Goncharov's novel and one archetype for the nineteenth-century Russian 'useless man':

Here I ligg, Sydney Slugabed Godless Smith,
The Smith, the Faber, Ποιητης and Makar,
And Oblomov has nocht to learn me,
Auld Oblomov has nocht on me [...]
A cauld, scummie, hauf-drunk cup o' tea
        At my bed-side,
        Luntan Virginian fags. (p. 154)

This Russian analogy enables Smith to mock politics and left-wing political verse. What would Stalin say if he saw me? asks the Speaker, and what sermon would he give? For sermonizing, one tyrant equals another, and the Speaker compares John Knox and Joseph Stalin. On the one hand, it took four centuries of capitalism and Scottish culture to produce the slugabed wallowing in his cigar ash. On the other hand, no doubt Stalin also can take a drink. As can 'Hugh,' cited in an ironic allusion to Mac-Diarmid's East-West synthesis.

Under the Eildon Tree is an example of the modern erotic elegy, of how Catullus, Propertius, and Tibullus can be made vital in our time. On the one hand, we find the lover as poet and the poet as lover, both undergoing a quest for love and the lady, a quest which is both adventure and artistic creation. Hence the allusions to great quest heroes of literature: Ulysses, Aeneas, Cú Chulainn, and Tristan. Hence also allusions to the great poets of love, from Catullus, Virgil, the troubadours, and the trouvères to the Renaissance and Burns and today. Hero, lover, and poet fuse in the eternal desire for the White Lady and the Dark Lady, in the eternal story of desire, betrayal, guilt, and death. This is then fused with or juxtaposed to a continuous process of undermining in the low style, *genus humile*, according to which grand sentiment and grand rhetoric always comprise their own counter-argument and counter-statement. The love is traditional and archetypal, and also powerfully modern and local, exalted, learned, and bawdy all at the same time. In the end the Speaker damns himself to hell, in despair at the loss of his lass and of love. He also returns to the beginning of his text, for although the lover may be damned and the artist as well, the artist will (have) create(d) the story of his love ('O, my great follie and my granderie'), quest, and damnation. That is the cursed gift of the poet – True Thomas condemned to tell the truth and Sydney Goodsir Smith condemned to write about telling the truth in *Under the Eildon Tree.*[41]

TOM SCOTT

Tom Scott occupies a line in the modern Scots tradition different from those of Garioch and Goodsir Smith. A self-made man from relatively humble background, he followed the example of the later, didactic Mac-Diarmid. Scott was a convinced Scottish nationalist and socialist; he advocated social poetry, in which the message takes precedence over the medium and the ideal medium should be the long poem, a kind of modern epic in which the poet could become (again) the spiritual legislator of mankind. Always a figure of controversy, he is considered by some to be a major poet and by others, no less authoritative, to be all but worthless.[42]

A university graduate and scholar who never held a formal academic position (and hated the university), Scott had a wide cultural range, comparable to those of Garioch and Smith. He translated Dante, Villon, Ronsard, Baudelaire, and Ungaretti. He cultivated the Horatian voice with an *Epistle to David Morrison* followed by a *Second Epistle to David Morrison*. He composed in Scots two didactic, allegorical long poems, *The Ship* and *At the Shrine o the Unkent Sodger* (At the Shrine of the Unknown Soldier).[43] The first is a commentary on the sinking of the *Titanic* as the culminating achievement of capitalism and Western civilization. The second is a protest against war. Despite fine passages in the satirical vein and despite the author's (occasionally blatant) sincerity, I feel that the social epistles and social epics do not come through as works of art.

Resembling Victor Hugo in ideology and in manner, Scott also shares Hugo's unevenness in poetic creation. Much the same can be said for his significant production in English.

Tom Scott does achieve poetic heights, in my opinion, when the social or ideological is fused with other concerns, which give it roundness and life. Such is the case in the long sequence *Brand the Builder*, published in 1975 with portions written as early as 1951.[44] This poem evokes Scott's family and the city of St Andrews, where he grew up, after a Glasgow childhood. The central figure, Malcolm Brand, is a version of Scott's father, Elsie Brand is the mother, and young Johnie Brand is himself. Whatever the biographical reality, these three elements take on life as literary characters – the mimesis of genuine people – and as symbolic or allegorical entities, each an individual and each helping to make up the family unit.

The family exists in a state of tension, a reality of tension that senti-mental verse would veil. Brand is, in some ways, pleased that his son is educated and wants to be a writer (there can be money in it) yet also worries that Jock spends too much time reading. Elsie shouts at the over-sensitive boy in order to harden him. Brand and Elsie also shout at each other, trading insults. Returning home from work tired at the end of the day, Brand goes out for a smoke to escape the noise made by Elsie and the children. He wants a few minutes of peace and quiet. While smoking and looking over the sea-front, he daydreams. This is the central passage of the sequence 'Brand Soliloquises.'

Some critics have attacked this section because the ideas expressed and the culture revealed are out of character in an uneducated urban construction worker. I submit, on the contrary, that such critiques are mean-spirited and also sociologically inaccurate. Malcolm Brand, who has become a small businessman, the owner of his little enterprise, is a member of the 'Keep-Left Club' and attends discussion groups at the university. A working man is capable of having ideas and meditating on them. As Bold has observed, we find here a mind limited by its environ-ment yet on the edge of full consciousness.[45] It is Scott's talent, by voic-ing a number of his own ideas through Brand and later Elsie, to have created successful mimetic characters who do embody the spirit of the masses. They are genuine human minds as well as rhetorical or medita-tive voices.

Brand reflects the implied author Tom Scott as well as Scott's bio-graphical father. One of his modes is what we can call left-wing satire. We find the same brand of satire in the speeches of Elsie and Johnie.

Malcolm and Johnie denounce the university for its intellectual squalor; Elsie denounces the schools for their practice of corporal punishment. If the university is so dreadful, this is because of anglicization; the institution has totally sold out to the English. English occupation and English mastery have corrupted life in St Andrews. That this could happen is the fault of capitalism. With 'siller' (money) the only god, corruption, exploitation, and war inevitably follow. The workers are all right, even the small owners, but the rest of St Andrews is rotten to the core. In answer to this, Malcolm sees little to counter the decline he has observed. Yet he retains, to shore up his ruins, personal integrity and the dream of socialism. Elsie shares his hatreds and his dreams. In addition, she is a feminist who blames men. They are such a bother, they (and the Kirk) insult us women with lies about Adam and Eve, and unlike women, they kill for their ideas.

The Brand family speaks not uniquely in the present. Their vision is grounded in personal experience, having endured through time, and their discourse is above all one of memory. Malcolm and Elsie meditate on what they have lived and how the world has changed around them. Elsie, in particular, recalls her breakdown in childhood when physically beaten by the dominie. These reminiscences add roundness and dignity to an otherwise seemingly insignificant existence. In 'Johnie Brand's Prologue,' the youngster and intellectual, instead of reflecting on his own life – he hasn't lived enough – evokes a more general sense of history and duration. Like his father, Johnie's sense of history is circumscribed by and also profoundly anchored in St Andrews and its magnificent stone monuments.

A builder in stone, Malcolm Brand hates the ruins of war he has seen. Johnie's 'Prologue' is a panoramic evocation of the city as it appears from the seaside. Here he meditates on the ruins of the ancient cathedral, pulled down by Protestant zealots:

> And yonder, doun by the pends whaur time hes duin
> Havoc on the auld toun waas, is Scotland's Shame,
> Hame nou for the daws, the doos and the craws,
> The jauggy ruins o whit wes in its time
> Europe's grandest cathedral. (p. 103)

Nothing is more tragic than the ruins of beauty, Johnie affirms. And he equates, as history and as symbol, the fall of the cathedral with the fall of Scotland, the decline of its university and its enslavement to England,

then and today, compounded by the phenomenon of young men leaving St Andrews to make a life somewhere else and coming home only to
be buried in a graveyard, another image of lifeless stone. The Presbyterian Reformation, the rise of capitalism, and the English ascendancy are
envisaged as a fall from grace, a symbolic Original Sin that has led to the
defilement of the Scottish land and people. Hence the importance of
Elsie's discourse, for Elsie, mother of Johnie, is a *figura* of Eve, Mother
of Mankind. Elsie denies the traditional misogynistic explanation of the
Fall, for which the Kirk is responsible, replacing it by her own, that men
learned from Satan to worship the god Power, his Word ('siller'), and
his Creed (war); as a result they have sold their mother Scotland into
whoredom.

As a counter to the imagery of oppression and enslavement, Tom
Scott offers two positive structures. Johnie's discourse begins and ends
with an evocation of the sea, the sea air, and the receding tide:

> The sea crines aye awa alang the sands
> And tint youth crines wi it, crines awa,
> Yonder the rocks' lang fingers harp the tide
> As aye they've duin, as aye they ever will,
> Heron-sprayed amang their slimy weeds [...] (p. 107)

He beholds the city from the vantage-point of the ocean. For him, the
city and its stone monuments are meant to contrast with the beauty
and the perenniality of the natural site which surrounds them and will
outlast them. Similarly, Malcolm quits his noisy, disruptive little family
community for a good smoke and deep thought, alone, overlooking
the water. At the end of his discourse, he asks what is man in contrast
again to the clean wind and the sea birds which survive where no man
could.

On the other hand, aside from the cathedral, the stone monuments
of St Andrews have survived and are things of beauty. They have survived because Malcolm Brand the mason restored most of them himself.
He spent his life building things, ships in Glasgow and houses in St
Andrews. Although no one gives him the credit, he the master builder
reconstructs what was destroyed by others. Here Scott states a biographical fact yet also delivers an allegorical statement. The little people, the
masses, make their contribution to society and culture. When properly
harnessed, they are capable of productive labour, negating the baleful
influence of power and money.

Malcolm's trade as a builder in the present precedes and prefigures, in a secular sense, Johnie's eventual career as a writer and, of course, the implied author's actual present creation of *Brand the Builder*, which recalls the father-figure in the past. The son continues the father and fulfils his vision, voicing what the father thought and keeping the faith of the mother, who still loves books in spite of her traumatic experience of school. Johnie (and, behind him, the implied author) holds the same radical political convictions as Malcolm and Elsie. Johnie will try to build in verse what Malcolm succeeded in building in stone. Art, whether visual and spatial or verbal and discursive, is one answer to the alienation of the Scots over the centuries.

Indeed, in one respect Johnie – that is, Tom Scott – succeeds where Malcolm and Elsie may have failed. One aspect of 'reality' in the implied diegesis is the problematic nature of marriage. Basically, Malcolm and Elsie growl at each other, exchanging insults. Yet, as Grassic Gibbon, among others, was to show, this sort of marital flyting is a typically Scottish way of communicating and of expressing tenderness, in a manner which diverges intentionally from what the Scots would deem to be English sentimentality. The extent, then, to which Malcolm and Elsie communicate, and to which either communicates with Johnie, remains veiled, one aspect of the marriage problematic. We can have no doubt, however, that all three characters communicate with the implied reader because the implied author wanted it so and created them as speakers, giving voice to their otherwise voiceless thoughts with that purpose in mind.

This ambiguous, problematic vision shapes the final section, 'The Daeth o Brand,' a song with refrain, ultimately of medieval French provenance (the *ballade* or the *chant royal*), in the manner of Dunbar. It is a threnody on Malcolm's death, praising him as Dunbar would praise a Makar. The beauty and the pathos are then undercut by the refrain, 'But nae tears coorse frae the hert o stane' (But no tears flow from the heart of stone) (p. 130). Life comes and goes, people come and go, whereas physical reality abides, indifferent. This is true for the sea and sea wind surrounding bad St Andrews; it is no less true for the good St Andrews built by Malcolm Brand. Not only is the mason's work not recognized; even the work itself, the houses and churches he made, his creation (Bachelard's hard earth of the will), remain indifferent, immune to human sentiment, as immune and mute as the man's own gravestone. But this is not the case for his other creation, his son Johnie, the implied Speaker who weeps and who loves. Common humanity, shared by Mal-

colm, Elsie, and Johnie, shared by Tom Scott, proves as vital and enduring as sea and rock, as nature in the raw and cities built by men.
Common humanity lives, creates, and loves. It also makes its mark in the
universe.[46]

'The Paschal Candill' is a splendid long poem, composed after the
author attended an Easter mass in the Vatican.[47] Although it was a rous-
ing success – read three times on the BBC – Scott refused to publish it,
indeed suppressed the text until 1987. He did this for what today we
would call reasons of political correctness, because, as a radical, a Marxist, and a non-Christian, he felt embarrassed, even oppressed, by the
poem and by the aesthetic and mystical experience which gave rise to it.
As Herdman puts it, Scott 'objects to his own religious stance.'[48] Unlike
their counterparts in Brittany and the South of France, poets in modern
Scots are not at all oriented toward the sacred mode, nor do they partake of the specifically Christian tradition. This is the case for a number
of reasons, which include their stance on the Left and, more important
still, their belief that the Christian tradition, embodied in the Church of
Scotland, is responsible for much of the narrowness and provinciality in
the land and for the historical phenomenon of anglicization. In this,
Scott is the direct heir of MacDiarmid. It is nonetheless striking that the
greatest Christian poem of the Scottish Renaissance in Scots should
have been disavowed by its author, and that the author, while claiming
to revere Jesus, denies that he ever was or is a Christian.

The Speaker locates his mystical experience in Rome, at the Vatican,
on the eve of Easter Sunday. The *erzählte Zeit* of his text, its implied narrative, covers the period of time which elapses between the lighting of
the Easter candles and the moment in the mass when the priest absolves
the faithful and they say the Lord's Prayer. For the Speaker, this is the
climax, the point at which Christ himself, embodied in the priest, laves
the Speaker and all others present – including the implied reader – of
sin. This shriving by the priest allows the Speaker to meditate on sin.
And, because he is a version of Tom Scott, the Speaker indulges, here
and throughout the text, in fierce, nobly expressed indignation on and
satire of human suffering and exploitation. In this, Scott's Christian
poetry resembles the oeuvre of that greatest of Christian satirists,
Agrippa d'Aubigné. Like D'Aubigné, Scott brings in much of sacred history and the Bible to reinforce his argument, in a manner that resembles typological exegesis of Scripture. The sacrifice of Isaac leads him to
evoke all our young slain in the wars. The Children of Israel turning

away from Moses to worship the Calf of Gold are postfigured, as it were, by the children of Scotland – 'O my kintraemen' – who sell their souls for money. The many mansions in the House of the Lord are interpreted by the Speaker to comprise the beauty and richness of pristine Scottish nature, defiled by pollution. Nature is defiled, the animals die off, and the land is ruined when Prometheus rises to give us the Bomb, and Jason crosses the seas to bring back gold. Love from Christ on the Cross and the love of the three Marys weeping for him are caricatured in our modern 'love,' when whores fight over a client and the Grove of Diana is defiled by the coupling of beastlike humans:

> In the citie parks
> Whures with nae skirts on ablow their coats
> To save time
> For the five-bob jerk on the boole of a tree
> In Diana's wood nearby [...] (p. 38)

Even the Lord's Prayer itself – Scott cites a fine version in early Medieval Scots – gives rise to the Speaker's commentary, a denunciation of evil – especially idolatry (modern science and technology) and greed (modern capitalism) – the sins against which the Pater Noster warns and from which it delivers.

Yet, against all this corruption and defilement, Scott offers hope, first of all because the Speaker is implicitly a Scot speaking Scots to a community of Scots. He addresses his 'kintraemen' because of what they share – space, a land of stone which is their house, a land which once was pristine and can regain its lost beauty and innocence; and time, centuries of shared history, for good and ill. They also share language, the Scots tongue which is the medium for this text. The Speaker is willing to assume a role in the regeneration, in his stance as the bard – a poet of facts and ideas, deeply involved in society, a force for change and renewal.

Second, whatever may be Tom Scott's opinions on the subject, his Speaker is undergoing a Christian experience in the course of Holy Mass and is in the process of uttering a Christian poem. The Lord's Prayer is a statement of faith, a credo. It is also a hymn of praise to the Creator. Most of all, it is a plea for God's mercy, which reaches a climax with the cry 'libera nos a malo.' In conjunction with the Pater Noster, the Speaker depicts for us the priest, who is the Living Christ, shriving us of sin:

Dae ye renounce the Tempter and his warks?
We dae renounce them.
Surrender all ye ken for this unkennable?
For saik of the Licht we dree the mirk.
Will ye be made baith clean and haill?
We will be made sae.
A promise is given ye, no a guarantee.
Lat it be sae. (p. 39)

Holy Mass is a sacrament, and it is in the mystery of this sacrament, which includes the shriving of sin, that the individual is healed and is guided toward salvation. What is possible for the individual Christian becomes then possible for the community – mankind as a whole and/or that special part of mankind dwelling north of the English.

Central to the imagery of healing and regeneration is light. The candles of the Easter mass cast light in darkness, fulfilling in typological terms the creation, when God created light ('Dixitque Deus: Fiat lux. Et facta est lux.') out of darkness and over the waters. In absolving us of sin, the priest grants spiritual light in place of spiritual darkness. At one time in the past God unleashed the Flood in its darkness, a horror post-figured in the Second World War, when fine young men are torpedoed in the waters. For them, unlike Isaac, God does not offer a substitute sacrifice; they drink fully his cup of wrath.

The Speaker observes that, although God promised his creatures no further punishment by water, he made no guarantee for fire. The Easter candle casts light and is fire. Yet, at the same time, the priest washes away our sins and we are cleansed, like Phaëthon falling into a river or Jesus immersed in the Jordan. Water, light, and fire can punish us, as the objective correlative of our own evil. As symbols and manifestations of God's love, they also offer hope, the only hope humanity can expect.

In a Christian world, fire and water are never static entities. They move, as we move, up or down, and our movement, like theirs, is fraught with meaning. We have seen the Speaker recount Jason's trip over the waters in search of gold and Prometheus's quest upwards to return with fire. These are false, twisted, demonic quests bringing modern horrors: capitalism and war. In contrast, that other wayfarer, Christ, wandered to and through Jerusalem and climbed onto the hill of Golgotha, a glorious, beneficent quest, his feat greater than the conquest of Everest. Because of him and because of his victorious adventure, he is fire and light, he is the candle, the cross in the Vatican (and in ancient Palestine), and the Speaker's own soul soaring aloft. Since, allegorically, Jason and Prometheus prefigure the Saviour, *in malo*, the hope is that the Speaker and his people (the Scottish chosen people following after the Chosen People of Israel) postfigure him *in bono*, in the tropological or moral level of exegesis, in this most moral of poems by a moralist poet.

We have seen, in further elaboration of Christian imagery, the allusion to modern sex polluting the Grove of Diana. The tree or woodland motif is amplified when the Speaker invokes the Holy Rood, Christ's cross which soars to heaven. The cross itself, a tree, is redeemed, as is its figural prototype, Adam's tree of the knowledge of good and evil. Similarly, in Christian typology, Adam is the *vetus homo* who prefigures the *homo novus*, Christ, who in turn redeems Adam and all mankind. Thus is explained the Speaker's twofold comment that, by bearing the cross and by climbing on it, Christ has restored the fruit to Adam's tree and Christ is crowned (*rex Iudaeorum*) with Adam's thorns.

We also hear of Eve being defiled by our defilement of nature. Eve, of course, prefigures the Virgin Mary as Adam prefigures Christ, and Christ's redemption of Adam is comparable to Mary's redemption of Eve (Eva transformed by Ave), and Ecclesia's redemption of Synagoga. Mary is the queen who forms the wax of the hive; she is the star (*stella maris*) who steers the ship; she leads the baby Jesus to Adam's tree; she is the Speaker's dream bride. And hers is the love which, in a Dantean image, moves the stars.

The result, for the Speaker as an individual and for the larger community of Scots or of humankind, is the possibility of healing. Just as Orestes was cured by Athena and Apollo, so too Mary and the Living Christ make us whole again. Water washing away our sins (Christ's blood in the mass) is the remedy offered by the priest in Rome, and by Christ in Jerusalem and throughout history. This is the miracle of the real presence in the Eucharist. Because of it, the Speaker remembers Ezekiel's vision of dead bones taking on life. The Speaker's own soul soars aloft, following the candle and the cross. He recognizes the non-entity, the nothingness of death. He discovers eternal life, which conquers death and which is Christ.

Tom Scott, as a poet, is surely at his most effective in exploiting the possibilities of extended narrative. He is a poet of archetype and myth, granting new meaning to the stories of the old culture heroes, Adam and Christ in addition to Orpheus and Odysseus. He exploits sacred imagery in his quest for social justice, fusing, for a time at least, the two great visions of the modern West – the Christian and the Marxist. His stance is far from the hermetic, fragmented, tortured gropings of so many modernists since Mallarmé and Valéry. Yet, along with Aragon's, Eluard's, and Neruda's, along with MacDiarmid's, his radical humanism is no less valid as social vision and as the creation of art in the twentieth century.[49]

NOVEL

LEWIS GRASSIC GIBBON

The triumph of Scots poetry does not carry over into the novel. The Scottish vernacular has not given rise to anything like the quantity and quality of modern prose fiction in Breton and Occitan. A developing practice of historical writing in prose graced the sixteenth century yet did not continue over the ages of neglect. For ages it was assumed that although Scots could be employed for certain kinds of lyricism, all serious writing – eventually, this came to include the novel – would have to be cast in English. Quite a bit of Scots prose was published yet limited to the popular, local press, especially in the northeast. As a result, the Scottish novel, back to Scott, even to Smollett, was composed in standard English, the narrative and reflective passages uniquely in English, with Scots – each writer's own version of it – reserved to passages of dialogue uttered by comic, old-fashioned, or lower-class characters. Some sort of fusion of English and Scots in the narrative-reflective passages was attempted by a few writers, Galt, for example, and, as we shall see, Grassic Gibbon. It also has to be said that, over the last two or three decades, a major effort to cultivate Scots prose of all sorts has been launched, especially in the pages of *Lallans* (since 1973), the review in Scotland which corresponds to the Breton *Al Liamm* and the Southern French *Oc.* Robert McLellan's *Linmill Stories* is one of the summits of this movement, the other being William Lorimer's translation of the New Testament.[50] Expository prose has been illustrated by J.K. Annand, Donald Campbell, Thomas Law, William Neill, and Alexander Scott, among others. Parallel to the Lallans compositions by McLellan and Lorimer, we find another current, disavowed by some Scots enthusiasts yet ultimately perhaps of greater importance for the future of the language. Here I allude to the urban demotic cultivated as a medium of contestatory homodiegetic discourse by writers such as James Kelman and Irvine Welsh. *How Late It Was, How Late* and *Trainspotting*, to cite two of the most talked-about contemporary novels, are representative of this current.[51] Important as they are, and as indicative of a dynamic Scots prose tradition in the making, they take us out of the chronological and historical parameters of this study.

One major book in a version of Scots did burst forth in the days of the literary Renaissance and has become a classic: Lewis Grassic Gibbon's / James Leslie Mitchell's trilogy, *A Scots Quair* (A Scots Book) (1932–4). From 1927 to his early death in February 1935, writing under both names, Gibbon / Mitchell composed some seventeen books, thirteen of them during his last three years. These cover a number of genres, which include exploration, archaeology, biography, and utopian/dystopian romance. His writing is partially inspired by diffusionism, the notion that mankind enjoyed a golden age of innocence during the eras of food-gathering but then was corrupted by evil, represented by food-production, agriculture, and its accompanying civilization, unleashed on mankind by ancient Egypt. Gibbon's most important book in this vein is the left-wing historical romance *Spartacus*, influenced by Flaubert's *Salammbô*. He also collaborated with Hugh MacDiarmid on a collection of essays, *Scottish Scene*, a book of superb satire and denunciation that also includes five excellent short stories.[52]

Although all this is of value, Gibbon's masterpiece remains *A Scots Quair*, made up of the three novels *Sunset Song*, *Cloud Howe*, and *Grey Granite*, which trace the adventures of a young Scotswoman, Chris Guthrie, born to the land, married to a farm labourer / foreman, then to a minister, then to a carpenter / urban worker as she evolves on the croft of Blawearie, the burgh of Segget, and the city of Duncairn. Most of Gibbon's prose is composed in standard literary English. With *A Scots Quair* and with some of the stories and a novel left unfinished, fiction dealing with Scotland and treating the Scottish experience, he adopted a different and quite original approach. (He also adopted, for the first time, the pseudonym Grassic Gibbon). The language of *A Scots Quair* has been characterized, and by the author himself, as English enhanced by a Scottish lexicon and a Scottish lilt and cadence. Others argue that much of the prose, especially in the first two volumes, is Scots recorded according to English orthographic conventions.[53] According to Wittig, this is the first effort to employ the Scottish language throughout an extended work of fiction, in the narrative as well as the 'spoken' passages. Thus, pages of the text have been transcribed as Scots, according to Scottish conventions, without 'changing' a word. After all, a Scottish lilt and cadence is one way of alluding to yet also occulting the phenomenon of

Scots syntax and word order. I find most convincing Campbell's thesis that, although the text is written and meant to be read silently by the implied reader, it has a tangible oral component. For the American reader it can reverberate as American, for the English reader as English, whereas the Scottish reader will recast it, will hear it, so to speak, as Scots. On another level, it does bring 'to the silent reader an approximation of the experience of *hearing* a version of Scots'[54] – at least to the sensitive, inquisitive reader – and can be considered Gibbon's own contribution to the phenomenon of Synthetic Scots.

Sunset Song, the first novel in the trilogy, is the most famous, the one which has enjoyed the widest public acclaim and has received most praise from the critics, including being listed as a set text in the schools.[55] *Sunset Song* exudes the atmosphere of poetry, beauty, and commemoration of the rural past which people associate with Grassic Gibbon as a writer. In this first volume we see Chris and her family arrive at the croft, in the parish of Kinraddie, and we see her grow up. Chris's mother and father die, her brother leaves for Argentina, and she marries Ewan Tavendale, the foreman at Upperhill. Chris and Ewan are happily in love, and they give birth to a baby boy. With the coming of the Great War, eventually Ewan enlists. He dies in France as do others from Kinraddie. The new minister, a man of compassion and understanding, unveils a memorial for the fallen and the passing of an age. He and Chris will marry.

The protagonist and central focalizing consciousness of *Sunset Song* is Chris Guthrie. One function of the narrative is to recount, mirror, and objectify, as it were, growth in her consciousness, her course of personal self-discovery. We observe her path from girlhood to womanhood to motherhood, in something like a female, rural *Bildungsroman*, as Chris undergoes rites of passage from innocence to experience and from happiness to disillusionment. On the one hand, her voyage is external and public: from a dependent schoolgirl and dutiful daughter she evolves into an independent young woman who chooses to stay on the croft, to wed Ewan, and to bear his child. The voyage is no less internal and private, as Chris becomes aware of her body at puberty, looks at herself in the mirror, and explores her budding sexuality. From a gender-oriented perspective, she differs from the men around her and much of society because of her frank, open, yet dignified and discreet recognition of the body and its place in nature. Chris wins freedom from the constraints of a tyrannical father. Yet a moment of epiphany concerning the family occurs at John Guthrie's funeral. Then Chris weeps with insight, recognizing the fact that her father, whatever his faults, had been a fighter – an authentic rebel and a fierce individualist – before life broke him. She chooses the land over becoming a schoolteacher. And it is as a farm wife and mother – the wife of Ewan, the mother of young Ewan, working the land with Ewan – that she is fulfilled. Her old family had caused her pain as well as joy. The new family – with the planting and harvesting of crops, of herself, and of her baby – brings joy. Then, after Ewan is corrupted by the war, Chris has a second moment of epiphany. She could never credit a situation whereby her husband fell in battle, dying for king and country or other nonsense. However, she is deeply moved when informed that he has been shot as a deserter. This means that he gave up the nonsense in order to return to her and to Blawearie. As the symbol of her discovery, Ewan's ghost or something like it comes over the grass and enters her heart:

> And then something made her raise her eyes, she stood awful and rigid, fronting him, coming up the path through the broom. Laired with glaur was his uniform, his face was white and the great hole sagged and opened, sagged and opened, red-glazed and black, at every upwards step he took. Up through the broom: she saw the grass wave with no press below his feet, her lad, the light in his eyes that aye she could bring.
>
> The snipe stilled their calling, a cloud came over the sun. He was close to her now and she held out her hands to him, blind with tears and bright her eyes, the bright weather in their faces, her voice shaping a question that she heard him answer in the rustle of the loch-side rushes as closer his soundless feet carried him to her lips and hands.
>
> *Oh lassie, I've come home!* he said, and went into the heart that was his forever. (*SS*, p. 241)

Thus she integrates the *animus*, the masculine element in her psyche, thus she attains maturation and individuation, and in full consciousness. And thus a specifically Scottish type of female subjectivity enters the genre of prose fiction.

Gibbon delves into Chris's consciousness, making the implied reader comprehend and sympathize with Chris and her thought processes, by a masterful exploitation of narrative technique in the spirit of modernism. Much of the narrative is filtered through Chris's own thinking, focalized through her consciousness; and even though *Sunset Song* and its sequels are third-person heterodiegetic narratives, much of the narrative is recounted in her own (silent) voice. He does this in two ways. Each major section of narrative and commentary on it is presented as Chris's recollection of what occurred in her life and in Kinraddie over the previous six months or nine months or six years. And the identification with Chris's point of view is maintained by frequent use of the second person singular (brilliantly anticipating Butor and the *nouveau roman*), as if Chris were speaking to herself. Trengove and Campbell have analysed how this 'you' grants the narrative a sense of orality proper to rural Scotland and, in addition, a sense of drama, sympathy, and identification.[56] Furthermore, it facilitates the introduction of *style indirect libre* or *erlebte Rede*, which again enables Gibbon to focalize through Chris, her point of view, and her point of thought.

The second-person device is also exploited when the author wishes the implied reader to hear the voice of the community. In the 'Prelude' it is the voice of the folk, a communal perception of history. In the narrative proper it becomes the voice of 'today's' Kinraddie, the 'bodies' as they gossip about events which comprise the narrative. We see harmful tattle-tale concerning Chris's brother Will and his girl, or that Chris is marrying a low-class man too soon after her father's funeral, or how terrible the Germans are and how glorious it is to go thrash them. This perception of things is often contrasted ironically to Chris's perception, for she receives the approbation of the implied author and, because the narrative technique permits him to mould the implied reader's response, the reader's approbation as well.

On other occasions, the community voice of Kinraddie joins with Chris's voice and the implied author's. The implied reader submits to a bond of sympathetic identification. He perceives this voice to embody a still integrated rural society, grounded in the land and in history, maintaining an organic wholeness which city-dwellers and intellectuals have lost. Indeed, although some of Chris's neighbours are comic or eccentric stereotypes, the two most vital and solidly drawn are admirable figures – Chae Strachan, the socialist, and Long Rob of the Mill, the freethinker. These two are profoundly good, decent human beings, friends to Chris and to anyone else in Kinraddie who is also decent. The positive sense of community is revealed in a series of episodes – a storm, a wedding, a funeral, the harvest, a New Year's drink – when people come together in fellowship. It is most apparent when Chae's barn catches fire and everyone gives his all to succour Chae, his family, and his stock. The organic world of *Sunset Song* is visible in concentric circles – the self, the couple, the family with children, and the parish – each bound to the other, each contributing to the total structure.

The structure is profoundly, inherently poetic. A series of image patterns or archetypes constitute the literariness of *Sunset Song* as much as the story line or the characters and their interrelations. The most important of these patterns concerns the land itself, related to the seasons of the agricultural year. The four principal sections of the narrative are entitled 'Ploughing,' 'Drilling,' 'Seed-Time,' and 'Harvest.' This cyclical structure functions on two levels: one referring to the actual farming of Blawearie, the other to Chris's evolution from girlhood into full splendour as a woman. Not long after the Guthries arrive at the croft, Chris is portrayed at age fifteen or so, with some of her clothes removed, in total innocence. The text comments that she is ploughed but not yet drilled and hasn't yet found her way. Later, at the time of the 'harvest madness,' Chris's physicality awakens and she discovers her other self, what Freud would call her id and its accompanying will to the pleasure principle. Now, states the text, she is drilled. Still later, during and after a storm, Chris and Ewan kiss for the first time. In the traditional manner of Romanticism, for that matter as in Virgil, the storm serves as a metaphor for the awakening of Chris's desire. The couple are married on New Year's Eve, after which they perform winter farming and the February ploughing. With Chris pregnant, the narrative voice waxes lyrical in imagery of sowing, tending, and reaping. Then, in the summer, wheat is harvested and young Ewan born. Although the Great War is also harvested, several years later, when Long Rob helps Chris with the harvest, they make love afterwards in a sort of secular epiphany.

On the one hand, the author posits a structural, symbolic, and archetypal bond between Chris and her land. In the Western tradition of the four elements, the earth is the one always depicted in feminine terms. Gibbon proclaims maternal fecundity in the earth and in Chris, the total woman. Both function properly and are fulfilled when they are ploughed, drilled, seeded, and made ready for harvest. In Bachelardian terms, Chris herself is assimilated to the soft earth of rest, earth conceived in terms of feminine imagery – the vagina, the womb – teeming with riches, waiting to be explored and impregnated. This is Chris's body, as revealed to her and Ewan, and in giving birth to their son. Hence Ewan's declaration of independence from the war – masculine doings – in his quest to return to Chris and Blawearie, the two fused in his consciousness as they are metaphorically in the text.

However, we must not fall into the error of envisaging Chris uniquely as a mother-figure or as an icon of rural life. Her identification with *terra* is not limited to the croft she herself works. At a number of points in the narrative, including the periods of reverie and thus of consciousness and recollection, Chris climbs the brae to the standing stones which rise behind Blawearie. These are, in phenomenological terms, the antithesis of the soft, fecund earth of the croft. This is Bachelard's hard earth of the will. In one sense they are phallic, symbols of the early primitive food-gatherers. They also symbolize a different Chris – her coolness and reserve, her splendid quiet dignity, her will to live life on her own terms, and, given the consciousness and recollection, her capacity for another kind of fecundity, in the spirit. After all, Blawearie itself is called, by the others in Kinraddie, not of this world. Therefore, it partakes, metaphorically, of the Otherworld, the object of the quest – for the Guthrie family concretely, in the beginning, and for Chris spiritually, throughout. It is not a coincidence that Chris climbs to the standing stones, that they are on a height, and that it is from on high that Chris views Kinraddie physically and her recent life in memory. Just as Ewan learns to accept a fusion of the masculine and feminine, so too Chris, all her life, embodies that fusion. For she is a woman, physical in her body and her maternity, physical also in her capacity to work the croft, yet she partakes of traditionally masculine traits of fierceness, independence, rebellion, memory, and thought.

Chris's metamorphosis, like Blawearie's, occurs as part of a cycle: for her the cycle of life, for the croft the cycle of the year. The yearly cycle is articulated by a series of ritual events – threshing, harvesting, and reaping; or funeral and wedding; or celebrating the New Year. Time is sacred, as Chris and others partake of something akin to the sacred. Cyclical time is also articulated by a metaphor emanating from the title *Sunset Song*, the cycle of the day. For we envisage Chris's life and that of Kinraddie beginning in struggle and hardship, culminating in a high noon moment of splendour – the splendour of Eros in the individual, the family, the croft, and the parish – only to decline with the coming of war and to end in death and dislocation. This is also the cycle of history, beginning in a Golden Age of Pictish hunters and ending in a golden sunset of Anglo-German slaughter. It is at sunset that the new minister unveils the memorial, explaining to all that, carved into the stones, it commemorates the war dead and, beyond them, the old peasant life of the Mearns. Both are now gone forever. Thus, what is cyclical – the cycles of the day, the year, and people's lives, ever since the time of the food-gatherers – is also linear. This cycle of history is now closed.

The croft life is ended, and ended as well is whatever was good, in terms of dignity, community, labour, and love, in rural Scotland.

Finally, we are made aware of the thematics of the song in this *Sunset Song*. Chris's favourite tune as a child is 'The Flowers of the Forest,' a terribly sad lament for the fallen at the battle of Flodden (1513). At Chris's wedding feast, amid the personal and communal joy, songs are sung, often sad songs. Chae, one of the good friends, sings 'The Flowers of the Forest.' And, at the end, as part of the memorial service, Ewan's friend and best man at the wedding marches around the stones piping 'The Flowers of the Forest':

> And then [...] the Highlandman McIvor tuned up his pipes and began to step slow round the stone circle by Blawearie Loch, slow and quiet, and folk watched him, the dark was near, it lifted your hair and was eerie and uncanny, the *Flowers of the Forest* as he played it.
>
> It rose and rose and wept and cried, that crying for the men that fell in battle, and there was Kirsty Strachan weeping quietly and others with her [...] (*SS*, p. 257)

An intertextual bond is created between the battle which ended Scottish independence and the war which ends Scottish traditional life, both shedding the blood of young men. History repeats itself cyclically even when it ends in linear terms.

But does it? For all our nostalgia for the old peasant life celebrated by Gibbon, life does go on. Chris will marry the new minister, Robert Colquhoun. Ewan will grow up. And the earth abides. For, as Chris has observed more than once in the course of her story, people come and go, people live and die, but the land – Scotland – will outlast them all. It is eternal. The piper circling the circle of standing stones, playing music in harmony with the spheres, offers the last image of *Sunset Song* – the cycle itself as a measure of fulfilment and of eternity.

Cloud Howe (1933) and *Grey Granite* (1934) continue the story of *Sunset Song* to make up the complete *Scots Quair*.[57] In *Cloud Howe*, Chris, now Mrs Robert Colquhoun, goes with her husband to the burgh of Segget. Robert, a liberal, modern pastor, identifies more and more with the fortunes of the poor. Sympathetic to socialism, he supports the General Strike of 1926. Disillusioned, he then becomes, to Chris's disgust, a sort of religious mystic and dies in the pulpit, his lungs deteriorated from an old war wound. In *Grey Granite* Chris and her son, now a lad of eighteen, inhabit the industrial city, Duncairn. Chris becomes a partner in the boarding-house where she and Ewan dwell. Ewan earns his living first as an apprentice steelworker, then as a labourer at the stonemasons. He becomes politically active, gets involved in union activity including strikes, and, finally, will join the hunger march to London and remain there as an organizer for the Communist party. Meanwhile, Chris will return to the land, to the croft her father worked prior to leasing Blawearie.

Although both novels have also been published in paperback and televised, they have not been given the same reception by critics and scholars as *Sunset Song*. *Cloud Howe* has been criticized because of the breakdown of the community voice and because Gibbon pays a great deal of attention to Robert's intellectual odyssey. *Grey Granite* has been attacked, in a more totalizing manner, because of the new centrality accorded to Ewan. Gibbon, allegedly, does not understand urban life and depicts it in extreme terms – of idealized communism or what has been called 'Communist Kailyard.'

On the contrary, I agree with those who believe that *A Scots Quair* is a unity and that the reader must consider *Sunset Song* as part and parcel of that unified, total artistic vision and not as a great single novel with inferior sequels.[58] The phenomenon is widespread in the history of literature – a magnificent first book followed by other fine books. The author evolves, but not necessarily his public, which, having identified him with the first book, expects the others to resemble it. In terms of the aesthetics of reception, the public welcomes that its horizon of expectations be expanded – once – but not necessarily more than once, by the same writer. This phenomenon is compounded by the fact that, for an Anglo-Saxon public, a book of poetry and seeming nostalgia exalting Kinraddie will, in any case, be more digestible than the ferocious satire of Segget and the class-oriented political analysis of Duncairn. *Grey Granite* would not normally enjoy any more recognition than the other left-wing urban novels of the 1930s. It has received attention because it finishes the adventures of Chris Guthrie, the fay of Blawearie.

I believe that satire and politics are as legitimate subjects for fiction as poetry and the quest, and that Gibbon succeeded in these other modes as well as in rural romance. One gives way to the standard colonial stereotypes if one assumes that the poetic, the feminine, and the rural are more appropriate to Scotland and Scottishness than, say, political satire. In addition, the themes of satire and politics are already present in *Sunset Song*, making it a more problematic text than the average reader might realize. Gibbon, who knows the savagery and the misery of the peasant classes, despises Kailyard nostalgia at all levels. His uncompromising vision of life permeates all three volumes.

In *Sunset Song*, the 'Prelude: The Unfurrowed Field' sketches the history of Kinraddie; we are informed that the tenant farming of the present, that is, 1914, is the outcome of centuries of violence and oppression. Then, this 'present' croft life will be destroyed, once and for all, by the Great War. Tragic irony is generated when Gibbon has Chris marry on 31 December 1913, and give birth in the fall of 1914; the implied reader sees what is coming whereas the characters, of course, do not. As a result of history, the best of the crofters – Chae, Rob, even Ewan – are slain; as a result of economic constraints imposed by the war – cutting down the trees, consolidating the land, installing tractors and sheep – the land is ruined and only profiteers remain.

This process then continues, amplified, in the other two novels. The war killed the best of Kinraddie; years later, it snuffs out Robert as well. History itself proclaims the change in locus, for Scotland and Western culture generally, from country to town and from town trade to city industry. In Segget the nineteenth century saw the jute factory and the spinners. The twentieth century sees increasing poverty, the old tradesmen ground out one by one, the mills closed down one by one, and the spinners sacked and reduced to squalor. This decline is punctuated by the General Strike of 1926 and the depression of the early 1930s.

Duncairn, from 1933 to 1935, is the locus of strikes, rallies, and hunger marches – genuine proletarian resistance. One episode turns on discovery by the workers that the plant manufactures armaments, including canisters for poison gas; on another occasion, people are killed by an explosion. I agree with Craig that if Chris consistently turns away from history by insisting on the perenniality of the seasons and the land over mere human agitation, young Ewan, on the contrary, is caught up in that very agitation.[59] He becomes a communist, fights the police, and leaves Duncairn for London, as his way of coming to terms with social reality, which is history. According to Jim Pease, the communist, Ewan *is* history. In this sense, history is linear not cyclical. Chris and everyone around her grow into the present, becoming more and more aware of present reality as they are caught up in it, as Chris's eternal time proves to be a vicious past that is now transformed into an even worse present.

From one perspective, history is an imposition from without. Otherwise decent people are ruined by external forces – wars, depressions –

which disrupt life in Scotland. Neither the croft nor the parish, neither the burgh nor the town can be separated from the greater world of England and Europe. At the same time, sociohistorical forces enter into the relatively small, intimate Scottish space and disrupt it from within. Within the community of Kinraddie we find, as soon as war is declared, dissension between the good people opposed to combat or indifferent to it, and the others, who indulge in cruel, stupid jingoism and also, sooner or later, profit from the carnage and their own destruction. The situation becomes worse in Segget, where the old inhabitants – the old tradesmen – a vicious, bigoted lot, are physically separated from the spinners, the urban proletariat slaving in the mills. Hence the New Town (the old semi-poor) is set against the Old Town (the new very poor). And in Duncairn the neighbourhoods are set so far apart spatially that people from different walks of life may have no physical contact with each other save in moments of crisis.

A romantic revolutionary such as Gibbon, who also considered himself a communist, never allows his readers to forget that history means the struggle of class and the workings of politics and money. The destruction of the old crofter class in Kinraddie is due as much to the deforestation and the monopolization of the land, transformed into grazing for sheep, as to the war itself. Needless to say, Chae and Rob leave no one in the dark concerning the capitalist undercurrent which created the war in the first place. In Segget class struggle is shown to be overt, between a declining petty bourgeoisie and the labourers of the mills. Symbolic of this state of affairs is Chris's dream of the betterment of mankind, her reverie broken by the screech of the mill horn calling the men to work:

> Was there a new time coming to the earth, when nowhere a bairn would cry in the night, or a woman go bowed as her mother had done, or a man turn into a tormented beast, as her father, or into a bullet-torn corpse, as had Ewan? A time when those folk down there in Segget might be what Robert said all men might be, companions with God on a terrible adventure? [...]
>
> Suddenly, far down and beyond the toun there came a screech as the morning grew, a screech like an hungered beast in pain. The hooters were blowing in the Segget Mills. (*CH*, p. 34)

The workers are organized by the Cronin family; the Cronins and the minister believe in Labour and give themselves to the General Strike. It

fails as do their aspirations, countered by powerful opposition figures –
a bitter, indifferent schoolmaster and the corrupt, neofascist absentee
laird. The mills close, the people breed and drink, and the old town rad-
icals die as did John Guthrie at Blawearie. As a result, in *Grey Granite*
only one class, the industrial proletariat, and only one doctrine, revolutionary communism, remain viable options for progress. Peasant individualism is replaced by collective urban consciousness. And the last
novel explores the slow but sure development of this consciousness in
Ewan, his girlfriend Ellen, and a few others, as the line is drawn between
the decent young men of the foundry and the forces of oppression –
bosses, scabs, police, army, newspapers – arrayed against them. Violence
becomes an element in the struggle as people are beaten, tortured, and
even killed.

The violence is one outcome of, and also one image which depicts,
the collapse of the community. The collapse or disintegration is seen to
occur in direct proportion to the numbers of people inhabiting the
same space. In the progression of the trilogy, this means that community
is lost as the author, the reader, Chris Guthrie, and Scotland move from
country to burgh and from burgh to city. We observe also a change in
the quality of ritual, the harvesting and reaping of Kinraddie giving way
to the Agricultural Show and Armistice Day in Segget and then to a
Young League New Year's dance and the moving picture show in
Duncairn, each pattern of ritual entailing greater alienation and a more
blatant artificiality and distance from the soil.

Yes, in Kinraddie people gossip and say silly things about the war. Yet a
genuine kinship exists and a sense of mutual loyalty and respect. In Segget there is no kinship or loyalty or respect. Malicious gossip dominates
the village and the people who dwell therein, with accusations of sexual
promiscuity tossed at random but especially at Chris and Robert
because, in a genuine sense, they are better than the others and incapable of even imagining what they are accused of. Chris herself is an isolated member of the community, as the minister's wife alienated from
the social groupings, and her consciousness is distinct from the 'Segget
Voice,' the perspective of the petty bourgeoisie which the author
moulds us to interpret with irony, *a contrario*. Of course the Segget Voice
takes itself as moral arbiter. Yet always – in part because of this moral
pretentiousness – Chris and Robert think and speak the opposite.

In Duncairn the community voice, good or bad, ceases to be heard.
Gibbon offers his implied readers a juxtaposition of voices and of points
of view, intentionally fragmented and chaotic. These are anonymous

voices. We are not informed whose they are. Chris herself no longer functions as a focus for thought or action, as if in the city no one, not even Chris Guthrie, can conserve enlightened individualism. In place of Chris and in place of Ewan, we find an indistinct urban perspective which is in the process of becoming an urban class consciousness, what, one day, could be a new homogeneous community. In Duncairn the family no longer exists. The home is transformed into a boarding-house, and what home a Ewan will know he creates himself in the factory or on the road. The fragmentation here is an objective correlative for the fragmentation of modern life as a whole and also the modernist aesthetic which mirrors and demystifies it.

In *A Scots Quair* alienation and disintegration are ever linked to sexuality and expressed in sexual-gender terms. It was, in part, the author's openness and disillusionment in sexual matters which gave rise to the negative local reviews in the 1930s. On the one hand, yes, Chris has three marriages. Although all three break down, each time Chris grows and learns, attaining an ever-deeper understanding of the cosmos. On the other hand, the marriages are structured in a descending order. Chris and Ewan attain plenitude and give birth to a son. Although disharmony occurs because of the war, Chris is reconciled to her husband's memory. Chris and Robert enjoy years of sexual harmony. Yet they never have a child. When Chris finally accepts pregnancy, the foetus is stillborn, as a result of her exertions during the General Strike. For years following, they remain distant sexually, because of Robert's new mysticism. For Chris, this mysticism is literally filth. Chris cannot forgive him the filth, and they are never reconciled. In *Grey Granite* Chris weds Ake Ogilvie because he offers to help keep the boarding-house and because he lost his job defending Ewan. Although Ake is a good man, she does not love him and feels only disgust in submitting to his desire. Love is not possible under these conditions, and Ake leaves for Canada. Total love becomes intermittent love becomes no love. And a son gives way to a stillborn foetus which gives way to sterility. Gibbon shows his readers, symbolically and as concrete events in the narrative, the extent to which love, fertility, and even simple desire are progressively deadened under the pressure of the city and capitalist exploitation.

However, this genuine yet relatively simple allegorical reading of the trilogy has to be problematized by the dark, cruel, tragically lucid picture of sex painted throughout the *Quair*. It is in *Sunset Song* that we find a corrupt, lecherous minister and one of the 'dafties' out to rape girls. And we find the portrait of John Guthrie, a religious fanatic torn by his

fleshly desires and who always gives way to them. Among the highlights
of the first volume, then, are the terrifying, torture-laden birth of twin
babies, Chris's mother poisoning herself and the twins when John made
her pregnant again, and Guthrie's incestuous desire for Chris, even in
his last days as a dying, paralysed doddard. The horror is gripping. This
horror then turns to disgust in *Cloud Howe* when the obese sixty-year-old
farmer rapes his servant-girls and when one of the local bodies recounts
proudly his own vile erotic feats in London. Similar vile feats occur in
Duncairn, where a girl is made pregnant and the wrong man suffers for
it, and another lecherous minister defiles his servant. Even with the best
will, Ewan and Ellen Johns cannot make a go of it. When she gives up
the movement and asks him to settle down, he calls her a whore, and it
is over. Gibbon's vision of love and desire is magnificently tragic, worthy
of the great novelists in the tradition of realism – Balzac, Flaubert, Zola.
It is powerful and unforgettable. One reason for its power lies in the fact
that, like the French realists, Gibbon demystifies love by ever assimilating it to the social forces, especially class, which shape it and in which it
grows.

The desire, frustrated or not, is associated with violence and death,
Eros and Thanatos. Chris's mother goes mad before committing infanti-
cide and suicide. Old Guthrie indulges in sadistic violence against his
son as well as sexual violence against his wife. At his worst, Ewan is violent to Chris and half mad, as was her father. Although Robert Colquohoun survives the war, his mind as well as his lungs are tainted, hence
the fits of darkness, his black days, when the traditional element of melancholia – black bile – corrupts his intellectual's psyche. Chris would
wonder to what extent Robert remained sane during the years of mysticism prior to his death, a Thanatos of the body which had long since
possessed the mind, once Eros had been thrust out. In the end, all of
Duncairn's modern life is distorted by violence from which love has
gone. Although Ewan and Ellen do know intimacy, the climax of the narrative occurs when Ewan is tortured by the police. This will to power – a
symbolic rape – defiles his body so that, even though physical potency
remains, he cannot love, not in the way his father and mother did, and
his dismissal of Ellen is a gesture of violence superimposed on the incapacity to love. It can be said that Gibbon distinguishes between his
female characters, endowed with natural sexuality, who are capable of
loving, and his male characters, tortured by lust, who find ways to spurn
tenderness. True enough, yet the author's own stance remains ambiva-
lent. It would be a mistake to assume he automatically and uncondition-

ally prefers feminine intimacy to masculine striving. Such is today's petty-bourgeois mind-set, not his.

Cloud Howe and *Grey Granite* explore two cases of this masculine striving accompanied by patterns of masculine imagery. In *Cloud Howe*, as the title indicates, the more or less solid, concrete nature images of the first novel – the land, the sun, the round of the day and round of the year – give way to imagery of clouds, as always in the realm of nature, yet, from a human perspective, more evanescent. The progression of clouds, from cirrus to cumulus to stratus to nimbus (the four sections of the novel), represents the progression of life from calm after the war to the General Strike and the Great Depression, storms which crush Gibbon's characters and Scotland. Even more, for Chris, the cloud formations represent her husband's ideals. The man's social protestantism, his socialism, and his mysticism – to her, these are fragile and intangible, of no importance. So also, thinks Chris, are Mowat's fascism and Moultrie's Labour. Yet men follow the pillars of cloud by day, worshipping them as if they were gods. Robert gives himself to one, then another, and then another, in terror that he may have to face life without a dream, his head out of the clouds. Again, archetypally, Gibbon renews the tradition of the four elements, with masculine fire and air opposed to feminine earth and water. The clouds are an aerial phenomenon, associated with and propelled on the winds. Like the wind, they symbolize man's spiritual nature, literally the spirit, which, for all its fecundity, remains ever changeable and evanescent. With poor Robert, as he changes from a liberal minister to a labourite to a mystic, each change proves to be for the worse, leading to the nimbus storm at the end, not fecund but destructive – self-destructive – in its essence.

In the biblical overtones of following pillars of clouds and in the conditions of Robert's demise, we can see with what care Gibbon introduces Christian imagery into *Cloud Howe*, which, paradoxically, underscores his negative judgment on Christ and the Kirk.

Robert looks good – very good – in comparison to the ministers of *Sunset Song* and *Grey Granite*, who are sex-crazed degenerates. Indeed, before degenerating in his turn, he wins the implied reader's sympathy. Yet, for all his admirable traits, the man suffers from bouts of melancholia, the black bile of the cleric, born under the sign of Saturn and subject to the sin of acedia. His lungs damaged by gas in the war, he spits blood; then he dies in the pulpit, declaiming a last great sermon, upon which Chris herself proclaims, 'It is finished' (*CH*, p. 211), the translation of Jesus' own 'Consummatum est.' Robert is meant to be taken as, in some sense of the term, a Christ-figure. This is by no means an excessively daring notion, given the age-old tradition – both Protestant and Catholic – that the pastor leads his flock as the Pastor of Men led and leads all humanity. Robert's life, his repeated endeavours to reach the people with the Good Word in order to make Segget a better place, and his failure with both the upper and the lower classes are a tragically ironic reading of Christ's own ministry, relived in twentieth-century Scotland. Gibbon thinks in terms comparable to those of the MacDiarmid of *A Drunk Man*. Robert's last sermon alludes to a spinner family, turned out of their home, reduced to wallowing in a pigsty, where the baby's thumb is eaten by a rat. The spinner family recalls Jesus, Mary, and Joseph at the inn, yet this baby is not protected by angels, nor is it worshipped by kings. The baby is a martyr, as is the wealthy farmer Dalziel's horse, impaled on a stake, which the man allows to be tortured to death in order to collect the insurance. The horse, the baby, and the minister are all martyrs to life – real life – where there is no recompense and no hope, and where the Lamb of God himself would be tortured by the people of Segget for pleasure or profit. The pillars of clouds do not bring this Moses to the *terra repromissionis*. In the end, more lucid than Christ (*dixit* Gibbon), Robert abandons the Old and calls for the New, a new hard-cutting faith in place of the Kirk's: 'There is no hope for the world at all [...] except it forget the dream of the Christ [...] and turn and seek with unclouded eyes, not that sad vision that leaves hunger unfed, the wail of children in unending dark, the cry of human flesh eaten by beasts ... But a stark, sure creed that will cut like a knife, a surgeon's knife through the doubt and disease' (*CH*, p. 210). It is in this faith – revolutionary communism – that the new Joshua, Chris's son Ewan, will attain Duncairn and, beyond Duncairn, London. Yet are Duncairn and London the equivalents of Canaan? Will they ever become lands of milk and honey? In *Grey Granite* the clouds of Howe are now soot-carrying fog, filthy oil, and greasy slime, redolent with the smell of cats, diapers, and the sewers. The fecund earth of Kinraddie has been transmuted into the granite emblematic of the city Duncairn (Aberdeen) or, some would say, into the granite-like Scottish national character. Perhaps, from another perspective, the lifeless, soulless granite of the city secretes the vile, disgusting viscous matter – slime, soot, oil, ordure – a fetid ooze that *is* the soul of the city. The granite resembles the standing stones in its harsh masculine power. Yet, unlike the stones, it has been constructed by evil for the sake of evil, and it serves as the dominant image of a world in which, no war having been declared, youths are cut down at home, beaten, tortured, and murdered by their own. Violence is the thematic of this last novel of the trilogy, committed by policemen and strikers in turn and culminating in the scene of Ewan's torture.

Yet, as Gibbon demonstrates (almost too overtly), the answer to the grey granite of oppression is to be found in the grey granite of men's wills, the power, persistence, and militancy of a new man who dares to wield the sword of the new faith Robert Colquohoun called for in his Passion. This *homo novus* is, of course, young Ewan Tavendale who, from his early years (in *Cloud Howe*), was described by Chris and by the implied author as one with eyes of granite or a body made of stone. As a boy, he collected the granite flints of the old nomads on the hill. In town he becomes a worker in the foundry, then a labourer for the granite mason. He abandons a boy's hobby and dreams of the past for reality in the present, which means social commitment and the social action without which commitment cannot but be sterile. Just as the sections of *Grey Granite* are assimilated to purer and purer strata of granite created by subterranean pressure and heat (epidote, sphene, apatite, and zircon), so too, we are led to believe, Ewan undergoes a quasi-alchemical process of purification, positive growth in contrast to the slow but sure decline of his stepfather in the preceding novel. Only at the end, when he *is* pure granite and when, in the name of the cause, he casts off the distracting girlfriend Ellen Johns (petty-bourgeoise and English), does he prove to be the descendant of the Pictish hunters who, in their harshness and purity, wielded granite also, the granite that Ewan once collected in his room and now has subsumed into his body and soul. In his renunciation and self-sacrifice, in his proletarian zeal, Ewan evolves into a communist epic hero, Gibbon's modern Scottish urban answer in the present and for the future to the heroes – Achilles, Aeneas, Cú Chulainn, Roland – of the dead past.

Critics disagree over how we are to read the ending of *Grey Granite* and, therefore, how we should interpret the novel, the trilogy, and Grassic Gibbon *in toto*. Ewan breaks up with Ellen and leaves for his new function in the Communist party, to organize in London. And Chris returns to Cairndhu, to work by herself, in her solitude, the croft her father worked prior to the story of *A Scots Quair*. There she climbs the Barmekin, has a last moment of epiphany with the land and the cosmos, and actually dies there or undergoes a death experience.

There are those, admittedly a minority, who insist upon the author's creed of revolutionary socialism or anarchist communism.[60] According to this view, Chris embodies the past and Ewan the present and the future. His granite symbolizes a new reality, more vital, more authentic than her old croft. Against her ultimately sterile passivity, he speaks and acts for change. As a strong young male, he can help bring about a future world that will preserve or, rather, reconstitute the best of the early world of the food-gatherers. Grey granite is necessary to fight grey granite, and a violent, revolutionary spirit to remove the slime and hypocrisy of industrial capitalism.

Another current insists upon the fact that Chris remains the focalizing consciousness of the trilogy and that she is given the last word.[61] The scholars who emphasize this point also observe Ewan's willingness to lie concerning the cause of an explosion in the plant and his disregard of values as he struggles for the revolution. He proclaims that the ends justify any and all means. Finally, these readers underscore the brutality with which Ewan dismisses Ellen. According to this view, Gibbon would then be criticizing (or misrepresenting) communist militancy by indicating that, in the end, the cold, unemotional Ewan has truly become grey granite, for he has lost all humanity, and, therefore, that his religion of communism is as cloudlike as Robert's Christianity.

I side instead with those who posit an open rather than a closed ending, with Chris and Ewan, both authentic, both committed totally to their respective visions of life, free to continue their lives beyond the mimetic frame of the narrative, and open to the future. In a final, dignified, deeply respectful encounter, Chris and Ewan each agree to go their separate ways, for, as Ewan puts it (it is he who has the last word): 'There will always be you and I, I think, Mother. It's the old fight that maybe will never have a finish, whatever the names we give to it – the fight in the end between FREEDOM and GOD' (*GG*, p. 202). Chris remains Scottish to the end, whereas Ewan quits Scotland and Scottishness to partake of an international revolutionary movement. The history of Scotland is not over. It continues, in Chris, in Ewan, and in countless others; only the future can tell in what direction lies 'reality' and who, the mother or the son, follows it more closely. Such a denouement – open, inconclusive, and deferred – would also, in its way, anticipate more recent aesthetic developments, in the same direction as the complexity in point of view and narrative voice.

A final word on the genre or mode of *A Scots Quair*, a question that has generated as much controversy as the ending. A number of early scholars including Wittig emphasized the symbolic and even allegorical character of the trilogy.[62] Wittig, inspired by Robert's remark in *Cloud Howe* 'Oh Chris Caledonia, I've married a nation!' (p. 139), suggests that the novels be read on three levels: personal, social, and mythical. The mythical level has especially appealed to adherents of the diffusionist interpretation. More recent scholars often object to the notion of allegory, insisting that the *Quair* is first and foremost a novel, a good story well told with magnificent, sharply drawn characters.[63]

As I see it, those who denigrate allegory are not perhaps fully aware of its generic traits. By definition, allegory exists on two or more levels. Of these, the first level, the literal, is expected to be a good story well told with sharply drawn characters. Otherwise, the work of art will fail, no less than it would were the allegorical level(s) insignificant or outlandish. Now, what is striking about the *Quair* is the presence – juxtaposition or fusion – of powerful, dense, concrete realism ('das Kreatürlich' in Auerbach's terminology) with no less powerful poetry and symbolism. The symbolism, when elaborated throughout the text with a reasonable degree of consistency, can develop into or be read as allegory. Thus, 'Chris Caledonia' (who dwells in Kinraddie, 'the Scots countryside itself' *SS*, p. 24), is both an individualized woman, born in 1897, and a figure for Scotland. Like the country or nation, she is torn between the two languages, Scots and English, as she is torn between the croft and the town and between farm labour and book-learning. Her marriages reflect the history of Scotland: first, union of Highland and Lowland in a rural economy; then domination by the Kirk; then the coming of the Industrial Revolution. The centre of life changes, for her and for the nation, from farm and hamlet to the burgh to the industrial city; and the decline of values is expressed by a decline in value of Chris's vantage-points – the standing stones, the ruins of the Kaimes, and the Windmill Brae – which also testify to stonework more recent and more artificial. That *A Scots Quair* is both realism and symbol, or realism and romance, at the same time, should not surprise readers familiar with Scott, Galt, Gunn, and Gray, a Scottish tradition in narrative which diverges from nineteenth-century English and French norms. More significant, I believe, is the fact that something like the structure and texture of the *Quair* is to be found in the modern novel in Breton and Occitan, as in recent fiction in Latin America and much of the developing world. Gibbon's trilogy, dating from the 1930s, anticipates a worldwide current in literature – magical realism – which was to become the dominant mode in the narrative of the postcolonial peoples. I believe *A Scots Quair* to be, then, an early example of magical realism. The question of genre, which must remain dormant for now, will be raised again, in other portions of this study.

THEATRE

As early as 1922 Hugh MacDiarmid called for the renewal of the Scottish theatre.[64] Subsequently, the creation of a living, vital, modern drama in Scots remained a central plank of the New Makars' program. Up to Hutchison writing in 1977 and beyond, the judgment on this theatre has been relatively harsh, bemoaning the absence of a tradition and of acknowledged masterpieces.[65] I see a number of reasons for the relative lack of enthusiasm. The critics generally put the Scots and English drama of Scotland together and weigh them against the total artistic theatrical production in England or France or Germany – not against Holland or Denmark. On an individual level as well, it is true, one cannot place Bridie in the same league with O'Casey or Beckett or Brecht or Ionesco. The specialists are sensitive to the immensely greater production difficulties in Edinburgh or Glasgow vis-à-vis London – commercial pressures, of course, yet which go beyond the strictly commercial to include questions of aesthetics and taste, all decided in England. The Scottish theatre, in general, is indicted for parochialism and provincialism. And for some, no play, however artistic, can be deemed a total achievement if it neglects social problems in the present.

More recent critics appreciate with a finer eye the theatrical output in the early 1970s and the late 1980s and 1990s.[66] However, my opinion is that no apologies are needed. In striking contrast to the novel, the theatre in modern Scots, when compared to theatre in Brittany and the Occitan regions, is very successful indeed, in terms of quantity, quality, and production. Leaving aside MacDiarmid himself, the major poets – Garioch, Goodsir Smith, Alexander Reid, Alexander Scott – wrote for the stage and for radio and television as well. So also did Robert Kemp and, more recently, Stewart Conn and Liz Lochhead. Goodsir Smith's *The Wallace: A Triumph* (1950) enjoyed a striking success at the Edinburgh Festival, in its opening season and in subsequent revivals. *The Wallace* is but one example among many of the Scots dramatists' specialization in period pieces (that is, historical plays); these could be tragic or comic; and they could be bilingual, according to the convention that characters who historically would have spoken Scots – Wallace, Robert the Bruce, and so on – speak a version of Scots as do the lower classes, whereas characters who historically would have spoken English – an English ambassador, an anglicized minister or courtier – speak English. The result is an attractive manifestation of bilingualism which enables the production to attain a relatively wide audience and allows the spoken language to offer social commentary and symbolism and even, metatextually, to play a role in the plot.

ROBERT McLELLAN

The greatest of the modern dramatists in Scots – called by his disciple Donald Campbell the father of that drama – is Robert McLellan, whose *Linmill Stories* make a serious contribution to prose narrative as well.[67] McLellan authored some sixteen or so plays, long and short. His specialty is historical comedy, delightful comedy with a serious undercurrent. McLellan's first major success came in 1937 with *Jamie the Saxt* (James the Sixth), performed at the Curtain Theatre in Glasgow and revived a number of times subsequently, as recently as 1996.[68] The plot concerns two years in the reign of King James VI, from 1592 to 1594, when he faced a number of troublesome questions, the most serious a rebellion by Francis, Earl of Bothwell. We follow some of the highlights of this contest. Act II depicts the nadir in Jamie's fortunes, when Bothwell and his henchmen slip into Holyrood, seize the king, and extort from him humiliating concessions. Act IV depicts Jamie's ultimate victory, with Bothwell discredited and the king secure on his own throne and in line to succeed Elizabeth of England.

A first impression given by this play, an aspect of its texture, so to speak, is a phenomenon we saw in Gibbon's *Scots Quair*: dense, concrete, material reality, aspects of the physical world which Auerbach ranged under the category *Kreatürlich*. For all his brains, Jamie is a man subject to the physical, perhaps subject to the physical because of his brains. He is, at crucial moments, violently hungry and thirsty. The thirst will be quenched by tankards of ale, not water. Bothwell's clique catch the monarch in his nightshirt, with more than a little of his discomfort due to semi-nakedness and exposure of the body. Jamie's physical relationship with the queen (Annie) and with Morton's daughter, as well as Annie's relationship, more or less platonic, with one of the earls, is subject to discussion, debate, and insult, with jealousy one among a number of sentiments which contribute to a rich, complex pattern of court life. To this should be added the presence of violence – naked swords drawn in the royal presence, whether directed against the king or in secondary intra-court rivalries – and Jamie's own cowardice in response to the violence. Finally, the rich, complex pattern of court life is mirrored in its language, conducted sometimes in the high register of debate and diplomacy, yet also in the low register of insult and invective.

This juxtaposition of *genus grande* and *genus humile* is also made apparent in the juxtaposition of social class, according to which king and courtiers mix with the burgesses of the town, and Jamie seeks information from an apprentice as readily as from one of his counsellors.

This creature-like, physical reality is generated intertextually, I believe, both as a demystification of the relatively spiritual, idealized, high-intellectual vision which most moderns have of the Renaissance, and to make a statement about Scottish reality compared to those idealizations. It also provides the frame for some rich comedy. As in Garioch's verse, the comic is developed by, in Bergsonian terms, the juxtaposition of the mechanical and the living ('du mécanique plaqué sur du vivant') or, if you prefer, the physical and the spiritual. The Renaissance prince, like the medieval knight, is expected to be a paragon of the virtues, with courage and steadfastness ever supported by courtliness and urbanity, a figure of *fortitudo et sapientia*. Now, Jamie has all the *sapientia* one could want; it is *fortitudo* which he lacks. Much of the comedy is derived from the ideal of chivalric virtue and the absence of such virtue in the King of the Scots. According to the code, the warrior is expected to be courageous and a victor in combat, chivalric to women, elegant in manner, and immune to the call of hunger and thirst. Jamie proves to be the antitype of the ideal, given his cowardice, his non-participation in war, his jealousy over his wife and willingness to seduce a courtier's virgin daughter, the absurd performance in his nightshirt, and, finally, his quasi-enslavement to meat and ale. For all its court spectacle, this is indeed a play of the body. The physical and the literary stand in conflict, with the physical undermining the validity of the literary ideal and the ideal pointing up the limits we have to place on physical reality. Much the same is true when McLellan generates comedy from the *sapientia* order of affairs, by having old Melville or, for that matter, Bruce the Presbyterian minister deliver long, boring, moralizing speeches out of place on the political stage, or by having Jamie himself argue and argue over kingship and sorcery. It is comic that he takes witchcraft as seriously as statecraft. It is also comic that these debates interrupt the seemingly more important issues of court and kingdom. And the very repetition of a comic trait, be it physical or mental, renders it still more comic, in that the quasi-mechanical repetition makes manifest a person's obsession, and obsessions are always mechanical and funny.

The comedy and the representation of physical reality veil yet also help grant substance to the play's kernel. This kernel is political and

ideological. It is very much to McLellan's credit that he involves the
implied spectator in a most complex political situation, and he does so
with brio and the elegance of indirection. Slowly, progressively, incre-
mentally to the plot, we are made aware of social class, the king opposed
by the more unruly earls and supported by the burgesses, with the nobility itself divided, some loyal to the king, some in open rebellion, and
some (the majority) shifting back and forth or simply waiting, eager to
weaken Jamie's power but never to permit one of their own to wield it in
his stead. There is the question of family, with one earl supporting Jamie
and another undermining him because of some right or wrong that
happened to one of their kin a month or a decade previously. Jamie's
wife, the queen, has her own courtiers and political preferences
grounded in the history of her family and in her own (sexual?) personal
preferences. There is the question of religion, with the Kirk, the burgesses, and the Protestant lairds pushing Jamie to root out the Catholic
lairds and fomenting insurrection because he won't do it, and he won't
do it because he depends on the Catholic lairds to help put down the
plots of the Protestant lairds. Then there is England – the distant, powerful mistrusted Other – nominally encouraging Protestantism but in
fact also involved in turning one side against another and fomenting
disorder at will.

McLellan makes it clear, and King Jamie knows all too well, that,
behind the public façade of faith and crown, lies the reality of power
and money. The earls wish to unseat Jamie's present counsellors in
order to become counsellors themselves. The ministers, the earls, the
burgesses, and the English all scheme with one goal in mind – power,
their hegemonic domination of Scotland. Meanwhile, Jamie has to navi-
gate among these threatening and ever-moving obstacles, simply in
order to survive. His task is made still more difficult because of finance,
Scotland being a poor country. Jamie stands in debt to his burgesses. He
cannot suppress either Protestants or Catholics because he lacks funds.
And it is this quasi-universal Scottish lack of funds which permits the
English ambassador to play so nefarious a role. Jamie is literally dependent on Queen Elizabeth's subsidization. And English gold permits the
ambassador to subsidize (i.e., to bribe) any and all of the factions at will.

The very physicality of life in sixteenth-century Edinburgh is thus
problematized by a socio-politico-economic structure of which everyone
(except the queen) is aware. Jamie's is also a world of disguise and
deceit, where secret alliances abound and people change sides at will,
where neither Jamie nor Bothwell can count on supporters, and the for-

tunes of war and peace vary from week to week. Thus, although everyone suspects the English of double-dealing, and rightly so, the Scots act with identical secrecy and identically shifting positions.

This state of affairs is underscored by the spatial and temporal patterns in the play. The scene shifts between Holyrood Palace (Acts II, III) and the home of Nicoll Edward, a cloth merchant (Acts I, IV). Jamie is, seemingly, democratically at home in both loci. In fact, he is democratically afraid in both loci, and everywhere else. Jamie can be assaulted by a mob in the streets or by a laird's invasion of the palace and his royal bed chamber. He exerts a fair amount of energy to escape a bad refuge 'here' in favour of a good refuge somewhere else, which will, in its turn, become a bad refuge. His goal is to survive. And, over the two years of the *erzählte Zeit*, survive he does. Time passes, survivors survive, and the fate of politics and money can be altered. Because he survived, because of the passage of time, Jamie discovers that Bothwell had been bribed by the English; armed with this knowledge, Jamie is now in a position to be bribed in turn. The Wheel of Dame Fortuna (the virgin Queen of England?) turns, with time, for those who are patient enough to benefit from it.

To be patient enough and intelligent enough brings us back to Jamie's strength – his *sapientia*, not Christian wisdom but, more important, McLellan would claim, the shrewdness and canniness of a master Scottish political tactician. Jamie's shrewdness and canniness, his mental capacity to hold out and then triumph over those stronger and wealthier than himself, recalls to my mind the paradigm of *Le Roman de Renart*, where the relatively small fox outwits the wolf, the lion, and the other great beasts, always in the trappings of a feudal court devoted to questions of war and the law.

McLellan portrays his Scottish king, then, as a little man of intelligence, a Reynard, who outwits the bigger, stronger creatures around him. One aspect of Jamie's intelligence is made manifest, intertextually, in the form of book culture, of the books we associate historically with the cultivated Stuart monarch. In the play allusions are made to his sonnets and to the treatise he is writing on witchcraft. He argues at length with the Presbyterian minister and the English ambassador concerning the rights and duties of kingship, uttering language taken directly from his later *Basilicon Doron*. Significantly, the climax of the play and the moment of anagnorisis occur when he unveils a secret message which confirms the English plot to assist Bothwell: 'Ay ay, Sir Robert, wark up yer indignation! But ye dinna ken what's comin! Dae ye see that airn?

Dae ye see that bit o flannel? Dae ye see this letter? Ay, Sir Robert, ye
may weill turn pale. Ye may weill gowp like a frichtent fish. Ye're a
proved plotter, a briber o traitors, a hirer o murderers!' (p. 126). It is by
means of textual discovery and textual mastery that Jamie triumphs over
his enemies, the rebellious earls and the conniving English.

This textual discovery also reveals the role played by language, not
just as the medium but also as part of the message. All the characters
speak Scots but for Bowes, the ambassador, and his messenger. The messenger, who utters Shakespearean *genus humile* in a Cockney accent, is
simply not understood by the Scottish gentles. Queen Anne, from Denmark, pronounces her broken Scots with a comic Danish accent. And
Jamie himself, the master of discourse, argues and debates with brio,
wielding his magnificently supple, fecund Lallans for all uses worthy of a
king. The author demonstrates his own command of the vernacular and
his joy in its uses. He also evokes a sixteenth-century sociolinguistic situation, one still enjoyed today by French and English but which Scots has
lost. Normal discourse takes place in Scots. Foreigners, even foreign roy-
als, make an effort to learn it. Foreigners speaking another language
cannot be understood; speaking Scots with an accent, or uttering their
own tongue, they evoke laughter. The lesson on what once was and one
day could and should be again is not lost. Nor is the fact that the winner
and most intelligent character in the play is a Scotsman who enjoys con-
summate mastery of his language, which, in this play, *is* language.

Jamie is the winner in a comic plot which diverges from the tradition.
Jamie the Saxt does not evoke the traditional comic world of boy and girl,
blocked by older parent-figures, who break free from the law of the
fathers to restore to their society the natural world of young love. If anything, Jamie, furious at Lennox's paying court to and taking the side of
Annie, adopts the role of the blocking figure, the *senex iratus* torn by
jealousy. It is Lennox and Bothwell who embody fierce young manhood,
against which Jamie appears, at worst, as the cuckolded husband and
impotent monarch (Arthur vis-à-vis a cohort of Lancelots and Mor-
dreds), at best as an *eiron*-figure and *dolosus servus*, an older hero of the
mind opposed to these young heroes of the body. In traditional comedy,
the *dolosus servus* would be assisting the young hero, but here, in McLellan's world, he does it on his own, for himself. Actantially, Jamie is the
subject. The object has nothing to do with women or love; it is to maintain his position as king and, if possible, make it more secure. He does
this in the name of Scotland and according to the precepts of kingship,
surely, but also because it is what he wills to do. Driven by a will to power

and a will to know – libido sublimated? – this protagonist young in years acts the role of the eiron and *dolosus servus*, in addition to the Molière *barbon*, and thus defeats his opposants, who are genuine *blondins* – young, erotic men who lack his will and brains. Paradoxically, this is brought about – Jamie wins – because of an act derived from the nature of Eros. Annie is pregnant. Because of the pregnancy, which presumably came about prior to the business in Act I and which is all but non-existent in traditional comedy, Jamie has an heir: he and his line can be counted upon, not only to rule Scotland but to inherit England as well. In a last bit of demystification, Jamie wonders who the father may be, then accepts the explanations offered and, rejoicing in his political good fortune, gives up his mistress to return to his wife:

> THE KING: It's what I hae hoped for wi aa my hairt. But I'm sair bothert wi douts, Sir Jamie. If I could juist be shair I'll be the faither!
>
> MELVILLE: Yer Grace!
>
> THE KING: Dinna be an auld wife! Ye ken as weill as mysell that the bairn micht belang to Lennox!
>
> ...
>
> THE KING: Ye're richt, Sir Jamie. Ye're richt. I see it nou. Puir sowl, I haena been guid to her. [...] I didna pey her eneugh attention. [...] I'll stert aa ower again. I'll coort her like a laddie. (pp. 81–2)

The structure of *Jamie the Saxt* can be seen to revel in paradox. The family unit is restored and Scotland unified by a traditional marriage – long after the marriage has stormed its way, however, and with doubts as to the legitimacy of the royal line. It should also be noticed that, in this worldly and cynical court, but for Jamie's own momentary jealousy, nobody is concerned with the legitimacy of the royal line.

Jamie wins, first of all, by conceiving an heir, an event which occurred prior to the diegesis and for which he may not have been responsible, and which occurred 'accidentally,' so to speak, without premeditation on his part. Jamie wins, second, by reading the ciphered message, which reveals treachery from the English. The English made mistakes. The earls made mistakes. Jamie simply held his own and survived. In the last analysis, is that the secret of his vaunted intellect and kingship?

One last vestige of ambiguity concerns the denouement. This witty, urbáne, intelligent, and cultured protagonist, an intellectual before his time, expects confidently to inherit the kingdom of England from 'the auld bitch' (p. 129) – Queen Elizabeth, the icon of English history. A

victory for intellect over brute force and for Scotland over England.
And, extradiegetically, historically, Jamie will inherit. Yet every educated
person in the audience also knows that this witty, urbane, intelligent,
and cultured Scottish monarch will take his court to London, speak
English, and write the *Basilicon Doron* in English. His victory will constitute a major step in the decline and fall of Scottish culture and of Scotland as a nation. That is one of the ambiguities of history and a final
ironic, intertextual ambiguity from Robert McLellan.

The Flouers o Edinburgh was first produced at the Unity Theatre, Edinburgh, in 1947 and has been revived several times, including performances at the Edinburgh Festival and on the radio.[69] This is one of a
number of plays McLellan locates in the eighteenth century, a great
period in Scottish cultural history and also one in which the conflict
between the English and the Scots languages became an issue in the
public sphere.

Unlike *Jamie the Saxt, The Flouers o Edinburgh* conforms (or appears to
conform) more immediately to the traditional structures of comedy.
Love and marriage are central motivating forces in the plot. Lady Athelstane wants to marry off her niece, and Lord Stanebyres's son is the
most likely candidate. Although Chairlie and Kate quarrel most of the
time, and although Kate appears to prefer and is squired by Captain
Simkin, an English military man, in the end she and Chairlie will be
married, as will Kate's Aunt Girzie and Stanebyres. A double wedding,
so to speak, of parent-figures and children constitutes the denouement
of a play in which, superficially, love breaks down barriers and overcomes obstacles, creating a new world of decorum and harmony.

This happy ending of love remains, however, as superficial to the genuine issues raised by the play, in McLellan as in, say, Bernard Shaw. *The
Flouers o Edinburgh* is dominated by questions of language, and it treats
language overtly – in its social and cultural manifestations – in contrast
to the relative indirection of *Jamie the Saxt.* Although Chairlie and Kate
are attracted to each other, language keeps them apart. Chairlie is the
new, anglicized Scot, home from a stay in London and speaking
(accented) English. He professes to scorn Scottish girls and the Scots
tongue and looks down on Kate for not being a lady and for ignoring
the latest fashion. Kate, who speaks only the vernacular, is deeply hurt
and sends him packing. In the end, she will not grant him her hand
until he proposes to her in good Braid Scots. This, against his will, he
does:

KATE: Are ye desperate to hae me?
CHARLES: Yes.
KATE: Ye'll hae to prove it. I'll tak ye if ye ask me in Scots. [...]
KATE: I'm waitin, then.
CHARLES: Oh yes.
KATE: Come on. Try. Ye'll no fin it as bad as ye think.
CHARLES: It will sound so silly.
KATE: I daursay aa proposals soond gey silly. Try.
CHARLES: Kate?
KATE: Ay?
CHARLES: Will ye mairry me? (p. 239)

It is a speech act which recalls the outburst in Act I when, enraged by Kate's behaviour, he bursts out in the demotic 'Ye whitterick!' (p. 190). Following this, Aunt Girzie accepts Stanebyres's proposal because, as conservative, unreconstructed Scots-speakers, they can grow old together. Speech can separate people and can bring them together. McLellan portrays Scots as being threatened by English yet also offering registers of expression – of social intercourse and of the range of affections – absent from the foreign, imposed tongue. The old remain faithful to the their language; the young are attracted to the idiom of newness, fashion, wealth, and power. Yet even in Chairlie the vernacular, which remains close to the surface, can erupt at any time. Whenever it does, it manifests authenticity in the face of imposed, most likely self-imposed, artificiality.

The language question permeates the drama. It becomes the main issue at stake for the secondary characters, all of whom, in one way or another, must decide between English and Scots. In a bit of linguistic poetic justice, Chairlie is outdone in his political aspirations by a nabob home from India. The latter obtains the seat in Parliament Chairlie hoped for and, rolling in coin and unaware of changing fashion, sees no reason not to speak the Braid Scots of his childhood. More significant, perhaps, is the case of poor Dr Dowie (a caricature of Thomson and Young), a Scottish divine who has just published a magnum opus, *The Tomb*, in English heroic couplets. Dowie, who reads English but speaks Scots, has committed false rhymes (rhyming English *à l'écossaise*) and feels humiliated by the criticism. The solution for Dr Dowie and others like him is either to take lessons in English elocution from an Irish (!) stage actor at the Select Society or to make the pilgrimage to London. Dowie returns from his pilgrimage uttering a comic mixture of English

and Scots. Having corrected his rhymes, he proclaims with assurance
that Allan Ramsay will be the last Scot ever to write in dialect. McLellan
dramatizes a genuine language quarrel and language dilemma which
divided the Edinburgh *beau monde* in the eighteenth century. Of course,
Scots was in decline and would continue to decline. Yet McLellan scores
points by having Dowie proclaim the literary demise of a language
when, in the near future, in Dowie's own presumed lifetime, Fergusson
and Burns would grant it a whole new artistic cachet, and by discussing
this demise in a play written and performed two centuries later in the
allegedly dead tongue – Scots. Language as metalanguage and the language of the play becoming the subject of the play – these are McLellan's strong suits, and, by playing them, he anticipates more than one
innovation in recent theatre.

In spite of their differences in language, Chairlie the anglophile
resembles the anglophobe Jamie the Saxt in a number of ways. Like King
James, Chairlie is a wily young man, a master of ruse and, more than a
master, a genius at politics. In his case, to be a genius at politics means
the ability, without money (therefore, without the capacity to bribe
overtly), to offer something to everyone in order to win the backing for
his electoral campaign. Chairlie's chief foible, roughly akin to Jamie's
cowardice, is snobbery, closely allied to his anglophilia and English
speech-habits. Social comedy is generated when Chairlie questions
whether Kate is a true lady and how, dwelling in Edinburgh, she could
ever be one. He is furious with the innkeeper's wife, who knows him
from childhood and persists in addressing him as 'Maister Chairlie' and
not 'Sir.' The social comedy is augmented by the fact that Chairlie insists
on speaking English to all and sundry when everyone around him speaks
Scots. His mania for gentility and for English takes on the obsessive
mechanical quality of Bergsonian fixation. Also partaking of Bergsonian
fixation is the other focus of comedy, Chairlie's opposite number as it
were – Jock the butler. Jock's insolence to Lady Athelstane is as much
subject to humour as Chairlie's insolence to Kate or to the innkeeper.
The difference lies in the fact that Jock is a truly productive individual –
no one on the planet can bake scones like his – and that his carping contributes to a pattern of flyting between master and servant that is
accepted by both as an inherent part of their lives. The flyting is also presumed to be authentically Scottish. No less authentic is Jock's vigorous,
earthy Braid Scots, in contrast to Chairlie's English. Yet, as always, Chairlie is a master and lives for the future, in town, while Jock the servant
joins Girzie and Stanebyres, who will grow old together in the country.

The social comedy and the social antithesis, grounded in language, veil but do not hide serious issues of power and money which also shape the plot. In line with Chairlie's political ambitions and bound to them is his project to acquire Girzie's land for his London cronies, in order to contract a mill. Chairlie, speaking English, argues with his father over the need for 'improvements.' As opposed to the old Scottish virtues of individualism and feudal loyalty, defended by Stanebyres in Scots, Chairlie promotes the improvements, which mean ruining the land and reducing the tenants to wage slavery. In this class war, Chairlie lies to his father, denying his role in the expropriation. Then, having lost one battle to the nabob, Chairlie perseveres in the war. At the end of the play his new project is to help exploit the Highlands; he will contribute to the Clearances, one of the darkest pages in the history of Scotland.

Power and money also contribute thematically to the denouement, making it even more ambiguous than the ending of *Jamie the Saxt*. Yes, Chairlie and Kate do like each other and are attracted to each other. Is this Scottish love *sans* English sentiment? Is this the happy ending of comedy? Perhaps. Yet Chairlie is eager to wed the Edinburgh girl because he has lost the election and run out of money. And Kate is eager to wed him because, now that everyone knows that Captain Simkin has a wife in England, she must marry someone or be socially disgraced. While Girzie, Stanebyres, and Jock retire to the country, Chairlie will use Kate's wealth to finance the 'improvements' in the Highlands. Presumably, sooner or later Kate will learn English. And Chairlie and Kate will enact the future of their land.

A final word about the title of the play. 'The Flouers o Edinburgh' alludes to a dance tune from c.1740 in praise of the belles of the town. The belles we see are Kate and her aunt, who possess any number of positive qualities and are sought after, but not by Chairlie, who questions whether an Edinburgh belle can be a lady. Yet he weds his, asking for her hand in Scots. The flowers also allude to the old Edinburgh custom of tossing the contents of chamber pots out of the window onto the public streets, where the little piles remain. Captain Simkin alludes to the custom, not objecting in aesthetic terms but for the sake of agriculture – the 'flowers' could prove to be useful and profitable if taken to the fields. A last contrast between England and Scotland? And a last, ambiguous comment on life in 'the Athens of the North' during its Golden Age?

A more ferocious demystification of the Athens of the North occurs in *The Hypocrite*, first performed at the Edinburgh Lyceum in 1967.[70] The plot is centred on the efforts of some 'good' Scots – urbane and cultured – to help an Italian engraver, Giorgio Barocci, exhibit his collection of old master paintings and his own engravings, which are also reproductions of old masterpieces. They are countered and, eventually, defeated by the exertions of the Rev. Samuel Skinner, the title-figure, a Presbyterian divine who dashes about the countryside stirring up the clergy and the people to resist papist obscenity.

McLellan, as always, plays with language, eliciting, as always, delightful effects of bilingualism and contrast in the use of language. However, in *The Hypocrite*, language choice bears less ideological weight than in the two previous dramas. Skinner and his rascally son Joseph speak English, but so also do the urbane, cultivated supporters of the arts Simon Adair and Lucy Lindsay. An equally cultivated patron of the arts, Lord Kilmardinny (Lucy's uncle), speaks Scots, as does Joseph Skinner's crude mother-in-law, Lady Kilgallon. People of lower social class or from the country – Skinner's henchmen and Adair's retainers – speak the vernacular. At this turning-point in history (Edinburgh, 1760), English versus Scots takes the form of young versus old, city versus country, and gentry versus the mass. By what is, after all, a theatrical convention (in real life, diglossia or no diglossia, people don't address each other in distinct and different languages), McLellan evokes the complex, problematic linguistic situation in eighteenth-century Scotland, in all its social aspects. He also assigns a formal, Latinate English to the villain.

The language question, as ideology, gives way to or is displaced onto the question of art. The English-speaking minister of the Kirk hates Barocci's paintings and engravings and will do all he can to prevent the planned exhibitions. His instinctive repulsion has two sources – the religious and the moral. Skinner censors the art because it comes from a papist land, therefore encourages the faithful to worship icons, therefore is idolatrous and sacrilegious. He censors the art also because it depicts figures in the nude, therefore is filthy, therefore will deprave public morals. Skinner does not merely wish to cancel the showings; he stirs up a mob to seize and destroy the exhibition pieces. Furthermore, the good Reverend's militancy is not limited to the visual arts. He also opposes the theatre and dangerous books; he is the enemy of Kilmardinny, who encourages Allan Ramsay's library and the Musical Society; and, at the end of Act V, he sets out to shut down Ramsay's theatre.

All this serves to problematize our vision of the Scottish Enlightenment. Yes, Edinburgh was the city of Hume and Adam Smith. It was also the city of the Kirk, where Ramsay's theatre was indeed shut down and an authentic, native, Scottish tradition in the drama never allowed to flourish. More than a little historical irony is generated when Barocci, bullied by Calvinist thugs, insists on returning to London, where the people are more tolerant: 'I cannot forget the rabble on the bridge at Perth, crying filthy, and sacrilege, and idolatry, and burn them at the cross [...] But Dundee. It was worse. The rabble on the harbour wall. Drown him, they cried. Sink the boat and all that is in it. [...] No, I am sorry. I return to England. The people there are more tolerant' (p. 92). Thus, in Scotland's Golden Age, the hated English are said to be both more humane and more cultured.

As in Molière and Jonson, the comic protagonist is the blocking figure, the man humorous because dominated by a humour, and much of the comedy is generated by the contrast between the humorous man's extremism, given over mechanically to his humour, and the other characters who live the supple, natural richness of ordinary life. In Molière as in McLellan, comedy is enriched by the additional contrast between the man of humour as he is and the role, as hypocrite, he tries to play in society, once again the mechanical and the vitally alive juxtaposed. That Skinner stands so opposed to the arts forms part of a larger pattern, that of the strict, highly moral clergyman immune to sin and to even the hint of impropriety. Skinner's diatribes against the paintings reveal one of his seeming obsessions – horror of the naked body and of everything connected with it, a revulsion from and, at the same time, an obsession with sex. The comic and the hypocritical are joined, given that Dr Skinner has the reputation of being a friend to rich widows and that, in the course of the plot, we observe him in the act of trying to seduce Lucy and in fact of seducing or allowing himself to be seduced by Lady Kilgallon. He is therefore a strict puritanical moralist and an active practising lecher at the same time.

The hypocrisy requires that the clergyman and everyone else keep their sexual activities hidden, given the moralism which dominates the Athens of the North. Skinner therefore has a weak point, and it is because of this weakness that he can be discomfited. Lady Kilgallon was observed leaving his bedchamber. Once this is known, Lord Kilgallon plans to divorce her, with the certain outcome that Skinner, exposed as a fornicator contributing to a married woman's adultery and committing near-incest, will be destroyed. This is the hope entertained by Skinner's adversaries, and the reason they are sanguine about exhibiting Barocci's art and continuing the theatre.

We must note that the sexual vulnerability cuts several ways and that everyone (especially the women) can be made victims. Lady Kilgallon risks dishonour. So does Lucy, if only for giving tea parties to actors and painters; and Lucy is vulnerable because she also is a married woman, whose husband went off to the Bahamas. Furthermore, the sexual skirmishing, as always with McLellan, is allied to more basic struggles for power and money. Lucy would like to divorce yet cannot, because she would lose her pension. Skinner seduces Lady Kilgallon to ensure that her fortune will descend intact to his son – her son-in-law – which it would not do should she take some other lover and/or, after her husband dies, some other husband. Although Joseph has nothing like his father's brains or will-power, both Skinners share the same love of money, a quasi-absolute greed. The greed (*avaritia*) is an additional capital sin, as vicious as lechery (*luxuria*), which the man of the cloth has to keep hidden.

As in King Jamie's bygone age, here, two centuries later, whatever may appear to be crude in Scottish life is belied by the subtlety and the intelligence these characters employ to veil their own vulnerability and to expose that of their adversary. Lucy is a charming, lovable flirt. She flirts with her uncle, to keep the pension. Then she flirts with Skinner, to protect Barocci and, in the end, to force the hypocrite to drop his mask. The uncharming, unlovable clergyman also flirts, in order to seduce Lucy and Lady Kilgallon. Whereas failure with Lucy deflates only his vanity, success with the soon-to-be merry widow inflates his son Joseph's purse. In the end, threatened with exposure and public disgrace, Skinner imagines the seemingly mad expedient of pretending to have died, and then to begin life abroad. The intertextual homage to Jonson's *Volpone* indicates the extent to which manipulation and deceit reign in Skinner's world and the extent to which he himself, perhaps unconsciously, is shown to be a fanatic of manipulation and deceit.

As, in the course of the drama, Skinner's presence comes to dominate the stage, so also the character is revealed to be deeper, stronger, more powerful, and more problematic than are any of the others. As a result, the genre of the play is slowly transformed from worldly comedy into the equivalent of Frye's irony – still comedy, perhaps, yet verging on the tragic. When Lucy defies Skinner, Skinner replies by defying the world: 'So you think I'm ruined? And no doubt young Adair and that Italian think I'm ruined. And Sir Colin Kilgallon. And your uncle, the generous patron of the arts. You'll all have to think again, my dear. There will be no scandal. No one is going to ruin the Reverend Samuel Skinner. There's too much at stake' (p. 102). He then imagines the Volpone gambit, and when he has triumphed (Lord Kilgallon dies, therefore there will be no divorce and no scandal), the hypocrite praises God and prepares for his next project – to destroy the theatre. The implied audience, impressed, perhaps even seduced, by the man's will and energy, cannot also but wonder whether or not he is entirely sane. The monomania may well be a symptom of madness, a madness which triumphs over weaker men's health. And the implied audience may also question whether Dr Skinner is an authentic hypocrite – that is, a conscious liar and scoundrel – or whether, given the madness, he may suffer from Sartrean Bad Faith and actually believe in everything he says and does.

This type of question forms one staple of the criticism devoted to Molière's *Tartuffe*, McLellan's primary source. I suggest that, in reworking Molière and adapting him to Scotland, McLellan goes beyond the French playwright or, if you prefer, writes a twentieth-century *Tartuffe* that Molière might have written had he had the freedom of expression to do so. We see that, whereas Tartuffe mastered one household (due to Orgon's weakness), failed to seduce a married woman, and, in the end, was discomfited by King Louis, Dr Skinner holds in his power an entire city and the neighbouring towns, does seduce one woman out of two, and, in the end, is a winner. McLellan tells us, I believe, that whereas the Church of Rome never really harmed French culture, the same is not true for the Kirk in Scotland. Ramsay's theatre *was* closed. It is reopened, so to speak, by McLellan himself, who writes the classical comedy that the Scottish Enlightenment never saw and brings to life the clergyman who suppressed the stage and, therefore, suppressed himself until McLellan resurrects it and him.

DONALD CAMPBELL

Robert McLellan's most notable disciple is Donald Campbell, the leading dramatist in Scots of the post-McLellan generation. Campbell published three historical plays in the late 1970s: *The Jesuit, Somerville the Soldier,* and *The Widows of Clyth,* dramas much closer to the tragic mode than McLellan's pieces are.[71] He also wrote a number of subsequent plays for the stage and for BBC Radio Scotland and has built a genuine reputation as poet, journalist, and man of letters.[72]

The public acclaimed *The Jesuit* upon its appearance in 1976, first at the Traverse Theatre and then at the Edinburgh Festival Fringe, seeing in this exciting, superbly crafted drama a breakthrough in the Scottish stage and in the stage possibilities for use of the Scots language. It has since then been revived in Scotland and Ireland and adapted for radio.[73]

The title figure is a genuinely historical Catholic priest, Father John Ogilvie, who, performing covert missionary activity in what was then Anglican-Protestant Scotland, was captured, tried, and hanged in 1615. As it turns out, one coincidental reason for debate in 1976 concerned the fact that, in that very year, Ogilvie was declared a saint by the Church of Rome.

The plot concentrates on the struggle between Ogilvie and the Anglican archbishop of Glasgow, John Spottiswoode. Spottiswoode strives in every way to persuade Ogilvie to change his deposition vis-à-vis the temporal power and thus save his life. Ogilvie strives in every way to resist Spottiswoode's pleas and threats. He has to resist the fear of physical torture, actual torture by sleep deprivation, the fear of his trial, and the fear of execution.

It is of significance that the implied audience never beholds the torture itself or the trial or the execution. Time is concentrated into the last few months of Ogilvie's life. The action is largely confined to the confrontation between Ogilvie and Spottiswoode *intra muros*, a confrontation that includes running debates on politics and theology. Compared to McLellan's comedies, this is a more intense, austere work of art, with a strong intellectual kernel. Spottiswoode's seduction is more intellectual than emotive, as is Ogilvie's response. The result is a play which recalls – in its intellectuality and in its classical intensity and restraint – some French dramas of the period of existentialism, and it thus contrasted powerfully with the kind of West End–oriented theatre so common then in Edinburgh.

Because much of the play's baggage, so to speak, is borne by the Jesuit and the archbishop, these characters as characters dominate the stage performance and have dominated much of the comment on the play. One question asked by a number of critics concerns which of the two men is 'the hero' and which of them wins the author's and/or the audience's sympathy.

One key to the secret of the conflict between Ogilvie and Spottiswoode lies in the question of age. In the modern popular culture saints are often depicted as aged and gentle, perhaps feminine, the Mother Teresa paradigm. Like Bernanos, Campbell turns this stereotype on end by portraying his saint and martyr as a young Jesuit father, young in his fierceness and military élan, a warrior in the Church Militant. As with the heroes of medieval epic, Ogilvie displays the pure, magnifi-

cent, total gift of self to an ideal, that absolute gift of self and oblivious-
ness to all else that characterizes *joven*. Here the intransigence of youth
joins the intransigence of a traditional Christian faith that takes literally
Christ's command to abandon family and worldly goods to follow him,
and to treasure God's law over the laws of men. Within the diegesis,
Ogilvie wins the devotion of one of the soldiers because of his courage
under duress and his profoundly human response to torture. As we witness the man's degradation, the breaking of his mind and body, so does
Ogilvie himself. He knows that, with all else lost, he retains and will
retain faith and the dignity and integrity of maintaining that faith: 'You
are driving me mad! You take my mind, you take my body, you take my
reason, you take my comfort. Very well, then! Take it – take it all! I have
no use for it, for any of it! I tell you only this. *You shall not have my faith!*'
(p. 49).

Bishop Spottiswoode, on the contrary, is a relatively older man, married, who plays a fatherly role with one of the soldiers and even with
Ogilvie. In contrast to Ogilvie's élan, he displays humanity and wisdom,
traits associated, at their best, with age. Spottiswoode is not a paragon of
sectarian loyalty: he has already changed religion once. He is a true
moderate. And, for all his goodwill, he is willing to subject Ogilvie to
sleep deprivation. Yet his is as deep an idealism as the Jesuit's. The
bishop dreams of a Christian Scotland where all people can live
together in peace: 'I want a Kirk in Scotland that will serve aa men. I
want a Kirk in Scotland that will bring Catholic and Protestant thegither
in the ae faith, in the ae life; I want peace in the land and britherhood
and guidwill amang aa men – as the Guid Lord aye intended it should
be!' (pp. 70–1). He tries to win over Ogilvie in order that the man not
be martyred and, therefore, that the Catholic-leaning masses not be
stirred up. Thus, as Ogilvie stands and resists with his will, Spottiswoode
turns about him, employing arguments of reason. And, as Ogilvie stands
alone, Spottiswoode does not mind seeking help from everyone – the
king, Andrew the soldier, his own wife, and the epistles of Saint Paul.
Whereas in epic *fortitudo* and *sapientia* can be joined, here in this tragedy
they are separate, each dominating the psyche of a man. This *conflictus
oppositorum* cannot be resolved.

The intellectual issues posed by the play include yet are not limited to
our contemporary secularist questions (posed by reviewers) as to the
nature of fanaticism and bigotry or the price, moral as well as physical,
paid by intransigence. Spottiswoode appears modern in his very moder-
ation and in his concern for building a commonwealth that will not be

torn apart by sectarian bickering. Yet Ogilvie also is modern in his insistence that the individual conscience be placed before loyalty to a mere
king and that convictions cannot be suppressed by mere *raison d'Etat.*
Ogilvie's commitment to an older world-view in which spiritual concerns transcend material ones and the international community of the
Church transcends the national community of Scotsmen or the feudal
community of lords and bishops is set in antithesis to Spottiswoode's
more modern-seeming dream of a secular commonwealth where peace
and contentment hold pride of place. Partially anachronistic, perhaps,
though not entirely so vis-à-vis the twentieth century, Ogilvie evokes
some of the best of Western civilization, magnificent traits that have
been lost. After all, in another guise, his is the quarrel of Antigone with
Creon, and most versions of the Antigone story take her side against the
wise, statesmanlike older man.

To ask, as I have done, to what extent Ogilvie and Spottiswoode are
'modern,' and whether or not their visions correspond to or are valid
for our contemporary mind-set, is not to traduce the spirit of Campbell's play. The intentionally anachronistic use of levels of discourse,
especially the obscene contemporary Edinburgh demotic of the soldiers, reminds the audience that the early seventeenth and late twentieth centuries converge, both occurring in the Scottish capital. Also, the
audience realizes that Spottiswoode's fear became and is historical fact,
for that Scotland was to be torn apart by sectarian strife for a good three
centuries, strife, which, in Glasgow and in the West as in Ulster, has not
ceased today. Campbell indicates this by having the soldiers be slowly
but surely dragged into the religious strife, which, in principle, affects
them less than it does the gentles, but which they also cannot escape.

Who is the protagonist? Who wins? Father Ogilvie wins, he is the victor. In a very real sense, he wills his martrydom and ensures that his
vision of right and principle triumphs over Spottiswoode's vision of
compromise and tolerance both in the fictional *erzählte Zeit* of the play
and in the historical reality which was to ensue. However, the first question – one of actantial structure and audience response – remains more
problematic. The audience has the right to sympathize either with Spottiswoode or with Ogilvie or with both at the same time and to envisage
the action as concerning either Spottiswoode as a tragic hero (actant)
who fails to impose his idealism and generosity spiritually on his adversary (opposant), or Ogilvie as a tragic hero (actant) who remains true to
himself and to God while being physically crushed by his adversary
(opposant).

The audience can also envisage the play as having two heroes, literally two protagonists – Aristotle might object, yet the twentieth century revels in defying Aristotle – and the subject of the play their confrontation. Underlying the confrontation is the fact that the two men cannot communicate. And, underlying the non-communication, we find another paradox: Spottiswoode, the empowered master, is desperate to communicate, and he fails, whereas Ogilvie, one lone priest, has no interest in communicating, and he succeeds. The inability to communicate can be explained by a number of features, among which stands the all-but-absolute antithesis between the two men – youth versus age, will versus reason, innocence versus maturity, principle versus compromise, and sacred versus secular.

Furthermore, because communication is normally possible only through speech, oral or written, the non-communicating raises issues of both language and textuality. The two men speak literally different languages. Symbolic and ideological capital is made from this and from the fact that, of all the characters in the play, Father Ogilvie is the only one who utters standard English. This is because, we are informed, extradiegetically he left his family and went into exile at a young age. All the others speak the vernacular, and Bishop Spottiswoode, proficient in linguistic bipolarism, has the richest command of his idiom, from a broad Scots when chatting with men-at-arms to a thin register when debating with Ogilvie. Linguistically, Spottiswoode is the better man, and he makes the point that the Jesuit – all but a foreigner – cannot speak the tongue of the people he has come to disrupt. Linguistically, Ogilvie stands alone. He stands alone textually as well, given that we observe him (the only writer in the play; the bishop is an avid reader) writing alone his deposition in response to a series of questions from the king. The torture, the trial, and the martyrdom all occur because he refuses to alter the deposition, to create ambiguities and the possibility of a broad interpretation when, for him, language, the deposition, and his faith are clear and unproblematic. On the one hand, Spottiswoode is carried away when he accuses Ogilvie's faith of being just words and rhetoric, given that most of the words and rhetoric come not from Ogilvie but from Spottiswoode himself. On the other hand, Ogilvie's relatively simple, unproblematic notion of language is belied by the entire theatrical performance which creates and contains him, grounded as it is in an exploration of the problematic, ambiguous structure of language and belief. Like so many fine tragedies, like the best of the plays on Antigone and Creon, the ending remains open in hermeneutic terms, even when we know who perishes and who survives. The competing visions of Father Ogilvie and of Bishop Spottiswoode are competing mental structures of history and of the human condition. Their complex, problematic confrontation provides exciting theatre and a vital intellectual experience. Donald Campbell asks the questions. It is for each spectator and each reader to answer, as best he can.

The historical drama reached a summit with McLellan and Campbell, and also with Goodsir Smith, R.S. Silver, and Stewart Conn. However, their example could not be followed into the 1980s and 1990s. This is because, already in the 1970s, new currents were having an impact on the Scottish stage, currents that would reshape in a decisive way the tradition of stagecraft and the use of language. One of these new currents will be discussed in the chapter on postmodernism.

BRITTANY

INTRODUCTION

Roparz Hemon / Louis-Paul Némo is the Hugh MacDiarmid of Brittany. As much as MacDiarmid, perhaps more than MacDiarmid, he devoted a lifetime to the defence and illustration of the Breton language and a modern Breton literature. In addition to producing a magnificent corpus of artistic literary works in all genres, Hemon worked hard as a scholar, organizer, and leader. He founded a number of journals, including *Gwalarn*, *Kannadig Gwalarn*, *Arvor*, *Sterenn*, and *Ar Bed Keltiek*; he also founded the Celtic Institute and programs in Breton on the radio (Roazon-Breiz) during the war, as well as programs for the teaching of Breton to children, *Brezoneg ar Vugale*, and a Basic Breton to be taught to foreigners and learners of the language. Of all these achievements, the most important for the history of Breton literature is the founding in 1925 of the review *Gwalarn*, which Hemon edited until its demise in 1944. This review revolutionized Breton literature and modern Breton culture. In it Hemon published his own writings of the prewar years; he also published and gathered around him those who were to become the best writers of that generation. They make up the Skol Walarn (Gwalarn School). In Hemon's words, 'A la différence des autres périodiques existant jusqu'alors, il [*Gwalarn*] s'adressait aux seuls lettrés. Son but était de relever, dans tous les domaines, le niveau de la littérature. Il eut la chance de rassembler une pléiade de jeunes écrivains de talent, qui ne cessèrent de lui prêter leur concours.'[1] This review published poetry, stories, novels, plays, and also literary criticism, scientific writing, history, philology, including grammars and dictionaries, and translations of world literature. *Gwalarn* succeeded in raising Breton to the level of all literary and intellectual uses, to an extent that the Scots could only imagine for their vernacular. Finally,

Gwalarn contained a good, proper dose of polemical writing. In
Gwalarn, Arvor, and their successor, *Al Liamm*, as in a number of books
such as *Eur Breizad oc'h adkavout Breiz* (A Breton Discovers Brittany) and
La Langue bretonne et ses combats, Hemon voiced his ideas for a modern
Breton culture.[2]

First of all, Roparz Hemon and his associates react with passion
against the false, condescending, alienating stereotypes of Bretons and
Brittany current in French cultural life and which the Bretons themselves adopted. These include, first of all, the sentimental, romantic
vision of Brittany to be found in turn-of-the-century Breton writers such
as Le Goffic and Le Braz – the 'feminine' Celtic soul manifest in a people of dreamers and mystics, Christian, melancholic, deeply serious,
given to sacrifice and lost causes, bound to their past and its traditions,
and incapable of functioning in the present-day real world. More
recently, Bretons and French both speak of the region's allegedly inherent sense of fatality, black romance, guilt, failure, quest for the absolute,
and quest for death. Far less noble are the more popular clichés, as Piriou denounces them in the recipe:

> On prend un calvaire, deux clochers à jour, trois coiffes, quelques notes de
> biniou; on agrémente d'un bouquet d'ajonc d'or, d'une touffe de bruyère,
> d'un brin de genêt; on brasse du vent, de la pluie et de la brume; on marie
> le cidre doux aux crêpes dentelle. Les korrigans de la lande interviennent
> alors qui assurent la transfiguration mystique du décor en y associant une
> duchesse, deux chouans, un pêcheur d'Islande, quelques cols bleus,
> une couple de boniches, un trio de bonnes soeurs, un recteur de paroisse,
> une demi-douzaine d'anciens combattants et un quarteron de ministres
> inconditionnellement devoués à la cause de la France éternelle.[3]

Roparz Hemon and his followers repudiate all that smacks of nineteenth-century Breton provincialism, including the old traditions and
the more recent sentimental attachment to those traditions. The past
as a corrupt, alienating Other has to be overcome just as those
moderns who indulge in nostalgia for that past. Also to be overcome is
the France – the central, Parisian, hegemonic presence – that has
created the alienating past and the alienating present nostalgia for it.

For all these reasons Roparz Hemon was a Breton nationalist precisely
as Hugh MacDiarmid was a Scottish nationalist. *Gwalarn* began as a literary supplement to *Breiz Atao*, the paper of the Breton nationalist movement. Hemon and his associates played a central role in the second

phase of the Emsav (Movement/Awakening), which dominated Breton cultural life in the 1920s and 1930s. He and his associates are to be numbered among the *emsaverien* (militants). It is also true that, for any number of reasons, again like MacDiarmid, Hemon was a writer and man of culture, not a politician, and that he always placed literature ahead of politics. As early as 1927 he wrote that Brittany will never be saved by a revolution or by political struggle. Brittany will be saved when the Breton people read and write in their language, learn their history, and create their own schools and their own literature.

Hemon's deepest commitment is to the Breton people and a Breton nation. As he sees it, a great people deserve a great literature, or, rather, a people cannot be great without a great literature. And to have a great literature, a people must be endowed with one, unified, literary language, the only possible medium for such a literature, which will then become, by its very existence, the language of the nation.

Given the demands of literature and culture, and given the precept that you can teach a language in the schools only if it is a standard and not a hodgepodge of local regional dialects, Roparz Hemon wanted, above all else, a single, unified, enriched, and purified tongue. The first *Gwalarn* manifesto called for literature in a literary language and not the dialects: 'des travaux d'une irréprochable tenue littéraire, et fermant la porte aux patois (même décorés du nom de dialectes).'[4] In 1943 he wrote, 'Al levrioù-skol, al levrioù gouiziegezh, al lezennoù ha kement skrid uhel a zo ret e buhez ur bobl ne vezont savet e bro ebet e yezh ar gwrac'hed kozh'[5] (School books, scholarly books, the laws, and all writing of importance necessary for the life of a people will never, in any country, be written in the language of little old ladies). Later, looking back on his life's work, Hemon stated:

Hep ur yezh lennek reizhet-strizh ne oa spi ebet da sevel ul lennegezh uhel. Dre eurvad, ar yezh lennek-se a oa bet prientet. [Here he praises the work of François Vallée.] Eno e kaved ur brezhoneg diazezet war un hengoun milvloaziek, maget koulskoude gant lavar bev ar bobl. Ar pep gwellañ a oa bet tennet eus an testennoù kozh, eus ar reolennoù stabiliet gant rummadoù yezhadourourien ha geriadourourien, eus ar gerioù ha troioù-lavar dastumet e pep rannvro, hag ar gerioù nevez rekis a oa bet stummet-reizh.[6]

(Without a strictly correct language there was no hope for creating a high-culture literature. Fortunately, that literary language had been prepared [...] There was to be found a Breton language grounded in a thousand-year-old tradition, yet nourished by the living speech of the people. All the best was drawn from old texts, from rules established by generations of grammarians and lexicographers, words and expressions gathered from each region, and neologisms, when necessary, formed correctly.)

Nonetheless, unification would not be possible until there was one and only one orthography. On 8 July 1941 a group of Breton writers and scholars, Roparz Hemon in the lead, proclaimed the Unified Spelling called 'peurunvan.' Although a number of people have contested it, often for political or pedagogical reasons, and other systems were proposed, nowadays some 85 per cent of the writing in Breton adheres to Hemon's system. Hemon is right when he proclaims: '"Gwalarn" en deus sevenet e bennañ kefridi, stabilaat ur yezh klasel. Dismegañset e vez a-wechoù ar glaselezh. Ar vardell eo koulskoude a harz ouzh rouestl ha dizurzh'[7] (Gwalarn fulfilled its primary mission, to stabilize a classical language. At times classicism will be despised. Nonetheless it is the barrier against confusion and disorder). And he is right to insist upon the role of individual will in the process: 'Dans un pays comme la Bretagne [...] pas d'Etat, pas de centre. Un seul élément sérieux d'unification: la volonté de quelques-uns de triompher de l'anarchie. C'est l'esprit de lutte de quelques hommes, linguistes et écrivains, qui a unifié le breton.'[8]

With a modern, regularized, enriched, and unified language, Breton writers will be able to liberate themselves from the past, made up of a degenerate populism and historical failure, in order to create a dynamic, wholly modern literature in the present. The *Gwalarn* manifesto states in no uncertain terms:

> L'avènement de *Gwalarn* marquera en Bretagne dans le domaine littéraire ce que l'avènement de *Breiz Atao* a marqué dans le domaine politique: réaction violente et raisonnée de la jeunesse cultivée contre les modes surannées et la fausse paysannerie mises en honneur par le régionalisme. [...] Il s'agit de savoir s'il existe en Bretagne un public assez instruit du breton pour pouvoir comprendre la langue littéraire (aussi distante du langage du paysan breton que la langue de M. France l'est de celle du paysan français).[9]

He and the Skol Walarn called for a modern literature that would be modern and modernist in all senses of the term and that could, therefore, treat all aspects of modern life in all the modern literary genres.

Among the critiques levelled against the Skol Walarn (as against the New Makars in Scotland) was the accusation that these young men were attempting to force the Breton tongue into uses for which it had no precedents and traditions, and for which it was purportedly unfit. Hemon and his associates would have agreed; that is precisely what they wanted to do, and succeeded in doing. Like Hugh MacDiarmid, Hemon brought ideas and a quality of intellectuality into a literary tradition from which they had been hitherto absent.

Roparz Hemon's notion of universality is not limited to the high literary. In 1941, in *Arvor* (under the pseudonym Pendaran), he calls for the use of Breton in all aspects of journalistic life: 'Son [*Arvor's*] but est de devenir, le plus vite possible, un journal complet, un journal où l'on trouve en breton [...] tout ce que l'on doit trouver dans un journal moderne. Il nous faut une chronique de tout, une rubrique se rapportant à tout ce qui importe et qui intéresse.'[10] Later in that year he writes; 'C'est l'affirmation de l'existence de notre langue dans la vie sociale du pays: l'encouragement donné à son usage, oral et écrit, dans la rue, dans les magasins, dans les administrations publiques.'[11]

As a result, Breton will have, for the first time in history, a truly European literature worthy of interchange and mutual fertilization with the other European literatures. This will be the proof of its quality and its universality. In an oft-quoted passage that dates from 1929, Hemon declares:

> Si ces braves Bretons francisants [...] savaient combien cette littérature a peu le souci de 'faire breton,' s'ils savaient combien, au contraire, elle recherche l'universel et répugne à toute emprise du terroir, combien elle suit l'idéal de Goethe – ou plus modestement de Boileau – ils en seraient navrés. [...] Qu'ils l'accusent de n'être pas bretonne, d'être anti-bretonne. Elle n'en a cure. Elle est écrite en breton![12]

Like MacDiarmid on the Left, Hemon on the Right is, in some sense of the term, an elitist. He feels obliged to spurn the populist features of the old poetry and the dialect spoken by grandmother in the village. Up to 1925, with few exceptions, people wrote only for the mass. As we have seen, *Gwalarn* was created for a more cultured public, again to cite the manifesto, 'une revue littéraire, destinée à l'élite du public bretonnant ... déclencher un mouvement général dans l'élite bretonnante.'

This said, Hemon then and his followers today are eager to work with the masses in the process of cultivating a national Breton culture. After all, without the acceptance, in some sense of the term, of the project by Breton-speaking people, there can be no hope of success. The *Breiz Atao* and *Gwalarn* ideal of educated, intellectual torch-bearers, leading the mass, showing them the way, is, after all, not incongruent with the praxis of classical Marxism-Leninism.

Given this position, we can readily understand the emphasis Hemon gave to teaching the language and teaching in the language, and to the creation of a network of schools and other educational entities. As early as 1928 *Gwalarn* launched *Brezoneg ar Vugale* (Breton for Children), to raise funds in order to publish children's books for teachers. In 1934 Yann Fouéré had the idea of a campaign for 'Ar Brezoneg er Skol' (Breton in the Schools). Inspired by the example of the 'folkehøjskole' in nineteenth-century Schleswig, Hemon planned for a series of Breton schools, at all levels, parallel to the official French institutions in place. This is one of the main reasons for the creation of the Framm Keltiek Breizh (Celtic Institute of Brittany) during the Second World War. His program was stated in the following terms:

> Nous rendrons plus parfaites nos oeuvres d'enseignement, en appuyant et en coordenant leurs efforts. Nous agirons sur la jeunesse scolaire, à l'école même; en dehors de l'école, s'il le faut. Avant que ne se termine cette année scolaire 1940–41, nous aurons créé les éléments d'une Université bretonne [...] Si l'on ne veut pas d'elle, elle poursuivra son chemin et se développera toute seule. Mais on enseignera le breton.[13]

Furthermore, and in this he goes beyond the Scots and the Occitanians, Hemon calls for the teaching of Breton to non-celtophones. On the one hand, he considers French-speaking Bretons, the majority of the people who inhabit 'Haute-Bretagne,' including Rennes and Nantes, to be 100 per cent Bretons deprived of their Celtic heritage yet who will play a role in national Breton life. Second, he is convinced that these Bretons – he himself was born a French-speaker – will contribute in large measure to the cadre of writers and scholars because, unlike those who chatter in dialect on the farm, they will be happy to learn and practise the new literary standard. It is for them that he had the idea for a sort of Basic Breton ('Brezoneg eeun') limited to a thousand words, to publish the list *Alc'houez ar Brezoneg eeun* (The Key to Basic Breton), and to publish articles in it and school manuals employing it.

Last of all, Hemon calls for the publication of everything of significance written in Breton:

Hag evit echui: embannit an abreta ma c'hellit kement skrid a dalvoudegez
a zo en ho kerz. Eur skrid moulet, skignet dre Vreiz a-bez, ha zoken dre ar
bed-holl, a vo saveteet, goudoret diouz gwallreustlou ar bed ha fallagriez an
dud, arboellet evit oadveziou a studi hag a beoc'h, evit rummadou len-
neien ha gouizieien a denno dioutañ dudi, kened ha madelez.[14]

(In conclusion, publish as soon as possible all your significant writings.
Writings which are printed and distributed throughout Brittany, even
throughout the world, will be saved, sheltered from natural disasters and
from human wickedness, preserved for ages of study and peace, for generations of readers and scholars who will draw from them pleasure, beauty,
and goodness.)

This passage alludes to the tragedy that struck Roparz Hemon personally when, on 15 April 1941, Allied bombs destroyed his home in Brest,
including all his books and papers plus manuscripts by other writers that
he planned to publish. It also underscores the fragility of minority languages, how important to their survival and their just assessment are
writings, and how these writings deserve the authority granted by the
printing press. To survive they must be printed, and to attain respectability they must be printed. Orality is doomed. The book lives.[15]

POETRY

ROPARZ HEMON

Roparz Hemon stands as the Breton MacDiarmid. As we have seen, he
was the founder of Breton modernism and the principal ideologue for
reform in the language and literature. In some measure, he went
beyond MacDiarmid, devoting over five decades – from the mid-1920s
to the mid-1970s – to the Emsav and to writing in Breton. Although he
did not create any one text comparable to *A Drunk Man Looks at the Thistle* (nor did anyone else), Hemon's lifetime production was enormous
and of consistently high quality: approximately ten novels, one hundred
nouvelles, eighteen plays, fifty poems, one hundred songs, and a mass of
translation from foreign classics. This, alongside a lifetime of editorial,
organizational, and scholarly activity, the indispensable *Geriadur istorel ar
brezhoneg* (Historical Dictionary of Breton, 1958–78) in thirty-six fasci-
cles comparable only to Von Wartburg's *Französisches Etymologisches
Wörterbuch*.[16]

Hemon's *Barzhonegoù* (Poems) is one of his most noteworthy achievements.[17] The collection contains two long poems grounded in Celtic myth which treat characters from early Irish literature, and a selection of brilliant adaptations (re-creations in every sense) into Breton of selections from FitzGerald's *Omar Khayyám*. We find, in my opinion, Hemon at his very best in another sort of verse, a series of meditations on the human condition and, more particularly, on the condition of the freedom fighter – himself – struggling to awaken Brittany, the Breton people, the language, and its literature.

The masterpiece in this line, and one of the great poems of modern Europe, is the elegy 'Pirc'hirin ar Mor' (Pilgrim of the Sea), completed in the early 1930s.[18] In this text the Pilgrim, after a lifetime of struggle, arrives at the sea and, addressing her, himself, and those who come after, recounts his life, draws lessons from it, and proclaims what will be his future.

The negative aspects stand out, the sense of defeat and of loss. The Pilgrim has suffered from injustice and solitude and from the fact that, by his calling, he can never be one man among many. There are the practical types who know how to live, who avoid excess, who bend with the wind and settle down to house, family, friends, and the good quiet life. The Pilgrim cannot join them, not while the world is mud. And there are others, little people who understand nothing; they do not notice the blood on your feet. These creatures have no time for your spiritual cause. Theirs is the world of power, fame, and wealth. They ask for clothes at their measure. You only serve as their jester, to make them laugh when they are sick of weeping.

You have no reward from them. Even if they understood you, they wouldn't toss you a penny. Rewards go to a different sort of versifier, one who prattles of romantic nonsense: boys and flutes, girls dancing, fountains and flowers, the murmur of oars on a lake at the foot of a castle. That is what they call poetry!

Friends? Partisans? Yes, you have them one day and lose them the next. All humans are capricious and self-centred; in the outside world they seek only the mirror of their own rotten heart. Your life means no more to them than a burst pimple.

Family? I am a stranger in my own land. From my kin I receive only scorn, mockery, and hatred. A cold fog snuffed out the flame of affection for my brother. Love? How I suffered, alone in the dark, during the long winter nights and, still worse, the summer nights hearing women laugh and seeing their outline in the woods and by the sea. I stumble always on the rocks and gravel, surrounded by people who are despicable.

So, a life of solitude and pain, and of ascetic renunciation. Yet one is committed and one never gives up, one cannot give up. Each idea in my boiling mind becomes truth, and each thought becomes action. Each word flies like the seed. It is transmuted into flesh, it is my flesh. I cannot deny my desire or give only part of me to the mission:

> Pep Ger 'zo Kig.
> Va c'hig.
>> Ha n' hallan ober tra hep gouzañv
> Poanioù dre 'm c'horf evel dre 'm ene.
>>> Biken
> Ne ouezin nac'h va c'hoant, na reiñ hepken
> Un darn ac'hanon d' ar gefridi veur
> On ganet da seveniñ.
>> Pe da vervel. (pp. 16–17)

(Each word is Flesh. My Flesh. And I can do nothing without enduring pain in my body as in my soul. Never will I go against my desire nor give only one part of me to the great mission that I was born to fulfil. Or to die.)

The Thing and the Work are all. So, Pilgrim, you continue to walk, to march, to go forward. You cannot stop, whatever the pain and the obstacle. Your quest is to climb high onto peaks which no man has known, standing in the wind with white light gleaming in red clouds, a domain of thunder, rocks, and the glare of the sun. Your heart beats, your lips are dry.

Hemon evokes in majestic terms the Nietzschean ideal of the Superman and embodies the Superman's vocation in Bachelardian (and Nietzschean) imagery of fire, air, and the harsh earth of the will. He also recalls, with the Pilgrim's quest, the archetypal quest of the knight-errant in medieval romance, which celebrates heroes such as Lancelot, Perceval, and Gawain, whose origins are to be found in Celtic myth.[19] This is a literature and these are archetypes of masculine heroism, of a virile life of quest and conquest, juxtaposed with the effeminate, viscous, putrid existence of those who are mediocre and those who betray. Also juxtaposed are the heroic, authentic life of the Master and the treacherous, inauthentic death-in-life of the Slave.

Although the Pilgrim's life is one of travail, he does enjoy rewards. The Pilgrim is a quiet lake in daytime that comes to life at night and shivers under the harsh eyes of the moon. Even the bitterness of the road grants him peace as his heart is made young again by the beloved Breton horizons and the bells he does not hear. The fountains of joy remain hidden? So what! It is enough that he will have sought them out and called for them by dawn from afar. He will be a master not a slave.

Finally, there is the sea, the *imago* of the Mother and of Brittany. The Pilgrim belongs to the sea, he has sought her all his life. She is a cruel goddess yet also his muse, for she mirrors his childhood, her depths and grottos echo his songs of youth, and the beat of the waves his music. Now, in the winter of his discontent, the Pilgrim speaks only to her. The sea, embodying the feminine element, stands for Brittany – the Breton soul – and, as a Great Mother, she stands as the source of all. The Pilgrim turns to her in place of the other, cruel God (Christ? Mammon?). As a Magna Mater, as a telluric goddess, she recalls perhaps the pagan past of Brittany; she could be a Celtic divinity worshipped prior to the advent of Christianity in a free land before invasion and subjugation by Latins. At any rate, after failing to commune with the dancing boys and singing girls of the common, pedestrian world, the idyllic fantasies of the mediocre, and after a solitary life of struggle and torment, the Pilgrim does commune with the Mother Goddess. Like a hero of *geste*, he will love only the sea and be loved by her. Thus and thus only will this masculine warrior, who struggles, panting, up virgin mountains and breathes in the radiance of the sun, integrate the *anima* into his psyche and, after so long a quest, become a total human being. He will commune with the goddess and, in a state of Hölderlin-like *tremendum*, become imbued with some of the godhead in turn.

That the Pilgrim addresses the sea as if in old age raises the problematic of time, so important in this text. On the one hand, he has wandered through the world, blood on his feet, and suffered the insults of the rabble for so long. His pride in art and his phantasms of recognition occurred in youth, so long ago. So long ago, also, the possibility of joining the laughing girls on summer nights and of living a normal life with wife, children, and friends. The illusions and the temptations of youth are long gone. Yet, as he states his credo – he addresses himself more than he does the sea – the Pilgrim exhorts himself (and other pilgrims) to persevere, to continue walking, studying, marching, voyaging, and questing. He will persevere, he will continue on his path, however rocky and tortuous it proves to be. The

Pilgrim has a future as much as he has a past, just as Brittany lives for the future and not just her storied past.

We are not told the future of Brittany. The Pilgrim knows his own future, the end of his path. After a brief life, with no peace and so little pleasure, await the talons of cruel death. His bones will dry out in the corner of a graveyard, his flesh decomposed in the earth. And the future after that? On the one hand, the heart-wrenching vision of other bards striding over his traces, alone, unaware of his existence and unaware of the phantoms who one day will stride over their traces – all encased in the stone shroud of pride. Yet, in the last section, the Pilgrim imagines a scene that will occur 'thousands and thousands of leagues from your time. A cultured little man, quiet like you – like the Pilgrim? like the real Roparz Hemon? – will open a little old book, yellowed with age. And as when the squall rips the clouds, in an instant you will rise up before him, in flesh and in the spirit. He the foreigner will find the path of his heart. And he will be thunderstruck.'

> Mil ha mil lev diouzh da amzer [...]
> Un denig seven, sioul eveldout,
>   [...] e tigoro
> Al levrig kozh deut melen gant an oad.
> Ha 'vel pa rog ur barrad gwent ar c'hoabr,
> E vezi trumm dirazañ, kig hag ene.
>   [...] Eñ, an estren, [...]
> A gavo hent e galon hag a chomo
> Sebezet. (p. 21)

'Pirc'hirin ar Mor' offers a pattern of imagery traditional to epic literature everywhere, and, in France, from the *chansons de geste* to Ronsard (*Les Discours*) and D'Aubigné (*Les Tragiques*) and then to Vigny, Hugo, and St-John Perse. The Pilgrim spurns the earthly feminine, portrayed in terms of the viscous and the rotten or, simply, the vulgar quotidian, in favour of a life of heroism and adventure, conceived as stone, rock, fire, open spaces, mountain peaks, and the harsh pure light of the sun. By progression in space – by wandering and striding – he frees himself from the flawed locus of ordinary life in order to proceed – even in defeat – to a higher, finer, better kingdom where he will be prince and bard. With this movement, plus its accompanying motifs of fire and hard earth, the Pilgrim establishes a masculine identity, which then gives birth to works of the spirit. And he, who would be frustrated by the all-too-momentary satisfaction of libido, is rewarded by the spiritual embrace of the land and the sea – his Brittany, she for whom he undertakes the quest and has renounced all else. He is a man of the spirit – a poet and bard – yet his quest is conceived also in martial terms (Aragon and Eluard were to do the same, later and on the other side, in French) as that of a knight-errant living only for his lady. Thus, poetically, the Pilgrim does integrate the *anima* into his psyche to become a total human being, just as, by disdaining everyday compromise and everyday comfort, he lives a life truly authentic and – whether he wins or loses is of no account – that of a master not a slave. To be a master implies facing time and mortality without dread, as did Gilgamesh, Achilles, Roland, Lancelot, and Galahad. It also implies triumph over time and mortality. Like the heroes of deeds in arms, the Pilgrim undergoes a death-rebirth experience. For the Pilgrim, this assumes the form of the future liberation of Brittany but also – for he is a bard – recognition by posterity, if only by one little man, such as himself, who will peruse the book – 'Pirc'hirin ar Mor'? the *Barzhonegoù?* – and, as a result of his doing so, the dead bard will return to life. Thus, as *mise en abyme*, the poem plays a decisive role in the narrative it itself recounts and serves to ensure its own reception in extra-narrative time and space.

Two briefer poems, also from the prewar years, develop further the thematics of the voyage. Given the Celtic tradition of the *imram* (sea trek) as a structure and even a literary genre for the quest over water (the term usually appears in this, its Old Irish form), it is not surprising that both texts centre on ships. 'Al lestr' (The Ship) tells of a vessel coming into port.[20] The crew enjoy their brief shore leave. However, the bell rings and they must depart. 'Listri-noz' (Ships of the Night) tells of the Speaker in a boat at nighttime.[21] There he observes the dream vessels, *sans* oar, mast, and sail, which tell of exotic climes and past ages. Then comes day, and they disappear.

In both texts the sea voyage is conveyed in positive terms. In 'Al lestr' the Speaker proclaims how beautiful the sea is, along with its foam, its wind, and the gulls. In spite of the fact that the Masters of the World exploit the ship for commerce, the vessel retains its primal majesty. Rusty, eaten away, uncared for, it remains more beautiful than ever. In 'Listri-noz' the Speaker's maritime experience is set in antithesis to past seasons of idleness, pleasure, song, and sleep on land, now fortunately dead, and to the next morning, which contains the seeds of sadness and shame, the fog of day, and the murmur of chagrin. Now, he cries, the path is firm, the wind is steady, and the waves sing with joy.

Yet the Speaker's relation to the sea trek is recounted, as it were, as if in the conditional tense and subjunctive mood. In one poem, like an orphan, he watches the ship and its returned crew sail off into the horizon, a vision of kindred beauty lost. In the other, he has a vision of the dream ships, so beautiful and so mysterious – with no oars or masts or sails – sliding along silently in the peace of the stars. He cries out that, if only it could, his heart would rejoin the brothers. In both texts, whether standing on the shore (or in his room) or standing on a common, non-dream ship, the Speaker is denied the adventure and the quest. He can participate only in longing, in dreaming, and in the working of the imagination.

He can participate in dreaming. Just as 'Pirc'hirin ar Mor' is a poem of daylight, of pilgrimage and struggle in the harsh light of the sun, here the Speaker embellishes the night in texts of the sea. 'Al lestr' begins in the middle of the night with the Speaker asleep, subject to nightmares yet also cognizant of the sea and its power and beauty. In the morning the sailors come ashore to partake of their usual trivial pastimes: food, drink, and girls. It is presumably near or at dusk when the crew is called back and the ship takes off. In any case, the entire diegesis may well be an oneiric experience, made up in the Speaker's dream of the preceding night. 'Listri-noz' recounts a night world of night creatures, and specifically the ships called ships of the night. These magical vessels, in their silence, sing of expanded horizons in space and time. Time past means bygone sailors and ships from the past, and therefore the old Celtic saints and heroes and their tradition of sea voyage. Here, also, the best occurs at night, in a dreamlike experience with dream ships, in contrast to the sadness, pain, chagrin, and silence of the day.

In these two poems Hemon exalts the sea, *imago* of the Mother, conceived archetypally in feminine imagery. The sea, as *fons et origo* of life, is assimilated to other manifestations of the feminine in our culture: night, the dark, the body, the emotions, and the realm of dreams and of the imagination. Frustrated by his own incapacity to be a heroic mariner, the Speaker can nevertheless evoke through the imagination both the heroic life which he, a poet, cannot live and the anguish of his separation in space and time – by the shore, by the dawn – from that life. The life he can lead, because it is a life of dreams and of the night, recalls death. The silent boats gliding through the night are vessels of the centuries, and their tales are the tales of dead mariners from the

Celtic past, death assimilated to nighttime, poetry, and the sea. Similarly, in a poem from the 1960s, 'Izold a Vreizh' (Isolt of Brittany), the
Breton princess sings a lovely stitching song.[22] She so wishes to be the
Breton wind that blows to her beloved in Cornwall or the waves which
break against his boat. As the sun sets and the shadow of her tower falls
over the sea, she would also drown her heart in the sea, as the tower
does. In contrast to 'Pirc'hirin ar Mor,' these poems show that Hemon
exploits also that other side of the human spirit – dreams, darkness,
poetry, ships, water, and death – the feminine element which, according
to tradition, is especially pronounced in the Celtic peoples and their
literature.

Two splendid long poems from the postwar years register Hemon's culminating achievement in verse and his final evolution as a poet of the
Emsav. In 1943 the Abbé Perrot, a leader of the Catholic Breton cultural
movement, himself largely apolitical and never a collaborator, was murdered by communist thugs in the Resistance. Fascist figures in the
Emsav used this act of terrorism as an excuse to found the Bezen Perrot,
a so-called Breton militia in the line of the Vichy-sponsored 'milice,' to
combat the Free French. A maximum of seventy-two young men were
enrolled. At the liberation, during the French purge trials (the best
translation for 'l'épuration'), eight members of the Bezen Perrot were
executed. Hemon himself, also largely apolitical, was incarcerated for a
time and then deprived of his civil rights – hence the exile to Ireland,
where he spent the last three decades of his life.

This contextualization is necessary to understand the powerfully
beautiful elegy 'Kanenn evit Deiz an Anaon' (Song for the Day of the
Dead).[23] It is the First of November, the Old Irish Samain or the Gaulish
Samonios, the Celtic Day of the Dead. It is also All Saints' Day, the day
we honour the dead and reflect on the Communion of the Saints in
God, and it is the eve of All Souls' Day, 2 November. Hemon paints a
striking contrast between two kinds of dead, two kinds of dead young
men. On the one side are those buried under vast stone monuments,
covered with medals, honoured by prelates, celebrated with noise: high
masses, trumpets, drums, organs, the peeling of bells, and speech in
French. On the other, quiet and alone, a fearful priest utters a few words
in a corner of the church, in the presence of one forlorn sister, a rosary
on her lap. On the one side, flowers, wreaths, bronze crosses, and noble
gravestones; on the other, a mother alone in the cemetery, clasping
flowers, yet with no grave to decorate; she knows not where her son lies;

she can only toss her flowers into the air, one by one, in despair. Pomp is contrasted with humility, crowds of people with lone mourners, noise with whispers or silence, and dead bronze and stone with living flowers and people. Also contrasted, of course, is French with Breton and the French or Resistance soldiers with the Bretons of the Bezen. The hegemony of noise over whispers and of pomp over humility reflects, in Hemon's allegory, the imposed dominance of French and the French state upon a Celtic people.

In a moving appeal for compassion, the Speaker urges no hatred for either side and certainly no hatred for idealistic youths who gave their lives for what they thought was a just cause. How can you even say which was right and which was wrong? he asks. How can you distinguish between the leaves ripped from the branch and tossed by the wind, some into the current of a stream and others crushed under cart wheels in the mud? In the horror of war the Speaker perceives only the young men, enemies and comrades, separated by Breton field embankments, with only death between them:

Sell ouzh sell,
dir ouzh dir,
hennezh en tu all d' ar c'hleuz,
va enebour,
va c'henseurt,
war hon tro kened ar bed,
etrezomp netra,
nemet an Ankou. (pp. 92–3)

(Gaze against gaze, steel against steel, that one on the other side of the embankment, my foe, my comrade, around us the beauty of the world, between us nothing but Death.)

In death and in memory, the Speaker grants them dignity, forgiveness, and, above all, equality as humans and as soldiers of commitment.

Still, he concentrates on the weak, on the losers. And, in so doing, he assimilates them to the feminine. Hence the contrast between the harsh earth of the will (bronze and stone) and soft, gentle flowers close to nature. Hence the presence of the family, of women – the sister weeping alone with her rosary and the mother searching alone for a child's unmarked grave. The pathos and the suffering of the weak, of creatures associated with the emotions, is set off against official masculine bluster.

A return to the Mother does not always lead to defeat, according to the Speaker. He tells the mother she didn't have to purchase the flowers:

Ha pa ve o eskern en tu all d' an Douar,
emaint e Breizh,
ha Breizh 'zo dezho:
int 'zo Breizh,
ha Breizh 'zo int. (p. 97)

(Even if their bones are on the other side of the globe, they are in Brittany, and Brittany is theirs, they are Brittany, and Brittany is them.)

Her (his) fields, trees, and children will bloom. Similarly, the Speaker observes that the winners have their wreaths and monuments, the latter in stone cut from Breton rock. Much good it will do them; they are dead. The losers, on the contrary, live on, for Our Mother keeps uncut slabs of rocks in her womb for her sons, whom she loves. It matters not where they are buried, just as it matters not where the heroes from the past are buried. They sleep on the Mother's knees and – recalling the legend of King Arthur in the Blessed Isles, who one day will return – one day they will awake. The Day of the Dead is a festival of genealogy and origins; and, because the Otherworld is not separated from ours by impenetrable barriers, the two domains can and will join. Each blade of grass tells its story of a Breton from long ago, a story of sadness and the world's blood. As the Speaker envisages it, the winners stand alone, far from nature, alienated, and lacking a history. The losers have families, they descend from millenniums of countrymen on their own land, a sacred land of rock and mist, of field and flower. The land is sacred because it is the Mother – the goddess – who grants life meaning. She nurtures the quick and the dead and, like the sea in 'Pirc'hirin ar Mor,' is the measure of life. Because of the Mother, the losers are endowed with a future as well as a past. Because of her they participate totally in Being, because of her they are immortal.

Immortality and rebirth in the Otherworld are not uniquely pagan or paganoceltic. Hemon creates a powerful Breton synthesis of the pre-Christian and Christian traditions, for this Celtic Day of the Dead is also All Saints' Day, the eve of All Souls' Day, a theme which is developed at the beginning and end of the elegy, framing it. He addresses the modern Breton martyr, the Abbé Perrot, who lived and died a soldier.

Although the winners don't utter your name, proclaims the Speaker, it echoes wherever Breton is spoken and it is whispered on the fields and the waves. You dwell in the Happy Isles with the old Breton saints, ever young, you who bless the young of today who walk in your path to live and die for Brittany: 'da vevañ evit Breizh, / ha da vervel' (p. 98). Thus the Speaker bridges old and young and Christian and pagan. The Christian martyrs of Brittany live on in a uniquely Celtic paradise, their thoughts focused on the motherland. Furthermore, in addition to the fields and the waves who whisper, the Speaker, standing for Roparz Hemon the writer and apostle of the Emsav, proclaims high and afar the name of Yann-Vari Perrot and the young men who were shot for their commitment to his ideals.

Because of the holy day the blades of grass tell their stories and the mother offers her flowers. Because of the festival of purified white souls, the old saints in their niches smile down at the girl who will be the Mother of God. The scene shifts from Tir na nÓg back to a simple Breton church. The message is the same. The young Christ gave his life to renew the world, as the brave, pure young men gave theirs to renew Brittany. On this holy day seed germinates in the land, a last allusion to the losers, figures of Christ, who, in spite of or because of having lost, are closer to nature, the land, the martyred saints, and the martyred Saviour. They and all of us face death. We all must take the road beyond the seas. We can do so in joy, the joy of the day of the Communion of Saints, when all creatures live in joy. Thus Roparz Hemon ends his elegy, all the more moving, all the more exalted in the human spirit, for those of us, his readers, who are convinced that he was, politically, in the wrong.

'Galv ar beziou' (The Call of the Graves), which stands as a summit or last milestone on Hemon's quest, fuses the fierce, virile militancy of 'Pirc'hirin ar Mor' and the feminine, death-oriented texts of the later years.[24] The Speaker and a young Breton stand near some graves. A voice speaks forth, from the Otherworld, to encourage the young Breton (and the Speaker), and the Speaker continues the exhortation.

As in 'Kanenn evit Deiz an Anaon,' these are the graves of the defenders of Brittany. The bodies are now ashes. It is forbidden to honour or even visit the site; we find there no cross, wreath, or prayer, no regret or care. These scattered graves are mute (again, no headstones) and subject to the ravages of sun and rain. We find only grass, thorns, rust, and mud.

In this scene of the viscous, of rot, corruption, and death, stand male figures – the Youth and the Speaker. The Youth is tempted to go home, to forget the losers and to obey the winners. Yet a third masculine presence makes itself known. The Voice from the graves is a masculine voice, the voice of dead heroes.

As in 'Pirc'hirin ar Mor,' the dead Voice and the live Speaker condemn negative, non-committed, self-indulgent, presumably French-oriented Bretons. Life is not just singing and dancing. Fat dogs are rewarded with treasure, not us. The cities are arrogant and will be levelled. Others are idle, mere dreamers, and death will annihilate them. When, indeed, Bretons do not respond to the call, the magic castle is transformed into filth, tallow, dust, and ashes.

In contrast to the imagery of rot and corruption, the Voice and the Speaker, like prophets of Israel, bear witness to evildoers yet also exhort good men (the allegorical Breton Youth) to live the good life and do the right thing. In a powerful Freudian image, they call upon the Youth to strike forth, to press down and forward, hard, like a plough in the fields. In contrast to the rotten and the corrupt, they evoke a vision of air, fire, and the harsh earth of the will. We are told of martial activity – trumpet blasts, banners unfurled, and a castle awakening. We hear of a prison door broken, of bells and the bright sun of Pentecost. Hemon evokes the world of his Pilgrim – progression in space, combat, fierce activity, the life of reason symbolized by pure air and the sun, and the awakening, a reawakening.

In contrast to the masses of fat dogs, the idle, and the traitors, the Youth will endure solitude. Yet even though the castle collapses, down below on the Breton heath assemble a small crowd, a community of all classes and ages, who listen to a murmur in the heart, who comprehend the call from the graves. The Youth will not be alone. The Speaker does not stand alone. Others join him (them) in their good fight and long march.

The call from the graves comes not just from one person but from all the souls. There too is a community. The Youth is their son. Dead to us, they live on in the Otherworld, and when the Youth dies, these souls will welcome him. He will have friends, Breton friends, there in Arthur's Blessed Isles. There doubt and anguish will cease. And, because these are the Blessed Isles from which Arthur will return (as in 'Kanenn evit Deiz an Anaon'), they will behold the Sun of Pentecost. Just as Christ arose from the dead and assembled his followers, so too the Breton martyrs will rise again. According to the Voice, our dead bodies will tremble with life, and the Breton young will be the fruit of our chagrin.

The feminine is reintroduced, in positive terms, as germination, given that the warriors and martyrs, those who stride and wander, are granted new life. Unlike others who die, they will be immortal. As if to underscore this more hopeful vision – movement from the graves to the Happy Isles – at the end of 'Galv ar bezioù' Hemon returns to the feminine *imago*, the sea. Those who choose arrogant cities are in error, for the Masters of Earth will cast them down. However, the sea rolls on. She brings her song to the dune, the grass, and the stones, and in the beat of her waves cries out that the hope of the race be not lost. 'Galv ar bezioù,' constituted by the discourse from the graves and by the Speaker's own discourse, constituted by the speech of men, is contained, embedded if you wish, in a frame of feminine imagery, which encloses it. The feminine images are the graves and the sea. The graves evoke defeat and the past. The sea evokes victory and the future. In between, in the eternal present, heroes speak to heroes and poets to poets in the name of that Eternal Feminine – Breizh – manifest in both the land and the sea.

Roparz Hemon has been compared to Valéry, because of their shared intellectual austerity. I should like to raise the names Hölderlin, Vigny, George, St-John Perse, and Josef Weinheber. There is a particular cast to his verse: the thematics of solitude, duty, the struggle, and the quest; the sense of the individual alone, at odds with society and, despite good intentions, with his uncomprehending fellow men. And there is the imagery of blood and soil, of the land and the race, of heroes of deeds in arms, radiant with health, casting aside the effeminate and casting down the rot and corruption of cities and, when doomed, finding solace and exaltation in the call from the graves. Much of this is Romantic in heritage, and much of it partakes of a consciously masculine vision, the epic strain in French and European letters, including *Gilgamesh*, Homer, Virgil, the Prophets of Israel, the *chanson de geste*, D'Aubigné, Hugo, and, for the moderns, Yeats and St-John Perse. It also reflects a pattern of conservative, nationalist, and even national-socialist imagery also prevalent in this period.

What is the appropriate reader-response? I offer you mine. It is one of anguish. I will not condemn Roparz Hemon for a thematics and a world-vision which D'Aubigné and Isaiah would have understood, which I understand, but which happens to be out of fashion on American campuses. Nor should he be blamed for Breton patriotism, for doing and writing what so many Irish did and wrote after the English crushed the Easter Uprising. Still, he was wrong, so very wrong, and, in the 1940s and the 1950s, no cause, including the liberation of Brittany, can justify,

even obliquely, looking back upon the Occupation with political nostalgia. The fact that Roparz Hemon was so wrong adds a tragic grandeur to
his verse and to his life, those last thirty years of exile when he refused
ever to go home, when, I am convinced, he knew he was wrong and
knew that the tide of history was receding from him and his most deeply
held beliefs. Hence a tone of anguish in the elegies of defeat. Hence the
shift from proud certainty to the tragic acceptance of uncertainty, a shift
from day to night, land to sea, and from the quest to the grave. As far
back as the 1920s, in 'Pirc'hirin ar Mor' Roparz Hemon concedes that
all trace of the Pilgrim and his life will be uprooted and that bards after
him will not even guess at his existence. Yet, as we saw, he protests that,
thousands of leagues from his time, a little man, by the light, will open
the little old book yellowed from the years, and he will be thunderstruck. I am that little man.

The tragedy of Roparz Hemon's life and exile contributes even more
beauty to the reading of his verse. His Celtic identity is enriched and
problematized by a sense of history, a vision of the past and the future,
and of the tragic sense of life, the recognition of loss and defeat, the
conviction that progress is an obscene lie in the mouths of the winners.
Then, in contrast to the Romantic or post-Romantic subject-matter, the
formal quality, the 'feel' of the poetry, is classical. Employing a limited
register of imagery and a limited range of themes and motifs, Hemon
does not shy from repetition and renegotiation of the same problematic
and the same vision. All this is expressed in texts in which the imagery
attains archetypal power and the speaking voice a pathos and nobility rare in the twentieth century or any century. Like Hölderlin and
George, Hemon attains a sense of *tremendum*, of that borderland
between men and the gods. Like them, he attains something akin to the
sacred.

MAODEZ GLANNDOUR

A decade younger than Roparz Hemon, Maodez Glanndour / Louis Le
Floc'h / Loeiz ar Floc'h was both a disciple of the Skol Walarn and a fervent participant in its struggles. An ordained priest, Glanndour did yeo-
man work as a scholar and public intellectual, writing, like Hemon, a
vast amount of literary and journalistic material. He also translated into
Breton the New Testament and several books of the Old Testament.
Most important of all, a number of his poetic works, published from the

1940s on, make him the greatest poet of the modernist movement and, it is probable, the greatest poet who ever wrote in Breton.[25]

Glanndour is a quintessentially modernist writer. Fusing a deep, fervent, and learned Christian faith with a no less fervent faith in Brittany and the Emsav, he brings to these strivings all the formal complexity and innovation we find in Eliot and Pound or in Claudel, Valéry, Perse, and Aragon. Alliteration and internal rhyme, free verse, the prose poem, and the calligram; borrowings in structure and form from modern French and from medieval Welsh; lexical borrowing from Old and Middle Breton and from all the Celtic sisters and cousins – these account for some (but not all) of Glanndour's capacity to raise, to explode really, the horizon of expectations of the celtophone public, in verse of magnificent, splendiferous sheen and of a weight and a density comparable to those of his beloved Breton rocks and heath.

Dating from 1941, *Imram* (Sea Trek) is perhaps Glanndour's masterpiece.[26] This long poem – a version of modern, Christian epic – recounts the Speaker's spiritual quest, conceived as a sea voyage in the tradition of the heroes of Celtic myth: Bran the Blessed, for example, and his avatar Saint Brendan. Like Bran and Brendan, the Speaker visits a number of islands on the deep. The first of these is the isle of a giant, the Ogre of War. In powerful imagery of torture and mutilation, of rot and putrefaction, Glanndour depicts the monster asleep yet dreaming. When awakened, he devours hordes of people, crushing, nibbling, and gnawing at them. And, while he sleeps, his rats fill up on the remains:

Douar milliget, ur Ramz a zo roue warnout,
Ar Roñfl hudur, loudour,
Gourvezet teurek en e vougev goude re-gorfad
War bern eskern an dud en deus debret.
Hag e-pad ma roc'h o mestr e ra fest ar razhed. (p. 148)

(Accursed land, you have as king a Giant, the loathsome, filthy Ogre, lying bloated in his cave after having stuffed his belly, on the heap of bones of the people he has eaten. And while their master snores the rats have a banquet.)

This god of butchery dominates but does not uniquely personify what is an Island of Sin, where all seven Capital Vices ingest humans held captive in their talons and Ankoù (Death) stinks with the rot of corpses.

The Speaker's next stop is the Isle of Women, a direct intertextual allusion to the career of Bran. Here is evoked imagery of the *locus amoenus*, the pastoral tradition of flowing water, birds, and butterflies in the world of the fays. However, again appears Ankoù, who breaks all this beauty into smithereens. As the *memento mori* in a Dance of Death pageant, he addresses the Speaker. I ever follow you. With my nails I age young girls' features. In reality, they are witches and hags, and inside their hearts curdle witches' potions. Because of me, Ankoù says, flowers grow indeed, but from people's corpses.

Glanndour condemns the idyll of human happiness, as Roparz Hemon did, yet persists in travelling to a third island. This is the Isle of Nature, a region untouched by the human, no less idyllic than the Isle of Women except that the topography – rocks, creeks, and the forest – is more savage. Primitive untouched nature appeals to the romantic and modern imagination much as the pastoral one appeals to the medieval and Renaissance. However, the Speaker is refuted once again. The island/nature cry out that they also are poisoned. The gentle white foam of the waters is but the drool of a terrifying sea in anger. Nature brings both good and ill, she creates and destroys. Adam could have joyed in oranges from the Tree of Life. Instead, he chose the other fruit, and this fruit – our earth – is ever afterwards corroded, spoiled, and defiled by the marks of his teeth.

The message the Speaker draws from the islands is that his quest is misdirected from the beginning and that the lives of most men are equally misdirected. We seek happiness and fulfilment in our earthly lives. We believe in progress and in perfection or, at least, in the successful working toward perfection. We do so in the name of heroism, love, and nature. And we fail, says the Speaker, we have to fail, because Ankoù stands beside us, his stench with us, his rot and putrefaction our eventual rot and putrefaction.

In other passages of *Imram* the Speaker proceeds even further in demystifying our modern, secular quest for happiness. He learns that Satan himself offers us the illusion of satisfaction just as he offered Adam and Eve fruit from the wrong tree. Glanndour evokes this theme with two images. Sinners imprison themselves because of their selfishness; as flies caught in the web, they give themselves to the spider to be sucked alive. This is because they do not listen to the priest, who offers them the Pearl beyond Price, but instead heed the black angel, who tempts them with his poisonous philtre – an allusion, among other things, to the philtre that poisoned Tristan and Isolt.

The Speaker learns that happiness is not of this world, grounded in this world. It can be had, yet only with God and his Holy Spirit. In his 'Kan al leinoù' (Song of the Summits) and 'Kan an eilger' (Song of the Response), responding to the aborted quest of the 'Kanenn azrec'h' (Song of Contrition), Glanndour evokes what such happiness entails. He employs imagery of heroism and the quest, and of nature. However, following in the tradition of the Song of Songs and of mystical poets such as Teresa of Avila and Juan de la Cruz, he speaks of Christian love and of the divine Eros. On the one hand, the Speaker himself is both lover and beloved. He confesses that he has been unfaithful, a sinner and a whore. Yet now he loves Christ on the Cross, loves him for his thorns, wounds, and vinegar. He loves Christ in his great beauty and begs to be ravished by him:

O, deus! Mall am eus d' az kwelout,
Daoulagad ouzh daoulagad
Kalon ouzh kalon,
Diharz da viken, Hollgened!
Ennon e vi, ennout e vin da viken,
Soubet ez frond, o sunañ da zouster,
Evel ar wenanenn en kalon ar vleunienn. (p. 160)

(Oh, come! I long to behold you, eye to eye, heart to heart, totally, for ever more, All-beauty! You will be in me, I will be in you, forever, bathing in your fragrance, sucking your sweetness, like bees in the heart of the flower.)

And Christ returns the sinner's love, loving him and all mankind by means of the cross and the torture – thorns, wounds, vinegar – he endures. His torture is also ecstasy, his *passio* is also passion, as is, in return, the Speaker's love for him. It is in this thematic of the reciprocal love between man and God that Glanndour evokes Christ in Majesty, awaiting the Last Judgment, when the guilty – those flies sucked alive by the satanic spider – will feel the cutting edge of his Word, whereas he will embrace the good, compared to little ants. Similarly, God will then grant us resurrection of the body as well as of the soul, for he is a good father and can succour his children in all ways.

This personal bond, between God and humankind, of *amor* and *caritas* is then conflated to include God as the seminal force who created the universe by a divine act of love. Here the Holy Ghost is invoked in place of Christ. In an especially sublime passage the Speaker tells how the

Spirit created the cosmos, bringing the trembling of life onto the void by a metaphorically sexual gesture: his divine breathing (the potency of his Word) on the abyss, recalling the Gospel: 'In principio erat Verbum, et Verbum erat apud Deum, et Deus erat Verbum.' So, too, cries the Speaker, the Word gave me life, breath, and fire. This is the paternal love which moves the stars and the cosmos, the harmony of the spheres standing as a testimony to God's continuing, ever-present hope.

The Speaker draws a lesson from this meditation: because the cosmos is the creation of divine charity, it is not as flawed as he deemed it to be in the 'Kanenn azrec'h.' Once he views reality from a Christian perspective, his vista and the essence of reality itself are transformed. Seeing the world with new eyes, he recognizes that it is clad in a many-splendoured cloak, for it, like us, comes from God. In particular, the Speaker invokes his land, Brittany, as God's creation, a place whose beauty and harmony reflect the Lord's beauty and harmony, a land which helps him comprehend the Lord's truth. Therefore, as a Christian, he can speak in his own tongue – Breton – of truth and liberty, just as he hopes for the resurrection of the flesh, when he will also speak Breton and even the French will understand.

The Speaker understands these mysteries in terms of traditional Christian imagery and, with the same metaphors, tries to make his implied reader understand. The Speaker evokes Christ on the Cross, who listens to us and to the music of the spheres. There he gives his blood to us, for us his Sacred Heart bleeds. This is the ultimate gesture of sacrifice and of charity, in that God's own blood is shed, not just once, but again and again, whenever people take communion in the mass. This love is not the sugar-coated sentimentality of our century, says the Speaker, but a manifestation of fire. Elsewhere the Speaker develops fire imagery in his personal Song of Songs to evoke the faithful, a multitude of burning stars.

As in so much Christian poetry, Glanndour's Speaker adopts a number of stances and embodies a number of personae. Following the tradition of typological exegesis of Scripture, the Speaker is a twentieth-century man facing twentieth-century problems yet is also, foreshadowing himself, a witness to Christ's passion and even a witness to the Creation. His personal prefiguration and fulfilment are patterned on the third, tropological level of exegesis, which treats allegorical prefiguration and the fulfilment of history in the individual. Second, he is an ordained priest, who has the authority to instruct humankind in the mysteries of the faith yet who also, when he betrays Our Lord by sin-ning, does so in a greater agony of consciousness, given that he, more than most, is called to postfigure Christ as the good shepherd and to act as his deputy in the sacrament of the mass. Third, the speaker is a Breton, automatically one of the downtrodden of the planet. Furthermore, because he is a Breton priest and poet, Glanndour's Speaker assumes the stance of the medieval warrior-bard on a sea trek, in the Celtic tradition of Bran and Saint Brendan, as a Bran or Brendan who is also a Taliesen.

Therefore the Speaker, happy at home in port, is compelled to set out on his *imram*, in the course of which he visits the three cursed islands. Yet because this is the intellectual quest of a poet, we are told little of ships and sailing. Instead, metaphorically a boat with a sail and anchor, the Speaker is borne on the arms of the wind. It is this wind, his muse, who demands that he depart with her, for she is the master and he must yield to her desire. So much for the 'Kanenn azrec'h.' With the Christian vision of the 'Kan al leinoù' and the 'Kan an eilger' the imagery of *imram* is largely forgotten. Now the Speaker encounters a new, other wind, which wafts him directly upwards, where he enjoys a vision of divine truths. This is because the old muse (pagan inspiration) is replaced by the new muse, the wind of the Holy Spirit, God's breath and God's kiss, a winged muse in/through whom the flower of revelation pours forth from the Word. To make this happen, the Spirit purifies the Speaker by a javelin or lance which pierces his heart (the mystical penetration vouchsafed to Saint Teresa) and a hot coal which purifies his mouth, eyes, and heart. Thus the Speaker is granted absolution for his sins; more pertinent still, thus, like Moses, postfiguring Moses, he is purified and granted the inspiration not to be a mere versifier but to be a prophet, God's messenger to his fellow humans.

We are made aware that this sea trek concerns man in quest of salvation and Breton man in quest of his heritage; it also concerns a poet in quest of poetry. *Imram* contains, particularly in 'Kan an eilger,' notes for a Christian poetic. Glanndour tells his implied reader that God values the aesthetic sense, which, like all others, is derived from him, so that, when any thing of beauty dies, angels bring it to Jesus, who treasures it in his heart. The poet therefore has a role in the cosmos. It is his duty to perform his art. Given Christian revelation – the revelation granted to the Speaker and, secondarily, to his implied reader – art devoted uniquely to form and grounded in formal considerations only is but a poetry of butterflies. Furthermore, the art of those who have a message yet who preach only materialism and material pleasure is doomed to failure. This sort of poetry he calls classical and associates, no doubt, with the French tradition of Ronsard, La Fontaine, Voltaire, Verlaine, and Valéry. On the contrary, counsels the Speaker, the artist has to embrace the world, in its reality and totality, and to seek the light not darkness. Because of revelation, the Speaker can speak, in his Breton, from a tradition other than the classical French. His model will be Saint John the Apostle, the author of Revelation, he who knew of the divine war of good against evil, he who is the greatest of poets, a bird of fire in the thunder of divine speech. The Speaker will imitate him, calling out to the people and offering them the Pearl of Great Price, urging them to listen to God and not to the Dark Angel. And if they do not listen? And if they mistreat you? Cry out and scream anyway! The strings of a violin play only when stretched. The swan sings when people pluck out his feathers. The will of God will grant you the force of wings.

If a secular, materialist, classical Frenchness is oriented toward the light of day (its Enlightenment), Glanndour evokes opposite it a Christian and Celtic darkness. Following in the wake of Novalis, the Speaker delivers his own hymn, a Christian hymn, to their night. Daytime hides the constellations, he observes. The night is also part of God's plan. It is necessary for us to know evil, in the dark, in order to comprehend the splendour of the good. The darkness includes human reality and also, surely, the emotional, irrational, and artistic qualities of being a Celt which are inherent in the Christian tradition, the *credo quia absurdum*.

Then, in the last section, the 'Kanenn voug' (Song of Snuffing Out), the Speaker – as poet, priest, prophet, and mere man – invokes the coming of night at the end of a day or a life. Once again he invokes the wind, the element closest to the Spirit, the image of breath, voice, poetry, music, and life itself. He again evokes night, now as the sweetest of times. When flowers and souls perish, their aroma scatters. Who will collect it? in what? The bard will collect it, replies the wind, in the vase of his heart. Now, sweet wind, muse and Spirit, go away, murmurs the Speaker. Now I am tired. Come back tomorrow. Now it is time to snuff out the lamp. Thus ends an epic of Christian faith in the quiet mode, in imagery of peace and, even, good death in the peace of the Lord.

Vijelez an deiz diwezhañ (Doomsday Vigil), published in 1978, restates the thematics and vision of *Imram*.[27] The poem is inspired by, and takes as its locus, the chapel of Our Lady of Isquit (Kermaria an Iskuit) at Plouha, where the Speaker arrives on a Saturday night, in order to say mass the following day. This is a poor country church, partially in ruins, where the wind and rain pour through holes in the roof, and owls – the icon of Pallas Athena – deposit their droppings on the statues of the saints within. As Galand has observed, the chapel in disrepair evokes symbolically the material and spiritual disarray of Brittany.[28] Yet also, paradoxically, this wretched little all-but-abandoned chapel contains frescos painted on the walls and ceiling – frescos of the Prophets of Israel and of the Dance of Death.

The sight of the Prophets causes the Speaker to prophesy, that is, to denounce the wickedness in modern life against which he bears witness. A traditionalist, Glanndour has his Speaker focus on the sin of lechery. He denounces the lusts of the body using bull-cow imagery, to suggest that our fleshly desires drag us down to the level of beasts; in particular, the Speaker decries the inevitable outcome of such animal proclivities – the increase in abortion. Evoking implicitly the parable of the Seven Foolish Virgins, who slept through the coming of their Spouse – Christ – he appeals to those of us who sleep, who are rendered numb by the dark night of the soul, to wake up before it is too late. Those who cannot awaken are denizens of Babel (Babylon), with the triangle of lust fixed to their bellies, accursed of God because they defy him.

The Dance of Death inspires the priestly narrator to envision a gallery of figures celebrating the carnival and wearing carnival masks. The Speaker recounts what happens when the masks are lowered: in a sense, he himself unmasks the dancers. The masks gone, we behold skeletons and the rot of corpses:

Diwar ho preinadur
Tennit kuit ho maskloù! [...]

Flaperezh
Ha stlakerezh
Ar chagelloù

C'hoarzhadeg
Ha youc'hadeg
Pennoù maro.

(Pull off the masks covering your rot! Chattering and clattering of jaw bones. Peals of laughter and shouting of skulls.)

As in *Imram*, the Speaker declares the nullity of human, earthly, secular happiness. After the carnival come ashes – the ashes of Ash Wednesday and the dust of the grave, for Ankoù is ever there, leading the dance. In a later passage the Speaker returns to this theme, addressing the Thinking Reed (Pascal?), the Thinker (Rodin?), and Narcissus (Freud?), three manifestations of rational modern man. Haven't you wallowed enough? he asks. Don't you see the cosmetics which mask the decomposing corpse? The corpse is modernity in all its horror.

In contrast to these images of wickedness and oppression, Glanndour evokes, first of all, the Virgin Mary. This is her church, her home. The frescos show her seated on the Throne of Wisdom when her son, Christus Pantocrator, will judge the quick and the dead, on that Last Day, the *deiz diwezhañ*. Second, the Speaker beholds, hanging from the rafters, an ex-voto ship, a boat offered by a pilgrim to Our Lady. The Speaker deems himself to be, like that pilgrim, shipwrecked, and he occasionally fantasizes the boat and its skipper. The ship is an image of Brittany and of mankind, sailing upon the life-threatening waters of the deep yet able to count on Our Lady, *stella maris*, as succour and guide.

This notion of evil subject to redemption is explored in the central structure of *Vijelez* – the contrast and also the bond between Saturday night and Sunday morning. The Speaker arrives at Kermaria on a Saturday night and beholds – lives as it were – the Dance of Death and the call of the Prophets. He will undergo a series of meditations, in that night, prior to the coming of dawn, the dawn of Our Lord's Day, the Sabbath, which includes the exercise of the Speaker's ministry. Temporally, the sequence of night and day and of Saturday and Sunday alludes to the end and renewal of the cycle of the day and of the week. It also symbolizes the eventual death and hoped-for rebirth of the Speaker, of humankind, of Brittany, and of the cosmos. Glanndour's symbolism recalls sacred baroque epics by Guillaume Salluste du Bartas, *La Sepmaine* and *La seconde Sepmaine*, which develop a similar pattern grounded in typological exegesis. The life and death of the day and the week, including the week of creation, evoke Christ's own death and resurrection, and the death and resurrection of the universe at Doomsday as recounted in the Book of Revelation by Glanndour's avowed poetic model, Saint John. Throughout *Vijelez* and in the poem's title Glanndour alludes to the judgment that we all await, in our individual and collective vigils, throughout our lives. And, at the centre of his text, in the middle of his 'Night of the Soul,' the Speaker hears, in terror, the trumpet of Doomsday and, as a sinner, proclaims how he hates the stench of his old skin and burning sins, which he can neither cast off nor flee.

The typological structure of time includes the present – the tropological or moral level concerning the individual Christian in his life. Therefore, as with *Imram*, we are made aware of the Speaker. He is not at all uniquely a stance or a voice. He is a committed yet tortured and suffering Christian man and – as in *Imram* – his persona includes the implied author Maodez Glanndour, priest. Thus we recognize in him the priest come to say mass in this isolated, broken-down church, and we suffer for the church, for Brittany, and for the modern world, filtered as they are through the Speaker's consciousness. We also listen to the Speaker as he recounts his dreams – a lonely boat on the waves with its lone skipper, a figure in white, or the bells of the City of Is, or the grating of Ankoù's cart. The Speaker makes us participate in his quest, a pilgrimage quite different from Roparz Hemon's. This is a spiritual quest through the dark night of the soul, where the pilgrim slogs in mud, slime, nettles, and thorns, his lute broken, lost in the blackness. He chose the straight and narrow, and the fire of purgatory burns within him.

The fact that the lute is broken reminds us that this pilgrim is also a bard and that – as bard, priest, and Breton – he is a creature of the Word. Hence the pathos of the Speaker's cry to God – I call out to you, and you do not answer. Hence also, at dawn, his prayer and prophecy for Brittany, with the avowal that if Brittany cannot be exalted on earth, its exaltation may yet take place in heaven. The theme of communication is crucial to *Vijelez* – between the Speaker and his implied readers and between him, as narrator, and his diegetic narratee, God – a communication which takes place in the downtrodden, taboo language – brezhoneg – here on earth now and, later, in heaven at Doomsday.

In Breton the Speaker imitates the style of the Prophets, whom he has observed on the church walls, encouraging his implied readers – us – to follow him on his pilgrimage and not to be the flies imprisoned in the web, sucked alive by the demon spider. It is on this level of rhetoric that he castigates those of us who, crushed by our pride, die before we ever had the chance to live, and he pleads for the angel to come and deliver us. In this style he also refers to the gate – straight is the gate and narrow the way – through which rich people and camels will not pass, but the little people of the earth will, Christ's *pauperi*. This is a meditation on life and death, on what it means to live and to die, and on what will be eternal life in Christ (and the other possibility) after the Last Judgment.

The Speaker, on behalf of the little people, makes two final requests, two prayers. First, he invokes the Blessed Virgin Mary, Our Lady of Isquit. He calls upon the Bride of Christ to appear, in her divine light.

He calls for a pardon in the tradition of Brittany, which will be a sacred, divine procession, a triumph of the Church Militant. It will be made up of the Virgin and her baby, the saints and the martyrs, including her mother, Saint Anne of Brittany. Bless your people! they beg:

> Hag holl e kanont da Werc'hez an Iskuit:
> 'Poent eo! Diskuliit ho sekredoù,
> Ar re miret d'ho tud e madelezh ho Mab!
> Bennigit ho poblad ha difennit ho tomani!'

(And they all sing to the Virgin of Isquit: 'It is time! Reveal your secrets, those you keep for your people in the goodness of your Son! Bless your countrymen and defend your domain.')

Bless your people now or at Doomsday. We realize that the *pauperi* to be blessed are, on one level, all the meek and the poor in spirit, and, on another, as the poet Jean-Pierre Calloc'h also proclaimed, the people of Brittany, Saint Anne's children, those who remain, even in our corrupt, secular age, among the remnants of the faithful.

The second and last prayer asks that, after the Speaker dies, he might be buried in Brittany so that, when he is resurrected at Doomsday, his body will be made up of Breton earth, the substance of his country and the substance – the subject – of his song. The present and the future are joined. Brittany and the pilgrims of life – of a Christian life – will be redeemed, if not now then at the end of time. As in *Les Tragiques* by the Huguenot rebel D'Aubigné, that future time and final dimension, the anagogical level in typology, offers the reversal of injustice and defeat. There the Agnus Dei becomes the Lion of Judah, there the little people of women and children, the beloved of Saint Anne and Saint Mary, are accepted into the *civitas Dei*, whereas the tyrants and brutes, the tormentors and prefects, are turned back. This is the ultimate, definitive Christian anagnorisis, the reversal according to which tragedy is transmuted into comedy, hatred into love, and the discord of human life becomes the harmony of divine wisdom. Glanndour's Speaker – as priest, as Breton, and as man – will be there, his people with him. Thus ends another 'imram,' this one a voyage through time which reveals the deepest mysteries and offers the greatest hope, in poetry of supremely luminous beauty, which reflects doctrinally and artistically the *stella maris* and *lumen mundi*.

ANJELA DUVAL

Anjela Duval stands as an anomaly in modern Breton letters and in minority literature generally. She was a genuine peasant, working the land, a Breton-speaker from birth who combines the spoken and the written, and the life of the soil and the mind, as practically no one else does. Although of the same generation as the moderns of the Skol Walarn (born 1905), it was only in 1956, five years after the death of her mother, that Duval wrote to *Ar Bed Keltiek* for a missing issue, and thus began a literary vocation. She contributed letters, sketches, tales, and memoirs to the reviews, and also poems after 1962. Her first collection, *Kan an douar* (Song of the Earth), won a prize in 1973.[29] A selection of her later verse was published posthumously in book form as *Traoñ an dour* (The Vale of Water).[30] An important figure for activists in the 1970s, Duval also achieved a measure of fame in the French-speaking world as the subject of one program in André Voisin's television series 'Les conteurs,' broadcast 28 December 1971.[31]

Her intellectual life shaped by the 1960s and 1970s, Duval sat at the feet of the *emsavenen*, including Roparz Hemon, who wrote to her from Dublin. She thus became a political militant and cannot be faulted for not denouncing the French enough. One stream in her verse is political. It sets up an antithesis between rich and poor, city and country, strong and weak, them and us, and French-speaking and Breton-speaking. She denounces 'An douristed' (The Tourists) who seek rest from their life in the city, drowning out our rural sounds with the noise of their automobiles and transistors. Elsewhere she refers to the French as 'An alouberien' (The Conquerors) who despoil Brittany, proud supermen who claim to improve on nature, and as 'Roñfled' (Ogres), the masters who devour our flesh, suck our blood, and then insult us in French, a civilized tongue, when our cart blocks the road. The earth trembles at the horror, and the red sun weeps at these evils. Meanwhile, Duval thanks God for having made her a peasant, and she cries out for resistance – on the land, in the church, and in the schoolroom. Overcome by 'Kounnar ruz' (Red Anger) at the thought of the people being crushed, she predicts that the old tired mare and the enraged sheep will turn on their exploiters. As for herself, when her one love left the land for the city far away, she turned to a second love that would be her destiny: 'Va Bro, va Yezh ha va Frankiz' (My land, my tongue and my freedom) ('Karantez-vro' in *Traoñ an dour*, p. 67).

In spite of the 1960s patina on much of this verse, Duval is scarcely a progressive. She stands staunchly opposed to communism, atheism, and farm improvement. She would neither join an agricultural collective nor, even, introduce a tractor to replace her plough horse. She exalts the old rural ways, the old people and their wisdom, sacred memory, and the ancestors. Hence poems about the farmhouse in which she has dwelt for fifty years; about the sound of wind, water, and earth, which are the voices of ancestors calling for action; and, finally, imitating Roparz Hemon, in 'Noz an Anaon' (Night of the Dead) the sound of the wind is assimilated to young freedom fighters who descend from the ancestors.

The militancy and the nostalgia are not central to Duval's vision. They are peripheral, so to speak, symptoms not first causes. Although some of these poems are good, her finest efforts lie in another domain. The central ontological reality of the Speaker in Duval's corpus and the all-pervading atmosphere of these texts is one of solitude – loneliness and, on one level, alienation. It is scarcely a coincidence that, in the deeply moving 'Karantez-vro' (Love for a Country), the Speaker turned to her land and her language after the beloved man ran off. How many poems begin with the Speaker alone, seated at her hearth or at work in the fields or wandering about aimlessly! She is alone, indoors, recalling her dead mother or meditating on the fire. She is alone, out of doors, in the cold and darkness, invoking her star, or hard at work when she looks up and sees diapers hanging on a neighbour's line, or alone with the broom flowers and aware that this year people won't come to visit, or alone meditating on her sister's grave. The Speaker addresses a poem to her solitude as to a friend and, in another, discusses the case of Lellig (Little Anjela), whom her parents warned against everything in life, with the result that she is all alone and has no friend. No matter! says the Speaker, Lellig will find a friend in the Otherworld.

Anjela Duval's work as a poet measures the loneliness, this void she carries within her, and then subverts it, populating her world with living beings and thus bringing it to life. One effort lies in the family, to renew bonds with the dead and so give these dead loved ones life – vibrant life – in her. She speaks to her dear father, Tadig, who gave her life and taught her so much, imploring him to think of her from his resting place. She speaks to her sister, deceased at the age of ten, observing the fallen leaves on the grave and recalling the tears and leaves back then, as people and trees wept, so that the love and loss endured then are renewed today. Finally, the Speaker, alone at home,

thinks sadly of her dead mother, when a burst of young people fill the
house. Now the Speaker is a mother in turn! On all three occasions
communication is established, either with the dead or with the
Speaker's deepest feelings toward them, and because of poetry and love
the feelings come alive.

We observe a comparable functioning of the old farmhouse. The intimacy of hearth and home give rise to the same sort of reflection, communication, and tenderness made manifest both in memory and in
vision. The fire on the hearth and the hearth enclosing the fire redeem
loneliness, helping to fill the void. Sitting by the fire, the Speaker
receives the book of Roparz Hemon's songs, mailed to her from Dublin.
Meditating before the fire, she enjoys the song of crickets or considers
the sacredness of the oak log and its incense. Children renew a fire,
working the bellows, while grandmother sleeps. Finally, in bed at night,
the Speaker listens to sounds of 'Buhez an noz' (Night Life): the log
cracks on the hearth, rain falls, wind shakes the tree boughs, a clock
ticks, mice scurry in the cellar, and her cat sleeps, dreaming of his girlfriend:

> Koroll al logod er c'hrignol,
> Tra ma rouzmouz ar c'hazh rous,
> – Al luguder Bilu, – moredet, koHet
> En e hun ha 'n e huñvre,
> 'N e spered bepred skeudenn e garedig,
> Gwennig, ar gazhez vihan vistr,
> Koantik 'giz un erminig. (*Kan an douar,* p. 63)

(The dance of the mice in the cellar [attic?], / While the orange cat purrs,
/ That sluggard Bilu, – dozing, lost / In his sleep and his dreams, / In his
mind constantly the image of his beloved, / Gwennig, the elegant little
cat, / As lovely as an ermine.) (Timm, p. 222)

As is evident from reading 'Buhez an noz,' communication and intimacy are established with entities to be found in nature. Here are a few
examples.

Animals. The cat dreams of his girlfriend, or, on another occasion,
death is compared to a cat playing with the string of his life. Elegies are
written on the loss of the Speaker's dogs – Fousou, who, suffering in
pain, wandered off to die alone; and Fido, bound to her by a chain of
love not iron, a friend, for whom – as if he were a poet – she builds a

grave on her land, covered with Breton flowers, buried with living earth
and the holy water of a tear:

> Kousk bremañ, va loenig mat.
> Kousk e Peoc'h da viken.
> Graet eo ganit da vuhez ki
> Da zever a gi: karout ha beilhal,
> Kousk Fido! (*Traoñ an dour,* p. 58)

(Now sleep, good little animal. Sleep in Peace for ever more. You have fulfilled your dog's life, your dog's duty: to love and to keep watch, sleep
Fido!)

The Speaker also celebrates the old horse who for so many years woke
her up every morning, and writes of a still field in summer, its only
movement three cows lying in the shade of a tree, occasionally shaking
an ear to flick away the flies.

Birds. We read of the Speaker asking a black crow, What are you thinking? She also tells us of winter roses and birds: when a bird is killed by
the cat (as in Chrétien's *Perceval*), its red blood glitters on the snow.

Flowers. As with the winter flowers, who live and die, the Speaker
describes the little wild rose, clad like a queen, truly a queen, yet she
lives and dies in one day, and tomorrow there will be another. Duval also
weaves a tale about flowers competing for the love of the prancing,
dancing, and drunk butterfly. When he chooses the violet, the narcissus
is broken-hearted.

Trees. We read of two willow trees, princesses and sisters, who change
colour (their dresses) all the time. We read of the ash tree. Are you
dead? asks the Speaker. Wake up and put on your skirt, for the beeches
are already dressed. When the willow tosses its seed, it becomes summer
snow and the flakes of dreams. The Speaker identifies with trees. She
sits at their feet, listens to them, and embraces them. Was she a tree in a
former life? She who has a thousand mute friends will never cut down
her linden trees, for they are her organ and harp, played by the wind
and by birds. The worst thing the dreaded foreigners (the French) do is
to axe trees, sacred to the druids!

Lowly things. In addition, the poet finds a place in her heart and in her
imagination for the lowly. She gives a thought to the rye, its green the
only colour in a parched brown summer, a despised grain yet all that
poor people have; to crickets on the hearth or in the field; to mice in

the cellar; to the leaves that consecrate her sister's grave; to the paths
that cross to form the threads of life, a road sign, or a calvary. Her credo
and, secondarily, her imagination are given voice in 'Perak?' (Why?) in
which the Speaker – in contrast to city people, who don't care – explains
how she treads, so carefully, in order not to crush beetles, ants, or flowers, the little creatures on her path.

   Natural phenomena. A final series of poems gives life to phenomena
that we associate with the round of the day or the seasons. A storm
('Arnev') occurs when two black clouds, drunk, hurtle along, bump into
each other, and break out in a fight. The sun rising at dawn is depicted
as the prince of the morning who wakes up and draws open his curtains;
the Speaker perceives his eye through the window. Also portrayed as a
prince is the springtime ('Nevez-amzer'), who, cavorting through the
land on horseback, tosses onto the desolate fields his gift of jewels, coin,
and little bells. In winter, on the other hand, ice hangs from the trees. Is
this the angels' laundry hung out to dry, asks the Speaker, or perhaps
lace belonging to the fays?

   All these things have been endowed by God with life. They also have
been endowed with speech. In Anjela Duval's poetic universe, this
speech, which others do not hear, is of unique significance, it is all but
sacred. The language of mute beings – trees, plants, wind, stream, and
sea – tells of Arthur, Isolt, and Merlin. For the Speaker, Arthur, Isolt, and
Merlin, protagonists of medieval romance, are Breton and to be assimilated to the ancestors of the race. In other poems she invokes again the
voices of fire, wind, and water, which echo or literally are the voice of the
ancestors and therefore are to be preferred to the speech of humans.

   As Timm has observed, in Duval's work we see the equivalent of a
child's intimacy with nature.[32] This is a communion with the external
world, endowing it with life and near-divinity, in a mental structure
which approaches animism. The Speaker sees, hears, and communicates with these external elements, she captures them with her gaze and
her inner ear. They become one with her; she opens out to embrace and
assimilate them. Thus, paradoxically, the self-proclaimed old maid, the
woman of loneliness, because of that loneliness forms a community and
a communion with the universe in its diverse levels of being. Thus she
attains Being, a fruitful existence cognizant of others existing, in contrast to the city-dwellers, the conquerors, and the ogres, who are infi-
nitely more alienated than she is, for they, creatures of modernity,
encased in their automobiles and enslaved to their transistors, have not
eyes to see nor ears to hear.

That the Speaker has this gift, Anjela Duval would insist, is the wish of God. Her poetry reveals a deep, traditional Christian faith, less fierce than Glanndour's but no less all-encompassing. Like Maodez Glanndour, she is convinced that these little creatures show the way to God. We must not forget that the Speaker loves her dog Fido in the Lord's name, because God is the creator, and she and Fido, creatures in God's world, help alleviate each other's pain. Her hour of meditation before the fire is also an hour of prayer. And more than one of Duval's finest texts assume the form of prayer. The Speaker prays to God for rain. Yes, the drought humbles our pride and, therefore, is good. Yet, she begs the divinity, please end the drought so the animals won't have to suffer. In 'Gouel ar mammoù' (Mothers' Day), where, bereft of her mother, the Speaker becomes a mother to the young people entering her house, she invokes the Mother of God in the name of all mothers, urging her to succour the young in this old land. And, in 'Itron Varia Vreizh' (Our Lady of Brittany), invoking as in a litany 'O Mamm garet' (dear Mother), the Speaker reminds a Breton Virgin that her people, who love and serve her, suffer, both on the land and when forced into exile. Please help us, she urges, a woman praying to a woman, a virgin to the Virgin, and a spiritual mother of Breton youths to the Mother of God.

The Speaker also prays the Virgin to help the Bretons keep their language so they can pray to her in it:

O Mamm garet, ho pet truez
Breizh ' fell dezhi pediñ 'n he yezh
Ni fell dimp kanañ kantikoù
Er yezh e kane hon tadoù
    E pep pardon
    E pep chapel
Da heul pep kroaz ha pep banniel. (*Traoñ an dour*, p. 135)

(O beloved Mother, have mercy. Brittany wishes to pray in her language. We wish to sing our hymns in the language our fathers sung. In every pardon, in every chapel, and following every cross and banner.)

The golden key to the castle, she states elsewhere, is Breton speech. Throughout her corpus, the language of Brittany is assimilated to the land ('Va Bro, va Yezh ...'), the struggle, and the martyrdom, and also to a unique people who live a unique existence in harmony with nature. It is as if their Celtic tongue and their celticity contribute to a situation of elegiac harmony and also to the persecution they endure from the ogres and the conquerors, city people speaking French who have cut their roots and are encased in alienation.

It is not surprising, then, that the corpus contains a number of references to poetry and poetics. The Speaker assimilates the writing of poetry to the void of her life and her efforts to fill the void. Hence the imagery of one text, where she speaks of milling the shreds of wasted youth, beauty, and tears into dough, which is then transformed into pages on which she writes a second youth; or of another piece, where, a peasant born in the country, in spring, and in nature, she hopes to die the same – surrounded by flowers, birds, and song. The Ronsardian imagery underscores Duval's vision of the nature of poetry, and more specifically her own. Other texts state a humble, even denigrating view of her verse. She wishes her poetry to be like the ferns she collects – fruitless, light-weight plants, yet which have an aroma. They (endemic to Brittany) will help her daydream, and maybe she can imitate their purity. She addresses her pencil, abandoned for some time, lost in a corner, around which a spider has spun her web. Finally, the Speaker declares that, although the white notepaper asks to be caressed, she will sleep instead, to gather the flowers of dreams, or that, instead of pressing pen on paper weakly and clumsily, at night, she prefers in the day to cut the grain with her scythe or press a plough on the breast of her beloved farm.

The humility is genuine yet also problematic. After all, the ferns do give rise to a unique, Breton, pure poetry; the recovered pencil will be used again, it is used to inscribe the verse addressed to it; and the flowers of dreams are inscribed on the notepaper. We know of the Speaker's plough and scythe only because she does also darken the blank page. Furthermore, like Du Bellay vis-à-vis Ronsard, La Fontaine vis-à-vis Malherbe, or Apollinaire or Reverdy vis-à-vis Valéry, the aesthetics of humility make an aesthetic statement and constitute an aesthetic register on their own terms – that of the *genus medium* or *genus humile* in willed contrast to the *genus grande* of the high style. Such an authorial stance is especially appropriate in the person of a self-educated peasant woman writing in a minority language. In Duval's world of intimacy and *Dinglichkeit*, which has its own cosmic grandeur, the lower ranges of rhetoric help contribute to the elaboration of a totalizing work of art.

NOVEL

YOUENN DREZEN

Breton-language critics generally consider the *nouvelle* to be the strongest narrative genre in Breton; as a result, for a number of them, the novel does not rate very high. I disagree. From the 1940s on, literature in Breton has witnessed a flowering of the novel, with a production much richer than that in Scots and comparable to the creation of long fiction in Occitan yet preceding the Occitan by some two decades. By 1990 some twenty to thirty novels (depending on one's definition of the genre) had appeared, some of these of the highest rank.[33]

The first extended modern novel, and one of the best, was published in 1941 by Youenn Drezen, an associate of Hemon and member of the Skol Walarn, and a writer of *nouvelles* and poetry. This is *Itron Varia Garmez* (Our Lady of Carmel).[34] To begin with, it is a strike novel in the line of *Germinal* or Gorky's *The Mother*. It recounts the response to the economic crisis of 1933–4, the war, so to speak, waged by farmers and fishermen against the government, in the town of Pont-l'Abbé, near Quimper. This novel of protest is also a *Bildungsroman* and a *Künstlerroman*. Paol Tirili, a cobbler, is committed to the strike. Also, carving statuettes in wood as a hobby leads him to attempt a large statue in stone – of Our Lady for the church of Our Lady. The model will be Paol's girlfriend Jani Dreo. However, because of the strike and because of illness, Paol cannot finish his masterpiece. Dying in despair, he breaks the statue.

In scenes of charm and wit Drezen paints a realistic picture of Breton town life in the interwar period. More particularly, he emphasizes the local traits of Pont-l'Abbé, in the Bigouden region of Kernev (Breton Cornwall). We observe workers playing and arguing in the tavern and women chatting and gossiping at their washing. Drezen makes us aware that this is secular country where, for the most part, people are nonchurchgoers. They enjoy life to the full, they abound in good humour and, perhaps most of all, in living, good-humoured, truculent speech.

Itron Varia Garmez strips aside the veil covering exploitation, injustice, the class struggle, and what today we call internal colonialism. Drezen makes it clear that the local Breton depression of 1933–4 does not occur as a result of local conditions. The Bigouden fish and farm produce are excellent. The depression occurs because the government, in Paris, raised protective tariffs in support of the coal and wine industries and the regions affected by them. However, as a result of the tariffs and of foreign counter-tariffs, the Bretons can no longer sell produce to their traditional clients, England and Portugal. As a result of central economic planning, which neglects to take into account all the regions of France, the Bretons are brought to the edge of ruin – a classical example of internal colonialism.

Drezen therefore shapes his narrative in terms of rich versus poor, the poverty of the little people a theme resonating from beginning to end. Yet he emphasizes even more the conflict between the local Bretons, whatever their class, and the manifestations of power – mounted police, the *préfet* – come from the outside, emanations, so to speak, of a Parisian French hegemony which itself is never seen or heard. Thus Laorañs Larnikol, the very bourgeois mayor, elected on the 'red' ticket (he is anti-clerical and pro-republic), supports the agitators, for he would do anything to give them work and bread. In this he is allied with his arch-enemy, Kerdraoñ, the equally good *person* (parish priest). The entire narrative and all the dialogues take place in Breton, except for the speech of or in response to four strikebreakers from Paris and to Romanetto, the prefect in Quimper – by his name, shown to be one of the Provençals or Corsicans who filled the rolls of government service. They are the vilest creatures in the book, the only true villains. We also see a pattern of imagery developed around the mounted police, who misuse decent, good beasts to harm the people and run down the old and the infirm, and around the flag. For a major funeral, Romanetto will allow the red flag but not the Breton flag, for, as he explains to the mayor, the 'new Bretons' are even worse than Moscow. Ultimately, the mayor is demoted, he attends the funeral without his sash, and the procession is highlighted by Christian banners and crosses, the red flag, and the Breton Gwenn-ha-Du (white and black). This is the flag of the nationalist Breiz Atao movement, whose meeting Paol and his friends decided to attend, preferring symbolically its speeches to the Ave Maria and the *Internationale*.

The funeral commemorates the death of a seventy-eight-year-old woman, Naig Moal, run down (by mistake) during a police charge. It is a magnificent crowd scene, in the tradition of Zola, but with the particular Drezen stamp of little people triumphing over their brute enemies with wit and humour. When policemen block the procession route, the ceremony takes place on the road and people leave the coffin to the police, who discover that both the cemetery and the church doors are locked, and find themselves stuck with their unwanted trophy. Later, similar discomfiture is administered to the outsiders: an automobile is misdirected into a dead end; the police are doused with water; another, small contingent of police is captured, detrousered, and spanked with nettles; and, on a more sombre yet also Rabelaisian note, the strike-breakers are beaten to a pulp in the tavern.

Two climaxes mark the political structure of the narrative. The first is made up of Naig's death and funeral, the second of the detrousering and spanking of policemen at the hands of the wives and mothers. Drezen follows the tradition of Zola and Gorky in that the women contribute to the struggle for justice as much as the men do, and their actions bring the protesters some of their most glorious moments and their closest approach to victory.

Some critics have decried the absence of unity in *Itron Varia Garmez*, objecting that it is both disorganized and too long.[35] I believe, on the contrary, that the novel is a thematically and structurally coherent, unified work of art, albeit more in the tradition of Tolstoy than of Flaubert. One unifying element, which brings together the worlds of strife, love, and art, is woman, the feminine presence essential to all three realms. For example, a subplot is constituted by the thwarted amours of Joz Gouzien, Paol's best friend, and Mimi Andro. Gouzien, called Joz Taro (Joz the Bull), is a giant of a youth, a smith by trade, back from Paris where he had been laid off. Although Joz and Mimi are in love, their match is opposed by Tin Andro, a tavern-keeper who owns land in the country and cannot accept a misalliance for his daughter. The unemployed Joz is too poor to marry anyone. In somewhat melodramatic fashion (but not counter to the reality of courting and wedding), only when Mimi becomes pregnant and Paol informs the father, will the latter accept the notion of family solidarity, agree to the marriage, and set up Joz, who is a good worker and eager to work. Class division caused uniquely by money – nobody other than Tin imagines that Joz is not good enough for Mimi – and a father's power over his daughter mirror, in the private sphere, the public chaos unleashed by economic policies decided in Paris and the misuse of power by a Corsican prefect vis-à-vis the Breton mayor and by French mounted police vis-à-vis Breton workers and peasants. This occurs even though the two officials are of roughly the same social origin, as are the protesters and the police.

The subplot is shaped by the conflict between young lovers and a hostile old father-figure and by the conflict between natural, healthy Eros and the alienating, dehumanizing strictures imposed on Eros by the force of wealth and social prestige. In the main plot Paol Tirili suffers from a comparable opposition, in the realms of love and of art. In his case, the outcome is tragic.

Paol and Jani Dreo are a couple, in the sense that Joz and Mimi are. Although Paol is less 'physical' than Joz and no declarations of love, much less caresses, are exchanged (in this they adhere to the rural Breton tradition, in theory at least), they spend time together, they are seen together in public, and it is more or less assumed they will wed one day if and when Paol can afford a wife. Paol pays Jani the greatest compliment by choosing her as his model for the statue of the Virgin and, following the tradition of medieval *fin' amor*, she is his inspiration and muse. Without the image of her face in his consciousness would he ever have dreamed of making such a sculpture?

Again, as in the French Middle Ages or the Italian Renaissance, a fine line divides the secular and the sacred, the two organically joined yet distinct and in a constant state of tension. This state of affairs is borne out by the relationship established between Paol and the Pont-l'Abbé clergy, representing the worlds of art and of the church. When Paol first broaches his project for a statue of Our Lady in terms of a young Mary, a joyous mother, Father Kerdraoñ accepts, insisting, however, that the Virgin maintain her dignity and smile a smile of paradise:

> 'Va Gwerc'hez Vari-me a zo yaouank, ha barr gant al levenez, ha lorc'hus zoken, e-giz ar mammoù ugent vloaz a welit [...] Ar Vamm Yaouank, na petra!' [...]
> 'Ha ma kizellez Dezhi ur mousc'hoarzh war He diweuz ha war He dremm, ra vo mousc'hoarzh ar Baradoz.' (pp. 37–8)
> ('My Virgin Mary is young, and full to the brim with joy, even proud, like the twenty-year-old mothers you will see [...] The Young Mother, that's what!' 'If you chisel a smile on her lips and face, may it be the smile of Paradise.')

Later, when one of his vicars protests that Paol, coming from a 'red' family, is unclean, non-Christian, and incapable of creating sacred art, the wise old rector concludes that God chooses and takes where and from whom he wishes.

What appears to be a novel in the realist tradition, upon closer inspection reveals symbolism and even allegory. (Such, of course, is also the case for Zola, as it is for Lewis Grassic Gibbon.) The title of the book alludes to the subject of the statue and to the church for which Paol makes it, Our Lady of Carmel, which also identifies the town of Pont-

l'Abbé and the Bigouden region. In addition, it is assimilated to the girl
Jani Dreo, Paol's beloved and his muse. As we saw, he wishes to give
being to a young Virgin Mary, resplendent with life, a young mother
radiant with joy. Symbolically or allegorically, on one level at least, Paol's
labours are those of the new young Bretons refashioning a new, more
modern Brittany, an artistic task but which has repercussions for all
aspects of life, including the political.

It is significant that one of the townswomen, representative of an outside public voice, insults Paol's aunt, mocking the boy for being lazy and
charging that his artistic pretensions signify only that he is being subven-
tioned by the priests. Paol himself, who proceeds more slowly than he
would like, argues in his own mind whether he is pretentious or impotent or simply lazy. Provisionally, he decides that since he is working for
himself, he will enjoy life and will finish the statue when it pleases him.
In time it will please him to finish all but the face, and then all but the
eyes and the mouth. These are the hardest, for they reveal the soul, and
they remain rough, chaotic, uncarved stone. From this process, over a
period of months and eventually years, Paol and others raise the spectre
of the archetypal Breton lost in his dreams, his head in the clouds, and
of the stereotypical Breton who starts a project yet is incapable of finish-
ing it.

Youenn Drezen indicates that there are good reasons other than the
Celtic soul why Paol dreams and does not finish his statue. One is
derived from the thematic of the strike. Paol is embittered by injustice
and the repression of the little people. He, who was himself wounded by
the police, states at one point that, because there is so much misery, he
can no longer sculpt the head and give to his Virgin the radiant smile
that would move the people. Because of the strike, because he is committed to the strike, he cannot work. Later Paol comes to love his statue
more than the real Jani, in part because he assimilates his drive as an artist to the drive of the people to make a better life for their children. Still
later, in despair, he blames God for having failed, because the people
still suffer.

Another reason why Paol does not finish the sculpture is his illness, an
extended, debilitating malady resembling tuberculosis *cum* pneumonia.
It is the illness that prevents Paol from escaping, at a trot, from the
police. Because of the illness he cannot finish the head or the smile;
because of the illness, weak in the chest, he no longer takes joy in life
and laughter. For a century prior to the Second World War, tuberculosis
was deemed *the* sickness of the Breton people. Thus, again, in allegorical

terms Paol is a figure of Brittany. However, Drezen problematizes this motif. For one thing, it is the illness that cut short the life of Drezen's closest friend, the writer Jakez Riou. Also, the sickness is not endemic to Paol or his family. It is, in specific terms, caused by the very love for Jani that inspired him to attempt the statue in the first place. In a powerful scene, located near the midpoint of the novel, Paol, Joz, Jani, and Mimi go out on a lark, a day of pure affection and pleasure. This is an outing at sea, their furthest gesture of freedom and of both closeness to nature and distance from the town. However, their boat is grounded. When a storm blows in, Paol overexerts himself by carrying Jani in his arms to the shore.

We see that Eros inspires and slays. So does art. Near the end, Paol, the hapless dreamer, has a nightmare. In this powerfully symbolic oneiric vision, he relives the time he carried Jani to the shore. Weighing him down, she is transformed into stone; he carries the statue and, struggling in the mud, is brought to earth bearing a menhir in his arms (cf. Daudet's *Sapho*). As with Proust, Gide, and Mann, Eros and Thanatos are bound together, as are illness and artistic creativity. In terms of imagery, man is crushed by stone and drowned in water. The stone – faith, Eros, art, Brittany – crushes Paol. He cannot shape Bachelard's hard earth of the will; it breaks him, rendering him impotent. Also throttling him is the sea, the feminine maternal entity in nature. He is broken, throttled, and rendered impotent also, we are led to believe, by being Breton, by the menhir he cannot hold and the archetypal Breton sickness he bears within, plus their archetypal sense of destiny and denial of compromise in the face of the absolute.

This is the case because Paol dies from his tuberculosis/pneumonia but, even more, from a broken heart. Or, from another perspective, he chooses to die because his spirit is broken. Since Paol is a true artist, his statue has become his life. To break the statue is therefore an act of suicide, the wilful breaking of his life. These elements are raised for the first time shortly after the Jani-menhir nightmare. Father Kerdraoñ and the vicar visit Paol on his sickbed. Here Paol repudiates God for allowing the poor to suffer. He also despairs because he cannot complete his work. Refusing absolution, he blasphemes. If you wish to pray for me, pray that I live! he cries, close to death, to the old priest also close to death:

– Hor Salver Jezuz-Krist n'en deus ket talvet E Wad da galz a dra. Ar beorien a zo chomet o stad ker reuzeudik ha kent. [...] Gast! gast! gast! tri

mil c'hast ar voullc'hurun kac'het gant reor an Diaoul! [...] M'hoc'h eus
levezon en Neñv, ma selaouer ouzh ho pedennoù en Neñv, goulennit ma
vevin. (pp. 280, 283, 284)
(No doubt of it, the Blood of Our Saviour Jesus Christ was scarcely worth
the trouble. The poor remain in as wretched a state as before [...] Bitch!
bitch! bitch! three thousand bitches of the thunderball shitted from the
Devil's arse! If you have any influence in Heaven, if there is someone to
hear your prayers in Heaven, ask that I may live.)

Later, listening to the roll of the ocean, Paol meditates that the sea has
plenty of time to complete her work of art – to engulf us all. Meanwhile,
he had wasted his time; it and his life are now used up. The statue,
Paol's child, will not be born. Finally, on his last morning, Paol speaks to
his mother, bantering (oh so ironically!) the same cliché, 'amzer zo!'
(there's time / take your time), upon which the novel opened. The story
opened with Paol, happy in his youth, nurtured by his mother and his
aunt Katell. Now it ends, in the youth (morning) of the day, with a pre-
maturely aged and disillusioned Tirili, betrayed by Mother Earth and
Mother Sea, sending away his biological mother on an excuse in order
to die alone. Since he has wasted his time, since he cannot give body to
his dream, Paol is defeated. Being Breton and being a child of the Bigouden country, he will not accept defeat. He destroys the statue and
himself drops to the earth, dead. There is no consolation, no silver lin-
ing, at the end of this powerfully tragic novel. In this vision of life, the
tragic triumphs on all fronts. Paol and Father Kerdraoñ, the best of
their two worlds, go off to die, Joz lies in prison, and the strike, broken,
will lead nowhere. 'Amzer zo!' for the sea, the eternal sea, to reclaim
what men, in their little pride, have dared to wrest from her realm, the
only one that will endure.

In 1972–4 appeared the master work of Youenn Drezen's later years,
the three-volume *Skol-louarn Veig Trebern* (Little Hervé Trébern Plays
Hookey).[36] This rollicking comic narrative recounts the adventures, in
Pont-l'Abbé in approximately the year 1910, of two eight-year-olds who
succeed in evading contact with their school and schooling for an entire
month. Owing in part to the reading of Per Jakez Helias, who has his
own agenda concerning folklore and folk memory, this book has been
thought of by some critics as largely autobiographical, as a testimonial
to the reality of Bigouden life before the First World War and to the
author's own happy childhood.[37] I believe the autobiographical element

to be prominent, of course, yet no more and no less so than in Machaut's *Voir Dit*, Rousseau's *Nouvelle Héloïse*, and Proust's *Recherche*. The theme of childhood is prominent, as one literary element in a narrative which celebrates, in literary terms, the joy, innocence, freedom, and creative imagination which we humans seek with such passion and which we displace, so often, upon a wish-fulfilment fantasy realm – the Arthurian kingdom, the pastoral of Arcadia, the collective future, or the individual past.

In other words, the celebration of childhood and, along with it, the celebration of a relatively innocent, organic, small-town community in turn-of-the-century Pont-l'Abbé contribute to a thematic of poetry and the imagination, to something akin to magical realism, in a work of art which is, first and foremost, narrative fiction, that is, a novel, not *témoignage* and not memoir. The genre is partly adventure-romance, partly picaresque mock-epic. The heterodiegetic narration adopts a range of modality and focalization: often the story is focalized through the consciousness of a precocious eight-year-old; no less often it is envisaged from a distance, from the mature, urbane, and sympathetic narrator's vantage-point. Hervé or his best friend Paotr-Teo (Fat Boy) or the two together lose and recover their satchels, buy candy, steal apples and chestnuts, devour chocolate and get sick, are taken for a ride in a boat or in an automobile, catch lice, sprain an ankle, are chased by geese, are caught skinny-dipping, are kidnapped by a priest (for choir practice), and are imprisoned in a barn overnight. On one level, as with the medieval *Prose Lancelot* and the Renaissance *Orlando furioso*, the implied reader joys in the richness of the story and in storytelling for its own sake. Day after day, page after page, the implied reader queries in anticipation: What new scrapes will the narrative voice invent, and what new ruses will Veig concoct, to keep the story going and preserve the boys from their schoolroom? In the course of the narrative we perceive a number of structural elements exploited by Drezen to keep the story going. One is what we can call Veig's physicality, his presumably typical childlike inability to resist the call of candy, chocolate, apples, and chestnuts, or the call to go bathing in the stream by a mill. Another is Veig's fear. This powerfully bright, precocious, ingenious child – crafty Odysseus in the bud – also depends on his large, robust comrade Paotr-Teo. Without Paotr-Teo he is simply too afraid to return to school and brave the schoolmaster's wrath on his own. So whenever Paotr-Teo is absent, so to speak – he goes off with his father, he catches lice, he breaks an ankle – Veig stays with Paotr-Teo or does something else, anything to

ensure that the return will be postponed. These structural devices are
the precise equivalent of the ones which maintain the narrative in medieval romance, such as the arrival at court of a damsel in distress or a hostile wicked knight; or the setting out by knights in search of a knight
who has been lost on a quest, and their getting lost in their turn; or the
knights' combating with their visors down, thereby encouraging non-
recognition and other opportunities for misunderstanding.

Just as the *Prose Lancelot* and the *Orlando furioso* partake of the arch-
genre of romance yet also borrow traits from and can be associated with
heroic epic, in its non-classical development, so too the three-volume
saga of Veig and Paotr-Teo partakes of romance and of epic – it is epic
romance in miniature. On one occasion, the narrator-implied author
compares his eight-year-old protagonist to the Wandering Jew and to
Aeneas – he must brave so many obstacles on his path back to the
schoolroom! The theme of the voyage is indeed central. Since, during
this entire month, Veig pretends to his family to be attending school as
usual, and since it is the custom for him to return home for lunch, over
forty times he leaves the family house to go somewhere else. The path
from home to school runs through the centre of town, where there will
always be something – the rough equivalents of the harpies, Dido, Scylla
and Charybdis – to cause the boy(s) to wander from the straight and
narrow. Indeed, on more than one occasion errancy assumes the function of the quest in Arthurian romance, for example when Veig goes
wandering in the woods of Travenneg with no precise intention and no
project in mind. After stealing apples and almost stealing chestnuts, he
encounters an old peasant woman and then listens to her old stories
and popular lore. All this is new to Veig; he learns as he grows and grows
as he learns.

On three occasions the narrative expands, to the point where these
little trips assume archetypal proportions, become the equivalent of the
medieval voyage to the Otherworld. This occurs when, befriended by a
Norwegian skipper, Veig is given a ride in the great ship, from Pont-
l'Abbé down the channel to the sea; when an aristocrat rides into town,
to do business at the hôtel de ville on the back of his camel; and when
another aristocrat gives Veig a ride in his automobile, also to the sea. It
would hardly be appropriate for an eight-year-old to undergo ordeals
quite in the sense of medieval romance or to win a kingdom in battle or
to encounter the princess he will wed. In Drezen's story the emphasis is
on maturation, the boy's first experiences in the adult world and his pre-
cociously giant steps in becoming, in his way and at his level, a man.

Therefore, first place in importance is shifted from adversarial opposants (ogres) and sought-after objects (the princess) to the adjuvants and destinators who adopt a paternal role and become father-figures in Veig's new world. The most important of these is the Norwegian captain who befriends the boy, adopts him in a sense, gives him errands to run, rewards him with coin and a bottle, and, as a parting favour, takes him for a ride down the channel, which, the Narrator observes, makes of Veig a twentieth-century Columbus. The viscount of Koedgili assumes a similar function, for when his car breaks down and Veig and two of his buddies show up, he takes the three off on a rollicking overland trip to the same village of Loctudy on the coast. As benevolent father-surrogates (Veig's own papa is a mason and seldom at home) and external wielders of authority, they contribute to the boy's 'family romance' by opening up for him grand new vistas. Like the old peasant woman with her stories, the father-figures dispense wisdom and initiate to freedom.

For Veig the grand new life is to leave home, if only temporarily, and, if only temporarily, to discover a world beyond Pont-l'Abbé. This notion of freedom is symbolized, above all, by the sea. The ocean and its telluric equivalent, the desert – an ocean of sand where camels roam – is where the boy now wishes to roam in turn. And freedom is manifest not only as the capacity to wander the earth but also as the opening out of Veig's imagination, of his capacity to imagine and to dream. Thus, whereas Paotr-Teo can only think of growing up to become an agricultural labourer, Veig now yearns to be a bishop or an admiral or an officer leading his men on a camel charge.

Should the implied reader not have recognized the imagery of the quest, romance, and the equivalent of magical realism, he would finally be shaken out of the expectations of autobiography or low-mimetic realism in volume 3. Here all pretence at mimetic realism is broken when, possessed by the demon of intertextuality, Koedgili recites for the children lines from 'Pirc'hirin ar Mor' by Roparz Hemon and, we are told, verses by Maodez Glanndour, poems that will be written decades in the future, commenting that Hemon then was also (would also have been) about eight years old, and that he also must have played hookey:

– Da Lok-Tudi, aotrou, da welout ar mor.
– Sada!' eme an aotrou, 'Tri birc'hirin ar mor, en un taol, ha n'eo ket nemetken hini barzhoneg vrudet Roparz Hemon [...] N'eus den par d' ur barzh dimezet gant an Awen. [...] An hini [...] a zle bezañ a oad ganeoc'h,

ha, d'an ampoent, nemet gwall-fazi a rafen, o c'harzata, eveldoc'h-c'hwi,
lamponed.' (vol. 3, p. 25)
(– 'To Loctudy, Sir, to see the ocean.' – 'Well!' the gentleman said, 'Three
pilgrims of the sea, all at once, not just one as in the famous poem by
Roparz Hemon [...] Nobody equals a poet wed to Inspiration [...] He [...]
should be as old as you, and, at this moment, unless I am totally in error,
playing hookey as you are, you good-for-nothings.')

He calls Veig and the two others his 'Pilgrims of the Sea.' And he alludes
to Abeozen's volume on the history of modern Breton literature to be
published still more decades in the future. The viscount has a fine,
ironic wit (to say nothing of Youenn Drezen, acting behind the scenes).
At the same time, the father-figure offers his child the latter's very first
audition of poetry in Breton. If the reader's horizon of expectations is
suddenly expanded in a surprising way, it is even more so the case for
Veig, whose adventures are an extramural education and who, to the
extent that he is a version of the implied author Youenn Drezen, will
one day become a Breton writer in his turn.

The Breton term for playing hookey or for truancy is *skol-louarn* (fox
school / school of foxes, cf. Fr. *école buissonnière*). In the novel's title and
throughout the narrative, school imagery is pervasive. On the one
hand, Veig and Paotr-Teo free themselves from what they see, and what
to some extent the implied reader comes to see, as restrictive, boring,
and useless. The ineffectuality and the irrelevance of formal schooling
derive in part from the child's focalization, in part from the fact that,
although Veig's family is 'red,' his parents send him to the 'white,'
church school. The priests are depicted throughout as well-intentioned
but ultimately irrelevant and useless entities speaking a different language (they come from Léon!) and unable to communicate with or to
comprehend the genuine needs of Bigouden people. The rollicking
high points of such miscommunication occur when the choir director
seizes Veig, who has no idea why he is being seized yet manages to
escape in any case; and, at the end, when Aunt Katell marches Veig back
to school, where, to his utter stupefaction, he will not be punished –
Katell is pretty, and the new young schoolmaster flirts with her and
shows himself eager to please her.

In contrast to all of that, the three volumes of the *Skol-louarn* recount
how Veig learns and grows on the outside. He grows in terms of adventure
and the quest, as we have seen. He also grows in terms of literature –
books and language. In the beginning Veig is distracted from going to

school because he desperately wants the money to purchase children's penny romances – he is an avid reader – in the morning, and then read them in the afternoon. From this point on, he becomes, in reality or in his imagination, the protagonist of these romances. Then, when M. de Najac – a writer of boulevard comedies in Paris – comes to town on his camel, the gossips tell stories about Algeria, the desert, and soldiers chasing bandits. Veig is drunk with the joy of the (narrative) exotic.

On another level, this young student of life is made aware of language and of problems in interpretation. He and his friend the Norwegian skipper speak with their hands and a few words. Each trying to speak in a foreign tongue, Veig in French and the captain in English, they enact a delightful comedy of errors, in which Veig thinks he understands perfectly, and gets everything wrong. One example:

'You ... poor?,' e c'houlennas. Distaget en doa e c'her: pour.
'Oui! beaucoup.'
Va Doue, ya! Veig a gave mat pour ... hag e soñje dezhañ e komprene ar saozneg. (vol. 1, p. 68)
('You ... poor?' he asked. He pronounced it as if it were *pour* [Br. leeks].
'Oui, beaucoup.' My God, yes! Veig liked leeks ... and he imagined that he understood English.)

Twice – once with the choirmaster, a second time at mass on Sunday – Veig cannot comprehend the priests' Léon Breton, and also fails to communicate by sign with one of his buddies.

This said, the child does become a master of speech, in his own manner. He dreams – of ships and captains, of camels and colonels, and of automobiles and generals. His imagination constructs for him a life with open spaces – sea or sand – and errancy. Veig also invents the wildest stories to enhance his feats when recounting them to Paotr-Teo. For example, his running away, chased by a flock of geese, is transformed in the telling into a great victory. Poor Paotr-Teo, the ideal narratee, is wildly impressed by the inscribed narrator's inventions. He simply regrets that such marvels never occur when he is around. When they are together, even when nothing happens, Veig makes nothing appear so interesting that Paotr-Teo is happy anyway. In Veig, the narrator, a writer is born.

The fox imagery of the title relates to the natural world and, intertextually, to *Le Roman de Renart*. It is no accident that a number of Veig's adventures deal with animals: he is fascinated by a parrot, he is fascinated by Karabos the camel, he runs from a flock of geese, and he runs from a rat. Veig relates to these creatures much as he relates to people – as positive or negative entities of his world, whom he desires or dreads. In this he resembles perfectly Reynard the Fox and Tibert the Cat in the medieval beast epic. This is the case because the grown-ups, as much as the animals, are giant authority figures capable of causing harm and must be propitiated or tricked or run away from. Hence – again in the Reynardian mode – Veig not only avoids school but, when it proves necessary, consistently and repeatedly escapes, from a barber, from the priest, from a landowning lady and her dog, from peasants, and from the police.

The mode of comedy is underscored by the fact that Veig does not always operate alone. He and Paotr-Teo form a comic team, two child heroes in an adult world, a fox and a wolf (or, rather, a tiny shrewd fox and a big lovable bear) surrounded by dangerous humans and assorted beasts. Veig is Reynard – the leader, the inspirer of ideas and actions. When someone has to speak, it is he; and, as we have seen, he is a master of words, a storyteller and artist in the bud. Yet, also as we have seen, he feels timid and helpless without Paotr-Teo at his side. Paotr-Teo is robust for his age, loyal to a fault and, in perfect complementarity to Veig, somewhat heavy in the mind. Normally, whatever Veig proposes or declares is fine for Paotr-Teo; his response is always 'Me ivez' (Me too). Forming a comic pair, each contributes to the other and each arrives at his full potentiality with the other. As a team, they partake of a long tradition in literature and the other arts of comic interplay, which includes such teams as Reynard and Isengrin or Brun, Don Quixote and Sancho Panza, and, closer to us, Laurel and Hardy, Abbott and Costello, the Marx Brothers, and the Three Stooges.

At the court of King Noble the Lion, Reynard is the medieval trickster hero *par excellence*; Hervé Trebern assumes the same function in the little world of home and school at Pont-l'Abbé. He consistently has to lie or tell half-truths to deceive his family as to what he really does and where he goes each morning and afternoon. Furthermore, to satisfy his and Paotr-Teo's natural, 'animal' desires, as in the *Renart* branches, a good deal of what he does concerns obtaining food – stealing candy, apples, and chestnuts, or paying for chocolate, begging for bread, and being reduced to devouring raw eggs. He is a modern fox inhabiting a modern town, and Veig's animal desire for food or his less animal desire for reading-matter is filtered through the capitalist system of exchange, much as Reynard's and Isengrin's were through the rites of feudalism.

Veig needs money to purchase candy. He spends much comic time trying to spend or exchange a large Norwegian coin the skipper gave him.
And a nice policeman, instead of arresting Veig for one of his trespasses,
gives the lad two small pieces of money for candy.

In sum, like *Le Roman de Renart*, *Skol-louarn Veig Trebern* – to the extent
that it is an epic – is a comic epic, a mock-epic. The Aeneas with his Pallas or Achates, Roland with his Oliver, or Lancelot with his Gauvain is a
child. His adventures so often end in running away from threatening
grown-ups, geese, or rats. His yearning is satisfied by chocolate or a trip
in a boat, and the aim of his quest is to avoid submission to rote-learning
from a harmless old priest. Humour is generated by the continual
antithesis between the heroic archetypes in the tradition and the low-
mimetic, humble, and truly childlike embodiment of the archetypes in
Veig and Paotr-Teo. Finally, to the extent that the antithesis is literary
and, therefore, artificial, and that the implied author artificially imposes
on Veig's story his own intertextual command of a literary tradition, we
find an example of the Bergsonian comic, 'du mécanique plaqué sur du
vivant.' This is so because, in Veig's case, the *imagos* of Aeneas or Columbus or the Wandering Jew, for that matter of Reynard and Isengrin,
are absurd. Furthermore, in strictly Bergsonian terms, the comic is
increased by repetition, by the persistence of Veig's truancy, and by his
repetitive, mechanical re-enactment of the same responses – distraction
by a treat, distraction by the road – to everyday stimuli, and by the
extent to which trivial causes give rise to grandiose literary effects or, on
the contrary, grandiose literary structures give rise to trivial little
mimetic actions.

Drezen's last word, however, is, I believe, one of joy in escape, freedom, and living life to the full. From this perspective, we must restate
the role of physicality in the novel, especially the functioning of food
and drink. Not all is idyllic in this Rabelaisian fulfilment of the body.
Veig and Paotr-Teo gorge themselves on chocolate, then vomit. When
Veig's father discovers the bottle of spirits the skipper gave to Veig for
his family, he and his mates go on a binge and all but wreck the house.
Such also is Brittany or the caricature of Brittany that Drezen demystifies. Still, for three volumes, Veig and his friend live Bakhtinian carnival,
escaping from, defying, and mocking the official institutional culture –
our culture – that constrains them. Their adventures are a delightful,
carnivalesque demystification of so many of the clichés on Brittany and
the Bretons in 'official' literature and culture. They are also a Bakhtinian hymn to life and to protest, to the spiritual yearning and physical ful-

filment of young people everywhere, those young in years and those others, like Youenn Drezen in old age, who have never lost the spirit of *joven*.

ROPARZ HEMON

Roparz Hemon authored ten novels, more or less, and some one hundred pieces of shorter fiction. One of the most highly regarded of the novels, *Nenn Jani*, is conceived in the realist mode, telling of little people living little lives in Brest. However, in general (and in this he resembles his Occitan homologue Robert Lafont), Hemon chose to cultivate a variety of modes and genres: detective stories, children's fiction, historical novels, futurism, the fantastic, and the symbolic. *Mari Vorgan* (The Mermaid), one of Hemon's masterpieces, written in 1947–8 and published in 1962, was, I am convinced, directly influenced by Drezen's *Itron Varia Garmez* and furthers the exploitation of an allegorical-symbolic-poetic narrative.[38]

The text is homodiegetic, the purported diary of a ship's doctor, on mission on a man-of-war in the eighteenth century. The doctor keeps a diary, to be a gift for his wife upon his return and a special means of communicating with her. Hemon thus renews the tradition of eighteenth-century epistolary and memoir novels. The Mari-Vorgan is a sea siren or mermaid, and also the statue of a mermaid on the ship's poop. The ship is dogged by strange occurrences that become an obsession to the doctor. The model for the statue – Levenez, whose name means Joy – is present to celebrate the ship's departure. Then she disappears, and the statue disappears. Then Levenez or someone like Levenez appears at the various ports of call. The doctor finally encounters her on board, whereupon she tells him her story, a powerful imaginative projection of what it means to be a fish in water. The doctor, not the most lucid of men, discovers too late that he has fallen in love. In the throes of passion and madness, he falls overboard trying to stab a rival and, in fact, piercing repeatedly the wooden statue.

As with Drezen's Paol Tirili, the doctor is exalted and then crushed by his imagination and by thwarted desire – *fin' amor*, which thrives on obstacle and, as with Tristan and Lancelot, can end only in death. Like any number of medieval *domnas* and fays, Levenez assumes the traits of a goddess or a princess from the Otherworld. To the doctor she stands cold and forbidding, indifferent to him yet demanding his service. Loving her brings, we are led to believe, quasi-supernatural ecstasy yet also the risk of death. For both the doctor and his rival, Lieutenant Arzhur a Lezivi, Levenez is a creature of Eros and Thanatos, in that desiring her leads irrevocably to cultivation of the Freudian death instinct. The doctor appears both condemned and resigned to Thanatos from the moment he admits to the ship's cook that he indeed spoke to the mermaid in his cabin, thereby breaking her injunctions of secrecy. The doctor's indiscretion, his failure to demonstrate *mezura*, is one of the great sins against *fin' amor* in the medieval lyric and romance, forming a central increment in Marie de France's *Lanval*, for instance, and in *La Châtelaine de Vergi*.

Central to Hemon's vision of *fin' amor* is the power of woman and of passion over men, the power to disturb their orderly, male-oriented lives. As soon as the officers begin to chatter over the statue and its model, the captain dreads that this voyage will be dogged by bad luck, ill fortune directly attributable to the presence of the Mari-Vorgan in wood on the aft deck. And ill fortune does dog the ship. It takes the form of natural phenomena – a storm or an extended calm – as if Levenez the female has a bond with the forces of nature. More often it takes the form of disharmony among the men. On the one hand, the doctor and Arzhur become rivals in their – obviously libidinal – yearning for the girl. The competition evolves into distrust and eventually hatred. Yet the crew also become disruptive. The men on board – officers or crew – are divided by feelings of desire and dread, each individual on his own, separated from the others and driven into the most irrational depths of his own psyche. In their encounter with the feminine, lunatic principle (Hecate, Ishtar), both Arzhur and the doctor drift into insanity. So also do those crew members who leap into the sea or try to escape in a dinghy.

To the extent that the princess in Arthurian romance is, in some sense of the term, a fay from the Celtic Otherworld, and the hero's quest is to cross over to and, in some sense, conquer that Otherworld, Hemon's novel ironically partakes of the old archetype. The sea voyage – from Brittany to Portugal to Cape Verde to the South Atlantic – becomes such a quest, delving further and further into Levenez's domain of the waters. Significantly, the Celtic version of the quest, as in *Immram Brain* and *Navigatio sancti Brendani*, included a central maritime element. As in the *Tristan* romances, the seas are the realm of passion, the irrational, the unconscious, darkness, and death. The sea, subject to the powers of the moon, embodies the feminine *imago* above all others. And, in this novel of symbol and allegory, the traditional gender roles are underscored. We perceive the doctor to be a man of reason and culture, whose most treasured memory is his domestic garden (*cum* Adela, his domesticated wife) at home, the polar opposite to Levenez, half animal, a creature of the waters, sensual, irrational, unobtainable, and unknowable. When Levenez tells her story of having descended from a people of mermen and mermaids, formerly inhabitants of an Atlantis-type city who were condemned to their present state for having refused charity to Christ and Our Lady, her tale reminds the implied reader of Breton legends, especially the greatest legend of all, Kêr-Iz: the story of King Gradlon and his daughter Dahut, the latter whose lust destroyed a city and a kingdom. The intertextual presence of the Dahut story helps establish a structural antithesis of land versus sea comparable to the one of man versus woman. Arzhur and the doctor are threatened by madness and by being drawn over a cliff. The sinful, sexually dominant sea creatures are opposed to creatures on land and its equivalent, a ship, who desperately try to maintain lives of hierarchy, order, and duty. The collapse of this rational, male world lies at the heart of Hemon's narrative.[39]

The character of the doctor is more complex, however, than simply the embodiment of masculine rationality destroyed by feminine passion. In the diary he explains, at one point, that he goes to sea again, against his will, uniquely out of a sense of duty. Yet later he confesses that he accepted the call *because* he loves his wife so much. This man – Breton to the core? modern to the core? – is divided in himself, a nexus of antitheses. On the one hand, he yearns deeply for home, family, and the family garden patch. On the other hand, he relishes adventure and the quest. He thirsts and thirsts, knowing not for what, and is torn by what appears to be inherent, visceral non-satisfaction – desire never sated because it cannot be sated.

Without knowing it consciously, the doctor yearns for the absolute. Since he refuses normal expression of the libido, his desire is made manifest in the life of dreams. He dreams of a distant city of stone that he cannot enter. He dreams that he beholds the mermaid in his boat that sails through his oneiric city:

Adwelet em eus ar gêr iskis-hont a welen em huñvreoù. An *Agenor* a dreuze anezhi, o faoutañ e hent dre greiz an toennoù. Astennet war ar c'herdin dindan ar wern-veg e oa Levenez, evel en ur gwele-skourr. (p. 72)

(I saw again the strange, distant city that I used to see in my dreams. The *Agenor* was crossing it, splitting its way through the middle of the roofs.

Stretched out on the ropes, underneath the bowsprit, was Levenez, as in a hammock.)

And life itself assumes the quality of a dream, as when he follows Levenez but, try as he can, fails to overtake her, or as when, at the end, he tries to stab Levenez yet only pierces the wooden statue on the poop. The dreams and phantasms reflect, one could say, a classical Freudian pattern of desire and impotence, of Eros and Thanatos, and, most crucial of all, the disintegration of the psyche. Resembling his predecessor the dramatist Tanguy Malmanche, Hemon elaborates an imaginary whereby the flight into the oneiric, with the unreal seizing the ground of the real, leads to insanity.

The sea of dreams also assumes an aesthetic function. These images of passion, darkness, and the unconscious inspire the artist. The doctor gives way to desire and dreams yet also to the life of the imagination. He keeps Adela's portrait on the cabin wall. After beholding Levenez, he grasps the portrait to restore his sense of reason and duty. At one point, he recalls the wooden church sculptures back home in Brittany, sculptures so alive that they make people laugh and Adela pray. We are reminded that Levenez is or was also a statue, and therefore that, in the doctor's mind and in physical reality, she is or was also a work of art. The doctor himself is an artist to the extent that his diary, which, but for the extradiegetic frame, constitutes Hemon's novel, is a work of art in prose. He wonders, quite rightly, whether the diary will be all that remains of him. He speculates that, were he a writer, he would compose a story to be entitled 'al Lestr klañv gant ar Garantez' (The Ship Ill with Love) (p. 73), which, in a sense, he and his creator, Roparz Hemon, do compose. In an extradiegetic passage added by one of the ship's officers, it is stated that the diary should be considered one-half true and one-half madness or a novel. The bond between illness and art and between insanity and art, exploited by Drezen, is raised again here. For all these reasons it is possible to interpret the doctor's story, symbolically and/or allegorically, as that of the artist or of the dreamer who hopes to build a new Brittany grounded in language and culture (the Breton Levenez versus the Frenchified Adela) and which renews the mythical medieval past and the no less mythical Celtic soul.[40] These were the lifetime goals of Roparz Hemon. How powerful and how tragic, therefore, this story of defeat which can end only in madness and death.

We must not forget, however, that the doctor's is not the only story, nor the unique quest. Functioning as a subplot and in polyphonic parallelism to the doctor, Levenez recounts her story of quest and liberation. Restricted by hegemonic familial relations of one sort or another and threatened sexually, the girl manages to escape twice. She turns to water as her natural element, and in water – a lake or the ocean – she discovers freedom, joy, and fulfilment, the fusion of her spiritual and physical needs (or the fulfilment of her uniquely physical needs, which are redeemed in the process). She, the female, succeeds where the male doctor fails. Her temptation and initiation are positive episodes with positive overtones, to the extent that the implied reader is willing to distinguish the human from the demonic.

Levenez's story, recounted by the doctor, is an excellent example of embedded narrative, in this case a *mise en abyme* which treats the thematics and problematics of the embedding, enclosing novelistic whole. It is also a metadiegetic narrative in the *tiroir* tradition of eighteenth-century fiction. This narratological structure should remind us that – except for the editorial frame – the entire story (including Levenez's confession) is recounted in the doctor's voice, an *Ich-Erzählung* from his point of view and focalized through his consciousness. We the implied readers have no reason whatsoever to doubt his sincerity. He is painfully sincere. Yet we have every reason to question whether he is not, unconsciously of course, an unreliable narrator concerning the external facts of the case and concerning the workings of his own psyche. One example: whereas according to the doctor, the Mari-Vorgan disappeared from the poop after only a few days at sea, the ship's officer who recovers the diary notes that this is false; he certifies that the statue remained on the aftcastle from beginning to end. Indeed, as in Marivaux or Rousseau, the sundry extradiegetic elements of the frame – the inscribed editor is given a manuscript by a retired navy officer in Brest; the ship's officer, in an addendum, 'corrects' the doctor's narrative and offers his own interpretation of the events – underscore the literariness of the device (diary-novel) and the fact that we are reading a work of literature adhering to literary conventions and not a piece of documentary evidence.

Central, then, to Hemon's superb manipulation of narrative technique is the fact that the story is filtered through a limited focalizing consciousness: that of the (more and more) mad doctor. As a result, we do not know – we have no way of knowing – whether the girl seen on the boat is Levenez, who climbed on board in Portugal or was a stowaway from the beginning, or an enchanted statue come to life or a mermaid all along or a phantasm in the doctor's psyche. As it turns out, the doctor did not know either.

One theme of the novel concerns the doctor's quest to know, and the difficulties he and others encounter in interpreting ambiguous evidence. The doctor would like his diary to be a mirror of truth to Adela. Mirrors prove to be deceiving, however. We discover this, whether or not the doctor does, when he observes, for the first time, Levenez herself and, along with her, the statue in a mirror. Rumours spread that a servant on the Spanish coast beheld a mermaid dancing on the waves. Later, a page informs the doctor that sailors and the cook beheld a woman walking or swimming on the ocean. Furthermore, whatever he himself sees or thinks he sees, the doctor also wonders whether his rival, Arzhur, is an arrogant and over-sexed aristocrat, as he had presumed, or perhaps only a youth who drinks too much.

This ambiguity of sight is further complicated and problematized by ambiguity in speech. Here the problematizing element proves to be the ship's cook, who may or may not be a demonic manipulator of others, for no one knows what purposes. He is the fellow who claimed to see Levenez on the water but later explains to the doctor that he lied – he tricked the sailors. The cook along with the page spread rumours concerning Arzhur's madness and probably the doctor's also. The cook also seeks a relationship of complicity with the doctor, feeding his mind with stories about Levenez, for example the information that she stays in Arzhur's cabin and that she left a coral bracelet at his door. We the implied readers have no way of knowing how much of this is true, or whether any of it is true. The doctor appears capable of fantasizing at will and of creating demonic scapegoats in Arzhur and the cook. On the other hand, it is equally possible that the cook serves as an innocent catalyst to the doctor's ravings or, perhaps more likely, that this liar and manipulator is, in his own way, also an artist, and that he pounced upon the doctor as the ideal neurotic narratee for his narrative inventions.

Whatever we think of the facts of the case, I believe we recognize – unbeknown to the doctor himself – the slow but sure disintegration of his psyche in the course of the diegesis. The man is, from the beginning, a loner, alienated, set apart from the others, even before his quarrels with Arzhur. One reason for this alienation is an (unhealthy?) fastidiousness, manifest in his revulsion vis-à-vis the cook, who is alleged to be the captain's procurer, and, likewise, his contempt for the captain and his rage at the cheap sexual exploits of the others and their sexual jokes. This is the man who tries so hard to apply logic, science, and self-control in the face of the Mari-Vorgan, the man who endures dreams of paralysis in a boat far from his dream city. The outcome will be the doctor's own loss of innocence and, ultimately, his avowal of guilt and remorse when, toward the end, he confesses to his diary and, therefore, to Adela that he now loves Levenez:

> Fellout a rae din lakaat er c'haier-mañ va ene en noazh. N'em eus ket graet. Anzav a ran deoc'h n'em eus ket graet. Ha ma klaskfen, evit ur wech hepken, hen ober?
> Skrijañ a reot. Adela. Ne ran forzh. Ho touellet em eus, Adela, va muiañkaret. En ur skrivañ al linennou-mañ, ho touellañ a ran c'hoazh. N'oc'h ket va muiañ-karet. Hi eo, hounhont, ha na welan mui, hounhont ha n'am eus gwelet biskoazh marteze, a garan. Levenez! [...] Ret eo e vije anezhi, pa sonjañ enni noz-deiz. (pp. 161–2)
> (In this notebook I wanted to lay bare my soul. I did not do it. I confess to you that I did not do it. What if, just once, I were to? You will shudder, Adela. I don't care. I deceived you, Adela, my beloved. By writing these lines, I deceive you still. You are not my beloved. She is the one that I love, over there, whom I do not see any more, whom perhaps I never saw. Levenez! She has to be real, given that I dream of her night and day.)

Yet the implied reader has seen it coming. He has seen the doctor displace guilt onto his wife (a dream that Adela writes to everyone on board except himself), and seen the doctor wait a week, once Levenez appears to him, before writing about her in the diary, and seen the captain and others treat the doctor with contempt. Hemon's narratological triumph is to make us sympathize and empathize with the doctor in his tragedy while at the same time we recognize that he is an unreliable narrator, lacking lucidity, riddled with bad faith, and that the story recounts his failure to understand his failure, himself, and others. This is a major achievement in a major, truly beautiful novel.

Tangi Kerviler, like *Mari Vorgan,* is situated in the eighteenth century.[41] Whereas the history and historical time of the Enlightenment are tangential to the structures of archetype that shape the doctor and his mermaid, this second eighteenth-century novel is more present and also more problematic in its relationship to history and ideology. *Tangi Kerviler* is historical romance yet also utopian romance, with the utopia displaced from the future onto the past.

Roparz Hemon casts his story in the form of an I-narrative. In this homodiegetic text the protagonist sets down on paper, in the year 1833, his memoirs, the purported adventures which he underwent in his younger days. Tangi Kerviler is the scion of a poor but old family in the nobility. At the age of fourteen he is sponsored by the Crown Prince, who, one night, turns up at the manor door incognito. After training as a cadet and being incorporated into the Household Guards the young lieutenant serves the Queen Mother in her palace. There he has a liaison with Orwen, one of the ladies-in-waiting. Later, on manoeuvres, he is again befriended by the Prince. When the Revolution occurs, in 1789, Tangi defends the monarchy. The palace is stormed, the Queen Mother is slain, and Tangi is obliged to assume a disguise and go into hiding. He finds refuge with Helgoed, the loyal Kapellmeister. Tangi escapes a second incursion, during which Orwen is killed. Eventually he rejoins the Prince, distinguishes himself in combat, and becomes a captain. Back in the present, 1833, Tangi informs us that he has lived a happy life married to Lina, his childhood sweetheart. The Revolution was defeated, Prince Alan was crowned king, and the kingdom lived happily ever after.

Hemon manipulates reader-response with brio. The implied reader will or ought to be disturbed by one or two early increments in this historical novel presumably about the French Revolution. He might be surprised at the Crown Prince, never having heard of a modern dauphin baptized Alain. And of regiments of the Guards where everyone is Breton. Suspicions increase. Yet it is only at the beginning of chapter 4 that the Narrator chooses to recall to his implied reader the history of their country in the old days, that is, the previous century. Here we discover that in 1789 reigned King Hoel VI, son of old King Konan XIII and of the good Queen Mother, Izabel of Spain, and Hoel's evil wife, Queen Ingrid of Denmark, all this occurring in the royal capital, Radeneg (Rennes). In other words, although 1789 is 1789, it is not the French Revolution. It is the Breton Revolution. Hemon has imagined another history, a history of Brittany as an independent kingdom and what the Revolution might have been had it taken place in that other kingdom with its other history. Perhaps to be expected from the intransigent author of 'Kanenn evit Deiz an Anaon,' in the history of this imagined Western European region France is absent. There is no French impact because France and things French do not exist. The Rights of Man come from North America, the idea of a representative assembly from England, opera from Italy, and the rococo garden *à la chinoise* from Germany. Here the absence of France leaves its trace, screams its significance as aporia, in a book which struggles against Frenchness and the imposition of French history on Brittany.

It would be a mistake to ascribe to Roparz Hemon or to his novel nostalgia for the Old Brittany, the sort of nostalgia against which Hemon and *Gwalarn* struggled for decades. The elegant, refined, courtly, and urbane Bretons and their concerns, evoked in *Tangi Kerviler*, correspond neither to the genuine history of Rennes and Nantes during the Ancien Régime nor to the clichés and stereotypes – folklore, peasant life, Catholic faith, and the cult of sacrifice – which traditionally feed Breton nostalgia. Hemon's Brittany proclaims sameness vis-à-vis France or Germany, not a factitious, condescending, and colonialist alterity. Also, the language of the novel, composed in high modern literary Breton, in and of itself repudiates the clichés of nostalgia to be found in a Théodore Botrel, much as Sydney Goodsir Smith's Lallans repudiates the clichés of nostalgia to be found in Harry Lauder.[42]

On the contrary, a utopian vision of the future is displaced onto a fictional past, this fictional past a symbolic call to action to make the utopian future actual in somebody's present. Central, therefore, to Hemon's utopia is his fictionalized meditation on politics and history. As he sees it, the French have occupied and exploited Brittany for centuries. This historical domination is so pervasive that were the Bretons, by some miracle, offered their freedom, they would remain frenchified in culture as in language. Anticipating contemporary insights into colonialism and postcolonialism, Hemon offers the paradox that Brittany can be or become genuinely Breton only by the eradication and subsequent reconstruction of history and culture.

For Hemon to have chosen the eighteenth century and the Revolution can be interpreted, perhaps, as a belief that France became most horribly French because of the Lumières, the Revolution, the Republic, and the imperialist and universalist Jacobinism that resulted therefrom. As he sees it, Brittany has suffered most, in the last two centuries, from the militancy of a secular, democratic French state determined to subject Brittany to an internal colonization of the spirit worse than the external colonization of markets and resources. Therefore, he demystifies the Lumières and the Revolution, refuting them in the universe of his fiction.

Politics in *Tangi Kerviler* is depicted in terms of binomial antithesis. Allied with the Revolutionaries, encouraging them and profiting from their depredations, are Queen Ingrid, her degenerate son Prince Gourmelen, and turncoats such as Lieutenant Leian. Faithful to the monarchy and monarchical principles are the Queen Mother, Prince Alan, Tangi and his family, his friend Arzhur, the good officers, the good page, and Helgoed and his family. Although Orwen begins on the wrong side, as Leian's mistress, she then redeems herself through love and sacrifice, contributing to Tangi's survival and thus to the survival of the values he embodies.

This relatively simplistic antithesis is restated in other, more problematic aspects of the novel. Hemon sets up an opposition between the old, dignified court of Queen Izabel, grounded in etiquette, and the new, frivolous court of Queen Ingrid, grounded in pleasure. Even more, he opposes the relatively corrupt and deceitful court in an urban centre, Rennes or Nantes, to the pure, innocent family nexus in the country. Hospitality in the Kerviler manor house is opposed to the disruption of hostility in Helgoed's manor house or to a false, ostentatious hospitality in the royal palace, where family ties are broken or never exist in the first place and Tangi must face the world in isolation. Similarly, in the erotic sphere, the kiosk in a pseudo-Chinese rococo garden, where seduction reigns, is set off against a series of décors in the country – a shepherd's cabin or the open field beneath an oak tree – where Tangi and Lina commune in purity and innocence. Their *loci amoeni*, derived from an age-old tradition of pastoral, contrast with the artificial, modern, rococo-Enlightenment fleshpots of the court.

We are made aware that Hemon proposes a cultural and ideological alternative to the modern, Enlightenment-grounded ideal of France dominant both in the eighteenth century and in the twentieth. In my opinion, the alternative – the counter-ideal – can be assimilated to nineteenth-century Germany and the cultural current of Biedermeier in German-speaking lands. The hallmarks of this current are intimacy in the home, garden, and family, idyllic realism, gentle melancholy, loyalty to the establishment, and the upholding of a doctrine of *ora et labora* and *Sammeln und Hegen*. In a tiny world that is sentimental, conservative, and committed to the primacy of love and the family, the lives of little people are treated with high seriousness. These lives are, therefore, capable of universal significance and of a new kind of heroism.

In this sentimental décor, where the public and the private merge, the archetypal image is elaborated during the attempted assassination of King Hoel as reported in chapter 5. There Tangi is told only of the coup. What he sees, later on, is the opera house in flames, set on fire:

Ac'hano ez ae ar gwel pell war gêr Radeneg. En oabl teñval en em lede ur skleur ruz, ledan, dindan ar c'houmoul. Ur peuliad flammoù ha moged a save en ur blegañ gant an avel diouzh ur savadur bras, treset an drolinenn anezhañ war an tantad. [...] Ar grommdoenn a seblantas koeñviñ, ha

neuze e tarzhas en un taol, gant un tousmac'h a ruilhas betek ennomp.
(pp. 75–6)
(From there [where we were] the view went far over the city of Radeneg. In
the dark sky a broad red glimmering spread out beneath the clouds. Bend-
ing from the wind, a pillar of flames and smoke rose from a large building,
its silhouette traced onto the blazing fire. The vault appeared to swell up
and then to explode all at once, with a thunderclap which rolled up to us.)

The burning of the opera house serves as an emblem of the Revolution
or, at the least, of revolution-oriented activity – wanton destruction
which, whatever the intent, harms culture and the arts. Also, the opera
house is a structure allied to the court and town. An edifice possible
only in a refined, urban ambience, its existence and its destruction can
occur only in Rennes or Nantes; they escape the countryside inhabited
by the Kerviler family. Finally, the burning of the opera house, seen
from a distance as a spectacle in the night, itself creates an operatic
effect in an operatic décor. This *mise en abyme* reflects and underscores
the operatic, spectacular, sentimental, artistic structure of the novel and
of history as it is presented in the novel.

The symbolism of the opera house would remind us, should we have
forgotten, the extent to which Roparz Hemon is a man of culture, and
his books intellectual and cultural artefacts. *Tangi Kerviler* is grounded in a tradition of the historical novel or historical romance in the
nineteenth century that concentrates on its most vital, immediate past,
the eighteenth century. Central to this tradition are meditations on the
history of Scotland by Scott and Stevenson, the conservative *plaidoiries*
for the Ancien Régime in Vigny and Barbey d'Aurevilly, and semi-popu-
lar romances in the line of Dumas and Hugo. Hemon exploits this vein
for a number of reasons. One is to demonstrate that Breton can serve a
wide range of uses, including historical romance, science fiction, and
the detective story (genres later to be cultivated by Robert Lafont in
Occitan). Another is to give value to a marginal form, outside the
parameters of French realism, which the French denigrate yet which
other peoples enjoy and – in the case of the Scots – have cultivated for
profit. For Scotland, the eighteenth was the century of suppression of
national identity and a national culture by the 'British' army, a tragic
time that the celtophile Roparz Hemon could imagine also in a French
context. Finally, even a popular genre, which appeals, he hoped, to a
public greater than the subscription list to *Al Liamm*, can be enriched
doctrinally and aesthetically to become a significant work of art.

In the case of Scott, Stevenson, Vigny, Barbey, and the others, as with *Tangi Kerviler*, we observe a process whereby the structures of medieval quest romance are displaced onto the recent past, in low mimetic, to end with a sort of Biedermeier *Bildungsroman*. In this structure the young son of the bourgeoisie or petty nobility is swept up by notable events and mixes with exalted figures only to return, wiser and an adult, to his own circle. The quest mirrors the trip to the Otherworld and the combat for a kingdom and a bride that we find in Chrétien, the *Prose Lancelot*, and Malory. Hemon turns the ideological message against Sir Walter Scott by having his hero remain faithful to the old order, not the new, and by concretizing temptation in the New Revolution not the Old Monarchy. A bond with medieval romance and with Scottish modern romance is maintained, owing to the exploitation of traditional motifs: battle, duel, assassination, conspiracy, disguise, sacrifice, and sudden turns of fortune. Loyalty is opposed to treachery, and purity to corruption. Upon undergoing his quest, the symbolic romance hero, Tangi, is endowed with a faithful friend, Arzhur, a faithful page, Skouarneg, and a faithful master, the Prince. He and his land have to choose between good and bad mothers (Izabel, Ingrid), good and bad sons (Alan, Gourmelen), and good and bad love-objects (Lina, Orwen). Perhaps the most conspicuous medieval motif, borrowed by Hemon, an avid reader and translator of medieval literature, is the hospitable host and his daughter – Helgoed and Anita, who succour Tangi and Skouarneg after the storming of the palace.

As in medieval romance, Tangi undergoes a series of amorous experiences and grows in the amorous life as much as he does in martial activity. As in medieval and nineteenth-century romance, as in the *Prose Lancelot* and the prose of Walter Scott, the youth is torn between a dark lady and a white lady, between Orwen the temptress and Lina the virgin. Orwen is allied to the evil forces of revolution in the town, and Lina to the forces of good in the loyalist countryside. The norms of low-mimetic romance are respected by the novel's having Tangi experience both Orwen and Lina. Lina wins out, of course, yet Orwen is converted to the good and redeemed by an act of sacrifice which then frees Tangi for a life of exemplary bourgeois harmony with Lina. In the tradition of Waverley and Ivanhoe, Tangi, in order to become a man, has to know both Orwen and Lina. After having known both ladies, he becomes an adult worthy of marriage and fatherhood.

Tangi's growth into manhood is reflected in a picture on the wall in his old school, a picture that he remembers (as an aging narrator) and

inserts into the novel specifically when recounting how he was torn
between Orwen and Lina. It is an allegorical painting in the old style
which depicts the torrents of passion (hell), ordinary daily activities (the
century), and the pure light of the good (heaven). The *mise en abyme*
alludes, in the narrator's mind, to the sensuous Orwen and to Lina, clad
in white, and to Tangi's choice between them, but also, I submit, in a
larger sense to the structure of the *Bildungsroman*. Tangi experiences
hell, ordinary existence in the world, and heaven. To lead a full, rich life
he must undergo all three and profit from them. Because he is a good
man on the good side, and the protagonist in a genre in which virtue
is rewarded, he progresses from secular hell to secular paradise. The
secular paradise is embodied not just in the girl Lina. On the contrary,
paradise with Lina means individual and communal fulfilment in a traditional, organic society where the soldier loyal to his prince can flourish as a husband and father. Integration into the community is Jungian
and it is allegorical, in that Roparz Hemon the author paints a picture
and offers a message for his fictional Tangi and the land he inhabits,
Breizh. We can consider this an example of twentieth-century Biedermeier and twentieth-century wish-fulfilment. Yet, at the same time, the
implied reader never forgets (and Hemon never forgot) that this
organic, integrated, synthetic Breizh is a fictional land and a fictional
kingdom. It never existed. And the nineteenth-century German princi-
palities on which it is based evolved, as we know, into an entity less admirable than the French Republic. Roparz Hemon never forgot the dark
side. That dark side problematizes his writing and our reading, offering
a deeper, more tragic and more meaningful vision and art.

PER DENEZ

Among the most important writers of prose from the 1970s to today
stands Per Denez / Pierre Denis, a militant, an editor, and a (now
retired) distinguished university professor. In 1979 he published a powerful brief novel, which some consider to be his masterpiece – *Glas evel
daoulagad c'hlas na oant ket ma re* (Blue like Blue Eyes Which Were Not
My Own).[43] Denez exploits narrative technique in a way similar to, and
raises some of the same themes as, Roparz Hemon in *Mari Vorgan*. The
novel recounts the relatively recent, adult life of a pharmacist's wife,
narrated in her own voice. She adores her husband, lives only for him,
and her existence is bound by him. One Sunday he is lost in his little
sailing boat at sea. The wife falls into utter misery. Then, rummaging in

his papers, she discovers he was having an affair with a young girl, who had decided to leave for Latin America. Therefore, the husband had in fact, that Sunday, committed suicide. In cold rage the Narrator looks all over for young Kristina, finds her, and brings her into her home as a maid and companion. Then, at just the right moment the Narrator poisons Kristina with hemlock and buries her in the garden. However, now she is tortured by the thought that her husband and Kristina are happy together in the afterlife. She will take cyanide herself in order to join them and be with her beloved.

The manipulation of narrative technique is superb. *Glas evel daoulagad c'hlas* is an *Ich-Erzählung*, a homodiegetic narrative limited to the wife's point of view and filtered through her consciousness. She makes claims to objectivity and tells her story in chronological order, recounting the events as they occurred to her and her reaction to these events. It is only gradually and in the course of time that we discover that the husband died, that he loved another woman, that the wife is a murderess, and that she will commit suicide. In this sense, even though the story is recounted toward the end of the wife's existence and is terminated just prior to her suicide, the integrity of what Stanzel would call 'Auktorial-situation'[44] is maintained. The implied reader responds positively to the suspense, the unfolding of the various mysteries, and the introduction of new, unexpected action.

At the same time, the implied reader recognizes, or rather in the course of time discovers, that this story is told by an unreliable narrator. As in the case of Hemon's protagonist, the wife can be trusted for an accurate rendering of the major events as they occur, or rather as she perceives them to have occurred. She is painfully, miserably sincere. Yet the implied reader will also recognize not only that one or two occurrences are false – owing to the fragile state of her sanity – but also, and far more important, that she is unaware of so much that happens around her and of the nuances of psychology and the moral imagination.

For example, she insists again and again that she and her husband were happy and that one reason for their happiness was the fact that they always worked together in the pharmacy. She also mentions his mania for subscribing to newspapers he never read, for renewing his hi-fi equipment every three years, and – as if it were a charming caprice on his part – his efforts to remain young, to keep slim and to resist encroaching baldness. Does the Narrator ever make the connection between her husband's vanity in his person and his pursuing a love affair? Apparently not, although the reader can and possibly will. Would the husband agree that he and his wife were so very happy? And that they were happy because they spent so much time together running the pharmacy? Quite possibly not, according to the implied reader. Finally, the Narrator never gives much thought as to why the husband kills himself, except to blame the 'whore' Kristina. The implied reader does not necessarily know more than the Narrator does. However, the reader, endowed with more lucidity and imagination than the Narrator, may well provide his own scenario. One such 'secondary narrative' could entertain the notion that the pharmacist was disgusted by his wife, whom he perceived to be partially deranged. The derangement would explain why he remained with her while, at the same time, he sought refuge and a partial way out in his hi-fi, his boat, and, finally, Kristina. He might have committed suicide not only because he had to go on living without the girl but also because he had to go on living with his wife. The latter prospect would have been too much for him to bear.

Similar blindness in the Narrator, and, therefore, an occasion for secondary narrative in the reader, will relate to the girl. Did Kristina seduce the husband, and is she therefore entirely responsible for his death? If so, how can she be as naïve and trusting as the wife perceives her to be? Did she really, only upon the point of dying, manifest horror and despair? And, if so, is the cause of the horror and despair the wife's belief that she destroyed in Kristina's mind the husband's love for her by claiming he had had many girlfriends, all with the wife's knowledge and approval? It is also possible to hypothesize that the husband was very much responsible for the love affair because of his need to escape from the wife, and that the girl's horror may also reflect her discovery of what a monster her lover had married and why, when she left him, he turned to suicide.

The secondary narratives I have sketched are my own, my hypotheses, neither more nor less valid than others. Such scenarios form part and parcel of reader response to all fiction. Yet, as we know from Iser, the call for an active response from the implied reader, who is obliged to contribute to the elaboration of the narrative, is one hallmark of the modern novel. Such hypotheses are the inevitable response from such a reader because of the elements of rupture and suspense and because of the very absence of lucidity and imagination in the Narrator. Because of Denez's choice of narratology, the reader asks the questions the Narrator ought to have asked and asks them in the Narrator's place, in reaction to the Narrator.

The Narrator fails to ask these questions because – to put it bluntly – she is insane. It is, again, in the course of the narrative, in the temporal duration of the reading process (*Erzählzeit*) that the reader comes to realize that the Narrator has developed a pattern of neurosis that then evolves into criminal psychosis.

From the beginning the Narrator portrays herself in terms that her therapist, had she had one, might have characterized as anal-retentive. She is a fanatic for neatness, cleanliness, and order. She is obsessed with the family garden and home. She is obsessed by the roses she cultivates and the objects she and her husband collect: furniture, china, pictures, and tapes. She joys in that the hedge of thorns keeps out neighbours' dogs, cats, and children, and that there will be no disagreeable residue on her roses; she decides never to grow flowers indoors or to make a fire in the fireplace, thus avoiding comparable stains on the rugs and scorching the furniture. She can't stand the noise of her husband's type-writer and declares she is happy they never had a child, for it might have come between her and her husband. As it is, she is his wife and mother, at the same time. The Narrator's existence focuses on her husband – she lives to love him – but also on ordering her nest or web, imposing order on her world and the objects in it, including the husband, and protecting it and them. The fact that she is a pharmacist's wife – both are pharmacists – and, according to stereotype, the quintessential petty bourgeois, crowns her own, totally unconscious self-portrait.

In time, in the course of reading, we discover her failure. After her lit-tle world is broken and after the hedges and walls are pierced, after the cat gets in and the husband takes it as a mistress, the Narrator's frus-trated libido finds another channel, no less pathological than the first one – violence. The wife is fully conscious that her extreme love for the husband has been transmuted into extreme hate for the girl, and that finding Kristina has given her life meaning again, the meaning which was lost when the husband disappeared. We can note, in passing, that in both cases such violent extremes of love and hate are groundless. Just as there is no rational justification for the Narrator's obsessive passion for her husband, a seemingly colourless fellow who neglects her, so also there is no rational reason for her to pursue and torture Kristina with such maniacal energy. The implied reader will recognize that the love and hate have nothing explicitly to do with their objects and everything to do with the Narrator's inner psyche.

In any case, Eros is transmuted into Thanatos as the Narrator seduces Kristina into becoming a defenceless object in her web (like the prelapsarian husband), then penetrates her with the poisoned drink. Upon which, she disposes of the body, digging away at the earth, dropping the corpse into the cavity, and planting roses over the restored topsoil. This is desire partially reconfigured in masculine terms, as she possesses Kristina, and entirely redirected to inflict pain and to ensure dominance. Although the Narrator, with her very bourgeois, vaguely anglophile and celtophile culture, has presumably never read Sade, instinctively she rejoins the tribe of the Divine Marquis. She gives Kristina lodging and nurture in exchange for the pleasure she will enjoy from her. She fattens her up, as it were, and makes her as happy as possible, so the girl will have more to lose by dying. And, in typical Sadian fashion, she plans the deed carefully in advance, accounting for every detail, in a triumph of the will. Thus she ensures that, on the point of dying, Kristina has to be made conscious that she is being murdered (executed), why, and by whom:

> Neuze, bremañ ma oa evurus, e c'helle mervel. Un nebeut traoù a oa ezhomm, avat, evit ma vefen me ivez evurus: ret e oa d'he maro bezañ dizañjer evidon; ret e oa dezhi gouzout e oa o vervel, perak e varve, ha piv a lazhe anezhi. (p. 67)
>
> (Then, now that she was happy, she could die. A few things were needed, however, so that I too might be happy: her death had to present no danger to me; she had to know she was dying, why she was dying, and who was killing her.) (Press, p. 65)

She had to be made conscious of her own enslavement and of the wife's mastery.

I have suggested that the husband is simply one of the Narrator's objects, one among a number of pieces in her collection, in the ordered structure she has arranged around her in the net or web. Unable to accept the fact that he rebelled against her ordered world, unable even to pose the question, she displaces her rage onto the external force she would like to believe broke into the web and seized her object. However, to avenge the loss she has to bring the outside agent within, to incorporate her in the web and integrate her into a new realm of order – like everything else in her existence. Then, slaying her as in a sense she slayed her husband, the wife will succeed with her where she failed with him. By burying the girl in the garden, she will maintain control over the collected object even in death and maintain its remains forever in her web.

At this point, the husband, the girlfriend, and the roses are the same in her psyche; they all are objects to be possessed. We observe this obsessional mother-figure ordering and protecting and appropriating her husband, the girl, and the roses. Does she not say, when Kristina arrives, that she is as excited as a woman expecting a baby? Does she not talk to her roses, loving them again like a mother? Hence, it is a symptom of alienation yet by no means incongruous that the Narrator thinks of Kristina and the roses together, loving the roses (which replace the husband) as much as she hates the now deceased Kristina. For the wife attempts to reconstitute the old, prelapsarian web, concentrating her libido now on the roses. Unfortunately for her sanity, although it ought to be easier to control the roses than the people, they also begin to die. The original pattern holds good, whatever the spider woman touches is poisoned. Her will to order slays, her desire slays, all three entities perish, directly or indirectly, at her ministrations, and, once again, Eros leads to Thanatos.

Actually, all four entities perish – including the wife, given that she regresses still further, this time into narcissism. Since she has killed everything she loved (or hated, with the passion of love), it remains only for the Narrator to kill herself. She has to kill herself in order to maintain the order threatened once again. In her dementia, she imagines that the two dead objects – the husband and Kristina – because they are dead, have escaped her web and are free to love in something like a Celtic Otherworld:

Zoken ma oa aet da glask ar peoc'h er bed all ... Ha me sot a-walc'h evit kas dezhañ Kristina ... da vezañ evurus o-daou ... Kristina ken sklaer he daoula-gad c'hlas, ken karantezus he divorzhed ... N'hellen ket lezel anezho evel-se, ha me chom er-maez, er yenijenn hag er maro, pa oant int e tommder an douar hag e buhez ar mor, e-kreiz ur sklerijenn na c'helle ket mont da get ... (p. 101)
(Even if he had gone to seek peace in the other world ... And with me stupid enough to send Kristina to him ... for the two of them to be happy ... Kristina with her blue eyes so bright, her thighs so loving ... I couldn't leave them like that, with me outside, in the cold and in death, while they were in the warmth of the earth and the life of the sea, amid a brightness which could not disappear ...) (Press, pp. 100–1)

The Narrator will therefore poison herself, partly to maintain herself as an object in the web, partly to follow the two transgressors to the Otherworld, to extend her web there or to build a new one to imprison them, enclosing him within and binding her without, the domination now functioning on a quasi-cosmic scale.

The Narrator intentionally, explicitly buries Kristina beneath her roses. The rose, an image of love and of the beloved woman, embodies an archetype in world literature which goes back to Ronsard and, beyond him, to *Le Roman de la Rose*, Ovid, and the Greek Anthology. The Narrator, who quotes Burns – 'My love is like a red, red rose' – is aware of this in her little way. She fervently believes that the roses mirror her love for the husband and also his love for her, and therefore that because of their location, over Kristina's corpse, sucking life and beauty from her, they symbolize her triumph over the girl. The roses would be the displaced metaphor, the objective correlative of herself. It is also true that, as the wife states so openly, the bright red of the roses reflects her passion for the husband and, at the same time, her hatred for Kristina. In point of fact, in the literary tradition, secular and sacred, red is the colour of love and also of violence. Red is *passio, in sensu bono* and *in sensu malo*. Unfortunately for the Narrator, by employing the roses for hate as well as for love and by juxtaposing them to Kristina, she risks contamination. She risks that the roses, sucking life from Kristina, will be assimilated to her in place of the Narrator. In her diseased mind, the Narrator is convinced that all the roses die except some of those planted over the corpse, and that these, in their pattern of growth, sketch the form of Kristina's body, that they give off light, and that those at her head have been metamorphosed from red to blue. Blue is the colour of the drink, 'Blue Lagoon,' which the husband drank at a hotel in Guérande with his wife, and presumably with Kristina more recently. The wife therefore poisons the girl with the same drink. Blue is the colour of the sea, on which the husband sailed, perhaps with Kristina, to escape his wife, and of the sea around the Blessed Isles, where he now presumably dwells with her. Above all, blue is the colour of two violets, simple blooms picked on the road (in antithesis to the wife's ostentatious garden flowers) that the husband pressed in his wallet as a memory of the pretty young girl, whose eyes are blue and not like the Narrator's (cf. Denez's title). That the red roses turn blue means that they have become Kristina, they live for Kristina and denounce her murder just as the violets unwittingly reveal her love affair. The blue flowers exalt good love in nature, free from human manipulation. They share the husband's intimacy and the girl's beauty. They also escape the web. Just as, traditionally, red it the colour of love and of violence, blue is the

colour of purity and of fidelity. By slaying Kristina, the Narrator gave the
separated lovers a chance to be joined, faithfully, in the afterlife, on an
island surrounded by the blue sea. Therefore, she also swallows the blue
potion, fraudulently so to speak, adopting the colour blue – the colour
of Kristina's eyes and not hers – to reclaim her husband.

The husband had been planning a novel. Putting off the project
again and again, he never wrote it. Perhaps he was too mediocre a fellow
to be capable of artistic creation. Perhaps being trapped in the Narrator's web sucked the juices of creativity from his system. Perhaps loving
Kristina (and others prior to Kristina?) kept him too occupied to devote
himself to aesthetics. The Narrator, on the other hand, is neither mediocre nor occupied. Utterly without pretensions or a project, she recounts
her story, which, because it constitutes Denez's novel, is a work of art. As
in the romantic tradition, we find a bond between artistic creativity and
both illness and moral evil.

More important, perhaps, than the theme of art itself is the functioning of intertextuality. The Narrator, the bourgeoise, the pharmacist's
wife, displays her bits and pieces of bourgeois culture. She thinks of herself as an anglophile. She collects Chippendale furniture. She quotes a
line – a cliché – from Burns. She alludes to the Loch Ness monster, to
Irish folk-songs, and to Tristan Corbière. At the very end the Narrator
identifies with the medieval Tristan's Isolt and swallows the poison,
choosing, like Isolt, to die with her lover Tristan. Yet the Narrator rein-
scribes the Tristan and Isolt story; she gets it wrong. She identifies with
'black-haired' Isolt, the Queen of Cornwall, Tristan's beloved. Given her
relatively limited cultural baggage, she is not aware that the Queen of
Cornwall was known as Isolt the Blond or Isolt of Ireland. A dark-haired
Isolt, if she ever existed, would have to be the second Isolt, Isolt of the
White Hands, daughter of King Hoel of Brittany, Tristan's wife, whom
he never loved.

To the extent that the myth can be construed as objective correlative
or *mise en abyme* of the triangle in Denez's novel, blue-eyed Kristina functions as Isolt the Blond, the beloved mistress, and the Breton Narrator
functions as Isolt of Brittany, the second Isolt, the neglected wife, frustrated by Tristan's failure to respond to her, and who was responsible for
Tristan's death. The second Isolt was, in a sense, a murderess and pathological neurotic, as is the wife-Narrator. Denez's novel ends on this final,
ironic, cultural demystification of the wife. Were there to be a Celtic
Otherworld, were the husband to dwell there as Tristan and Kristina as
his mistress, the Narrator, upon arriving, would discover that she was the

wrong Isolt. She would discover that, in the Otherworld and in the realm of myth, she is as much the outsider, the unwanted, undesired third in the triangle, as in her twentieth-century earthly existence. And she would discover that, just as Isolt of Brittany's spinning never brought Tristan home to be a real husband, so the Narrator's web fails to hold the husband and the mistress – in this world, in another world, and in the novel.

Diougan Gwenc'hlan (Gwenc'hlan's Prophecy) tells the story of an elderly toy-maker in Birmingham who discovers that his workshop is haunted by the ghost of an ancestor who hanged himself in 1713.[45] The toy-maker then, in some manner, becomes his ancestor or is possessed by him, with the result that he also commits suicide.

Although John Augustus John Williams, the kind, simple, victimized protagonist of this novel, scarcely resembles the demonic wife in the preceding tale, the two works do bear striking resemblance in structure and theme. Both texts are homodiegetic I-narratives in which the protagonist slowly but surely learns about himself and others, this learning process leading to disaster. And, in spite of the learning, the protagonist retains relative blindness to the end, whereas the implied reader is enabled to understand and to pass judgment on a level never open to the narrator.

Somewhat like the wife in *Glas evel daoulagad c'hlas*, Denez's toy-maker inhabits a realm of domestic order which he himself has created according to his conscious will, in order to grant him security and happiness. In this respect he is a *pantouflard*, the comic petty-bourgeois analogue to the more tragic wife with her web of habit and collection. John Williams's equivalent of the web is concretized in his collection of clocks, which he winds at the same hour every morning, and his habit of reading in bed at night, at always the same hour, about history in general and the family genealogy in particular. The *pantouflard* behaviour is a family affair. While John Williams reads at night in bed, his wife knits. She is as much a creature of habit as he, for she always knits the same thing – sweaters for him, always in the same size and colour, whether they actually fit him or not.

The implied reader can observe from John's testimony that the man is obsessed with time. The clocks, the genealogical research, the habit and routine all betray the narrator's desire to control the passage of time, both the past time of his forebears and the present duration in which he dwells. A comparable sense of routine and of defence emanates from the man's spatial nexus. Wilfully, as if against the spirit of the present age, John lives in the same house and makes his living in the same workshop as the John Williams people have done since the beginning of the eighteenth century. To do so requires more than a little sacrifice on his part. Since coach-making, the family trade, is now obsolete, the man continues as best he can, by the manufacture of toy cars and trucks in wood. This quest for order and for security – the security of a petty-bourgeois nest impervious to the ravages of time – is symbolized by Mrs John Williams's insistence on the installation of a security system for the workshop. Intruders will be prevented by such a system from disturbing the routine of the nest.

However, the toy-maker's workshop proves to be no less impervious to change than the wife's rose garden in the preceding novel. The irrational, the mysterious, and the uncanny break into John Williams's world as they broke into the domain of the pharmacist. Here, the irrational assumes the guise of a recurring phenomenon that cannot be accounted for by the usual common-sense explanations. On the second Tuesday of each month the alarm is set off in the workshop. The police, security engineers, watchdogs, and the neighbours – these guardians of the community and representatives of order – stand helpless. They cannot account for the phenomenon, nor can they prevent it. On the contrary, it is their finest technology – the alarm system – that proclaims the anomaly without determining the secret or explaining its origin. The failure of the 'community' and of modern technology to explain the anomaly leads to fierce, irrational responses. Hence two engineers responsible for the security commit suicide; hence the neighbour and the neighbor's children develop epilepsy.

John Williams, obsessed with the family genealogy and with collecting and perusing historical documents, proves to be the only person able to fathom the mystery. Ironically, he who really doesn't care about alarms and alarm noises discovers the truth – an irrational, emotive, fantastic truth – indirectly, in the course of his private research. Fascinated by a missing link in the genealogical chain, he concentrates all his energy on a namesake, another John Augustus John Williams, who was the first in the family to quit Wales for Birmingham, where he founded the family coach-making trade. The toy-maker reverses his ancestor's trek; he travels from Birmingham to Wales, the Celtic source, from which he brings back photographs of parish registers and other documents. From these he discovers that, in 1713, the distant forebear hanged himself in the Birmingham workshop and therefore was not buried in hallowed ground. And he deduces that the disturbances in the alarm system must be caused by the suicide's ghost, his unhappy spirit imprisoned inside the workshop where his body was slain.

Also, as a result of his research, the toy-maker is enabled to account for anomalies in his space, details which otherwise defy explanation. These include the hook in the main beam over the entryway to the workshop (the hook from which the ancestor hanged himself) and, in a more humorous register, two ravens, birds of ill repute, who 'haunt' the man's garden and ultimately perch on his window-ledge. These also are features of the irrational that intrude into the otherwise calm, account-able life of the toy-maker, images from the past and traces of absence from a different world.

John Williams also seemingly finds a way to appease the ghost, suc-ceeding where the men of science and the law failed. He appeals to a Father O'Flaherty, who accompanies him to the shop and, on the sec-ond Tuesday of May, exorcises the ancestor. The exorcism works, to the extent that the alarm is no longer set off and the dog ceases to howl.

Although the ghost stops haunting John Williams's workshop, the man finds his life invaded by other inexplicable phenomena. In June he comes to the realization, when he and his wife are lying in bed, she knit-ting and he reading, that the click of her knitting needles registers his own heartbeat, and therefore the passage of his life. The toy-maker also discovers that he loses consciousness when the wife pauses in her knit-ting at the end of a row. Then, at the end of the summer, the wife inex-plicably knits smaller and smaller sweaters. With fewer stitches per row, she pauses more often, and the husband's heart ceases to beat corre-spondingly more often. As if this were not enough, during the same period the toy-maker's clocks, one by one, stop ticking, breaking down one after the other.

Faced with these symbols or premonitions of doom, John Williams responds in the same way he responded to the spectral phenomenon in the workshop. He refuses to worry about the problem, to excite his imagination as he says, and instead focuses his energy on genealogical studies, especially the life of the old John Williams who committed suicide:

Ne felle ket mui din, da noz, selaou ouzh ma c'halon o lammat: ne rafe kement-se nemet isañ ma faltazi en un doare sot. [...] Koulz din soñjal, n'eo ket ennon, met e John Augustus John – egile, anat eo. (p. 120)
(I did not want to listen any more to my heart beat at night: all that would

do nothing other than to excite my imagination in a crazy way. [...] Obviously, it was just as good for me to think about John Augustus John, the other, not myself.)

Yet by refusing to speculate on the present, be it spectral or not, and by concentrating with all his will on the Other, the other John Williams, does not the toy-maker in fact indulge in the greatest flights of the imagination? And by focusing on the historically verifiable, does he not fall into extremes of fantasy? In the course of time, as his own duration purportedly slows down, the toy-maker studies his ancestor – a man with the same name who dwelt in the same home – with such intensity that he senses he is becoming the old John Williams. From time to time, when half asleep, he reaches for his nightcap. Later, he actually feels the lace of a nightgown on his chest. These acts of sympathetic identification occur to the old man at night, in bed – the time of dreams, the body, the irrational, and the feminine, ascribed in popular imagination to the Celtic peoples. Also, for Per Denez, the Celtic peoples mean Celtic speech. No less significantly, therefore, the modern John Williams comes to understand the sermons delivered in his Welsh chapel and actually speaks an archaic form of Welsh.

Whatever the reality of his condition, at a point in the narrative the narrating toy-maker ceases to resist what he now recognizes as destiny. With a sense of resignation, John Williams accepts the silence of his clocks and of his wife's knitting implements. He who was obsessed by fixed time and order accepts the end of ordered time: 'Ne oan na chalet na spontet gant un amzer he doa paouezet evidon da redek, gant un amzer a oa chomet, war-bouez nebeut, a-sav, e didrouz ma horolajoù' (p. 131) (I was neither worried nor frightened by time which had ceased flowing for me, by time which had stopped, or nearly so, in the silence of my clocks). So he consents to die, at the same age as his Other, at the same time of the year as the Other, to commit suicide like the Other, employing the same rope on the same beam as the Other did.

John Williams the toy-maker is Welsh, as was his ancestor. He attends the Welsh chapel, is fascinated by Welsh local history, he learns (somehow) to speak and understand Welsh, and (a touch of delightful humour) he feeds the ravens Welsh cheese. Is his destiny specially, uniquely, symbolically Celtic and, in some sense, a commentary on the destiny of the Celtic people? Whether in a serious or a comic register, the answer would have to be yes, given the Celtic motifs scattered throughout and given the title of Per Denez's text. *Diougan Gwenc'hlan* refers directly to one of the most important poems in the *Barzaz Breiz* (itself a monument to Breton culture), also entitled 'Diougan Gwenc'hlan.' Roparz Hemon's 'arrangement' of this text was published in the 1969 *Al Liamm*, pages 183–5; the 'Diougan Gwenc'hlan' also formed the subject of one of Professor Per Denez's courses at the University of Rennes.[46] Hersart de la Villemarqué helped promulgate the notion that the original author of the poem was Gwenc'hlan, a purported Breton bard from the fifth century, who would have preceded Taliesin, Aneirin, and the other bards of Britain. Gwenc'hlan therefore radiates an aura in Breton culture as a mythical figure of the bard and the first one of whom we have a trace. His 'Prophecy' would have been the execration of a foreign prince who had blinded and imprisoned him. One couplet in particular – 'Red eo d'ann holl mervel teir gwes, / Kent evid arzao enn-divez' (All must die three times before they shall find rest) (p. 20) – alludes to the theme of metempsychosis in early Welsh myth. Denez takes the motif intertextually and elaborates it in his tale, where the sixty-four-year-old Welshman commits suicide as did his sixty-four-year-old Welsh ancestor. Has the early John Williams been reborn in his modern-day descendant? Or has his ghost seized the toy-maker's body after the exorcism, which could appease the ghost only a little? Is the exorcism, then, a second death and John Williams's suicide the third death, which will permit this Celtic Ur-phantom to rest once and for all? Should the suicides of the engineers figure also in the reckoning? Or is the analogy simply a manifestation of authorial fantasy, a fantastic intertextual connection which could have and perhaps did occur to the half-mad toy-maker, and which tells more about his mental state than about empirical reality? If, of course, there is empirical reality in his life? It is for the implied reader to answer, for, in this novel as in the novel *Glas evel daoulagad c'hlas*, readers have the right to interpret the tale according to their own wishes, norms, and beliefs, a tale told by an unreliable and possibly insane implied narrator. Something approaching the technique of *nouveau roman* and of magical realism is shown to be the most appropriate means of narrating Celtic reality and Celtic destiny, which begin with the mythical Gwenc'hlan, attain one summit in the *Barzaz Breiz*, and end or become present with the fictional toy-maker and the pharmacist's wife, in a universe of horror and the absurd, of the cruel and the fantastic, of the mad and the magnificently creative.

THEATRE

PER JAKEZ HELIAS

The theatre has always been a force in Brittany. Mystery plays, mostly adapted from the French, and other forms of popular theatre dominate the early written corpus of literature in Breton and are to be found in hundreds of manuscripts from the sixteenth to the nineteenth centuries. The dramatist Tanguy Malmanche was the leading writer of the pre-*Gwalarn* epoch. Radio drama thrived from the 1940s, and television drama from the 1980s. Various student and local companies also thrived in the wake of 1968. Roparz Hemon wrote some eighteen brief plays, and Jarl Priel another seventeen, many of Priel's being adaptations of prior work in French. However, the most brilliant and the most successful dramatist, in my opinion, is Per Jakez Helias, best known for his 'testimony' *Le Cheval d'orgueil.*[47]

With the publication of *Le Cheval d'orgueil*, Helias became world famous. Partaking of and helping to launch the 1970s current in France of ethnology and local history, of the commemoration of and a return to the peasant roots of society, Helias's books, which combine autobiography, witness, ethnography, storytelling, and folklore, sold, including foreign translations, millions of copies. He became a media figure, 'le Breton,' better known to the average cultured person than any other figure who appears in this book, with the exception only of MacDiarmid in his old age.

This vast, French, educated, bourgeois public is not aware that Helias is also a major creative writer in the Breton language, with a corpus sufficiently vast and varied to call for comparison with Roparz Hemon's. *A-berz eur bed all* (From an Other World), published in 1991, consists of collections of verse dating back to 1955. Famous himself as a public *conteur*, Helias published, in the periodicals and in book form, a vast number of tales and newspaper articles. *Le Cheval d'orgueil* appeared also in Breton in 1986 as *Marh al lorh.*[48]

Helias's favorite genre and first love has always been the theatre, in part because of his conviction that Breton reality is primarily oral and that one can capture it only in the form of spoken drama.[49] After a career in the wake of the Resistance (he was on the other side from Hemon, hence one explanation for his failure to acknowledge the greatness of the Skol Walarn), Helias was put in charge of a weekly program

in Breton on Radio-Kimerc'h (1946). With the assistance of Pierre Tré-
pos, he created hundreds of sketches and dialogues, the most important
being the never-ending give-and-take between two stock characters,
Jakez Kroc'hen and Gwilhou Vihan. In 1948 he cofounded Les Grandes
Fêtes de Cornouaille, which was then and remains one of the major
summer festivals of Breton folklore. And, for festival dramatic performances as for radio and television, Helias contributed his own one-act
and full-length plays, usually first in a French version. Subsequently, he
published the same plays in Breton. It would appear, according to
Favereau, that Helias composed a kernel in Breton, wrote up the script
in French, and then later returned to the kernel and the French text, to
write up the expanded, final Breton version.[50]

Helias's best-known drama and the one performed the most – since
1958 in French, since 1959 in Breton – is a finely crafted demystification
of rural life: *Mevel ar Gosker* (The Top Hand of Kosker Farm).[51] The
Kosker Farm is owned by rich old Yann Konan and managed and run by
the *mevel bras* (Fr. *grand valet*) Jakez Mazo. Yann has two daughters, God
and Maria. Two young men, Loeiz and Lan, both court Maria; Jakez also
cares for Maria, and God is in love with Loeiz. God convinces Lan and
Maria to elope to Quimper. As she sees it, her father will then have no
choice but to have Loeiz wed her. However, Jakez arranges for Loeiz to
overhear all this. In a fit of dementia, Loeiz shoots Lan. With both suit-
ors out of the way and the family the talk of the region, Jakez steps in.
He will be the new *mestr* (master/owner). It is agreed that he marry
God, and Maria will leave for the city.

It is understandable that Helias, who, in his autobiographical and eth-
nological writings, paid witness to and celebrated the dying rural culture of his native Bigouden country, should, in most of his plays, record
that same rural life in the process of extinction.[52] *Marh al lorh* speaks of
the old-style marriages decided by rank, social status, and the possession
or absence of land and money. It also evokes the passing of the institution of the *mevel*. The *mevel bras* is the most important of the farm workers. A manager and overseer, he is responsible for running the farm,
and it is assumed he will also be the strongest, most active worker. Traditionally, these men, who, at festival time, competed in their own sport-
ing events, were highly sought after. A farm would prosper or decline as
determined by the *mevel*, and the *mestr* would be praised or blamed concerning his choice of *mevel*. The *mevel* could enjoy any number of privileges, as Jakez does in the play – a contract of many years' duration, the

right to live in the farmhouse with the *mestr* and his family, and the respect and affection of the family. However, because he comes from a lower class and a lineage in that lower class and because he is not a land-owner, the *mevel*, like Jakez in the play, cannot even dream of marrying into the family. In the old Brittany what Jakez finally succeeds in doing – marrying God – is not only impossible, it is literally inconceivable. That Jakez conceives it and brings his conception to fruition provides evidence that the old Brittany is dying.

One problem posed by this fascinating play is generic: To which genre heading should it be assigned? It has been said that *Mevel ar Gosker* is a tragedy, one of a number of tragedies in Helias's repertory. It is true, one man is slain, another goes mad, and the old world is destroyed. *Mevel ar Gosker* is a serious drama; the spectators do not laugh. Yet, at the same time, the dramatic structure recalls the Roman New Comedy and its French inheritors, from Molière on. The title-figure of the play, the protagonist, is Jakez Mazo, and in the end he triumphs, winning the farm and a wife of the landholding class. In archetypal terms Yann and his neighbour, Loeiz's father, embody the order of old men who impose their will on the young – expecting to marry Maria to Loeiz, to force God to become an old maid, and to exclude Jakez from everything. They are the blocking figures. Opposed to them stand the young – Maria, God, Jakez, even Lan – who have their own lives to lead and their own desires to fulfil. Jakez's victory is the victory of the young over the old and, in part, of a more natural human condition over the rigidity of paternal law grounded in money and land. As comic archetypal functions, Yann plays the *senex iratus* and also the *agroikos*, a role he shares with poor Loeiz. Jakez plays the *dolosus servus* and the *eiron*; the latter function he shares with Maria and God. Helias has the tricky servant work on his own behalf, not that of another, Loeiz or Lan; the servant becomes the hero, a democratization of Roman comedy which goes back to Beaumarchais. More original and more democratic still, the women are not uniquely objects of desire. They themselves manifest desire, intellect, and subjectivity, and offer their own version of the events. Finally, the absurd rural world of Plautus or Molière, a laughable anomaly external to the action, becomes the central décor and is to be taken with high seriousness. In actantial terms, Jakez is not adjuvant to Lan or Loeiz, as he pretends, but the subject actant himself, and he will defy his opposants – Yann and, in her way, God.

Jakez the servant, who appears to work for Loeiz or Lan, for that matter Maria or God, works for himself. He neutralizes God's act of manipu-

lation by a series of feats of manipulation. Indeed, this *dolosus servus* is a
magnificent winner in the game he plays. He dons a mask and disguises
himself as the benevolent, neutral confidant of others. Others confide
in him and seek his advice. He then manipulates them (Loeiz, Lan,
God) into doing what he wants, not what they want, and what is in his
best interest, not theirs. Like McLellan's Jamie the Saxt, this manipulator and deceiver shows himself to be the trickster hero *par excellence*, a
man of deep intelligence and sharp wit, who turns the sharp God as
readily as the dull Loeiz. Accordingly, his role more than the others'
functions to underscore the play between illusion and reality. For what
to others is reality Jakez proves to be (or makes) illusion, and vice versa.
The trickster hero, by his power of will, employs illusion to mask reality
and himself transforms reality into illusion, determining what will be
real and what not. Because he is a winner, the others are compelled to
accept his version of reality.

Jakez Mazo – or rather Per Jakez Helias the dramatist acting through
him – works in much the same way on the implied audience. The audience hears only the dialogues between the sundry characters, including
those by which Jakez manipulates the others. The audience presumably
is not and cannot be aware of the story (*fable*). It will know the plot (*histoire*) only as it unfolds. More than a little suspense is created as the audience wonders what is going to happen and how the plot will end, but also,
once the audience discovers Jakez's role as trickster and manipulator,
what the *mevel* is doing and why he does it. The suspense concerns why
Jakez aids Lan, Loeiz, and God (self-contradictory, self-defeating acts in
themselves), and who will marry whom in the end and for what reasons.
Jakez's motivation – the man is masterly, cool under fire, and never
reveals one word more than he needs to – is a mystery solved only in the
final scene. It is only in the course of the play that the implied audience
and the other characters – the audience before the characters – discover
what a powerful man Jakez is.

Jakez's capacity for power and his successful wielding of power before
he is granted it legally are the discovery (anagnorisis, in classical terminology) that the characters and the audience make, and they determine
the drama's outcome. Jakez shows himself to be a master of people and
events, and thus worthy of being the *mestr* of Kosker Farm. The family
members accept this fact when they yield to his will – he will take over
the farm and wed one of the daughters – and when, in the last line of
the play, the most independent character other than Jakez himself,
Maria, who repudiates the land and all it stands for, responds to one of

his decisions, 'Ya, mestr' (Yes, master). Jakez is truly the master in a Hegelian sense. He, the former servant, not only asserts hegemony over the others, formerly his betters, now his inferiors (slaves in the Hegel-Sartre frame of reference). He does so because they recognize him as the master and consciously submit to him.

The submission does not occur until after a long ideological struggle. Jakez's adversary, on the most overt level, is the old master Yann, seconded, of course, by his friend and neighbour Ban. Yann embodies the closed world of the older generation and the old Brittany, actually those who got rich purchasing cheap lands under the Revolution. He lives and breathes a structure where marriage and everything else are shaped by considerations of money, land, rank, reputation, and honour. The strictly economic forces – wealth, with land commodified as a measure of wealth – are important, yet rank and reputation even more so. This is the shame culture Helias evokes so brilliantly in *Marh al lorh*, in which shame – *ar vezh* – is the determining taboo force in a society obsessed by what other people will think and what they will say. The antidote to shame is honour or pride, doing one's duty; honour under these conditions, however, means adherence to the community values of money and rank. Even God assumes that, whatever Jakez's virtues, he is not good enough to marry into the Konan family and that, were such a misalliance to occur, the family would lose status in the eyes of others and thus be dishonoured. Jakez, therefore, has to overcome the pride of the old men, shared by the community. He has to break open their closed world, symbolized, in a sense, by the constraints of the classical French drama that Helias adapts so well to *Mevel ar Gosker*. Old Yann has made up his mind to marry off Maria to Loeiz. The others, therefore, have to act immediately, for within only a few hours the patriarch will have worked his will, and it will be irreversible. Thus unity of time. Only one entity matters to the old man. This is the Kosker Farm, over which he has total hegemony. The farmhouse, therefore constitutes unity of place and action.

To disempower the *mestr*, the *mevel* has to dishonour the family and, consequently, make it impossible for either God or Maria to marry anyone but him. He treats the two young women as objects, counters on the game board, playing them as he plays everyone else. However, unlike the pitiful male figures in their entourage, these women are magnificent, powerful entities, capable of suffering (hence the tragic element) and of duelling with Jakez, creatures of will and ruse just as he is. God is furious that Maria has all the men at her feet. God not only feels humiliated in her libido. She also is a person of honour and shame in an honour and shame culture. She knows that, an old maid, she will live out the rest of her existence as an unpaid servant in Maria's or the father's home and as the object of condescending pity:

> GOD: Med kentoh e chomin da blah-yaouank-koz. Mond a rin da zerhel an traou e ti ma zad, er vourh, p'e-no dispeget diouz ar Gosker. Me a zeuio da veza an devodez treud, fonnuz he leve, ha n'eo mad nemed da zerhel bleu-niou war aoter ar Werhez, beteg kemer c'hwez an ezañs ha liou ar hoar [...] Ma flanedenn a zo da veza matez an oll, en ti-mañ. Gwasoh eged eur vatez, peogwir e vo dizoñjet zoken rei din ma gopr. (p. 37)
> (But I would rather stay an old maid. I will become my father's house-keeper at his place, in the village, when he gives up Kosker Farm. I will become a skinny churchhopper, with an abundant income, good only to keep putting flowers on the altar of the Virgin, until I take on the smell of incense and the colour of candle wax. My fate is to be the maidservant of all of them in this house. Worse than a maidservant, because they will even forget to pay my wages.)

God dreads loneliness. As for Maria, she would like a bit of it, for she is sick of the men. She seeks freedom, the freedom not to be a farm wife, the possibility of attempting another life in town:

> MARIA: [...] eo gand aon rag ar c'hoant d'en em zistruja. Ma unan-kaer ez an kuit ahann, ya, abalamour ma 'z on heuget gand ar vuhez a vevan, netra ken. Heuget ivez gand ar re a vev endro din. (p. 64)
> (... it is that I am afraid of wanting to destroy myself. Yes, I am going away from here alone, by myself, because I am disgusted by the life I lead, noth-ing else. Also disgusted by the people who live around me.)

After Loeiz kills Lan, she returns to Kosker for one reason – to sate her thirst for authenticity, so that everyone (specifically, God and Jakez) finally admit his or her truth and say it aloud.

Each of the daughters demystifies in turn the values of the patriarchal rural society embodied in Yann. The young women rebel against the world of law imposed by older men. And Jakez? In the end we realize, as Jakez did from the beginning, that in this world love destroys. God loves Loeiz who loves Maria who loves Lan (or her freedom). The classical Racinian chain of love leads to disaster. Although Jakez thought he loved Maria, he accepts marriage to God, because God will make a superb farm wife and because Maria hates the farm. In the end, we realize that he has acted all along not for a woman but for the land. Jakez loves the land. He is the actant subject, and his object is the integrity and survival of Kosker Farm. The donor is not love but empowerment. The land takes precedence over rank, reputation, and personal convenience. And, for that reason, perhaps *Mevel ar Gosker* is a tragedy after all. The *mevel*, who shares the title with *Kosker*, is a man. He becomes a master and a patriarch, more enlightened than Yann, yet master and patriarch nonetheless. In his lifetime the farm will survive, and so will its ways. The play ends, as comedies do, with an imminent wedding and, as tragedies do, with the acknowledgment of a new master, all passion spent: 'Ya, mestr.'

In my opinion, Helias's most powerful play is *Katrina Lenn-Zu* (Katrina of the Black Pond / Katrina of Black Pond Farm), performed for the first time in French in 1965 by Le Centre Dramatique National de l'Ouest (and as recently as 1992), performed later in Breton by the Strollad teatr Penn-ar-Bed, and published in 1994.[53] Katrina Lenn Zu, a beautiful widow and the mistress of Lenn Zu Farm, disappeared in 1945, presumably having committed suicide, leaving three sons. In 1950, the time of the plot, a young woman, Katrina Mezmeur, comes to replace Melani, the housekeeper who has quit. It turns out that the three sons constructed a doll or mannequin of straw and rags (hence the play's French title *La Femme de paille*) which they keep installed, as Katrina Lenn Zu, in her bedroom, treated as a taboo sacred space, and which they bring down once a year, on Katrina's saint's day, to speak to and honour. Katrina Mezmeur is accepted into the family and becomes far more than a cook and maid, for the three sons treat her as a reincarnation of their mother or, literally, as their mother and grant her authority in the home.

This is Act I. The remaining acts resolve a number of questions, concerning both plot and motivation. In this superbly crafted play, on one level a whodunit with Katrina Mezmeur the detective, Katrina herself and the implied audience discover that Katrina Lenn Zu had a lover, Commandant Meriadeg in the Resistance, that he was the father of Mikael the youngest son, that he was murdered, that old Katrina committed suicide by drowning in the Black Pond because of the murder, and, finally, that it was the second son, Visant La Marine, who killed Meriadeg. Among other questions asked are why old Katrina committed suicide: because her lover was killed? because only with the murder did she realize how vile and neurotic her sons (and Meriadeg) were, fighting over her like a commodity? as a gift, to release her sons from their bondage to her? or in despair, because Meriadeg allowed himself to be killed in order to escape his bondage to her? Still further mystery is elucidated as to who the young Katrina is and whether she will be killed in turn. We discover that she also fought in the Resistance, loved Meriadeg without return, and has come to Lenn Zu to find out the truth.

As with a good mystery story, in the end truth wins out over the unknown, and reality stands free from illusion. Also, in the end, accounts are rendered. Louis, the oldest brother, will marry Melani; together they will manage the farm and get on with their lives. Mikael, aware now who his real father was and how he died, leaves the farm for good. However, this mystery story partakes of the archetypes of tragedy not comedy. Mikael is free yet will probably wander the earth as Orestes did, tormented by his furies. Visant La Marine commits suicide by hanging, and, once all is known and all illusions are lost, young Katrina goes off to drown herself at the same spot in the Black Pond that old Katrina did, five years before.

Young Katrina is the investigator who discovers and makes us discover the solution to the mysteries of Lenn Zu. She also acts, within the household, as a teacher and a therapist. It is Katrina who persuades Louis to wed Melani; they will become a good farm couple and restore normal life to Lenn Zu. She brings Visant La Marine, the second son, to avow the murder he committed five years previously and to take responsibility for it. As for the youngest son, he had been known only as An hini Bihan (the Little One). Katrina is the first to call him by his name, Mikael, which was his father's name. Because of Katrina, he learns his name and his identity. Because of her, he arrives at adulthood and at a measure of legitimacy and, because he 'assumes' the memory of the Lenn Zu horror, is capable of breaking out, leaving the farm and living his life elsewhere. Katrina offers these people a message of freedom and the acceptance of reality, as opposed to slavery and illusion. From her they learn to think in the present and the future instead of the past. Uniquely owing to Katrina, the mannequin will be burned and the musty old taboo rooms of Lenn Zu opened up to let in the air. Above all, Katrina Mezmeur communicates with these people and persuades them to communicate with each other. The first walls to be broken down are the walls of their own psyches, isolating them each from the others as in Racine. Katrina's greatest feat in this line is opening up the crazy servant, Toussaint, who has not spoken a word since old Katrina's disappearance. Upon his beholding young Katrina his speech is restored, and, from beginning to end, he acts as a sort of Greek chorus, uttering discourse which is both mysterious and fraught with wisdom. It is more than a little uncanny how Katrina restores speech to Toussaint, and for that matter how she persuades the three brothers to accept her into the home and to substitute her for old Katrina, seating her in old Katrina's chair. Katrina Mezmeur resembles in more than one respect the fay of Celtic myth. Indeed, she can be considered a good fay, in contrast to her namesake, Katrina Lenn Zu, who imprisoned four men in her web, turning the farm into an Otherworld and maintaining the web from beyond the grave.

The quality of a mystery to be solved (the whodunit) and young Katrina's quality of detective, teacher, therapist, and fay in no way diminish the melodramatic or *guignol* structure of the plot and its ambience of passion, hatred, and jealousy, of violence, baroque horror, and family slaughter. Helias indulges in a relentless demystification of any and all platitudes associated with traditional rural life in Brittany. As in *Mevel ar Gosker, Lenn-Zu* portrays a doomed world and, more so than with the earlier play, the world of Lenn Zu is justly doomed.

Lenn Zu is, first of all, a locus of neurosis. The three sons fought over the love of their mother, the old Katrina. With the arrival of the new Katrina, they fight over her. This erotic sibling rivalry is performed in the name and on behalf of the dead father(s). Louis and Visant humiliate Mikael, denying him his name and calling him An hini Bihan. In a sense, they proclaim his bastard origins, his illegitimacy, in their eyes, in the family. This deprivation of name, stature, and status is a phallic assault, meant to castrate or render impotent (metaphorically) the son who had won their mother's regard. Similarly, Louis and Visant try to kill Katrina Mezmeur because she caresses Mikael in the same way Katrina Lenn Zu did; and Visant did kill Commandant Meriadeg after having observed the primal scene – Meriadeg with the mother in her bedroom. None of these phallic acts grants to the sons mastery or potency, however. All three were enslaved to old Katrina during her lifetime and after her death, and to the new Katrina, who replaces the old one. None seems to have led anything like what we would call a normal sex life, or for that matter to have had any contact with a woman other than the unavowed and totally frustrating adoration of a distant living mother *imago* and even more distant dead one. The regression to the oedipal stage is utterly destructive in these grown men, who remain, in psychic terms, pre-adolescent children who give life and libido to a cas-

trating superego – the doll – as dead as the mother and her lover are or
ever will be.

From oedipal neurosis these characters move swiftly to psychosis (one
murder, one attempted murder, and two suicides) and to insanity. To
keep a mannequin of straw and rags in Katrina Lenn Zu's room and to
bring it down and talk to it once a year is madness. With a superb innate
sense of criminal psychosis and of living theatre, Helias reveals to his
audience that the three brothers are half aware that the doll is only a
symbol, and half certain that it is the genuine mother still alive in their
home. Similarly, they are half aware that Katrina Mezmeur is the new
servant and a woman of brains and charm, and half given to the belief
that she is the old Katrina come home from her wanderings. Visant the
murderer is the most deranged of the three, no doubt because of
remorse for the murder he alone perpetrated, and he alone fantasizes
that old Katrina, young Katrina, and the doll are one and the same living person.

The central image – the arch-image – of the play is the straw and rags
mannequin. Without any semblance of life, it stands as a concrete metaphor for the impotence and living death that the three oedipal sons
have made of their lives and the lives of others. It is also a metaphor for
Katrina Lenn Zu and the non-life she led. Never having left her two
rooms and never having spoken to her sons, she also, in a sense, lived as
a lifeless mannequin or as a child in a child's dollhouse – hence the
appropriateness of the doll as her totem. We see her maleficent influence over the others in that the two rooms are compared to the centre
of a spider's web –

> KATRINA: Med an diou gambr-se oa kalon al Lenn Zu. El Lenn Zu, an dud
> koulz hag an traou a rede etrezeg an diou gambr-se e-giz gwiad eur gev-
> nidenn. Eur gevnidenn gaer ha mad deuz a glever. Koulskoude eo marvet
> 'blamour 'n-oa gwiet re vrao he loñj. Red eo distruj 'nezañ. (p. 147)
> (But those two rooms were the heart of Lenn Zu. In Lenn Zu, people and
> things flowed out toward those two rooms like the web of a spider. A beau-
> tiful and a good spider, so it appears. Still, she died because she weaved too
> fine a web. The flow has to be broken.)

– and to a cage, both of which imprison Katrina and her lover. From Act
I to Act III the décor of the play shifts from the main room downstairs to
Katrina's anteroom upstairs to her bedroom itself, from the outer fila-
ments to the centre of the web. The spider kills, especially the black

widow spider, this motionless and seemingly ageless, good, beautiful mistress of the Black Pond. In such a universe, Eros and Thanatos are constantly joined. Black is the colour of melancholia and black bile, the humour assimilated in the Middle Ages to lovers and poets (born under the sign of Saturn) and to the Celtic peoples. Following the tradition of suicide in rural Brittany evoked by Helias in *Marh al lorh,* Visant the male hangs himself, and the two Katrinas drown themselves. The two fays – the evil and the good – leave this world for the other (if there is another), at the same place and, presumably, in the same mood of despair. Events in the past hold primacy over a weak, helpless present, subject to the past and incapable of revising or reliving it. Celtic fatality and Celtic doom arrive at their ultimate tragic close, and the last voice in the tragedy is that of Toussaint, the madman granted speech by young Katrina, he who – in his insanity and in his function as the chorus – sees all yet is helpless to influence events. He can only bear witness and weep over the fatality and the doom.

In addition to dramas of rural Brittany, Helias has written a number of plays concerned with the past (as did the dramatists of Scotland), poetic visions for today of Breton history and legend. The two most innovative efforts in this line – *Le Jeu de Gradlon* and the supremely brilliant *Le roi Kado* – apparently exist only in the French. No complete Breton version has been found up to now. However, we do have a Breton version of the Tristan and Isolt story, the splendid tragedy *An Isild a-heul* (The Second Isolt).[54] This play was heard first on French radio in 1965 and since then has been performed in both tongues.

Helias takes the medieval *Roman de Tristan* and rewrites it from the Breton perspective. His play treats only those later episodes in the romance concerning Tristan's arrival in Brittany, his marriage to Isolt of the White Hands, daughter to King Hoel, his departure for the British Cornwall to see once again Isolt of Ireland, his return, illness, and death, the latter caused by Isolt of Brittany. Helias concentrates on the Breton Isolt, exploring the story from the loser's side, for she is the focus of action, and the plot revolves around her, not around Tristan nor Isolt of Ireland. She is the Second Isolt, literally the Isolt who follows or comes after ('a-heul'), the pale simulacrum of Isolt of Ireland, Tristan's archetypal mistress. Yet, as Guillemin-Young has observed, whereas the original romances portray Isolt of the White Hands as a frustrated virgin and cruel, vindictive murderess, Helias redeems her.[55] By redeeming the calumniated wife and the loser, Helias also redeems

Brittany and part of Breton cultural history. For, influenced by amateur Celtic enthusiasts such as Jean Markale, he embraces the myth whereby medieval French Arthurian romance, including the earliest Tristan romances by Beroul and Thomas, are in fact Celtic and Breton and were 'appropriated' by the French.

The intertextual weight of the medieval *Roman de Tristan* and Helias's endeavour to rework it are central to this play. As if to underscore the cultural importance of the intertext, the second Isolt, who is fascinated by the stranger from across the seas, learns his identity and his relationship to the first Isolt by questioning a Greek merchant expert in Greek eloquence. Then, in the Epilogue (Helias's equivalent of Act IV), she herself, who alone knows the entire story including her role in it, recognizes that she will be subjected to calumny after her death by people in the future who will assume she brought about Tristan's death out of jealousy. This metatextual allusion – a character in a myth referring to the various shapes the myth will take in future artistic re-creations of it, which calls attention to the myth as myth and as artistic re-creation – is endemic to modern theatre (one need think only of Giraudoux's *Electre* and *Amphitryon 38*). It is not endemic to minority theatre. Helias's successful exploitation of this device marks the spot and sets an example.

The majority of scholars who deal with medieval literature are of the opinion that the love portrayed in the Old French Tristan and Lancelot romances is *fin' amor*, the lyric *fin' amor* of the troubadours adapted to narrative – to flux in space and time. I agree with them. However, Helias, perhaps influenced by Celtic enthusiasts, envisages the Eros in his Tristan play as peculiarly Celtic and a Celtic cultural gift to the West. Tristan arrives in Brittany as a stranger who refuses to reveal his name or history. Different from the others and oblivious to them, he, who faints upon hearing the name of the beloved, 'Isild,' is obsessed with love, just as the others are obsessed with him. King Hoel recognizes that his ethos of war and martial honour, the old ethos of the old heroic class, will be shattered by the new tragic love that is passion. Similarly, Rozili, the wise bard, the counsellor, and Isolt of Brittany's tutor, a Merlin-figure of sorts – Helias introduces this supplementary character into the plot – also discovers the force of the new love. Rozili, like Tristan, is a poet and musician. Rozili loves Isolt as Isolt loves Tristan. Yet Rozili does not know passion. His love, deep and authentic, nonetheless cannot measure up to the metaphysical absoluteness in which live and breathe Tristan and the two Isolts. Just as Tristan surpasses Rozili in erotic terms, so also does he as an artist.

Eros is the unique source and guarantor of freedom, salvation, and the absolute. The second Isolt wills to partake of this unique essence, heretofore endured only by Tristan and the first Isolt. Whereas in the original romance by Thomas she weds Tristan out of love and filial obedience, and is presumed to be ignorant of his past, here the princess knows all about the lovers and marries Tristan because of what she knows. Whereas Tristan and Isolt of Ireland were forced into love by the philtre, Isolt of Brittany chooses to love. She declares more than once that, since she is a woman, she cannot go on quests or slay monsters:

ISILD: An dimezi a rin a vo ma zro-chañs din-me peogwir ma stad a vaouez a zivenn din ar marhekadennou, an enklaskou, an emgannou a ra ho puez deoh. An dro-chañs-se, felloud a ra din kas anezi evel ma plij din, ha pa rankfen mervel. (p. 36)
(My marriage will be my adventure, seeing that my condition as a woman rules out the horseback rides, quests, and battles which make up your life. This adventure, I want to undergo it by myself at my liking, even if I die for it.)

Her quest and her adventure will be love. She will marry Tristan because he alone is capable of absolute love, because he has demonstrated it with his supreme passion for another. She is totally lucid and never a dupe. She marries him in order to win him, to take him away from the first Isolt. She marries him as her quest for the absolute. Thus she responds to one of the prime demands of *fin' amor*, so comparable to love and glory in Corneille: the best love is granted only to those who are worthy of it, who are truly the best.

Isolt weds Tristan to partake of the adventure and to win him; Tristan weds Isolt to be cured. Helias explores all that is destructive and life-sapping in the new Eros. Tristan brings his obsession to Brittany. Because of him the Bretons lose their innocence and become riddled with *angst*, as he is. Tristan's misery, explained in Thomas's *Roman de Tristan* as longing for the absent Isolt of Ireland coupled with devouring physical jealousy of her life with King Mark, is granted perhaps a more profound, more metaphysical dimension by Helias. Helias's Tristan is the alienated hero *par excellence*, always a stranger, always the outsider. He is as torn between the two Isolts as he is between our world of mortals (King Hoel's court, King Mark's court) and the Otherworld, which he seeks in vain as a quest hero or which he seeks equally in vain to re-create here. Isolt of Brittany indeed ranks second to the first Isolt, yet the latter stands no less second to her lover's insatiable hunger and anxiety. Tristan needs both Isolts just as he must escape from them both, the escape and the denial – the obstacle – forming a central increment in *fin' amor* and in the Tristanian Eros.

Tristan married the second Isolt hoping that she might release him from bondage to the first Isolt. It can be maintained that Isolt of Brittany, having failed to win him for herself, succeeds in breaking the enchantment by slaying Tristan, and that she causes him to die in order to grant his request and thus fulfil her wifely duty. (She also causes him to die in order to discover how absolute are his love for the first Isolt and hers for him, and thus to measure her striving compared to theirs.) According to Helias, Tristan had himself wounded with the poisoned arrow in order to see if the second Isolt could save him and/or to force the first Isolt to come to Brittany to save him. However, the Breton princess and her husband both realize that healing a physical wound will resolve none of the problems of Eros manifest in spiritual wounding. Given that, according to Celtic myth, death is a continuance of life and its fulfilment on another plane, by killing Tristan (allowing him to die) the second Isolt does grant her husband the deliverance he seeks: 'Re vraz kalon a oa dezañ evid ar bed-mañ. Hirvoudi a ree da veza bahet ennañ. [...] warnon-me e fizie d'e zieubi. Kalon awalh 'm-eus bet d'henn ober' (p. 133) (He had too big a heart for this world. He lamented being imprisoned in it. He relied on me to deliver him. I had enough courage to do it). Because she kills him he can now go alone in his boat to the Happy Isles, the Otherworld he has sought throughout his life. Thus the second Isolt finally wins Tristan by losing him and thus lives her impossible love, never having touched her beloved, dead or alive.

The second Isolt's virginal passion is as strong as the first Isolt's adulterous one. Although she never touches Tristan, and Isolt of Ireland always did, none of this matters in the world of Eros and in the flow of destiny which brings the three figures from life to death at the same moment. For in this play Isolt of Brittany does join the other two in death. After Tristan perishes, she awaits the arrival of the first Isolt to observe her worthiness. When Isolt of Ireland then passes away, Isolt of Brittany is ready to do the same. She also will be worthy and will endure the quest and adventure to the end.

It ought to be clear that *An Isild a-heul* and *Katrina Lenn-Zu* explore the same problematic and develop a comparable dramatic structure. The young Katrina resembles the second Isolt in her desperate effort to live an impossible love in rivalry with an ever-absent queen from another realm. *Lenn-Zu*, like *An Isild*, is a reworking of the Tristan myth, conceived in modern terms for a modern audience. And, in parallel to the Black Pond of love and death, Helias develops a pattern of water imagery in his *Isild*, which also parallels the imagery in the original romances of Beroul, Thomas, and their continuers, and in early Irish literature also.

In Helias, as in Beroul and Thomas, water is the feminine element, associated with Isolt of Ireland and with the Eros that binds Tristan to her. Tristan and the first Isolt drank the philtre together. This potion, literally a drink ('beverage' in Beroul), is the symbolic cosmic force that unleashes their passion. Tristan and the second Isolt appear to fight against it, to neutralize its destructive powers. (In Beroul the term for the potion is also 'poison'). Yet Isolt of Brittany and Tristan both consider the possibility that the lovers are personally responsible for Eros, that the philtre may be only a symbol or only an excuse, and that Tristan and the first Isolt may have chosen physical separation in order to fan the flames of love and of jealousy.

Tristan drank the philtre on the ocean. As a result or, rather, as a cause, the sea itself, the *fons et origo*, the Eternal Feminine under the moon, offers Tristan an adventure no man in this life can complete. The stranger came from the sea; twice he quits the second Isolt to return to the sea. He is always on the waters in reality or in his dreams, and the sea is his philtre and his destiny. For Tristan is wounded by and on the sea and can only die or be saved on it. Yet since the ocean separates Tristan from both Isolts and since it is his only road to the Otherworld, it also evokes the world of dreams and the imagination, of heroism and the quest, which excludes both Isolts. It is fitting, therefore, that the first Isolt fails to reach him in time, on the sea, and that the second Isolt kills him with the lie concerning the sail: that the sail on Isolt's ship is black when in fact it is white. The sail is white yet it is also black, as is Tristan's love for both Isolts and their love for him, combining the ecstasy of joy and the tragedy of loss, the white and the black colours of Brittany.

In Helias's version of the story, the magnificent, raging, cosmic ocean and the magnificent queen from beyond the seas contrast with the little princess, Isolt of Brittany, given the nickname Dourig ar Housk (Little Sleeping Water), the best English equivalent being perhaps Still Waters, as in the expression 'still waters run deep.' Yet Little Sleeping Water, so quiet, apparently untouched by the tempests of life, in her way and on her terms joins the great ocean and the hero who navigates it. She too is worthy. In the end, unlike Katrina Mezmeur, who drowns herself in the

Black Pond in defeat, Little Sleeping Water, who had evoked a black sail, goes to sleep in utter serenity, having attained her wish and lived her adventure, her magnificent, impossible love. Rozili, condemned to live on, gazes at her in love and in awe, as she sleeps in death and wills her way to the Otherworld and to us.

Per Jakez Helias has created a genuine modern and – dare I say it? – classical theatre in Brittany and in the Breton language (Tanguy Malmanche being the great experimental pioneer). These plays are utterly Breton, in theme, motif, and subject-matter. Yet Helias, who always distances himself from his subject-matter, never gives way to nostalgia, nativism, or sentimentality. In the rural plays oriented toward demystification and in the history and legend plays oriented toward rehabilitation, we find the same exploration of pathology, Eros, madness, and fate. These are plays of high seriousness. Because of the high seriousness, because of the terrible honesty that emanates from the characters and their plight, Helias's dramas attain that universality which has to be the goal of all truly great art.

OCCITANIA

INTRODUCTION

The journal *Oc*, founded in 1924 by Camille Soula and Ismaël Girard and which served as the linguistic and cultural arm of Societat d'Estudis Occitans (Society of Occitan Studies) and, later, the Institut d'Estudis Occitans (Institute of Occitan Studies), corresponds exactly to the Breton reviews *Gwalarn* and *Al Liamm*. To this day, *Oc* remains the principal organ for the expression of Occitan modernity in literature, language, scholarship, and culture. Although he is of a younger generation and cannot be considered the founder of modern Occitan, Robert Lafont in other ways stands as the Southern French equivalent of Hugh MacDiarmid and Roparz Hemon. Since first entering on the scene in 1944 (present at the creation of the IEO), he has remained at the centre of the Occitan movement, as a participant and a leader in its literary and political manifestations. Among so much activity, we note simply that he was secretary general of the IEO in 1950–8, president in 1958–62, and editor-in-chief of *Oc* in 1957–62; that he launched a number of study and action groups including Comitat Occitan d'Estudis e d'Accion (Occitan Committee for Study and Action) and Lucha Occitana (Occitan Struggle); and that he was candidate for President of the Republic in 1974.

Like Roparz Hemon, Lafont has practised with *maestria* all literary genres and modes; in my opinion, he ranks as one of the best novelists in Oc and as the best playwright. Like MacDiarmid, he devoted much of his energy to presenting the Occitan position to the outside world, which resulted in a good dozen volumes in French treating cultural matter of the South. Having come to age at the end of the Second World War, Lafont inevitably inherited part of the Occitan ideology and, inevitably, shares the podium with a number of other writers.

As early as 1962 and perhaps earlier still, Occitan intellectuals conceived the notion of an inner or internal colonialism, applying it to the Occitan-speaking regions vis-à-vis northern France. Internal colonialism

appears vividly in Lafont's French books of socio-politico-economic
analysis, for example *La Révolution régionaliste* and *Décoloniser en France.*
Along with this, in *Sur la France*, he elaborates the idea of an Occitan
nation, of a kind with and no less legitimate than the French nation.[1]

In *Clefs pour l'Occitanie* and elsewhere Lafont dissects the clichés, cari-
catures, and stereotypes of the South promulgated by Parisians (and
accepted in the South) for centuries.[2] Writers such as D'Aubigné, Corneille, and Molière take relish in the caricature of the Gascon – a not
especially clever *miles gloriosus*, lacking the manners of the court, an
upstart who talks (too much) in an inexpressibly funny manner. The farcical Gascon then gives way, in the last two centuries, to the farcical
Provençal – lazy, hot-tempered, a braggart, and over-sexed. Whether
mocked at or treasured for his charm, the modern Provençal is, by definition, geographically, linguistically, psychologically, and socially provincial and low-class. Lafont, conscious of the Breton as well as the Occitan
alienation, draws the ultimate conclusion:

> Le Français de l'ethnie dominatrice et le Français breton ou occitan (dans
> la mesure, immense, où *ce dernier* aliénait son être dans la tyrannie nationa-
> liste) ont ainsi pensé que la Bretagne était *par nature humaine* un pays de
> sots en costumes folkloriques et le peuple méridional un peuple de doux
> fainéants. [...] Nous ne faisons qu'effleurer cet immense sujet, très difficile,
> mais que quelqu'un devra bien traiter un jour, d'un *racisme intérieur* qu'ali-
> mentait une réfraction régionaliste de l'occitanisme, perceptible chez Dau-
> det. (*La Révolution régionaliste*, pp. 206–7)

As in Scotland and Brittany, one manifestation of the modernist
credo is to repudiate folklore, a version of the popular that has no aspirations for or consciousness of high culture and that helps maintain the
negative stereotypes. In the 1957 'Manifèst de Nerac' published in *Oc*
and often reprinted, Bernard Manciet and Félix Castan state their pol-
icy in lapidary terms: 'Le culte et l'étude scientifique des traditions tels
que les conçoit le folklore constituent des activités dignes d'intérêt, mais
par nature distinctes de l'activité littéraire.'[3] Lafont argues the question,
as usual, in its socio-ideological context:

> On comprend que les écrivains en langues régionales les plus conscients
> aient des réactions parfois vives contre la vogue du folklore. [...] Nous
> savons que les pouvoirs colonisateurs ont favorisé le folklore des peuples
> soumis. Ce folklore ne peut être utilisé positivement par ces peuples

qu'une fois abolie la dépendance économique et reconstituée la véritable dignité culturelle. Pour l'instant il est à ranger parmi les phénomènes de déculturation que la colonisation entraîne avec elle. Déculturation et exotisme sont toujours synonymes. (*La Révolution régionaliste*, pp. 208–9)

Just as the fact that in Scotland literary folklore means Robert Burns and the Burns legacy, so also, I am convinced, in the South of France literary folklore means Gabriel Mistral and the Mistral legacy. History is made of such extraordinary coincidences – the equivalencies of Burns and Mistral, the Burns Cult and the Felibrige, the national poet of Scotland and the national poet of Provence, up to and including Burns Suppers and Sainte-Estelle Banquets with their food, drink, song, and grandiloquent speeches. The Occitan movement had to repudiate Mistral and the Felibrige for precisely the same reasons that MacDiarmid and his followers had to repudiate Burns, the Kailyard, and the Whistle-Binkie. Lafont's brilliant polemical and scholarly book *Mistral ou l'illusion* sounded the death knell to Provençal claims to cultural hegemony.[4] In this essay and elsewhere, Lafont praised Mistral as a poet and, prior to 1870, as a political man. He does blame Mistral for turning to the Right in his later years and for grounding Provençal identity in rural life and the past when urban centres were already the dynamic focus of the present and the future. The most powerful critiques, however, are reserved for the cliques who surrounded the Master and, after his death, perverted his message and his art:

C'est en fait un discours sectaire, brodé d'une symbolique dont la secte détient la clef: Sainte Etoile, Coupe Sainte, Saint Signal. Le Félibrige a été conçu comme une franc-maçonnerie dépositaire d'un 'Secret.' [...] Cette situation émotive est favorable à l'investissement du projet par l'irrationnel. Le Félibrige, dès ses premiers moments, décale idéologiquement la tâche très concrète qu'il se fixe: il en fait une mystique. [...] [un] discours souverainement inconscient, protégé d'optimisme initiatique, patiné d'esthétisme. [...] Le Félibrige ou tient un discours de libération bourgeoise que le peuple ne comprend pas, ou renfonce le peuple dans le provincialisme, l'archaïsme moral et culturel. [...] les félibres ont conçu les hommes de leurs pays en représentation de passé. Ils ont fabriqué une identité ethnique miroitante dans une bulle de temps, une éternité factice. [...] Le discours félibréen finit en représentation touristique. (*Clefs pour l'Occitanie*, pp. 121–2, 124, 129, 137–8)

In this register of satire Lafont follows a tradition. From its beginnings in the 1920s a constant theme in *Oc* is to denounce the Felibrige, who were always a generation behind, culturally immobile and turned to the past, a narrow-minded, self-centred clique dwelling in an ivory tower, or, in the words of Max Rouquette, his people sick 'de l'academisme feli-brenc, de son "passéisme", de son fetichisme mistralenc [...] enfin de son verbalisme e de sa mediocritat'[5] (of Felibrige academicism, its attachment to the past, its fetishism of Mistral, lastly its verbosity and mediocrity).

From the beginning *Oc* and its adherents sought to replace the fetish-izing of Mistral and a nineteenth-century nostalgia for the rural past with modernity and modernism in both the language and its literature. In 1943 René Nelli called on those adherents 'suscitar per tots los mejans una cultura autonoma e nova s'inspirant dins sas formas d'un modernisme de bona lei'[6] (to give rise, by every possible means, to a new and autonomous culture drawing its inspiration, in the forms it will assume, from legitimate modernism). Nelli also wants his modernity to be enriched by 'las nostras tradicións mai autenticas' (our most authen-tic traditions), and here he cites the troubadours and what was later to be called the Occitan Baroque or the Renaissance de Toulouse. Simi-larly, the 'Manifèst de Nerac' declares, 'L'importance d'une langue et d'une tradition de civilisation se mesurent non aux politiques de préser-vation (du type du Félibrige) qu'elles suscitent, mais à leur efficacité dans la pensée moderne.'

The Occitan writers are convinced that their language must not be employed uniquely in the domain of poetry – as pure form – but also used to give voice to ideas and history, to reach out to the life of the mind at all levels. To that end, Occitans will have to escape from the local dialect in order to cultivate the modern tongue, which is to be nor-mative and, therefore, universal. In the words of Lafont, 'La commu-nauté occitane d'écriture, dans l'espace et dans le temps, oblige notre poète à s'évader du local, où est sa vérité propre, pour atteindre la vérité de sa culture, le général, l'occitan.'[7] It is only with a unified, universal tongue that Occitan writers will arrive at cultural unity and a sufficiently broad public with the capability of reading them – only then can there be a flourishing book trade and genuine, vital journalism. And only then will cease Parisian condescension or Parisian scorn vis-à-vis the dia-lects, deemed incapable of modern uses and, therefore, inherently reac-tionary. Alibert, like MacDiarmid and like Hemon, cites the example of Dante, who forged literary Italian using as a base his own Tuscan, but

then forged onto it elements from the Italian dialects plus the troubadours' own Occitan.[8] And one manifestation of such unity and maturity
would be a vital, modern prose – in novels, drama, and intellectual writings – which would expand the all but uniquely poetic vocation of Occitan heretofore. This call for prose is a leitmotif which occurs again and
again in the pages of *Oc*.

A single, unified, normative literary language was the goal. It was necessary to simplify and purify the tongue, as was the case for Scots and
Breton. And to do so, as was the case for Scots and Breton, it was necessary to aim for a single, rational, unified orthography. This was to be the
Occitan or classical or Alibert spelling, grounded in the tradition of the
troubadours, as opposed to the French-like systems which had evolved
since the Middle Ages, including Mistral's own orthography for
Provençal. As Alibert puts it:

> Per la [Occitan] tornar rendre apta a expremir totas las ideas e aténher lo
> vast public indispensable a sa vida, caldrà donc unificar la grafia e lo voca-
> bulari dins la mesura de las possibilitats e far caire totas las barralhas que
> separan los parlars de Niça a Pau e de Limoges a Valéncia. [...] Unificar e
> depurar de lenga [...] Dotar l'occitàn d'un vocabulari scientific e tecnic
> rigorosament comun.[9]
>
> (In order to restore to Occitan the capacity of expressing all ideas and of
> reaching the large public essential to its existence, it will therefore be nec-
> essary to unify the spelling and vocabulary to the extent that is possible and
> to break down the barriers that separate the dialects between Nice and Pau
> and between Limoges and Valence. To unify and to purify the language, to
> equip Occitan with a scientific and technical vocabulary strictly common to
> all.)

Lafont also argued that the classical graphic system of the Middle Ages
can be applied to all the dialects, no matter how they are pronounced.
When you seek to approximate local pronunciation, as the Felibres did,
the sense of total community is broken and, in any case, your spelling
will be only a pastiche of the French. And, as the Scots and Bretons proclaimed again and again, the Occitans understood that only with a unified spelling can you hope for writing in the public sphere and for
something approaching mass education, for you can justify teaching
and maintaining a single standard language capable of dialogue with
other standard languages, but not several languages or dialects.

Significantly, this concern for the international standing of Occitan and for Occitan taking its place as a modern standard alongside of other standards pervaded the theoretical writing from the beginning. Just as the Bretons looked to Ireland and Wales for inspiration, the Occitans turned toward the south. Alibert specifically called for scientific and technical vocabulary to be borrowed from Catalan. Especially in the 1920s and 1930s, those who wrote in *Oc* were inspired by the Catalan success in forging a vital modern all-purpose language and in attaining some measure of political power. Along with the Catalans and superimposed onto them, in the 1940s and 1950s Occitan writers turned to the troubadours (as the Scots New Makars had turned to the Old Makars) for the example of a dense, purified, and high-culture language manifest in dense, purified, and high-culture literature, authentic in the past and capable of becoming authentic again in the present.

For all these reasons, the new literature had to adhere to the high modernist norms of the international European market-place and, therefore, to be a literature of intellectuals not of the mass. In general, the Occitans were less consciously elitist than MacDiarmid and the Bretons. However, Castan, the co-author of the 'Manifèst de Nerac,' does make the claim in the strongest terms: 'Ni la littérature occitane ni la revendication occitane n'étaient d'origine populaire. On ne peut imaginer hiatus plus profond entre une création et son peuple. [...] la culture occitane, qui est sans doute plus que toute autre une culture à dominante savante. Littérature d'aristocrates et de lettrés.'[10]

Others, today, support the Castan thesis in imagining that, even were Occitan to die out as a grass-roots language, it would survive in what they believe is its most authentic form – as the medium of literature and the function of art.

The internationalism is expressed splendidly in the 'Manifèst de Nerac': 'En revanche par une interrogation constante des littératures de civilisations française et étrangères, sans distinction de siècle ni de situation, – et surtout par l'interprétation des créations littéraires d'avant-garde, – les écrivains d'Oc espèrent trouver en toutes circonstances une solution au renouveau de leurs traditions et un mode d'expression de valeur universelle.' Occitan literature comes from writers' ambition to create works of universal quality, and a literature, therefore, that is at the level of the other literatures. In other words, as the editorial of *Oc* claims in 1991, 'Las nòstras letras devon demorar vigorosas, joves, vitalistas, en s'obrent als escambis critics amb totas las literaturas estrangièras, prèpas o lunhanas'[11] (Our literature must remain robust, young, vital, open to critical exchanges with all foreign literatures, near or distant).

Last of all, as with Roparz Hemon, Charles Camproux calls for an act of the will, which is the sign of life ('una volontat qu'es signe de vida')[12] and which alone can bring about a situation whereby the language will live again, oriented toward the future and not languishing as an embittered meditation on the past.[13]

POETRY

MAX-PHILIPPE DELAVOUËT

Max-Philippe Delavouët is the greatest poet in the Mistralian or Provençal school. He spent much of his adult existence tending a farm in the hills of Provence, a bit of a recluse; he read much of world literature and published, from 1971 to 1983, four volumes of a vast lyrico-epic panorama entitled simply *Pouèmo* (Poem) (volume 5 came out posthumously).[14] Given that a number of the texts later collected in 1971 appeared independently, in reviews or in plaquettes going back to the 1940s, *Pouèmo* in its totality encompasses the production of a lifetime. It is one of the more prodigious and coherent artistic monuments of our age, the most obvious parallels being *Une Somme de poésie* by Patrice de la Tour du Pin and *Canto general* by Pablo Neruda.

The sections that make up *Pouèmo* are lyrical or lyrico-narrative entities. The same or similar 'characters' recur in the corpus: the Speaker is a poetic persona entitled the Prince; his beloved is an archetypal Lady-princess-queen-goddess; he has an alter ego–brother, the Other Prince; they dwell in an archetypal Provence in an archetypally mythical past. Many of the same themes, images, and motifs recur. Nonetheless, each entity also stands on its own. There is, no doubt, a total vision and poetic voice yet not a single, univocal narrative line. Part of the modernity of the text lies in its complicated, problematic elaboration, of voice and point of view. The spirit of *Pouèmo* is one of incantation and celebration, not one of telling a story.

In this mode of celebration or incantation Delavouët joins, intentionally I believe, Pindar, Ronsard, Hölderlin, and St-John Perse. Considering more particularly the block of texts contained in the first two volumes, a sequence that recounts or corresponds to the four seasons and ages of man, we observe that the Prince also assumes the roles of

Adam, Odysseus, Tristan, Mistral's Prince of Orange, and, no doubt, the implied author Max-Philippe Delavouët. The Prince leads a hieratic existence, grounded to a large extent in the Middle Ages or, rather, in our literary myth of the Middle Ages. He undergoes quests, encounters dead cities, hermits, buffoons, or his alter ego, the other prince, but most often a version of the Eternal Feminine. Central to Delavouët's imaginative world is the libido. Two metaphoric structures of desire pervade these first sections of *Pouèmo*. One clusters around what I call the Lady of the City, the other around the Lady of the Sea.

The seduction of the Lady of the City occurs in 'Courtege de la bello sesoun' (Procession in Spring). There the Princess lies asleep in her palace, dreaming of her future love. He, the Prince, sets out on horseback, grasping a rose and bearing a flag emblazoned with a crimson heart. At the end of his quest the Prince discovers a white city and castle by the sea. He shakes his rose, the petals rise and scatter, and a flock of birds rises and scatters from the battlements. The Princess, who in the dream had offered to her phantom lover the Grail, presents her chalice to the Prince, who pours his wine into it and drinks.

What appears to be a charming, elegant, vaguely nostalgic evocation of the medieval past in fact functions as a powerful metaphor of desire. A pattern of male, phallic imagery is evoked by the Prince, his horse, his rose, his wine, his movement, and the colour red. A pattern of vaginal imagery is evoked by the Princess, her stone castle, city, dreams, cup, and immobility, and the colour white. The slow, majestic, hieratic roll of the text mirrors the no less slow, majestic, hieratic union of the lovers. It veils yet also reveals the ritual of Eros in all its splendour.

Other occurrences of the imagery are to be found in passages where the Prince (or Adam?) desires a woman (another? the same?) in a stone medieval castle – her eyes are his light, she is his land, his island, and his repose; where Tristan dreams of the port city which awaits his coming, offering him trees and foliage in exchange for his light and song; where, in 'Blasoun de la dono d'estiéu' (Blazon of the Lady of Summer), the Prince calls on his beloved to quit her dreams of the dusk in order to accompany him to a new realm of light, in the sky, on the heights.

The second structure, the Lady of the Sea, is first announced in 'Pouèmo pèr Evo' (Poem for Eve). What is the apple in the garden of Eden? Either the sun – Adam's own libido – as it sets literally into the Tree of Life; or Eve's breasts, her female, maternal libido. In any event, Eve is not born of Adam's rib. Instead, Adam proceeds to the sea. There, like Venus, the image of Venus, Eve is born of the waves and strides forth onto the strand, where she and Adam make love. This thematic is reworked in 'Dono d'estiéu,' where the Prince offers the Lady his heart, in the form of a fruit, which he places on her breast. She bites into it, then, having tasted, gives it back. Bitter and painful as a wound is the taste of this sun on the branch. Later, the Lady, nude, having bathed in the ocean, returns to the Prince, whereupon they fall asleep in the grass.

Tristan also partakes of the myth. As with Achilles, Tristan's mother had plunged him into the sea as an infant. However, she held Tristan by the heart. The heart is his weak spot, his glass heart vulnerable to Cupid's golden arrows:

Aqui, dins d'àutris oundo, à la mar me neguè,
un tèms, coume li pèis qu'aviéu dins moun astrado.
    Mai, dins l'aussado que rènd fort,
ma maire me tenié 'm'uno man sus moun cor.

[...] i bras de ma maire, veniéu plus lourd
coume lou fru gounfla que courbo au sòu sa broundo,
    e la terro touquère alor,
baiant un cor de vèire à milo flècho d'or. (I, pp. 174, 176)

(There, for a moment, in other waves, she plunged me into the sea, like the fish in my horoscope. But in the swell which grants strength, my mother held me by one hand on my heart. In my mother's arms I became heavier, like swollen fruit that bends its branch to the ground, and so I hit the earth, baring a heart to a thousand arrows of gold.)

Assimilated to Ulysses as well as to Achilles, Tristan is a mariner, a man of the sea, joined to the sea and, like Eve, born from the unconscious and the all. An older Prince will dream of his lost youth in 'Lusernàri dóu cor flecha' (Lucernary of the Pierced Heart). Meanwhile, as an adult, Tristan dreams ever of the sea; in one such dream he imagines landing on a desert island, then diving into the waters to recover pieces of slate. As in the previous sequence, we behold a coherent pattern of erotic imagery. The man is associated with the sun, the Father, the physical and intellectual potency of the Logos; the woman with the ocean, *magna mater, fons et origo* of life in the realm of the Mothers. His desire is also embodied in the fiery, bleeding heart that she is so eager to ingest. Nude, she welcomes him on the shore, at the frontier, the region that St-John Perse called 'Amers' (*aimer, amer, la mer*), a point of epiphany where land and sea, heaven and earth, and man and woman are joined in fleeting union.

The eroticism generated by the Prince and his beloved(s) is to be interpreted on other levels than that of a passing affair. Both Eve and the Lady of the Summer are portrayed as goddesses, Venus born from the waves and an earth deity, respectively. A goddess of nature, the 'dono d'estiéu' holds sway over beasts, birds, and fish, and her hands contain fire and retain the salamander. The Prince is a god to Eve in turn, for, at one point, not perceiving him in the flesh, she is touched by him only in her dreams, he who is her dream. Their union should be read as individual wish-fulfilment but also as an earthly and cosmic fertility rite, the nuptials of god and goddess, fire and water, gold and quicksilver, sun and earth, and, since we speak of Adam and Eve, the birth of our planet and the history of humankind.

As a last element of Eros, this time an *argumentum a contrario*, we might consider 'Danso de la pauro ensouleiado' (Dance of the Wretched Girl Who Is Sunstruck). Although the central image has been interpreted by Thunin allegorically as water from a fountain leaping at the sun,[15] on a literal level Delavouët tells with extraordinary power a story of demented female passion. The girl has literally fallen in love with the sun. Her blood is hot, she is desperate to reach the sun, her bird of desire, to soar like him and be made pregnant by him. Nude, she offers him roses from her blood:

> Tout passo à travers iéu coume l'aigo e lou fue
> e la lus sus mi sen vèn n'en flouri li pouncho
> en roso que sa sabo es l'eigagno di niue [...]
> Danse e dise li flour di mai secrèt jardin
> balançant si perfum sus li liano saunouso,
> semene autour de iéu li roso dóu dedins,
> en gèste lènt ma danso à fuioun li desnouso
>   e siéu l'auto semenairis
> que tiro de soun sang li roso qu'espandis. (II, p. 30)

(All goes through me like water and fire, and the light comes to blossom the thorns of my breasts into roses whose sap is nighttime dew. I dance and I tell the flowers of the most secret gardens, balancing their scent on creepers of blood, I sow around me roses from within, in slow movements my dance releases the petals, and I am the high sower who pulls out of her blood the roses that she flings.)

Later, at the end of the day, the sun, wounded, burns up and expires, its blood now devoured by her shadow. Having lost the sun and in terror of the beast (her shadow), the girl, in despair, sinks into the void.

The text is suffused with the imagery of *fin' amor*: the bird, flight, fire, roses, and blood. Yet these are largely phallic, not vaginal, images. If the 'Ensouleiado''s story turns out to be more tragic than Adam's and the Prince's, if she fails where they have succeeded, is it not because, in Delavouët's traditional, hieratic universe, desire, motion, flight, and fire are reserved for the man? By thrusting away her natural realm of darkness, water, and dreams, by proclaiming desire in her dance, by acting on her own, without guidance from a prince, does not the poor girl transgress against the cosmos? Does she not castrate instead of opening herself and giving birth? And thus, truly mad, is she not punished in her womanness, made 'lunatic' and therefore, as a moon-figure, deprived forever of joining with her sun?

With the exception, then, of the mad 'Ensouleiado,' the Lady – Eve, Penelope, Isolt, the Princess, later on Roland's queen – never comes to the Prince in his land, at his bidding. On each occasion it is he who quits his home with the goal of finding her. As Prince or as Adam, the male Speaker sets out on a quest in the direction of the sea, seeking the beloved of the sea or of the town. As Tristan or as Ulysses, he sails across the waves, dreaming of the port, village, and refuge, the port-city and its mistress that await his arrival. His is an inner quest and an inner conquest. The conquest of the Lady, at or upon the waters, is the conclusion to a rite of passage, the passage from childhood into manhood, through a process of individuation and maturation, through initiation into Eros.

In one passage Adam tells the implied reader that he dreamed of a beautiful 'oumbro' (shade/shadow), then followed it, his 'oumbro,' all summer:

Sounge, sounge trop viéu, contro iéu, fin finalo,
    te devistère sout ti tra:
toun bèu visage d'oumbro èro clar e daura.

Sounge trouva, bello oumbro [...] (I, p. 48)

(Dream, dream too vivid alive, against me, in the end / I stared at you beneath your features / beneath the darts you shot at me; your beautiful dream face was fair and golden. Dream found, beautiful dream.)

Later it was replaced by Eve, it had foreshadowed and prefigured Eve, the source of his dreams. Together they will be one flesh. As I read the text, Delavouët builds upon the Jungian notion of the *anima*. Each man projects or displaces the feminine element of his being – the unconscious and the irrational – upon a real or imaginary woman outside himself. He can succeed in the individuation process and attain wholeness only by coming to terms with the *anima*, by integrating the feminine *imago* that he lacks. Adam does so by 'creating' Eve, by dreaming of her, then drawing her from the waves (his unconscious) and uniting with her on the shore. The Prince undergoes the same psychic process by seeking the Princess, finding her in her castle by the sea, and metaphorically uniting with her on the shore (filling her cup with his wine). The Prince convinces the Lady of Summer to abandon her valley of dreams in order to accompany him to his realm of freedom, light, and adventure. Thus man will integrate into his psyche woman's world of darkness, intimacy, domestic peace, and the *Ewig-Weibliche*, yet with the proviso that the masculine principles of heroism, creativity, will-power, and the Logos shall prevail.

The 'oumbro' also evokes, in Jungian terms, the negative masculine aspects of the psyche that the Self must conquer before attaining wholeness. These the Self projects upon another man. In Delavouët we find no hostile martial adversary, no opposant. Instead, in 'Cansoun de la mai auto tourre' (Song of the Highest Tower), from his tower the Prince discovers or imagines an alter ego, another prince (poet, lover) identical to himself. The Other Prince is a brother, friend, and fellow poet. On the one hand, it is clear that, more than for the woman, the Other is a projection of the Prince, a part of him displaced upon the world or, if you prefer, part of the world created by the Prince in his image. This Other, perhaps embodying the more libidinal, unconscious elements of the id, the shadow ('oumbro'), is nonetheless treated with affection and respect. The Prince is proud of his (imaginary) brother. Now they are two! For, in terms of the medieval epic-romance tradition in which Delavouët grounds his text, winning a friend – Olivier, Bernier, Fouques, Guivret, Gauvain, Galehaut – is as important to the hero as winning a bride or conquering a throne.

Not only the man must integrate his *anima* and overcome his shadow. The same holds true for the woman. The 'Ensouleiado' wishes literally to escape her physical shadow, an enemy tracking her every move, and aligns herself with the Sun, on which she has projected her *animus*. However, the Sun tells her that he is to be found within her: his light shines in her blood, his wine in her grape. For, he points out, she is like a tree – dark underneath yet with flowers and the sun above. Driven by the irrational, by her female libido, the girl fails to understand that wholeness for her lies in a fusion of the masculine and the feminine, light and dark, and reason and madness, within herself, which she will attain only when she agrees to be bound to earth and to submit to the masculine Logos offered to her by her *animus*.

Delavouët gives expression to the ideal of wholeness and the desire that can lead to wholeness in patterns of archetypal imagery. Among the clusters are:

The tree. As we have seen, the 'Pauro Ensouleiado' is or ought to be a tree, the dark lower half representing her feminine Self, the sunny upper half her integrated *animus*. Adam's body also is as a tree, his blood is sap, and he gives birth to fruit. Finally, in 'Camin de la Crous' (Stations of the Cross), Christ nourishes his cross, is his cross, and the Holy Rood becomes Christ. The tree thus stands as an image of refuge in nature, of pastoral calm, but, still more, as a symbol of life and growth, of physical and spiritual striving, the burgeoning life-force that moves the cosmos.

Fruit. The tree exists in large measure to give birth to fruit. Adam's tree, his body, lodges the sun in its branches. The prince offers the Lady his heart, his fruit, which she may place in an orchard. Tristan's heart is his Achilles' heel. On the side of the woman, Eve's breasts are apples. The Prince urges Eve to pluck the fruits of the earth; by doing so she will offer him a gift from heaven. Delavouët transforms the evil apple of the tree forbidden by God into good fruit from the Tree of Life, created by men and women, their hearts beating in their bodies. The good fruit is a metaphor for desire, *jouissance*, the flesh, and the emotions, that which is bitter as well as sweet, and is spiritual as well as physical food.

Birds. The 'Ensouleiado' envisages her lover, the Sun, as a giant bird. She is eager to join him in flight, and also to become his nest. Penelope awaits the coming of a bird. 'Cansoun de la mai auto tourre' comes into existence because the Prince hears the cry of a bird which announces the arrival of autumn and causes him, the Prince, to meditate on birds and seasons. The Other Prince then sends him a bird as a gift. In Tristan's dream birds soar up from the church tower. His alter ego (Ulysses) shot down the eagles. Redemption for the poet will occur when he has created new eagles. These birds evoke masculine desire, as did the nightingale in medieval lyric. As with the medieval nightingale, Delavouët's birds also represent the power of the imagination, poetic inspiration, a spiritual power in harmony with nature. We can scarcely forget that Delavouët's Prince is a poet, an Adam-figure who names and orders his garden for Eve, and a Tristan-figure who brings his people light and song – a lover, prophet, and artist who desires, sees, and creates through the Logos, having become a secular *Verbum in principio*.

Delavouët's world is located, on one level, in the real Provence (allusions to Aigues-Mortes, les Alyscamps d'Arles, and the Rhône) but also, on another level, in a semi-mythical Provence of the spirit, an imaginary Provence of elemental space: the enclosed space of the village, valley, farm, the walled castle, and the port; or the open space of the road, mountains, and the sea.

Similarly, *Pouèmo* exists temporally in recognizable, school-manual Western history – the Middle Ages and the Ancien Régime. Yet Delavouët's time is also a semi-mythical, archetypal past: of princes and princesses, eagles and horses, swords and roses, a time of the imagination – the conflated fictional ages of Adam and Ulysses, Tristan and Perceval, Mistral's Prince of Orange and Max-Philippe Delavouët's Prince. Because *Pouèmo* gives the impression of being an ode or sacred text from an ancient, indeterminate civilization, recounting events that occurred in the past, perhaps the distant past, but that exist in archetypal or mythical time, the reader enjoys an intense participation in the *hic et nunc*, duration compressed into the *nunc stans* of a living, sacred, eternal present.

I speak of the sacred, in part because of the overtones of rite and ritual that pervade Delavouët's text, especially in 'Courtege' but also with Adam and Eve's nuptials and with the 'Ensouleiado''s passion (her desire and immolation); in part because Adam and Christ are vital participants in the diegesis. After a sleep of centuries, Adam, *vetus homo*, awakens as the Prince, a secular *homo novus*. The Prince is Adam, and Adam speaks through the voice of the Prince. Both seek an ever-present and ever-distant eternal Eve. Present time – itself a mythical duration located in the past – re-enacts the foundation of the race. Somewhat akin to the way it does in medieval typology, the time of Adam and Eve prefigures the ages of Christ and of the Prince; all three eras are fulfilled and postfigured by Max-Philippe Delavouët, the speaker elaborating his 'pouèmo' in his (our) present. Thus, all four eras coexist, superimposed, like a palimpsest, and the palimpsest is the deep structure of *Pouèmo*.

In addition, not only does Adam wake up after a sleep of centuries, but the girl of 'Courtege' sleeps and dreams, then wakes up at dawn and sets forth on the run: spring has returned. The Prince of the Spring in 'Courtege,' by the time of 'Mai auto tourre' having loved a 'Dono d'estiéu,' regrets the end of summer in his castle. He meditates on winter and death, and dreams that his body is assimilated to the funeral stones in a church ('Pèiro escricho de la roso'; Stone Written from a Rose), then, in 'Istòri dóu rèi mort qu'anavo à la desciso' (Story of the Dead King Who Went Down River), the dead king's body is literally transformed into its own funeral stone descending the Rhône in winter.

These early sections of *Pouèmo*, that re-enact the passing of the seasons, contribute to the elaboration of a modern cosmological myth, the equivalent of Ronsard's *Quatre Saisons de l'an*. With, as the principal characters, embodiments of Adam, Ulysses, and Tristan, the passing of the four seasons corresponds to the passing of the Four Ages of Man – the evolution of man as an individual, from birth to death, and of humanity in history, from Creation (by man) to Judgment (by Delavouët), a judgment that is provisional not final, ending in life not death, since our life in the present is eternally present because it contains within it its (our) past and it throbs with its own Eros and Ever-becoming.

Pouèmo is that: a poem, in the complete sense of the term, the poem as total work of art: lyric, pseudo-autobiography, philosophy, confession, history, cosmology, and myth. The recurrence of the Delavouët stanza mirrors the continuity of the seasons and the roll of the sea. It evokes intertextually the long ode à la Ronsard and Hölderlin and the long poem à la Mistral, Péguy, and Perse. For the first time in Occitan we find the equivalent of the sublime Attic lyric, the lyric treated with high seriousness and in the sublime style, elevated to the level of epic. For Delavouët the world is real, pulsating with frenetic, explosive life, subject to change yet also the measure of the human at its most sublime. A world worthy of celebration, sacred, evoking rapture in the beholder, and which exalts all seasons, times, places, and persons. As with Mistral, there is a Homeric quality to Delavouët's verse, given its quasi-atemporal and unproblematic sublime. Delavouët recounts the struggle of the lone individual in quest of love and adventure, the inner exile of humans who have to overcome the greatest of obstacles including their own selves, and the triumph of those who learn to live as, to be, a Prince. He also recounts that only such people deserve to be commemorated in and to be the narrative voices of an extended work of art. The struggle, the exile, the triumph, and the written commemoration are fixed forever in *Pouèmo*.

RENÉ NELLI

René Nelli is generally considered to be the greatest poet in modern Occitan, a modern classic in all senses of the term. A scholar, an authority on the troubadours, *fin' amor*, Catharism, and the history of Southern France, he taught for years at the University of Toulouse without, however, having been offered a permanent university position. Nelli was one of the early adherents to the Occitan movement; more than any, he insisted that a minority literature has to grasp the modern world in its modernity and has, therefore, to partake totally of modernism. Nelli wrote difficult, arcane verse in the style of Valéry and Char, Montale and Quasimodo. Like them, he sought to attain a new Mediterranean classicism, a *monumentum aere perennius* that would fuse the rigour of Greece and Rome with the rigour of high modernist *trobar clus*. Publishing as early as 1931, Nelli produced a number of collections from 1942 on, the most important of which is the 1952 *Arma de vertat* (Soul/Weapon of Truth). These, along with other, newer texts, were brought together in 1981: the *Òbra poëtica occitana* (Poetical Works in Occitan).[16]

Despite evolution in form and subject-matter over a period of five decades, Nelli's corpus exhibits a remarkable coherence. Phenomenologically, his is, to begin with, a nightmare world of aggression and terror. Sometimes we read of an inside space – a room, a reading lamp, presumably a desk and books, and a window – set in contrast to, and menaced by, the unfathomable or hostile outside space. Thus trees in the garden below prevent the Speaker indoors from hearing the words under his lamp, and a star ravages him with pity. In another poem the cypress tree, outside, stands like an owl or a pagan idol with a necklace made of skulls, exhaling the odour of a dried-up well; also, green skeletons of ferns crouch beneath the window, and stars comb their ashes. The cypress invades the Speaker's room and seats its shadow on his chair.[17]

More often, no refuge is provided by a room and no mediation by a window. The Speaker stands in the open, his subjectivity opened to the external reality that presses in on him. In 'Lo Sòm' (Sleep) water, in rage, transformed into diamonds or tears, abducts a child; a dead castle tosses a stone into a well and howls so as not to fly away yet flies off anyhow, moonless; pine trees become a forest of wolves; and water again strangles, seeking to drink the darkness. In this poem of sleep the Speaker cannot sleep, he endures the torture of insomnia:

lo sòm qu'ablandís nòstras dònas
e nos agaita sus la dralha
tornar tristes solets jos nòstres capulets. (p. 45)

(the sleep that caresses our wives and watches us wander on the road sad all
alone beneath our hoods.)

Other texts tell of the living who believe they are dead, and of the
dead who weep without forgiveness of love; so many gaze with cruelty
while dead dogs howl. Or of the swallows who, this spring, did not
return; this spring there comes a dawn of blood, and the dead rise from
the earth, captives of the living. Or of suns that are crucified in the smile
of blood, and (since this is late autumn or winter) colour is gone from
the leaves, a residue of arsenic, while we perceive a petrified tree, lik-
ened to a man's phallus. Finally, in 'Òda als salamandrins' (Ode to Sala-
manders), we hear of a bouquet of tortured bodies, the cry of wounded
goddesses, a woman whose shades/shadows/ghosts are older than
death, and ghosts who leave their dead bodies and speak yet remain
unaware of who is what.

The nightmare world is derived, in part, from French surrealism and,
also perhaps, German expressionism; in part from Nelli's preoccupation
with Catharism as a manifestation of Occitan culture and his own neo-
Catharist, dualist philosophy. From the Catharist perspective, the world
as we know it was created by Satan and is, therefore, in its essence
doomed to chaos.

Certainly, the outer space – all that is nature and almost all that is
human – is depicted with what Frye called 'demonic imagery.' It is
nighttime, the realm of Hecate. We hear of howling dogs and wolves, of
menacing ferns and trees, of blood and dying suns, of water seizing and
strangling, of pagan idols, skulls and skeletons, of hostile stone and hostile women. Whatever in nature or the outer world in other literary
genres or registers – the classical pastoral or the romantic nature portrait – appears benevolent or, at least, indifferent to humankind, here
cries out and forces itself onto the Speaker's subjectivity: the inanimate
comes alive, and that which surrounds him is shown to be aggressive,
threatening, and hostile. The Speaker cannot defend himself, since his
thought processes and his perception of this hostile universe lack coherence; all is fragmented, disjointed, and liminal. The landscape is his
inner state. And, given the presence of stone, of Bachelard's hard earth
of the will – a castle casting stones, a petrified tree compared to man's

sex – the Speaker is metaphorically wounded, he suffers *regressus ad uterum* (but there is no womb, the windowed refuge cannot protect him), and symbolic castration or impotence. Finally, just as death is a metaphor for castration, so castration is a metaphor for death. These nightmare texts are pervaded by the presence of the dead – as spirits or in the flesh – returned to life or to a sickly, non-human half-life. They come not in peace, nor do they bring consolation. They come in hatred and rage. Once the barriers between the living and the dead are broken and the world of the dead is shown to be as demonic as our own, the Speaker, in his tortured waking state (assimilated to insomnia), walks and thinks as one of the living dead.

One cause of insomnia, nightmare, and self-petrification is the presence of Woman as Other. Given that Nelli was a medievalist and that he edited the troubadours and published an influential book on courtly love (*L'Erotique des troubadours*), it will come as no surprise that a good portion of his opus – especially in *Arma de vertat* but not limited to that volume – is constituted by a meditation on *fin' amor* as he envisages it, in itself and in modern terms for the modern world.[18]

In the beginning, so to speak, there is desire, assimilated to fire. In Strophe I of the long poem 'L'interna consolacion' (The Inner/Intrinsic Consolation) the Speaker exploits the imagery of thirst: he drinks to sate his thirst in the girl's heart, during midnight's burning, when even the stars are athirst; and the girl's cheek shines in pleasure like a forest fire. With Nelli, love and desire can be portrayed in positive terms. Thus, in a number of poems, we discover that the girl blushes and loves, new and innocent, in a night illuminated by the light and whiteness of her thighs in the pale grass, while the Speaker will pluck hope from her lips. Or the girl sings, nude in her voice like a flower on her dress, from a 'polida boca' (pretty mouth). Or she is a rose and has the lips of a flower, her blondness hidden under a black moth corolla, she who stretches nude under the moon. Or her body, a young flower, made the morning cool as the joy of her limbs renewed the Speaker's flesh. Or, in a lost farmhouse at the end of a white path, the unknown girl, nude, sleeps in a dream state, her loveliness of and in burning darkness.

Nelli renews an old convention, dating back to Ronsard and, before him, to *Le Roman de la Rose* and, before it, to Horace, Ovid, and the Greek Anthology. This is the analogy (exploited by Sydney Goodsir Smith in modern Scots) between girls and flowers, the flower personified as a girl and the girl 'vegetalized' as a flower. The archetype, vital in Western culture (the rose, the lily) and in the East (the lotus blossom),

can be attributed to intertextuality, a process of poets reading and copy-
ing other poets over the centuries, in a golden line extending from the
Greek Anthology to Aragon, Eluard, and Nelli himself; or, in more
immediate Freudian terms, as a vaginal image in which the structure of
the rose or lotus mirrors the structure of the female sex (which Nelli displaces onto the girl's mouth). The vaginal reading is stated openly by
Jean de Meun and by the author of the *Chin P'ing Mei*. Nelli wishes to
ascribe to the woman the traits we habitually find in flowers: sweetness,
goodness, purity, beauty, and evanescence, all that is true, good, and
beautiful in the green world. He then reinforces the flower imagery by
insisting upon the girl's nakedness and innocence, and the whiteness
and light which she extracts from or imposes upon an otherwise dark
night.

However positive the desire and/or the experience, the ideal of *fin'
amor* and the reality of life itself impose an obstacle, the obstacle inherent in *fin' amor* which helps to maintain it at its peak yet also dooms it to
tragedy and loss. Sometimes in Nelli the female presence exudes the
demonic imagery of the nightmare, and there is no shared libido. This
is the case when, in one text, although the sacred mountain waits to
kneel to Diana, the proud goddess with a cruel smile is gone, never to
return, so that the hearts who adored her are dead hopes; or when, in
another text, although Eve waits for the night to love, we hear no more
of the love but only that there is no sun and no garden and that a mad
tree unleashes the wind and the melting of stars.

Even when love occurs, when it is shared, and when the Speaker does
joy in flower lips and shining thighs, Eros proves to be fragile and fragmented, as ephemeral as the rest of life, with the result that lovers are
separated by time, space, or death. Instants of bliss pass and are then
reduced to torture. Memory preserves something of Eros but also fails
to resurrect what is lost, indeed contributes to the destruction, granting
pain in addition to joy. Thus, the Speaker knew a siren ('la Serena'), he
knew the cry of her ravished flesh, the music of the abyss. She still
enchants him, for he dreams of her all his life and, because of memory,
though gone she remains with him. Still, she is not there, she flees, and
he beholds her presence (in memory) without hope. The character of
the wind collects white speech from light (happy?) hearts, then steals it
from lovers, also torn between hope and absence. At night, permeated
by the smell of rain and thunder, time distances our hearts; between the
morn and flocks in the field stands only a garden of stone. A summer
day turns from us, says the Speaker, our paths will never meet again in

spite of the joy your limbs gave me, an instant of your life. The thirst will
be quenched only with death, by a loveless God; the wound is first
desire; love and the Speaker's heart are in ashes.

In the end, or perhaps ontologically from the beginning, each human
is a unique element, in time and space, between life and death. Each
human consciousness is a Self, alone, doomed to solitude, incapable of
merging with the Other. This is the lesson – one lesson – of 'L'interna
consolacion.' The poem speaks of our loneliness that plunges in wind
and digs in sand, to find an arid tomb; there remain only ashes and
stars:

> Es la soletat nòstra
> qu'afonsa dins lo vent
> e cava dins l'arena
> son aride clauson.
>
> Remanh pas que de cendre
> remanh pas que d'estelas. (p. 69)

It also speaks of a sweet love, now in the autumn; will I know you, who
are foreign? Even in the past, the good days, you lied. Now we part and
give back the evil we have endured. In hope, death, and sadness our two
solitudes abide. Later, alluding to his dead 'sister,' the Speaker grieves
that, in her other life, she bears love for no one, so that their solitudes
are doubled. *Fin' amor*, then, a burning, spiritual longing for the Other,
in fire, can be satisfied only in instants of time. Continuity, certainty, stasis remain impossible because time, absence, and death are more powerful than desire, and because the very essence of our created world
contains and is eroded by the fragmentary and the chaotic. Man is
doomed to be a lone, solitary consciousness. Finally, since love even at
its best is grounded in the desires of the body, how can it overcome the
physical and, from the crucible of Eros, purged of its dross, rise in purified light to a higher level?

Is there then no hope? no answer? no higher level, for a purified
desire or other quests of the human? In my opinion, Nelli does not offer
a single answer or series of answers. His is not a poetry of doctrine. However, he does offer, after infinite struggle and pain, the glimpse of a
glimpse of the possibility of hope.

In 'L'interna consolacion,' Antistrophe III tells of a struggle against
the gods in sacred-profane night. Did we create them or they us? asks

the Speaker. Let me breathe my fatality and dream of gods! Then, in Antistrophe IV, in gnomic fashion the Speaker calls out: Don't be a slave! Live, embody what and whom you love! Fling your cry against the sea! Be pure and generous! Finally, in the first of the 1970–6 *Òdas* (Odes), addressing his dear, departed friend, the writer Joë Bousquet, the Speaker states, following Kafka's *Der Prozess*, that there is a door behind which stands a god who will not answer, or a greater Terrible, or the Void. Yet Joë Bousquet opened that door for deliverance from death. These are statements of our striving, heroism, and simple human dignity in the face of the greater Terrible and Void.

The last section of 'L'interna consolacion,' the text which despairs of rejoining the dead sister, ends on a brighter note. I am faithful to you, cries the Speaker, and I am truly myself to haunt you. You who cannot hide your heart or my desire for you, guide me in the shadows. Guide me to the threshold of glory. Spirit, choose that your broken beauty becomes charity.

I disagree with those who insist that Nelli's neo-Catharism determines the intellectual content and the shape of his entire corpus. That would result in reductionism and the oversimplification of an oeuvre so magnificent in its problematic complexity. However, it is true that the 'Catharist question' is central to Nelli's vision and is the subject of a number of his finest poems. Catharism is the heresy stamped out by the Albigension Crusade in the early thirteenth century. A number of Occitan writers, Nelli in the forefront, have created a new, twentieth-century Catharist myth (anticipated by writers in the nineteenth), the fall of Catharism perceived as a turning-point in history, an allegory for the fall of the South – according to the myth promulgated by Lafont, the assault on a unified Occitan nation – the end of freedom and the decline of humane values under the boots of invading, colonizing hordes from Paris. At the heart of this fascinating cultural phenomenon is to be found the arch-image of Montségur, the mountain citadel which held the remnant of Catharist resistance and was eventually stormed by the Count of Toulouse, who had by then joined the French.

Nelli evokes the Catharist question head on in *Beatrís de Planissòlas*, a playlet one-third to one-half the length of a Racinian tragedy, evoking the characters and issues we know best from Le Roy Ladurie's *Montaillou*.[19] (In a shortened version, it served as the libretto for an opera by Jacques Charpentier, performed at the Festival of Aix-en-Provence in 1971.) Nelli reconstitutes, in noble blank verse, the confrontation between the châtelaine Beatrice, her erstwhile lover Peire Clergue, and the inquisitor Jacques Fournier, Bishop of Pamiers, who in 1334 became Pope Benedict XII. Beatrice speaks for courtly love, Clergue for Catharist spirituality, and the bishop for Catholic orthodoxy. When I read *Montaillou*, I thought the inquisitor the only sensible person in a universe of rustic psychotics. Nelli is more 'politically correct' than I am; he gives the good lines to the adulteress and the heretic, and they are very good lines indeed.

In a moving passage, Beatrice insists that, although Clergue raped her the first time, they both felt pity and tenderness afterward. Yes, love is fire and hate, she says, yet beauty, pleasure, and hate give rise to the good, and fire creates light. Beatrice never took pleasure in the sexual act; her pleasure was giving pleasure to him, and he, in her, was as pure as a child. His destiny acted on mine, she says, and the void was cancelled by love, for love and virtue free themselves from destiny and hell. Love is pure and true ('fin,' 'coral') when he gazes in my eyes.

Clergue, on the other hand, insists this love was of the body only, and the body, my false soul, is already dead. That body and soul exist only in the past; they are ashes I abandon to the false Double (the Other Me) at the stake, as ashes and silence. Yes, God is absent, and, yes, now I seek only the Spirit.

It would be wrong to credit either Beatrice's conviction of love purified or Clergue's sense of the good soul freed from the body as a resolution of the problem. On the contrary, the strength of this text lies in the unresolved, ever-deferred conflict among all three voices. What might appear to be a symposium of allegories is transmitted into a moving, heart-rending *dialogue de sourds*, three possessed yet vulnerable human beings who cannot communicate. Each goes alone to the end, an end chosen and willed in the fire of the spirit.

Given that, twice, Nelli tells of climbing the narrow, winding, medieval streets of Carcassonne, from dusk to the stars, it was quasi-inevitable that his poetic persona, the Speaker, would also climb Montségur. Two masterpieces – 'La nuèit de Montsegur' (Montségur Night) and 'Òda a Montsegur' (Ode to Montségur) – treat this theme. Montségur is a sacred mountain (Frye would call it a point of epiphany), a temple which the Speaker climbs, preceded by an invisible procession of souls who flee to the beyond of love. These are the martyrs from centuries ago who, unchained, themselves seek out the flaming stake. Love wishes to die in the light of the flames. These spectres in the wind of hate, in a sky of glass that Evil broke, may they be reborn from the ashes of the dead, freed as a dove from the shadows! Esclarmonde rejoins her essence in the matrix of grace; the prettiest of the girls slept for seven centuries in an ark of stone; now, in a red mantle, she quits her dream to climb stairs in the clouds. The rocks – the ruins of the citadel – at the mountain top form an altar which no longer hears the waves of change or the rumours of the century. The angel brings love and fire to the rock, and God himself takes light from the burning, from infinite rigour extracting eternal patience. All will cease, all will perish. Yet we can still dream of righting wrongs, for, if we do, fear, hatred, and evil will flame away. In thunder and lightning the Speaker approaches the portal of the castle where God is Other, a God Unknown from beyond the stars.

Nelli offers no easy answers. He explores with the greatest intensity and rigour the human quest for love and for God, arriving at the glimmer of a glimmer of comprehension and of hope. He does so in a sequence of magnificently dense, cosmogonic lyricism, in which ideas and history are cast into the crucible of language. As with Valéry, these moments of intensity, comprehension, and quasi-alchemical transmutation mark the triumph of modern art as it struggles with and, in some sense, conquers the dislocation of our modern life, our vision of the universe, and our art.

BERNARD MANCIET

Bernard Manciet from Gascony is no doubt the greatest living poet of Oc. He served in the Diplomatic Corps and then returned to his village in the Landes region, where, from 1955 on, he ran the family business and then retired. Manciet's real business is and always has been writing. A number of tiny books and pamphlets appeared over the years, containing powerful, violent verse in free or the most rigorously fixed forms: odes, sonnets, *chants royaux*, panegyrics, dirges, and, in *Gesta* (Deeds), poems of combat. There also appeared a series of novels and shorter fiction which have contributed in a significant way to the revival of prose. Manciet has been one of the most outspoken apostles of modernism, calling for a language whose worth is determined by its literature, and a literature open to all of Europe and to the avant-garde, on as high a level as that of the troubadours. In the name of that literature and of the high culture it embodies, he co-authored the 1957 'Manifèst de Nerác' and, since 1978, has served as editor-in-chief of *Oc*.[20]

Manciet's masterpiece is *L'Enterrament a Sabres* (Burial in Sabres), published in 1989.[21] This long lyrical epic or epic lyric depicts the burial of la Dauna, an old lady in the village: the procession to the church, the traditional Catholic requiem mass, and the procession to the cemetery. A simple, trivial, and eminently marginal subject, it would appear, but one to which Manciet brings the same gravity and *tremendum* that his forefathers brought to the Battle of Rencesvals and the Fall of King Arthur. What is Sabres? A little village in the Landes, a region south of Bordeaux, best known to us from the novels of Mauriac, a bit of swamp and sand off the main roads, of no interest, on the margins of French life, for that matter on the margins of Occitan life.[22] Yet for Manciet it becomes the centre of the cosmos, a sacred locus (Frye's point of epiphany again) where God makes manifest his presence, where God speaks to man and man to God. And la Dauna? One-half a village notable, one-half the local witch, she also is nothing, a rustic on the margins of society, yet at the same time she is the life and soul of the village and of Gascon tradition. The people, the little people of the village, are a flock of losers: Paula the whore, Armant de Malichec the drummer, Arnaut the old priest, Maria de la Neta the bell-ringer and town drunk, the mule drivers, and the mourners. These drunkards, sluts, and buffoons embody the land and the race, they are the heirs of centuries of history. Behind them, fused in them, stand those who made Gascony – kings and queens, dukes and duchesses, popes and bishops, mercenaries and slave traders. In them we perceive as well the suffering of the centuries, of victims cut to pieces by war (especially the Great War) and by machines (factories come from the north), and by the Beast, image of Napoleon III. Focusing to the utmost on this patch of swamp and sand, the centre of the cosmos, Manciet brings to the two or three hours of the *erzählte Zeit* a power and intensity of *nunc stans*, containing centuries of history, in the eternal present of sacred time.

The third book of *L'Enterrament* is called 'Dies Irae.' In it la Dauna and all the dwellers of the Landes, past and present, are called to the seat of judgment. It can be said that judgment is the dominant theme of the poem, that la Dauna and the others die in order to be judged, and that the plot of *L'Enterrament*, to the extent that there is a plot, leads to a cosmological climax, the end of time, when all men, the quick and the dead, stand before Christ in Majesty. After so many centuries of culture and of Christendom, it is perhaps fitting that the centre of gravity be displaced from the life of Christ (the past) to the Last Judgment (the future), in Manciet's sardonic vision our only future as individuals and as a race: 'Dies irae, dies illa.'

God reproaches la Dauna for having been a harlot on the roads.

Although he sent her his Spirit, she disdained to answer. Oh! he will force her to speak, he will seize her and break her:

liri esconvirat vau te tirar de la caudèira
esborentada viva e viva esplumaishada
se vam vrenhar
dalhar e talhar
carn vertadèra deu saunei tirada (p. 257)

(dishevelled lily I will drag you out of the pot boiled alive plucked alive we will harvest mow and cut real flesh taken from a dream)

He will boil and pluck her alive like a chicken. God accuses humankind of physical and spiritual weakness, of corruption, softness, and rot. You refused me sacrifices, he says. So be it. I will myself make burnt offerings – you! I will drink your blood and teach you the wrath of God:

volotz pas mès me har gresilhar la vianda
la grèisha de las cueishas me la har humar
a l'autar de Baiona
volotz pas m'escanar la sang deu hilh
e en voloi pas mès deus vòstes maseths
me sui hèit a jo medish lo sacrifici (p. 169)

(you refused to grill the meat for me to smoke the fat from thighs for me on the Bayonne altar you refused to spill the blood of a son for me so I did not want any more of your slaughterhouses to myself I made the sacrifice)

Manciet revels in apocalyptic and demonic imagery. Christ on the Cross endures cosmic pain and agonies of thirst. Kyrie brings the winds. Blessings from saints and the souls in purgatory are manifest in rain and hail. Elsewhere, we are told that God's Peace comes with water, and with water come also vermin and the plague. And his love brings fire. Forest fire and locusts are mine, not Satan's, he cries. Although storm, thunder, lightning, and flames evoke God's creative seminal power – *Deus faber et pater* – more often they manifest his wrath. For the poor folk of the Landes, which is covered with pine trees, forest fire is an obsession.[23] They are chastised, therefore, in their obsession. Again and again are re-enacted the fall of Sodom and Gomorrah and the end of the world, apocalypse in fire, a drama in which God is lightning, 'Eslumbric.'

The poet's metaphoric Doomsday is portrayed not in terms of monologue but as dialogue, or rather a combat in words, verbal confrontation
which resembles Jacob's wrestling with the Angel. The author of *Gesta*,
who wrote 'la gai de la batalha' (the joy of battle) and 'Ma patria es la
batalha' (My native land is battle), lives for combat.[24] In our culture,
since Hugo and Vigny the combat is waged between human beings and
God, and for the little people it can be only a battle of words, words
incarnate in our flesh, in God, and in the poem, 'La lenga que ditz a la
lenga' (The tongue speaking to the tongue).

La Dauna never yields before the divinity's reiterated blasts. On the
contrary, she rebels against the Lord God of Hosts, she brings him as an
offering war: 't'i pòrti guèrra' (p. 161). Her voice and the voices of the
villagers and of the Narrator accuse God of never having been present,
of never having spoken to them and always waited too long before helping them. In Heideggerian terms, she accuses him of Being-ever-in-
absence, a Transcendent Other who abandoned his flock. We the little
people have suffered more than you ever did on the cross! she cries. You
need us more than we need you:

es pas la tua fauta es belèu la nòsta car
as dau d'estar sauvat
e embaumat e cohintat de la nòsta estadissa
la lana [...] pòt pas mès plorar
a fòrça de sorelh au sable (p. 79)

(it's not your fault maybe it is ours for you need to be saved and incensed
and cradled by our exhaustion our *lande* can weep no more by dint of sun
on sand)

Take back your shoes and return to us our feet, the little people ask. All
we want is a little light and warmth, the memory of love, and the chance
to work. (Later, the mule drivers, bursting with truculence, demand
some bread and lots of wine and sex!)[25]

More than once the text calls for a Hegelian reading of the master
and the slave. God is the Lord; we are his servants. His power is absolute, ours is a void. Yet he needs us, he cannot function without us. He
must have our consciousness and need and hunger for him in our
misery, as he thirsted for us on the cross in his misery. These meditations align *L'Enterrament a Sabres* with the central problem of the twentieth century, the *Seinsfrage*: the anxiety of being, the ontological void

endured by all who are, who are conscious of being, yet who can never fathom the totality of existence.

From *Roland* to *Lancelot* to Balzac, Zola, and Proust, for that matter to Camus and Gracq, the hero of literature is a young man, and the diegesis recounts his exploits and his inner growth, modulated by a structure of conventions ranged under the term *Bildungsroman*. Manciet, on the other hand, is powerfully modernist, even anticipates postmodernism; for his text tells of a marginal anti-protagonist functioning in an anti-narrative that depicts marginal anti-heroism. This 'hero,' la Dauna, in herself and in her social and linguistic contextualization, evokes a problematic of marginality and also one of undermining and of derision vis-à-vis the grand archetypes of literature. La Dauna is a woman, old, tiny (a hag really), in the village, surrounded by her servants, her gossips, and her mourners, mouthing the patois of Sabres, itself on the marginality of Gascon, which is marginal to central literary Occitan – all this set off against male heroes of epics, romances, and novels, young, strong, dwelling in Paris (or Camelot), speaking French, and anchored in and contributing to European universality. La Dauna can be a creature of horror, her body all insect and scales. The villagers don't want her back. And she is afraid to go without her servant, whom she berates in a series of mock farewells à la Villon: Did you put away my money? Now you can sleep late mornings! She is old, old with centuries of village life and Gascon history. She is a woman and, as such, recalling the martyr heroes of Baroque epic (in D'Aubigné and Saint-Amant), she suffers and endures. Her actantial function is to suffer and endure, in her subjectivity and in her universality. As a woman she also is symbol and allegory, of the *landes*, the village, the little people of Gascony, and their language.

In addition, in this Gascon night punctuated by blasts of thunder and lightning, in the archetypal feminine night of passion and the irrational, under the feminine moon, occur a series of lunatic combats – not Jacob wrestling with the Angel, but la Dauna struggling directly with the Creator in erotic battle. As with Delavouët, as with Nelli, Manciet establishes a sexual register derived from *fin' amor* and from the Song of Songs, where Eros presides at the core of the human experience and is the Way, the Truth, and the Life. On one hand la Dauna may well be an insect, all scales; on another, the stars are her breasts and sex, and she is a rose. God finds her comely, he is stunned by her beauty, and he becomes her sun, stallion, and tree. Yet God also cherishes her in fire and sword, in breaking her and burning her. As with the Catholic poets writing in French, Claudel, Jouve, and Emmanuel among others, for that matter as with the poets of courtly love, death is assimilated to love and love to death. Eros and Thanatos stamp the human condition in its rites of passage: at birth, in the nuptial bed, and, in the last passage of all, Christ's embrace.

Again, as with Delavouët, Manciet renews the peculiarly medieval, typological sense of time, with la Dauna (we can translate her name as Ma Dame or Madonna) an *imago* of the old widowed mother; a traditional village 'type,' transformed by the workings of typology into a figure of Eve, the mother of mankind, and of Mary, Mother of God. Manciet underscores la Dauna's maternal role. God impregnates her, and, as a telluric goddess, suffering the birth pangs Mary suffered, she gives birth to all around her, and she stands for the land, containing the people in her. Manciet also underscores la Dauna's role as *mediatrix*, for, again resembling the Mother of God, she intercedes for the Gascon people and begs for mercy on their behalf. Herself a sinner, Whore of Babylon, seduced by the Serpent and seducing men in turn, she perpetuates the worst of Eve; yet she also redeems her sins and those of her race, for, as a woman, she is the Bride of Christ (the Church) in the Canticles and she postfigures the Virgin Mary as much as she does the First Mother. She is Eva fulfilled and crowned by Ave, the New Covenant which redeems the Old Covenant, Ecclesia now in place of Synagoga.

Nevertheless, the redeemed Synagogue remains, because of the bond which unites the village of Sabres to Jehovah. How often the Narrator proclaims that these little folk of Gascony are the Chosen People, beloved by God, and that 'we the race of Levi, God is our only inheritance' ('nosautis de la traca de Leví / n'am pas sonque Diu com erteratge') (p. 189). They are the Children of Israel in bondage in Egypt; their Dauna (judge, prophet) stops the sun like Joshua. And they praise God because of their suffering, not in spite of it. The people and their prophet ask from God what he gave the Children of Israel: chastisement as love and torment in consciousness. The Eternal then responds positively. As in the Old Testament, as in D'Aubigné, God's love wounds, and one endures it in pain. The Lord loves his people in chastising them, he is thirsty, so he drinks Gascon blood.

He loves in blasting and breaking. And his wretched beloveds are reduced to asking questions (Job) or condemning themselves (the Prophets) or – in this we moderns break out of the biblical frame – condemning God in turn. They are worthy, these little children of the Tribe of Israel. They reply also in fire, they shout back the flame of speech and of love: 'la lenga que ditz a la lenga.' The Old Testament, the New Testament, Occitan history, and contemporary life – as in the mystery plays, as in D'Aubigné, all is present, all is included in this Legend of the Centuries that Victor Hugo never wrote but should have wanted to write.

After all this, in the end, what happens? What is the end? After struggle and pain, the old woman dies partly as a good Catholic and partly as a pagan witch, one-half soaring into the skies as flower and light and one-half borne off to Charon's boat, on the swamp to the seas. And it is over. Is this then a closed narrative, the battle ended, all said and done? The death of the old Gascony, its villages, language, and culture? In one sense, yes. Manciet adheres to the structure and the symbolism of the mass, according to which Christians, the quick and the dead, find a stasis of peace in Christ and are blessed. This *pax Christi* is also the benediction of the implied author on the Daunas he has known, the village, the land, the language, and the history and people of Gascony. La Dauna is dead. Yet the others? All the others, including the implied author, Bernard Manciet? Every line of the poem cries 'No!' All that I know of this semi-mythical village and land and their author cries 'No!' Remember that the Lord's benediction is manifest in thunder, lightning, rain, and hail. The sacraments are storm, and the storm is a sacrament. For Manciet, faith, hope, and love are always grounded in, and associated with, transgression and excess. These are a truculent people of rebels, always given to transgression and excess. Did not la Dauna entreat the Lord – demand from him – instead of a soft death *à la provençale*, death in ecstasy, to be torn apart by his lightning? It is then the ultimate thunderstorm, God's rage/rape, ecstasy in the eternal present – lightning blasts that fall like wood, joy in stabbing, lovely tears, white tears – that end this song of *geste*. Dead, laboured and ploughed with whiteness, 'la Dauna tota lana la Dauna' proclaims, 'Now leave me be' ('que me pòdetz adara atau deishar tranquil',' p. 433). The last voice we hear is hers – the bride, the mother, the whore, the human woman who questions and denounces her male creator up to her and the text's final breath. Such is this allegory – Manciet's vision is powerfully allegorical, more in the spirit of Dante, Digulleville, D'Aubigné, and Langland than in romances about roses – the life and death of one frightful hag, who is also Gascony, the Gascon people, the Gascon language, and all of humanity, all the daughters of Eve and Mary.

For Bernard Manciet, poet and human being, for the Narrator of his book, for the people of the Landes, for the Landes, for all who dwell in Sabres, in the flesh or in the spirit, the struggle continues. A struggle which began with Roland and Charlemagne, or with Gilgamesh and

Enkidu. A struggle which will endure, in rage and transgression, in quest and introspection, for all of us who see only as in a glass, darkly. Such is the human condition.

NOVEL

JEAN BOUDOU

Jean Boudou (Occ. Joan Bodon) is, by general acclaim, the greatest writer of prose in Occitan and the first and best modern novelist. A tragic, solitary figure with a tragic, solitary vision of life, he spent much of his adult existence as an itinerant schoolteacher and died in Algeria, in his fifties. Boudou published a number of story collections, derived in part from the oral tradition of his native Rouergue, and five novels, with a sixth left unfinished at his death in 1975.[26]

Boudou's first novel, the 1956 La Grava sul camin (The Gravel on the Roadbed), recounts the life of a peasant.[27] The plot is resolutely modern, with no indulgence in clichés and the sentimental nostalgia endemic in so much of the writing on country life. The protagonist is Enric de Savinhac, a rural anti-hero, who fails the entrance exams to the Ecole Normale, is sent off to Germany in the work battalions (1942), returns home after the war to people who treat him almost as if he had been a collaborator, agrees to a disastrous marriage, and then, on the day of his wedding, runs off in an even more disastrous flight.

Savinhac is the very embodiment of alienation. As his mother says, 'Eras pas coma los autres' (You were not like the others). He can neither work the land in the old way as a member of the community nor leave the village. Since his studies led nowhere, he is riveted to the farm socially as well as spatially. Manipulated and exploited by others, he dreams of brotherhood with the people around him but cannot live that dream. For Enric, there is no exit.

Boudou demonstrates courage and generosity in writing, with sympathy, about a loser, a young man enrolled in the STO (Service du Travail Obligatoire), who was not a hero of the Resistance and not a committed, engaged idealist. He writes with sympathy and generosity concerning the misery of the poor, little people oppressed in their daily lives yet scarcely conscious of the oppression, outsiders who seek only a little happiness and whose only redeeming virtue is their dignity in the face of pain.[28]

One image of Enric's pain and his alienation is created by patterns of space. The title of the novel alludes to the sharp stones on the roadbed of the railway and, by extension, to the road of life. Part 1 of *La Grava* tells of Enric's return from Silesia after 1945, a trip punctuated by a series of brusque movements – oblique, incoherent, contradictory, going nowhere. The ex-prisoners are rounded up, pushed here, herded there, taken on railway cars and then taken off, starting and stopping with no sense and no logic. This structure is then repeated later in the novel. The three other parts are made up of little trips, desperate efforts to get away from home and to escape boredom and fatigue: Enric gets drunk at a dance, at the fair, or at a baptism, and on Sundays he roams the countryside. Each section ends with a voyage: Enric tries the 'cours complémentaire' and the exams; he visits a wealthy farmer, meets the daughter, and gets engaged; he runs away, drops into a whorehouse, finds a bicycle, and breaks his leg. In each section, at a moment of crisis, he undertakes a quest, dreaming of diplomas, money, friendship, and love. The only way to free himself from his closed, traditional, ancestral world is by breaking out. Progression in space is a metaphor for psychic progression, Enric's capacity to grow and evolve, to relish simply being. Significantly, therefore, in each section, at each crisis, the quest is aborted. Savinhac never attains his dreams. Except at the end, he always returns, forced to return home. The external exile to Germany is complemented by an internal exile in his own land, in his own family, where, again and again, he proves to be a failure, incapable of rebelling yet equally unwilling to submit.

The morning he leaves for Germany, Enric and his father wander off from the train station. To return, they walk directly following the railway tracks. However, the gravel – the sharp rocks on the roadbed – would hinder their progress, so they tread only on the wooden ties:

Trimèrem benlèu una ora. Lo solelh donava. I aviá pas cap de vial lo long de la linha. Susàvem. Cada travèrsa un pas. Cada travèrsa un pas. Voliàm pas trescambar sus la grava reganhuda, la grava sul camin. (p. 109)
(We slogged at it for maybe an hour. The sun beat down. There was no path along the railway line. We were sweating. For each tie a step. For each tie a step. We didn't want to stumble on the exposed pebbles, the gravel on the roadbed.)

The gravel is the obstacle. Later, on another road also covered with gravel, Savinhac loses control of his bicycle and breaks his leg.

This is not the only image of stone in the novel. The cathedral at Rodez marks the young man's failure in his studies and in his love life; the church in the village is a locus for social exclusion and hypocrisy. In Silesia, Enric dreams of the family farmhouse, associated with the image of the mother. Part 3 of the novel is entitled 'Al meu ostal' (At Home). Yet, ironically, immediately upon his return, the house ceases to be a home. In Occitan, *ostal* refers to the family unit, the kinship community as much as to a building, and Enric no longer belongs to the one and only eats and sleeps in the other. No less ironically, on his wedding day the protagonist wanders into what he thinks is an inn, which turns out to be a brothel, a quite different kind of *ostal,* 'l'ostal de las filhas' (whorehouse), where he wallows in degradation. Significantly, prior to entering the brothel, Enric had reached the railway station (again!), but this time the train had already left. Gravel, monument, bridge, church, headstone, train station, classroom, inn, house, and whorehouse – all are built of stone and all stand against the young Enric. Boudou has created his own structure of imagery, a Bachelardian pattern as it turns out, dominated by the harsh earth of the will, the Rouergue earth which Enric knows so well, which is central to his heritage; yet, because it is his imposed heritage, he cannot cope with it and it breaks his body and his spirit.

The last section is entitled 'Lo vent d'autan' (The South Wind). Reinforcing the imagery of stone, the wind dominates these last episodes. Enric's decision to run away coincides with the rise of this blast from the sea. He strides, runs, and cycles, always against the wind: 'Val mai sègre lo vent; e lo capval me tira. Davali ... davali ... [...] Lo vent lo còpi, lo vent me pren, puèi de longa l'ai contra ieu' (pp. 157, 176) (It's better to go with the wind; and the downgrade pulls at me. I go down ... I go down ... I slice through the wind, the wind seizes me, then I have it constantly against me). It is the wind which knocks him backwards, the immediate cause of his accident. The wind can be interpreted on a number of levels, as a symbol of liberty or will to power, or the loss of rational consciousness or panic or insanity, or the hostile force of nature and destiny. In any case, Enric struggles ever again and again against wind and stone, and ever is the loser. Ever tortured in his lonely ontological Self, no matter how hard he tries, he cannot escape the inner exile, which is as punishing as was life in a Silesian camp. A Freudian reading would state, validly I believe, that the struggle of the psyche against the obstacle, the breaking of the Self by the obstacle, relates to a structure of desire in which the libido is blunted, frustrated, and denied in imagery of metaphoric castration.

The structure of desire is central to Enric's and Boudou's world.[29] Vis-à-vis the female principle of his society, Enric always loses and always is in the wrong. He is basically a decent chap who treats a Polish prostitute and a German woman kindly. Back home, ill at ease with women and equally ill at ease in the rural community, he cannot find a place for himself where the unique modalities for sexual activity are located in marriage and prostitution. Unable to adapt, subject to trauma from the beginning, Enric follows a quasi-obsessional pattern. He seeks out girls who are rich, pretty, and highly prized, girls for whom he literally does not exist, whereas the two young women who seek him out do not exist for him; he rejects them because, partially handicapped, they don't mirror his dreams and don't adhere to the canons of beauty, and therefore of respectability, of his world. As a result, he ends up with, and is disgusted by, sluts and whores. Social barriers apparently (Enric does nothing to infringe them) forbid a relationship with Rotlanda, the good student who passes her exams, and with Marinon, the girl next door whose family has been feuding ('pas d'acòrdi') with the Savinhacs. Enric's own misplaced pride, his dread of what the others will say, forbids him to accept creatures as miserable as he is and who therefore could love him: the hunchbacked Melia he meets at a dance and the limping Cristiana he is supposed to wed. The novel begins with the evocation of a poor Polish whore, her life destroyed by the Germans; it ends with the evocation of a Southern French whore, who also 'served' in the camps. Enric fails to relate to these girls as to everyone else, and his isolation in the rural community is determined by his failure to find a wife, in a universe where standing is granted by the family, marriage, and home – the *ostal* – and where, for the man as well as the woman, solitude is treated as a social lack and is unforgivable.

One reason for Enric's failure, with women and elsewhere, lies in his inability to communicate. As Feliçon and Suson prattle and chatter, poor Enric feels inundated by their flow of words. Himself the strong silent type, he speaks rarely and with difficulty. Is his a specifically Occitan problem, and does he, in some sense, stand for the man of the South, deprived of his speech? It is certain that background, education, and social class all contribute to making Enric the person he is. As the inscribed narrator of his own story, he speaks in Occitan, 'la lenga del trimadís,' the language of the home and the farm, the language forbidden in school. German and French, in equal measure, are seen to be foreign tongues, the one ('alemand dels camps') used to communicate – more or less – with Poles and Russians in Silesia and with German prisoners of war in France; the latter appearing as orders from a loudspeaker or insults from rich tourists or as the medium for conversation with a prostitute until it is discovered they both come from the South. Enric does his best when relating to marginals like himself: the prostitutes, drunkards, foreigners, and the handicapped. Still, failure to communicate becomes tragic when the men from the village beat a German prisoner because they think he has been singing a Nazi war song. Savinhac is the only one present who actually knows some German, and he protests that the poor fellow is innocent but fails to convince the others, who, on the contrary, are ready to beat him for being more German than the Germans. People from the South, in their own Occitan, are no more able to communicate or to lead authentic lives than anyone else. Indeed, these brutes from the farm are shown to be more violent and pig-headed than the French schoolteachers, the German prisoners, and the Russian officers. In the end, Savinhac succeeds in communicating – to the extent that he does – only as the narrator of his book, with his narratees – us the implied readers.

I say to the extent that he does, because one of the more disconcerting and exciting aspects of the text lies in its use of narrative technique. *La Grava sul camin* is an *Ich-Erzählung*, a homodiegetic narrative, told directly by Enric de Savinhac, the protagonist of his own story. The implied reader sympathizes with this narrator-hero for a number of reasons. The story and the world it evokes are filtered uniquely through his consciousness, since his point of view, however limited, is the only one we have, and since his intelligence, however limited, alone provides us with the evidence to respond to the people and events.

Furthermore, three of the four main sections are narrated in the present tense, which creates an aura of drama and suspense, of immediacy and authenticity. The distance between the *erlebendes Ich* and the *erzählendes Ich* – between the 'I' as protagonist and the 'I' as narrator – is therefore narrowed, as is the distance between the two of them and the implied reader.

Finally, Boudou moulds the reader's response in his hero's favour by dropping a number of metanarrative signals that will appeal to the known, presumed horizon of expectations in the public and will both appeal to and help shape its response. Thus, a French intellectual and/ or a literate Occitan public will become positively disposed toward a character of peasant background who does his best in school, tries for the Ecole Normale, doesn't go to church, is conscious of clerical hypocrisy, is nice to 'las filhas dels camps,' sings the *Internationale*, and wears a cap with the red star.

All this granted, a level of ambiguity remains, due to questions of point of view and focalization. Enric tells his story in brief, truncated, paratactic sentences. He tells the facts, all that he sees, but rarely does he analyse the psychology or motivation behind the facts. Although he dreams often enough and of politics, he never interprets events, and only rarely will he admit his personal reactions. Savinhac the narrator tells of the encounter with the Polish prostitute without revealing what he now thinks of the event or what Savinhac the character thought of it at the time. Savinhac the narrator tells us that Savinhac the character was fearless when once arrested by the Russians yet leaves it to the implied reader to interpret the character's behaviour as courage, confidence, nonchalance, indifference, insensibility, or sheer stupidity. Again and again Enric's veritable, profound emotions – if he has veritable, profound emotions – remain hidden and perhaps unconscious. It becomes then the reader's task to fill in the gaps in the text, to provide the appropriate psychological reading.

Boudou brings this about by employing a narrative technique to be found in Hemingway, Steinbeck, and Camus: the behaviourist mode, according to which the narrative records speeches, gestures, and acts – what a movie camera could register – but rarely or never the voice of a superior consciousness. The problem is, how can this technique be harmonized with a homodiegetic narrative where the *erzählendes Ich* displays, in theory, not only a point of view but also a focalizing consciousness and is the implied author? Camus did it successfully in *L'Etranger.* Here Boudou also succeeds, in part because, as with Camus, there are legitimate mimetic and historical reasons – the war, the fact of being a peasant, the fact of speaking and thinking in patois – to explain why Savinhac as narrator registers everything but is so inept at expressing what he feels in the domain of imagination and introspection (if and when he feels).

Moreover, because of the first-person behaviourism, Boudou establishes, in addition to the aura of authenticity, distance between his protagonist and the implied reader. The reader comes to discover faults and weaknesses in the hero – for instance, his failure to communicate – and all that belongs to motivation and psychology, of which Savinhac the character and Savinhac the narrator appear to be ignorant. By being obliged to contribute to the process of reception, indeed to the process of creation, the reader enters into a situation of complicity with the implied author against the protagonist. This disjunction between narrative voice and inner focalization gives rise to a sense of hermeneutic

ambiguity. The absence of narrative omniscience and of obtrusive consciousness deprives the story of the control in shaping beliefs and norms
that the reader relies upon in traditional fiction.

 La Grava sul camin is, therefore, untraditional and, because of the
ambiguity, powerfully modern. It is my conviction that the ambiguity
and the modernity extend to the novel's denouement, rendering it
more problematic than it at first appears. These last, quasi-picaresque
adventures end on a neutral, anti-climactic note. Yes, the protagonist
has lost Cristiana, for a time; yes, his leg is broken, for a time. But he has
found Lacòsta, his old comrade from the war; Lacòsta takes him in and
Lacòsta's mother receives him with as much warmth, more warmth actually, than he could expect in his own *ostal*. Enric having cried out his
fiancée's name, 'Cristiana!,' Lacòsta reassures him: he, Lacòsta, will go
the next day to her house: 'Cristiana, me dises: deman tanben anarai al
seu ostal' (p. 195). It is over. Yet, is it really over? Should we stop at the
surface of the text? Given the narrative distance, external focalization,
and behaviourist point of view, it is clear that we the implied readers do
not know Lacòsta, we are not made aware of his character, emotions,
and motivations, or for that matter the tone of his voice. And Enric does
not necessarily know any more than we do. The one creature in the cosmos who knows is Jean Boudou, who chooses to end his novel here. Perhaps he wants the reader to discover things never even imagined by
poor Enric. The narrator underscores Enric's tears, the mother's aston-
ishment, and Lacòsta's surprising lack of authority. Is it not possible that
Lacòsta will indeed go to Cristiana's *ostal* but not necessarily on his
friend's behalf? That, acting on his own, he may well supplant Enric in
the eyes of this girl, who is indeed handicapped yet, at the same time,
covered with gold in her affluent, opulent *ostal*? If I am right, here, at
the end, even friendship from the war proves to be contaminated, and
Enric's last illusions – his memory of the past, the only genuine adventure in his life – are lost forever. Even if we interpret Lacòsta's character
in a more favourable light, it is still possible for something to develop
between him and Cristiana, for him to be welcomed in a way now lost to
the disloyal, disgraced bridegroom. In any case, the lack of introspection on the part of the hero makes up one indispensable element in the
novel. The story ends at just the moment when Savinhac the narrator
begins to understand what Savinhac the character never knew and,
because of it, he is now ready to create. The ambiguity of the novel, the
ambiguity of the stone gravel on the road, becomes an essential theme
of the novel and the narrative technique of *La Grava*, a fundamental

contribution to *La Grava*. The Occitan person becomes an Occitan narrator-creator of Occitan characters, rejoining the tradition of European modernity.

After *La Grava sul camin*, Boudou continued to write novels. *La Santa Estèla del centenari* (The Felibrige Centennial) of 1960 and *Lo Libre dels grands jorns* (The Book of the Last Days) of 1964 are traditional in that they tell a story and present rounded characters. However, as with the Breton novel, Boudou shifts from realism to the realm of symbols, allegories, the poetic, the ludic, and the fantastic. Like the Bretons he turns to something approximating magical realism.

In *La Santa Estèla del centenari*, a man closely resembling Jean Boudou visits Rodez, where he is handed a manuscript by an inmate from the local asylum.[30] The novel will be his story. The inmate, Ambròsi Lorei, was a poor young man in the Rouergue country who worked as a postal delivery man and, in his spare time, wrote poetry in Occitan. He enters into contact with the writer Enric Molin (Fr. Henri Mouly) and is persuaded by Molin to attend the great Felibrige ceremony in Avignon (this is 1954), which will celebrate the movement's centennial. After a series of misadventures, including the loss of his poems, Ambròsi accompanies an Old Man ('lo vièlh'), who takes him to Nîmes, where he observes a man drowning in a fountain, and then to a deserted village back in Rouergue. Here Ambròsi falls in love with the Old Man's servant, Joseta, and they make love. The next morning they awake to discover that the Old Man – a brilliant engineer – has transformed them into robots (today we would say cyborgs), in order for them to reproduce and conquer the world as and for Occitan-speakers. The couple rebel. Ambròsi kills Joseta while attempting to saw off her metallic outer crust. The Old Man applies electricity to Ambròsi, who wakes up as the drowning man in the fountain and is interred in the asylum.

This strange narrative – half allegory, half science-fiction fantasy – builds on themes and motifs from *La Grava sul camin*. Here, again, Boudou writes of little people in the countryside, marginal people, losers in the eyes of the world. He makes us sympathize with the young postal carrier, who loves poetry and nature and his native language, and strives for a better life. And with a young man who falls in love and learns compassion and sacrifice. Ambròsi is an exile in his own land, as was Enric de Savinhac; and the Old Man, like Enric, suffers from having been a prisoner in Germany. More even than in *La Grava*, a pall hangs over Ambròsi's world, a sense of decline and death. The Old Man is obsessed

with the death of Old Europe and the coming of the Apocalypse, an
idea originally tossed out by a group of Jehovah's Witnesses and by a
self-proclaimed John the Apostle, who disrupt the Felibrige Celebration.[31] Boudou is especially concerned with the death of Occitan, which
is the Old Man's obsession and the reason for his mad experiments; yet
the decline and soon-to-be anticipated demise of the language also pre-
occupy Molin and serve as an ironic undertone to the chaotic, artificial
folklore of Provence.

In the style of medieval romance, Ambròsi undergoes a quest. Very
young, isolated, naïve, he resembles Perceval, the *nice* in Chrétien de
Troyes. In the course of the quest, in the tradition of the modern *Bildungsroman* (which goes back to Chrétien), Ambròsi learns, grows, and
evolves, as he travels from his home to Molin's house, then to Avignon,
Nîmes, the deserted Saint-Ferréol, back to Nîmes, and, finally, Rodez.
He is educated and initiated into the mysteries by a first father-figure,
Molin, and then by the Old Man, a father far more threatening, a
would-be god who acts as God. The Old Man also serves as a guide, a
force of nature, accompanying the hero on his voyage, without whom
the voyage would be impossible. Ambròsi falls in love, is initiated into
sexual fulfilment, and then learns the tragedy inherent in human passion, subject to time and death. He learns to rebel against a wicked
father, to stand up for freedom and the right to live, and, in the process,
undergoes a death-rebirth experience. Unlike Enric de Savinhac, always
acted upon, incapable of serious resistance or transgression, Ambròsi
Lorei strikes out on his own; he becomes, in part, a genuine hero of
romance.

Only in part, because the romance, the quest, and the *Bildungsroman*
are constantly undercut by a counterstructure of paradox, irony, the
grotesque, the *buffo*, and what Gardy calls Bakhtinian carnival.[32] To
begin with, each chapter has a title in Occitan yet also in French and
English. The French and English versions are comic amplifications of
the Occitan, in the style of newspaper headlines and advertising. Hence,
for chapter 8 of book 3, 'L'amor' becomes 'Découverte sensationnelle
du savant aveyronnais: Les robots seront désormais capables d'amour et
pourront engendrer' and 'Love among the Robots: Hearts Not of Iron.'

Poor Ambròsi's quest is made up of a series of broken, fragmented,
twisted train rides, from Villefranche-de-Rouergue to Toulouse to Nîmes
to Avignon to Nîmes to the Cévennes, then by car to Saint-Ferréol. One
quest and initiation culminate in the comic, folkloric, useless ceremony
of the Felibrige, which ends in a ruckus on the streets. The second quest

and initiation wind up and up yet lead our hero only to a deserted village in his own province. Here, the structures of romance and the mimetic, neo-realistic background are turned inside out by intrusion – invasion, one could say – from the domain of science fiction. However, in place of the potentially grandiose effects of, say, interaction with outer space, Boudou inserts into the heart of his narrative the futile inventions of one Old Man, who superbly embodies the archetype of the mad scientist, endemic to our culture over the last century and a half. It is pathetic yet also uproariously comic (à la Kafka) to see Ambròsi and Joseta, after their night of love, waking up to their new, cyborg state: human hearts beating in human flesh and anguished human minds, all encased in an outer shell of steel. After the two robots have intercourse (a kind of penetration in iron), it is again pathetic and uproariously comic when Ambròsi decides to restore Joseta to her human state by sawing off the metallic outer crust:

> 'Crenhas pas, Joseta. Pòrti los espleches que cal. Ressarai, limarai, dubrirai lo metal que nos plega. E tornarem coma davant, totes nuds. [...] E totara. Començarai per tu. Jai-te per tèrra! cridèri. Sul ventre.' (pp. 224, 227)
> (Don't be afraid, Joseta. I am bringing the tools we need. I will saw, I will file, I will cut open the metal that enshrouds us. And we'll return to how we were before, stark naked. Immediately. I'll begin with you. Lie down on the ground! I cried. Flat on your stomach.)

In the Bergsonian sense, comedy is produced by the juxtaposition of the mechanical and the dynamically human, as it is by the mechanical rigidity of the mad scientist who will go on to produce more and better cyborgs. The defence of the Occitan language and the desperate efforts by Occitanists to maintain their language, against history and against death, are noble endeavours. The nobility emanates from Molin and even from Ambròsi. However, that such a cause should give rise to the Old Man's fanaticism, that such a cause should bring him to become a hermit with the express purpose of creating mechanical monsters who will take over the earth and preserve Occitan by eradicating all humans who speak something else – this is indeed madness and farce. The language question, important on one level, is seen to be trivial as the justification for individual kidnapping and societal terror. Boudou, himself a member of the Felibrige and an Occitanist faithful to the IEO, shows that he can mock, undermine, and satirize all sides of the cause he himself so strongly believes in. Ambròsi's childish, useless little notebook of

'Flor de ginèst ... Poèmas' (Broom Poems) is sweet and endearing, and a joke. More catastrophic is the childish, useless, and joke-filled Sainte-Estelle Banquet of the Cup (Hugh MacDiarmid could scarcely invent comparable satire of a Burns Supper), where people doze through a long poem in Catalan that no one understands and then wake up to a street riot. Given these terms of the debate, can we not interpret the Old Man as one version – an allegorical, satirical caricature – of IEO extremism, the new Occitanists who will create their own artificial language and their own artificial high culture, far from genuine peasants, and somehow also bring about radical social change in Southern France, that is, create Occitan socialism, all by themselves? The two levels – of nobility or pathos and of farce – are maintained throughout, up to and including Ambròsi's sacred death and rebirth: he is resurrected as the drowned man in the fountain at Nîmes, alive yet incurably insane.

I employ the term 'sacred' because, throughout the novel, Boudou exploits the thematics of religion as one of his major structuring devices. The title – *La Santa Estèla del centenari* – alludes to the centennial celebration of the founding of the Felibrige movement, and to the annual commemorations that take place on one day of the year blessed by one saint in the calendar. At Molin's house and again on the train, a countercurrent of religious heresy is offered by two Jehovah's Witnesses, pests who annoy Molin and Ambròsi with their obsession with the end of the world and with the notion that language can be redeemed only in Christ. In Avignon, after Holy Mass (of the official church), the heretics take over; the Jehovah's Witnesses and a street messiah, who claims to be the John the Apostle of a new Christ, disrupt the proceedings and turn the farcical religiosity of the Mistralian ritual into a genuine farce of religion. It is also Pentecost Sunday, with inane disciples indeed howling in tongues. Then, after spending the night in a YMCA, the Old Man brings Ambròsi to his 'Òrt del Paradís,' a Garden of Paradise which serves as the title for the third and last section of the novel. High on a hill (as in Dante), this paradise proves to be only a sun-beaten, drought-infested deserted village. In a parody of the Book of Genesis, here dwells a mad scientist who, instead of creating human life, transforms humans into monsters, half human, half metal. He does so partially in the name of religion, for he is a new Cathar – in the line of Nelli and others. As the caricature of a new Cathar, the cyborgs reflect his Catharist doctrine, that all men are robots and that our bodies – evil, wicked flesh – are the equivalent of metal, imprisoning our souls within. For the new Catharist age, this god will create a *homo novus*, Ambròsi, who will replace the sons of Adam, *veteres homines*. However, the Fall recurs: Ambròsi and Joseta commit the sin of the flesh and are punished by symbolic castration, metamorphosis into stone, and Ambròsi's death-rebirth experience. Desire and the sexual act induce immediate shame, guilt, and their atonement. Yet his is a good sin, good rebellion against the fanatic. Resurrection occurs but in a state of madness, not Christian *sancta stultitia* but common, everyday insanity, and the poor Adam-Christ figure returns from the Otherworld to spend the rest of his days in an asylum. The arch-images mocked here are the standard archetypes in the West of nurture, creation, and idyllic peace: the garden and the fountain. They are undermined throughout.

Religious faith, doctrine, rituals, and ideals – all serve to twist, corrupt, and imprison mankind. All our mechanical overlaps rigidify the genuine vitality of life. All are, in one way or another, associated with insanity. An aura of madness runs through the book, from the beginning, when the inscribed editor, who in his youth was fascinated by the asylum at Rodez, encounters some of the inmates and is given the manuscript, to the end, when the inscribed narrator, Ambròsi, is raised from the dead and institutionalized. In between, Jehovah's Witnesses, the new John the Apostle, and the Old Man who wants to be God – all display psychotic tendencies. From a tale of seemingly autobiographical authenticity, we slowly but surely discover that not only is this a nightmare world, but it no longer adheres to our modern, empirical sense of what is physically possible and what is not. Life itself – not to speak of the Occitan condition – is seen to be an irrational sequence of events in which madness predominates, where power lies in the hands of the insane and the narrative itself may be the ravings of a maniac.

Indeed, the narrative frame makes us aware of the ambiguity inherent in this story, an ambiguity more explicit than in *La Grava sul camin*. Did these events actually take place? Did Ambròsi hallucinate them while drowning in the fountain? Are they his insane invention imagined during his years in the asylum? Is he the innocent victim of the mad scientist and an uncomprehending medical establishment? Was he mad from the beginning? Does it really matter, given Boudou's vision of the madness of our world and the mockery of existence? We do not know, nor ultimately does it make a difference in so powerfully imaginative, witty, and despairing a novel, which breaks all the rules – in the name of truth and in the name of art.

Lo Libre dels grands jorns (The Book of the Last Days) is the most stark, despairing, and tragic of Boudou's novels, and also his first exploration of an urban scene.[33] The Narrator has just discovered he is dying of cancer. Leaving his wife and children, he boards the Montpellier–Paris train and then, for no conscious reason, gets off at Clermont-Ferrand. He will spend the last weeks of his life in a strange city, impoverished, his life reduced to squalor. Thus the protagonist wanders aimlessly in the maze of little passages, bars, and brothels nestled about the train station. He encounters whores, a defrocked priest, and a half-communist, half-shepherd. As in Céline, this man looks for girls and drink, moving from bar to bar and from cheap hotel room to cheap hotel room. Boudou depicts modernity in all its tawdriness: statues of irrelevant figures from the past, war memorials, Michelin tire advertisements, a square named after some athlete who once won the Tour de France, and the suffering of North Africans. All this in a powerful, suffocating phenomenology of little rooms and hallways, cellars and staircases, dark streets at night, petrification and poison, softness, corruption, rot, and the viscous, all filtered through the lens of cheap alcohol and visceral physical pain. The wine and the cognac grant as much pain as joy and as much excruciating introspection as forgetfulness in a dream. And always, in counterpoint, we remember what wine should and does entail on a higher, sacred level: Christ's own blood, which he gave to humanity ('calix sanguinis mei') to preserve humanity from death. These little people of Clermont-Ferrand, Boudou tells us – the whores, bartenders, drinkers, and losers, including the dying narrator – all these poor in spirit have somehow been forgotten, left to endure their lives and deaths of quiet desperation in loneliness and misery. In this novel as elsewhere in Boudou, the presence of the sacred or its absence proves to be a crucial element in the narrative.

The Narrator is an intellectual. Throughout the narrative he recalls memories from the past, especially childhood. And he reflects on what we can designate as major questions: life, death, the afterlife, and religious faith. As we might expect, none of these reveries comes to a definitive conclusion, none gives him satisfaction, none seems to lead anywhere. His thought processes, his inner wanderings, so to speak, are as fragmented, disjointed, and chaotic as his outer rambles at night or the useless, insignificant flow of his life. The Narrator's memories, whether good or bad, idyllic or disillusioned, inevitably pale before the simple, overwhelming physical pain in his digestive tract, caused by alcohol and also, presumably, by cancer. In any case, he once observes, for all intents and purposes he had ceased to live, really live, long ago. He finds no meaning to life and death, is convinced there is none, and if he imagines a motif for comprehension and consolation, quickly undercuts it with sardonic mockery. The last and deepest meditation – which begins Part 3 – has one significant, meaningful outcome. Because of it, the Narrator loses his wallet.

Yet in the midst of the despair and the decay occurs an episode of overpowering tragedy, despair, and also love. The Narrator meets a defrocked priest, a man apparently as cynical and hopeless as himself, who sarcastically recounts the last words of wisdom of a saintly abbot on his death bed: 'Voldriái far pisson ...' (I have to go pipi) (p. 78). This same miserable creature (the defrocked priest), at the nadir of the ecclesiastical hierarchy, a nadir to which the Narrator wishes to descend in the secular world, is the only priest – the only one – willing to hear the confessions of dying whores here in the poor sections of Clermont. He does so because his grandfather, a good man and a 'red,' held out against all the 'whites' in the village, including his wife. Yet he died with a look on his face of terror, of unimaginable horror. In the end he believed the others, that he was going to hell. So the Narrator's friend became a priest in order to give all people, and especially the poor and the guilty, the comfort that they will not go to hell. This is all that Maïté the prostitute asks for after a life of living hell. The defrocked priest does this even though and because he believes in neither heaven nor hell:

'... quand vegèri lo meu pepin mòrt faguèri lo vòt d'èsser prèire. E dempuèi ai pas volgut que degun anès en infèrn ... degun d'aqueles que me sonarián ... [...] Pels autres, qu'impòrta çò que pòdi creire. [...] Maïté, sabi que morirà, ela, lo sorire als pòts, la claror als uèlhs, de mercé a la sia fe e de mercé a ieu.' (pp. 105–6)
(When I saw my grandfather dead I made the vow to be a priest. And since then I have not wanted anyone to go to hell, anyone of those who call on me. As for the others, what does it matter what I can believe? Maïté, I know that she will die with a smile on her lips and a light in her eyes, thanks to her faith and thanks to me.)

Like the Narrator he believes in nothing, yet he bears within himself the Love that, we are told, can move the stars.[34]

The Narrator is an intellectual, a man of education, and, as with Enric de Savinhac and Ambròsi Lorei, Occitan is his native tongue; it is also his passion. He is obsessed with his own death and with the death of Occitan. The two are associated in his mind, so that in his reveries and rambles, in his drunken stupors and illuminations, he worries and digs and burrows into the problematic of both deaths. His despair centres on the fact that although he, an Occitan writer, is exploring one of the great cities of the South, a home of the troubadours, he can find no one who speaks his tongue. He quotes and alludes to the troubadours and to figures in the history of Auvergne: Vercingetorix, Sidonius Apollinaris, Pope Urban II, and Pascal. His private myth of Auvergne is grounded in dreams of victory (Gergovia, the First Crusade) and in the multiple reality of defeat: the Gauls crushed by Rome at Alesia, then, still worse, the Occitan world crushed by Northern France at the time of the Albigensian Crusade, for, the Narrator implies, good crusades lead inevitably to bad ones, and evil always triumphs over good.

Here a rich pattern of intertextuality is woven into the text, granting it a complexity, in terms of history and culture, that we have not seen previously in Boudou. The quotations from Jaufre Rudel and Raimbaut of Orange structure a thematic of courtly love and chivalry, which is then undercut by the contemporary story of the dying narrator, who lives an ironic anti-quest in the manner of Kafka and Beckett. Instead of the *domna* in troubadour and trouvère song, we find poor prostitutes at the lowest register of their profession; in place of love service or acts of chivalry and valour, simple coupling (when the Narrator is not too inebriated) and, later on, the sex act as the centre of a pornographic show. The defrocked priest is shown to be our only modern – and how ironic – equivalent of the medieval warrior saint: Perceval or Galahad. Boudou elaborates a pattern of demonic imagery, also intertextual. His most prominent 'demonic' counter-symbol proves to be the fountain, one dried-up spring which emits noxious gas and another which petrifies. These recall the fountains of love, fertility, and adventure in medieval romance – Chrétien de Troyes's *Yvain*, for instance, or Guillaume de Lorris's *Roman de la Rose* – and Boudou's own ironic fountain in *La Santa Estèla del centenari*, which kills, restores, and brings on madness.

Boudou divides his novel into three parts, resembling the three notebooks in *La Santa Estèla*. These three parts are organized into a linear structure which reveals a shift in genre, each notebook couched in a distinct literary register and tone. Part 1 evokes the Narrator, alone, crushed in his isolation and obsessed with his own suffering and death. More than one reader will respond negatively to the fact that the Narrator begins by abandoning wife and children without a word. His narcissism is absolute. Then, Part 2, no less tragic, brings the Narrator into contact with others, especially the defrocked priest, who becomes his friend. In this form of human contact, he displays nobility and decency in the face of annihilation. In Part 3 the Narrator's social activities expand. He finds work, he engages with people committed to political change, he even leaves Clermont-Ferrand for some time in the country. Yet what could be considered reaching for a better life, even the opening out of this ironic parable into romance, is – as in *La Santa Estèla* – undercut by derision and mockery.

By the priest's good offices the Narrator gets a job in a castle named Marxilhat (Marxville). There he and the whore make love on stage. The shepherd explains to the Narrator, and shows him, how this utopian community succeeded in draining the swamps. Then the leader, Spallanzani, succeeded in granting immortality to his followers by severing their heads and keeping the heads alive. The sex show is to offer them some amusement, for otherwise they get bored. Spallanzani of Marxilhat severing heads and granting immortality is a magnificent satire on international communism and, especially, Stalin, the atheist who butchered tens of millions of his own people in the name of a future classless society. The mad scientist motif recalls the Old Man in *La Santa Estèla* and, like him, looks back to a tradition of demented inventors and technological fanatics in literature and film. The severed heads in this 'Otherworld' recall also rows of severed heads that identify demonic Otherworlds in medieval romance – Chrétien's *Erec et Enide*, for example, and the Occitan *Jaufre*. Following from this, Spallanzani also rejoins the Middle Ages: the Arthurian sorcerer Merlin and sundry monstrous adversaries of the hero in romance.

It is significant that the one genuine success of this futurist community was to drain the swamps; draining the swamps and reclaiming land from the waters was Faust's accomplishment, which made him proud and brought him to death. Goethe's idealistic yet tortured protagonist reappears in Mann's *Zauberberg* as Naphta but also as the idealistic, progressive agitator named Settembrini, so close phonologically to Spallanzani. Finally, Boudou's three-part novel, opening out from an individual hell to more social and uplifting concerns, cannot but recall Dante's voyage from the Inferno to Purgatorio to Paradiso. Boudou follows his hell with a sort of tragic Christian purgatory but then paradise – the wish-fulfilment paradise of the Motherland of Socialism and the secular paradise cherished by so many generations of intellectuals like Boudou's Narrator, including Boudou himself, who gave it their hearts and souls; this paradise is shown to be an obscene mockery of everything that is good, pure, and true.

The sardonic, sarcastic, and picaresque once again appear at the climax, triumphing over the rest. The secular answer proves to be as flawed as the religious one. As a result, after this one, last, definitive fiasco, the Narrator escapes his Otherworld; however, he has failed in the quest and can only stagger, dying, back to Clermont. After meditating on the past and the future, on the sacred and the secular, this intellectual faces the void alone, all illusions lost, his last recorded thought devoted to a folk-song. His last thought evokes once again the problematic relationship between past and present, and the problematic status of the language. Intertextually, historically, and in human terms the modern, both tragic and burlesque, parodies and undercuts the Middle Ages as well as the modern, proposing that our modern hell is the outcome of medieval folly and the failure of medieval dreams. And always, in counterpoint, we observe the Occitan writer, who finds no one to speak to, who sets down his miserable tale in simple prose (versus *trobar clus*, the *genus grande* of hard verse, back then), and who, dying, creates one of the last texts in a dying language and a dying culture, which will finally bring to an end, in the flesh, the language and culture which began to die centuries ago in the spirit.

ROBERT LAFONT

Like Hugh MacDiarmid and Roparz Hemon, Robert Lafont was and is an omnivorous writer. For years a professor at the University of Montpellier, he is credited with a dozen or more volumes of political, social, and economic analysis of the Occitan situation and another dozen or more of literary history and philology, all of these in French. In Occitan we have several collections of poetry, over fifteen volumes of fiction, seven full-length plays, and a number of brief ones. He sought and still seeks to build a tradition, to expand the uses of Oc for all genres and modes, in every possible way. Lafont is the Victor Hugo of modern Oc.

As a novelist, he stands in the front rank, alongside Boudou. *Vida de Joan Larsinhac* (The Life of J.L.) from 1951, the story of a young man who grows up in the city and joins the Resistance, is the first modern novel in Occitan.[35] Following upon this text and the succeeding one, Lafont, like Boudou and like Roparz Hemon, broke away from the tradition of realism à la Balzac and Maupassant in the direction of generic experimentation, with narrative in the style of (and sometimes labelled) romance, philosophical tale, fable, science fiction, and detective story. One of the best of these novels – a powerful, intense, magnificently poetic work of art – is the 1971 *L'Icòna dins l'iscla* (The Icon on the Island).[36]

In this futuristic dystopian anti-novel and anti-romance Lafont recounts the events subsequent to a nuclear apocalypse. As a result of the conflagration, the Narrator and his French companions, vacationing on a Greek isle, find themselves (with some Greeks) among the last inhabitants of the planet. They witness the end of the world and the end of Western civilization. Sought as a haven, the garden becomes a prison. The Narrator evolves in the course of the story. However, imprisoned as he is, he is incapable of seeking out adventures and undergoing a quest. On the contrary, the narrative begins with the protagonist and his companions already there – having attained the Otherworld, the sought-after centre – and continues with a series of assaults from without which threaten the band in what, for them, has become both a place of refuge and a mad, demonic incarceration. These assaults include the aftershock of the Bomb(s), tidal waves, a sea coat of oil, masses of dead and dying birds, masses of dead and dying fish, and the crushing weight of thirst and heat. Then comes the equivalent of a knight-errant, a quasi-divine saviour, Leif the Swedish aristocrat, master of the waters and dispenser of food. However, this romance hero proves to be an ogre in disguise, a sodomite and seducer of women, and an exploiter and manipulator of men. After Leif arrive other men, white masked monsters in helicopters with the gift of napalm, and, before and after them, armies of gigantic jellyfish, who, the new masters of the seas, destroy all. Only in the end will there be a sort of rescue, by black people from Africa, too late to revive the now dying Narrator.

Striking and monstrous as are these assaults from outside, and Lafont's grandiose imagery of apocalypse, more striking and monstrous still we discover to be the disintegration of the community within, the collapse of elementary human decency in the wake of the holocaust. One of Lafont's themes is the progressive degradation of the human spirit, torn apart by greed and sex. The planetary slaughter is launched by Arabs and Israelis but then quickly engulfs the great powers, who not only wipe out each other but also use the occasion to decimate their own contestatory minorities. This war of the macrocosm is then re-enacted on the Greek island in microcosm. When the cataclysm occurs, there exists a little community of seven French tourists and four Greeks: a simple local couple and two intellectuals, refugees from the Greek mainland. Inevitable suspicion between two social and ethnic subgroups brings about the first schism: the French and the Greeks each form their own centre and space. Then the strong impose on the weak, and violence erupts as people compete over food and sex. Leif creates still more tension: the men are jealous of his magnificent virility; one of the women lets him seduce her. Once he leaves, Didier seeks to take his place. Violence carries the day when the strong kill Ianni and rape and kill Bèti only to die of food poisoning, from the carcass of a dead monkey they kept selfishly for themselves. Lafont depicts slowly, surely, and in graphic detail how lust for food and lust for sex, how the will to conquer and the will to destroy, dehumanize this last residue of humanity, how these humans transform themselves into animals.

The descent into animality is both underscored and rendered problematic through a series of cultural and intertextual allusions, which never let us forget that the Narrator was and is an intellectual and that we are in the process of observing the end of a high culture that shone for millenniums.

An ironic reference to 'una comunitat de Robinsons' (a community of Robinsons) (p. 87), reminds us of Defoe's *Robinson Crusoe*. By locating his novel on an island, by telling the story of the will to survive on an island, Lafont constructs an anti-*Robinson* and a super-*Robinson*, rather in the way of Chrétien de Troyes and his anti-*Tristan* and super-*Tristan*. The island, assimilated to the mother and to life and death in some future time, was to be a constant in Lafont's career, witness a recent collection of two nouvelles entitled *Insularas*.[37] The Robinson theme becomes most acute once the others have died, and the Narrator remains on his island with Ianni's widow, Athanasia. This peasant woman assumes the role of Friday. Since she is a woman and an attractive one, an erotic bond develops between them, something not possible (unless latent and unconscious) in Defoe. Defoe's and Lafont's narrators describe the material conditions for, and circumstances surrounding, their decision to write and the fact that they do write. Athanasia resembles Friday in that the Narrator composes for and to her, and he reads aloud to her from his notebooks. As in Defoe, the Narrator is an intellectual and a creature of Logos; he is the creator and artist, whereas Athanasia, a simple peasant woman and the widow of a fisherman, stands as a creature of nature. However, Lafont's Narrator, a typical French Left-oriented intellectual, feels inferior to Athanasia's 'primitive' essence as a force of nature and a representative of the people, the lower classes that such intellectuals often fetishize. So, perhaps, also does Lafont, because, although the Narrator thinks and writes, Athanasia is physically stronger than he and better adapted to survival in the wild. She teaches, protects, and masters him, whereas he, very French and European, seemingly Robinson-like, in spite of tenacity and a genuine will to live, ultimately has to depend on her, to give himself over to her. He converts to her way of life, instead of her converting to his. In the end, she will survive and he will not. This is one of Lafont's statements on gender relations and the qualities that man and woman bring to human life or, at least, to a male consciousness of that life. As in the tradition, beginning with the troubadours and the trouvères of romance, man is the bearer of Logos, the creator of wisdom and art, and woman, more physical than he, closer to the earth, the sea, and the moon, exists in part as a maternal figure to love and protect him: 'Me pòrtas lo manjar, lo pèis brasucat dau vèspre [...] Me pòrtas l'aiga [...] Danças. Danças pèr me tornar aprene coma se manja, coma se beu [...]' (p. 118) (You bring me food, grilled fish for supper. You bring me water. You dance. You dance so I can learn again how to eat, how to drink). Thus, paradoxically, she is stronger and more heroic than he is. At the end of the novel, also stronger and more heroic than the Narrator are the genuine avatars of Friday; a band of Africans come in their simple boats to rescue what they can find of whatever remains. Their presence, their power, and their goodness are the ultimate turnabout or revenge of Friday and the post-colonial sense of Friday-ness over the traditional, archetypal, European Robinsons.

The juxtaposition of French, including one Occitan speaker, and Greeks on a Greek island near Crete brings to the fore issues of greater scope than Defoe's one eighteenth-century novel. Lafont, himself a 'demystifier' of the mythology surrounding Mistral and the Felibrige, erects a powerful ironic counterstructure to the classical yearnings endemic in Parisian intellectuals, and, even more so, in the Provençal heirs of Mistral who believed then and still believe in 'la raço latino' (the Latin race) and in 'l'empèri dóu soulèu' (the empire of the sun). It is not a coincidence that the Narrator – an ironic anti-Achilles – dies from a wound in the ankle, or that he attains communion with Athanasia, a woman from the present, simple and illiterate, embodying a vision of contemporary Greece far from the cliché-world of Electra and Medea. From this perspective, Leif, Swede though he is, caricature of Aryan supremacy that he is, also evokes classical figures such as Ulysses, Neptune, and Apollo. Extraordinarily beautiful, magnificent in his physical mastery and power of the will, contemptuous of politics and concerned only with the body, Leif turns out to be responsible for the destruction of Crete by fire (he made love to two shepherds who had been extinguishing the blaze) and the near self-immolation of the community on the Narrator's little isle. His penchant for sodomizing men and women indiscriminately (called 'Greek love' in French and Occitan as in English) and his amorality serve as a powerful condemnation of those who would fetishize classical antiquity. This contemporary equivalent of a Greek god personally wipes out the last vestiges of classical culture on the planet prior to being wiped out himself, by jellyfish.

A second, last vestige of classical culture – at one remove – is the Narrator himself, who writes in Occitan, the oldest high-culture vernacular (according to Lafont) in the modern West. The Narrator, with his Achilles' heel, is conscious of his role as the last cultured person on the planet, the last human to write. Writing gives him a sense of life, becoming more important than food. His little microlanguage will be the last speech, the last tongue, and the last witness to life and to culture; this will be its revenge on French, Latin, Greek, and all the others, all the dominant languages that no longer dominate, for in death (as is the case with people) they are all alike.

The power of this text derives, in part, from Lafont's vision of that death and of our transition into it, a vision of horror typically 'baroque' in the writings of a distinguished scholar of the Baroque. Thus Lafont, while demystifying the utopias of Defoe and Mistral, creates his own magnificent dystopian universe worthy of Grimmelshausen and D'Aubigné. To be included in his pattern of demonic imagery are the following: on the one hand, dryness and petrification from the rocks on the island, the machine and machine-like creatures who kill (white men in protective white garb dispensing napalm), the heat of the sun, and, of course, the people who die from thirst; and, on the other hand, corruption and rot from the snow of feathers and dead birds, the waters red with the blood of fish, the waters black with oil, the disgusting sweet smell of decomposing flesh, the armies of jellyfish that engulf all, and, of course, the bodies, all the dead and dying bodies of what once were men. This is the ultimate amplification (theme with variations) of Bachelard's hard earth of the will and soft earth of rest, juxtaposed and synthesized to build up to a climax of horror in the apocalypse, which stuns even the reader already familiar with the trappings of science fiction.

Yet, paradoxically, Lafont's vision is inherently more optimistic or, at least, less despairing than Boudou's. One finds in *L'Icòna dins l'iscla* a counterbalancing pattern of human solidarity, idealism, and hope. Set off against the rocks, the machines, and the jellyfish stands a 'cistèrna,' a reservoir from a well that taps water. People, and especially the Narrator, flock to this point at the centre, the equivalent of the nourishing fountain, metaphorically the nurturing mother, her breast and womb. Set off against the criminal selfishness, violence, and bestiality of so many, emerge better people – first the Narrator and his peasant girl-friend, and then the Africans who come as a community, singing, to rescue what remains to be rescued. The Narrator, a French intellectual, will die. The vigorous, earthy peasant woman will survive, in Africa and thanks to Africa, thanks to a people descended from slaves (in America and in antiquity). The new Third World will retain the best. It was Athanasia herself who placed in the cistern-well-fountain-temple a photo of Malcolm X. This photo becomes, for her in her Holy Orthodox faith and for others, a symbolic icon of the martyrs to history, all the martyrs in a post-Christian world. Then the Africans arrive, a picture of Christ on the sail fixed to the mast of their boat – it is a Black Christ:

> Es una granda cara d'òme, tiblada de sofréncia, ont an pintat li rugas coma de cèrcles maladrechs, una lagrema redona sota cada uèlh, e pasmens sèmbla que soritz. La cara es negra maugrat l'aura de mar que l'a passida. (p. 126)
> (It is a huge human face, hollowed out by suffering, on which they painted wrinkles as awkward circles, a round tear beneath each eye, and yet it appeared to smile. Despite the sea wind that had caused it to fade, the face is black.)

The Black Christ is the only appropriate Son to the Great Mother Earth, who will endure despite rape by advanced cultures – by American helicopters, bombs, and napalm, and by Scandinavian amoralists flaunting their self-indulgence. *L'Icòna dins l'iscla* partakes of a current we can call 1960s leftist utopianism or socialist romance. In this fascinating text, which contains a meditation on culture and history, and on the transition from the past to the future and from Europe to a global continuum, communal vision from the Left joins a sort of leftist primitivism. Thus the anti-Robinson is wedded to an anti- and hyper-Christianity in a visionary universe where the poor, the weak, the simple, and the female inherit the earth and terror appears, in the end, to give way to pastoral. This said, appearances are deceiving, and Lafont's novel remains in the end as complex and problematic as in the beginning. Yes, the Narrator undergoes a series of death-rebirth experi-

ences. Yes, he learns to love: first a discreet, undeclared *fin' amor*
for Bregida (one of the vacationers), later a genuine, fulfilled, quasi-
spousal relationship with Athanasia. Yes, he writes to and for Athanasia. Yet the beauty and the tragedy of their love resides, partially, in
their failure to communicate. For the Narrator speaks French and
Occitan, also perhaps a little English, and Athanasia speaks her
demotic Greek. The couple learn to love each other through glances,
gestures, body language, and the gaze. Eventually they exchange
words, with the Narrator presumably learning more Greek than Athanasia learns of his languages. Whatever Occitan Athanasia may have
picked up orally, she obviously cannot read his elaborate, rhetorical,
splendidly baroque writing. The beauty and the tragedy of the Narrator's career as a writer resides, partially, in the fact that he is writing a
book that, within the diegesis, has no public, a book that no one can
or will ever read. This then is the end of the book and of the world:
our last literary text is written in Occitan, the despised language of a
regional minority. The last book will never be read.

In 1983 Lafont published *La Festa* (The Festival), a two-volume novel
counting some nine hundred dense pages.[38] This work, which treats
much of contemporary history from the 1940s to 1973 plus makes forays
into the past, and which, centred in the South of France, reaches out to
Paris, Vienna, Salzburg, parts of Germany and Italy, and Algeria, is
surely the single most ambitious, most monumental work in the history
of Occitan and in the history of the minority languages treated in this
book. Composed in Lafont's habitually rich, concrete, baroque-like
prose (with passages in other languages and in their past literary registers) and exploiting a variety of narrative and intertextual strategies, *La
Festa* can also be considered the first New Novel in Occitan or, if you prefer, the first *après*–New Novel.

In volume 1 Amielh Ribiera purchases a manor called 'Lo Paradís'
(Paradise) at Mars in the Cévennes. There he discovers what purports
to be the correspondence and papers of an eighteenth-century Huguenot, the Cavalier de Març. The rest of this volume, 'Lo cavalier de
Març,' recounts Amielh's imaginative recasting of his own life up to
this 24 August 1973 and his imaginative musings on the Cavalier's life
from the man's own perspective. Volume 2, 'Lo libre de Joan' (Jean's
Book), recounts the life and inner musings of Joan Ventenac, Amielh's
friend and former teacher. The festival (*festa*) occurs the next day, on
25 August: the Harvest Festival of the Larzac, when leftists from all over,

including Amielh and Joan Ventenac, gather in the Occitan heathland to protest the installation of a military base.

Perhaps the central theme of 'Lo libre de Joan' is the eternal human quest for liberty, personal authenticity, and political commitment. We follow Joan Ventenac, a hero of the Resistance, through years in the Maquis and his postwar career in the Communist party, the Hungarian insurrection of 1956, and the FLN struggle for Algeria. A kind of modern knight-errant, Joan Ventenac mirrors his Camisard namesake, the eighteenth-century historical figure Joan Cavalier (Jean the Knight), who becomes Joan Ventenac's imagined alter ego, just as the Cavalier de Març does for Amielh. Through Joan Ventenac's consciousness and/or the consciousness of the narrator, Lafont explores the nature of the active life and contrasts bad heroism to good heroism or what one critic has called good outlawry.[39] It would appear that heroism can be justified only as transgression, never when it becomes co-opted by a government or an institution.

Allied to heroism and transgression is desire, and desire is assimilated to transgression and the exploration of the unconscious. One image of transgression occurs when Joan Cavalier, requested by God (in a dream) to map out the Divine City, places it in the centre of the Virgin Mary's sex. So much for the past. In the present Joan Ventenac experiences a series of passionate encounters: with the older woman Loïsa, who initiates him; with an intellectual and physical equal, Anna, his wife; and with the fifteen-year-old Margherita, whom he initiates. Amielh enjoys two comparable relationships: with an Algerian girl during the Algerian war, and with Anna. Whether licit or not, whether oedipal or not, these passions have an air of transgression, of the release of animal libido, and of striving into and attaining the unconscious.

From a gender-related perspective, the female figures and their bonds to Amielh and Joan are fascinatingly problematic. On the one hand is elaborated the ideal of the modern woman, free in body and in mind. Loïsa leads the pro-Algerian resistance in Toulouse. Sandra and Anna are both journalists, the one in Geneva and the other in Paris. Anna has a host of husbands and lovers. Loïsa initiates Joan to the pleasures of the body, as Anna does to Amielh. These are strong women, possessing greater powers of will and, for that matter, of heroism than the men.

However, it is no less true that, in the narrative and in the male narrators' consciousnesses, the women exist only in relation to men, for what they can do for or give to men. The men are central, the women peripheral. As mothers, virgins, whores, or partners, their role is largely arche-

typal. They function as temptresses or muses: Margherita almost destroys Joan; Loïsa encourages him to write in Occitan; Anna shows
Vienna to Amielh. Symbolic of the role of woman is the fact that Amielh
and Joan write extended letters, for years, to female confidantes (Wal-
traud and Sandra, respectively) but do not send them or dream about
the letters and do not write them. The confidante is a dream figure,
cherished in the imagination but carefully excluded from reality.

It is no less significant, then, that the women exist, in some sense, as
counters in the game played by the men and as icons that cement what
we nowadays call the homosocial bond between Joan and Amielh. Joan,
Amielh's teacher, serves as a father-surrogate and encourages his surro-
gate son to write in Occitan. Joan and Anna become a family for
Amielh, who reveres them as parent-figures. Later, Amielh enjoys a brief
affair with Anna – the great love of his life – fulfilling the oedipal dream;
he then loses her back to Joan, fulfilling oedipal reality. In the end,
Amielh also spends a night with Joan's daughter Bregida. Joan accepts
Amielh's invitation to the Paradise. Arriving, he has a reunion and communion with Amielh and also a coronary attack. Joan presumably will
die, bequeathing his world (and, partially, his women) to the son, who
will carry on.

This said, I do not agree with those who find Joan's heroism or his life
of knight-errantry especially admirable. I agree instead with those who
underscore his weakness and his neuroses.[40] One major neurosis is narcissism, the selfishness and incapacity to relate to women and to return
the love they offer as a gift. Unable to communicate, Joan is grounded
in himself, obsessed with *his* politics, activism, life of action, life of pleasure, and life of thought. He thinks of writing an *Essai sur le narcissisme
littéraire*, does compose a story in Occitan, 'Lo mirau que tua' (The Mirror That Kills), and later refers to his gigantic book in Occitan as a mad
project, nothing but narcissism. As we shall see, perhaps the narcissism
and the rejection of woman are necessary preconditions for artistic creativity and for saving one's soul, as so many creators and saints have
claimed.

Along with the narcissism, bound to it, we find, according to Forêt,
the gnawing of a terrible secret or memory – Joan killed a man during
the war; Amielh's Algerian girlfriend was executed because of her
involvement with him – that impedes heroism in the Lafontian hero.
Joan and Amielh suffer from their own nausea (a Sartrean touch),
sense of guilt, remorse, introversion, and symbolic masochism and castration. The self-destruction is most apparent in the artistic realm,

where, ultimately, the Cavalier de Març fails to write; Amielh and Joan Ventenac do write but give away their writing, in fact destroy it and their identity with it. Gemila died because of Amielh; Rudolph, Loïsa, and even Margherita die because of Joan Ventenac. Joan, the pillar of knight-errantry, suffers a coronary on the way to Amielh's house – Paradise – the only paradise he will ever know in this world and the next. Joan then gives away all his money to found a review and quits the Festival, Amielh's house, life, and the novel as naked as he came into life and the novel.

Eros then is bound to Thanatos, and both to the life of the mind and of art. What makes these men interesting and what distinguishes them from the usual postwar type of intellectual in Sartre, de Beauvoir, Camus, and the like is their complex, problematic relationship to language, in this case an occulted, subconscious, minority tongue, Occitan.[41] Loïsa urged Joan to write in Oc just as Joan urges Amielh. Joan meets Anna in 1947 at a course on the medieval romance *Flamenca*, and their first words are in Oc. Joan and Anna speak the language in the family, which entrances Amielh. Back in the eighteenth century the Cavalier de Març lives for Occitan as much as for the Reformed Faith. He wanders through Europe, assimilating Occitan and his land to the ideal of rebellion everywhere, as does Joan Ventenac two hundred years later. Joan Cavalier dies with words in Oc on his lips; Joan Ventenac and Amielh live the Festival of Larzac surrounded by young people speaking Occitan and defending their land and their tongue. Also on the Larzac we find the genuine Occitan writer Jean Boudou, busy at work on his novel *La Quimèra* (The Chimera). It is certain that Amielh, by opening a box and poring over the books and papers inside it, opens a door to the past through which flows the old language. *La Festa* becomes a quest for the language up to the point of writing the language and writing the novel, just as it is a novel of language which itself fills the absence it deplores.

This is the case because three of the four male protagonists are writers, first in French yet drawn also to Occitan, and because all three, unlike Boudou, are failures. Given the 'prison house of language,' their language, and their problematic status as bilinguals enduring involuntary diglossia, writing what they want to write is shown to be impossible. Although the Cavalier de Març is committed to an Occitan *Don Quixote*, only the title-page survives (in French) plus a few phrases here and there, all of which may be the imaginative creation of the nineteenth-century antiquarian Auguste Pujol, or the twentieth-century Amielh.

Amielh did write a novel in French on his tragic love affair in Algeria: *Djemila*. However, he ensures its destruction by mailing the only manuscript copy to a non-existent recipient at a non-existent address from a non-existent sender. He purchased 'Lo Paradís' in order to write, and this time in Oc, but is afraid of the ordeal, and we have no way of knowing what will come of it. Joan Ventenac, as usual, assumes the role of a hero. After failing at a number of aborted projects in French – a modern version of *L'Education sentimentale*, an *Essai sur le narcissisme littéraire* plus *Lettres à Sandra* – he does finally succeed in composing a two-volume novel in Occitan, 'Lo Libre de Joan' (superficially similar to *La Festa*), a unique book synonymous with its author, the insane manifestation of his narcissism, only to hand it over to Sandra. If it has any promise, he says, she can revise it and publish it under her name. Whatever the outcome, Joan will never again be associated with the text. And since we hear nothing of its publication, I think we can assume that 'Lo Libre de Joan' also joins the void of the Cavalier's *Quixote* and Amielh's *Djemila*.

The presence of language and of writing projects scattered over the centuries creates a problematic sense of time and space. Amielh discovers Pujol's books and the Cavalier de Març's papers on 24 August 1973; on 25 August 1973 he, Joan Ventenac, and the others celebrate on the Larzac. On the one hand, unity of time is respected with the rigour of a classical tragedy. On the other hand, because of the discovery, Amielh evokes the Cavalier de Març's eighteenth century and Joan Ventenac's and Amielh's own twentieth century. Through memory and imagination, and through letters they have (presumably) written, we discover Amielh's and Joan Ventenac's past lives since the 1940s and how their political activism relates to and fulfils Joan Cavalier's Camisard Occitanism (which we also discover), and how their struggles with the land and the language also relate to and fulfil his. We see in parallel great ages of Occitan triumph and defeat. We see how, only by imagining and recuperating the past, will it be possible to create in the present. For time is circular as well as linear in a novel that begins and ends in August 1973 with a premise of something like an eternal present for the secular, sacred time of the Larzac *festa*. As in Manciet's *Enterrament a Sabres*, one day in the present recapitulates and poeticizes duration in the past, both in the lives of individuals and in currents of history.

As with Manciet, the same is true of space. Yes, Joan Cavalier, Joan Ventenac, and Amielh roam over much of Europe. They are deterritorialized. Yet they do so for and in the name of a territory, a place, a *païs* which is their own, the South of France, land of Oc. Thus, when God appears to the Camisard guerrilla and orders him to map out the Divine City, he devises a series of concentric circles with, at the centre, his *país d'Oc* (plus the Virgin Mary's vagina). Similarly, Amielh purchases 'Lo Paradís' in order to write in Occitan, and write he will. This house in the Cévennes becomes a centre to which gravitate Joan Ventenac and a host of others, all prepared to march on the Larzac to defend their language and their *país*. Yet just as there are two historical levels and two centuries in time, so also Lafont, because of the deterritorialization, establishes a second spatial centre: Vienna. It is in Vienna that Amielh enjoys his brief liaison with Anna, in Vienna that both he and Joan Ventenac visit the museum and behold a painting which will change their lives (cf. below), and in Vienna that the mad clockmaker and creator Hans Frankl calls his city the centre of the Middle Empire, in the middle of Europe. Vienna, like the Occitan heathland, has lost its power and glory; it too feasts on the past; it too lives through and hopes to build again a vibrant multicultural openness to the world.[42]

In strictly narratological terms *La Festa* does indeed partake of the *nouveau roman* tradition. The implied reader is able, for the most part, to follow the narrative and to distinguish between eighteenth-century and twentieth-century people, events, and texts. *La Festa* becomes excitingly problematic, however, when we investigate narrative voice and point of view. The focalization is deeply internal; we know the conscious and even the unconscious feelings of the principals. But who is focalizing? A principal himself or an external consciousness? And whose is the external consciousness? Lafont even blurs the distinction between first- and third-person narrative. Example: Are the Cavalier de Març's musings and papers his own? Or have they been imagined by and are they projections from the unconscious of Auguste Pujol? Or by and from Amielh?

Dau pus sornarut de l'inconscient bombís la fantasiá sobeirana, lo Cavalier de Març. Mai de quin inconscient? Lo de Pujòl, lo mieu, ò aquela pasta de segles e d'òmes, çò pus misteriós de tot, teoricament insostenible, emotivament imparable, qu'es l'inconscient collectiu dau pòble d'òc? (I, p. 66)
(From the darkest of the unconscious leaps the supreme fantasy, the Cavalier de Març. But from whose unconscious? Pujol's? Mine? Or that dough of centuries and of men, the most mysterious of all, theoretically untenable, emotionally irrefutable, that is the collective unconscious of the Occitan people?)

Does Joan Ventenac perhaps imagine and narrate Amielh? Or does Amielh do the same for Joan? Or are both Amielh and Joan, in the twentieth century, and Joan Cavalier and the Cavalier de Març, in the eighteenth, *instances narratives* offered to the implied reader by a ludic implied author?[43] An obtrusive external voice (the implied author) intervenes – in the best eighteenth-century tradition – to inform us that Amielh is a preparation for Joan, that they are two versions of one hero in one novel, and therefore that perhaps he ought to make one of them leave. He also reminds us that he has the power to pick up the strands of the narrative where Anna and a certain Jiròni make their last appearances and to bring them back. Ambiguity lies at the heart of the narrating process. We do not know who is writing whom and, therefore, what is technically real and what is imaginary. What we do see is a complex of I-narrators who cross and negate each other, who create texts and comment on them and the texts of others, the novel being, in part, the narrative of their coming into being.

Lafont's modernity derives, in my opinion, from this narratological ambiguity and from his sophisticated, problematic employment of intertextuality and *mise en abyme*. In 1945 Joan Ventenac is in Vienna, in 1956 Amielh and Anna. Joan and Amielh visit independently (yet Anna takes Amielh, she who heard of it all from Joan) the Kunsthistorisches Museum, where they view a painting from the late sixteenth century – *Architektur mit vornehmen Besuchern* by the Frisian Netherlander Hans Vredeman de Vries. This work of art is concerned with the nature of architecture and was created to illustrate the workings of perspective. It shows a gallery and, at its centre, a man and a fountain, the man, an elegant courtier, facing two ladies. In the background a feast is being prepared, and the viewer is made aware, directly and by the play of mirrors, of additional galleries extending *ad infinitum*. As was the case for Sarraute's *Portrait d'un inconnu*, this painting is a classical *mise en abyme*: it is an artistic structure which reflects the problematics and thematics of the larger structure which contains it, and it has an impact on and helps to create those larger structures. The fountain at the centre is an *imago* of the land and tongue of Oc and the locus of desire in woman. The gentleman may well be the direct source, the generator (*texte générateur* or, in this case, *tableau générateur*), of the Cavalier de Març and the reason why Amielh meditates on the Cavalier, creating him in the image of Vredeman de Vries's character. He, like the Cavalier, Joan Ventenac, and Amielh, is torn among several women, joining totally with none. Finally, the complexity and ambiguity of architecture in the Dutch painting is adapted by Amielh in his imagining Joan or their implied author in his (their) elaboration of structure in the Occitan novel as a whole.

This artistic *mise en abyme* is then paralleled and enriched by a series of literary intertextual *mises en abyme*.

The Aeneid. Joan Ventenac has an adulterous affair with the older woman, Loïsa. When he decides to break with her, she attempts suicide. Years later he hears of the leader of the FLN cause in Toulouse, a woman code-named Didon (Dido); she turns out to be Loïsa, who is later slain by the police. Loïsa claims for herself the status and the tradition of Carthaginian Dido vis-à-vis Roman Aeneas. Hers is the life of Venus as opposed to Joan's commitment to Minerva – or so it would seem. Yet the irony of the situation, the fact that Loïsa is a more authentic and successful hero than he, and has become more wise in the process, is apparent to Joan and to the reader.

L'Education sentimentale. Joan Ventenac purchased a farm in order to settle down and compose a modern version of Flaubert's novel. He fails utterly. Yet, shortly thereafter, he lives the Flaubert narrative with Loïsa. In our age there are no scruples and no barriers: the oedipal incest-adultery occurs immediately. Yet the outcome is no happier than in Flaubert, and, in cultural terms, the older story simply reflects an older cultural myth.

Faust. In a number of the more exciting passages of 'Lo libre de Joan' Joan Ventenac meets the devil in the guise of an ancient beggar with a peg leg. This devil, called Giannicottu by the locals (we are in Italy), is another Joan and, therefore, a shadow alter ego of Ventenac. They apparently bargain over Joan's soul, the devil offering him, on various occasions, heroism, land (*lo païs*), and a book. There is no reason to believe that Joan, an atheist, agrees to any such pact. However, shortly thereafter Joan, in Sicily, purchases from her family a fifteen-year-old girl named Margherita and goes to dwell with her in Germany, where he calls her Grete. In time he also writes a two-volume book in Occitan and returns to the heart of Occitania. Perhaps the devil decided to tempt the man by giving him, without a contract, all he might have asked for, all that a modern Southern French Faust could ask for. And perhaps this explains Joan's self-effacement at the end: his destruction of the book and abandonment of his money, status, and identity. From an anarchist perspective, he will remain free and never, like the real Faust, accept status or stasis, for these would negate all he has lived for and ensure his damnation. Perhaps Joan was never aware of what Amielh had learned, that writing, because it is transgression, inevitably partakes of the dia-

bolic and the Faustian. As Amielh writes to a friend, 'Je te l'écrivais ce
matin, je te le récris dans cette nuit qui s'étire, pendant ce temps de
silence après l'orage où j'espère encore que va arriver mon ami Jean
Ventenac: j'entre en littérature sur un signe du diable, un bon diable
qui rend la jeunesse au docteur Faustus, lui offre de bien douces
Marguerite, Magali ou Grete, et lui ouvre le vrai savoir: l'héroïsme'
(I, p. 449).

   Don Quixote. The Cavalier's papers are covered by a title-page, 'Dom
Quichotte occitanien,' presumably a project which never comes to fruition; still worse, the title-page is in French. Amielh and the implied
author conceive that Joan Cavalier, the Cavalier de Març, and Joan Ventenac are knights and figures for the Occitan Don Quixote. According
to Andrieu:

> Pasmens, redreceire dei tòrts, siás romanesc e quichotesc. Ont es lo molin
> d'infamia que molineja ara? Rigam pas. Dòm Quichòt es un eròi mai ver-
> tadier que Cervantes o cresiá. O, au revers, tótei leis eròis vertadiers son de
> Quichòts. (II, p. 242)
>
> (Nevertheless, righter of wrongs, you are romantic and quixotic. Where is
> the windmill of infamy that grinds today? Don't laugh. Don Quixote is a
> more genuine hero than Cervantes thought. Or, on the contrary, all genu-
> ine heros are Don Quixotes.)

On the one hand, Lafont tells us that a life of heroism centred around
Occitan – the language and the region – is roughly equivalent to tilting
at windmills. Such Occitan heroics will always contain a measure of quix-
otism as well as narcissism. On the other hand, since *Don Quixote* is generally assumed to have been the first modern novel, Lafont also tells us
that Occitan will never become a truly modern, European, universal language until the Occitan Don Quixote comes into being as a book. Here
I propose that *La Festa* is that modern Occitan *Quixote*. It is nine hundred pages long, in two volumes, the second volume recasting material
in the first, and its hero is a narcissistic, absurd, and failure-prone yet
heroically romantic figure. One of Joan's failures is *his* two-volume Occitan novel, which never sees the light of day. It and he, however, are
redeemed by the genuine *La Festa*, perhaps imagined by Amielh, an
intellectual not a knight, and certainly written by Robert Lafont. As *Don
Quixote* was the first novel, *La Festa* will be the last, or at least the sum of
all preceding novels. (Finally, it can be noted that Cervantes is one of
the greatest writers of the Baroque, a period also epitomized by the city

of Vienna and its museums. Lafont turns to the Baroque seeking cultural roots, much as Garioch, Goodsir Smith, and McLellan turned to eighteenth-century Edinburgh; these later models supplement the Middle Ages as historical and cultural analogues.)

The Bible. Amielh dwells in 'Lo Paradís.' There he uncovers a treasure – the Cavalier de Març's papers, that is, the gift of language, history, and the imaginary, the gift of the knowledge of Oc, for both good and evil. For Amielh (like Adam), this is a *felix culpa*, which opens up the world; it is a gift of origins. After the Adam-figure in 'A' comes Joan Ventenac, a figure for John the Baptist and John the Apostle. With his (admittedly aborted) two-volume novel, he preaches the *Verbum in principio*. As a militant for Occitania, he heralds the coming of a better world. Paradise is lost, but then, in Lafont's powerfully secular vision, it is and will be regained. Synagoga is fulfilled not by Ecclesia but by militant *laicitat*, and the Occitan novel will contain all of Western civilization, all that it missed over the centuries.

It will be regained not from an individual saviour but through collective activity in an ambience of joy. Hence 'la festa.' Joan Ventenac returns to the Paradise and reunites with Amielh; it is located in the South not the East. In this paradise, according to Joan Cavalier, sex and the body are privileged. An outpouring of young people flock to the centre, a flock growing into an army. Speaking all the dialects of Oc, they come to defend mother earth against the ravisher – the French state. The next day they all will celebrate the harvest festival on the Larzac as an act of political defiance. For Lafont, the new apocalypse is grounded and will take shape in rebellion, outlawry, festivity, desire, and, above all, transgression. The transgression and its joy – physical and spiritual – are made manifest in the body (the joy of food, the joy of sex) and the mind (the joy of writing). For in this Bakhtinian carnival in which a despised minority tongue rebels against and displaces the grand languages of culture, freedom and desire are made incarnate in the literary text itself, the sprawling, picaresque, baroque, multi-registered Occitan 'Quixote' which is *La Festa*. And the ultimate *festa* of and in the novel is *La Festa*.

JEAN-CLAUDE FORÊT

Since 1983 Robert Lafont has continued to expand the parameters of fiction in Oc, including in his achievement a sequel to *La Festa*.[44] And, from the 1980s on, a new generation of writers has come of age who publish novels and novella collections, adhering either to *nouveau roman* or to the equivalent of magical realism. The two works of prose narrative from the younger generation most highly regarded are *Antonio Vidal* by Alain Surre-Garcia (1983) and *La Pèira d'asard* (The Stone of Chance) by Jean-Claude Forêt (1990).[45]

La Pèira d'asard is a linguistic and narratological tour de force, very much in the surfiction-metafiction line. An extra-diegetic 'editor,' one Leonard Jactefeu, has discovered three documents. Each document has a distinct narrator who is also a distinct central focusing protagonist. Each text is written in a separate variety of Occitan, to be distinguished from the others in space and time. An intellectual puzzle is offered early in Text 1 which Texts 1, 2, and 3 help to solve. Yet as each text completes the puzzle of the preceding text(s), it also adds to it.

Text 1 is the confession memoir of a young scholar and idealist, cast in twentieth-century central-Languedoc literary Occitan. Abel is ripped apart by the fact that the very day he discovers an ancient slate covered with writing in the Etruscan script, his girlfriend Cintia leaves him without warning. After an enormous expenditure of time and energy (learning all he can about Etruscan, discovering the slate is written in Proto-Basque, learning all he can about Basque), Abel finally deciphers the slate: he then realizes that the text is identical in meaning to the eight-line verse in patois that Cintia left him as her goodbye:

> Coma la nuèit tombava sul mieu sòmi,
> Ai quitat los camps mairenals,
> Los monts de la mieuna enfantesa,
> Bon astre a los que passan!
> Me'n vau cap a l'oblit,
> Un moment me sieguèri,
> Lo temps d'espillar qualques mots
> Per fins que sàpias que foguèri. (p. 83)

(As night fell on my dream, I left home, the family lands / our fields, the mountains of my childhood. Good luck to those who get through! I am going to oblivion. I sat down for a moment, just long enough to pin together some words, so that you know that I was.)

Text 2, in a medieval manuscript, is the fragmentary verse memoir of the Monk of Mazan, cast in his speech, thirteenth-century classical Occitan, the language of the troubadours. The Monk is ripped apart by what he reads in an ancient Latin manuscript. The latter preaches a doctrine, heretical from the Monk's perspective, that the universe is governed entirely and only by chance. As proof of the powers of chance, the presumed author of the text, a Roman sceptic, having heard a slave sing a song in some language from the East, has it translated into Euskera by a Basque slave and has this Basque version inscribed onto a piece of slate by an Etruscan slave. A Gallic merchant is instructed to drop it at a spot as far from Rome as he can.

Text 3 is the goodbye letter Cintia wrote to Abel but kept to herself, cast in the modern, popular Occitan speech of the Vivarais mountains, where they live. She recounts her life and the life of her family, including her uncle Joan, who made poems in dialect for her and who knew the story of the Monk of Mazan. The eight-line poem she does leave Abel is presumably one of these, which Joan adapted from the Monk's manuscript or, if not that, one of her grandmother's songs, part of an oral tradition dating back to the Monk.

The title of *La Pèira d'asard* provides a launching-point for discussion. The principal theme of the novel is the notion of chance. It is by coincidence that Cintia's farewell poem is identical in meaning to the text inscribed on Abel's slate. It is pure chance that Abel discovers the slate the same day that Cintia leaves him the poem. It is by chance that Cintia should have given her boyfriend the poem and not the prose memoir she intended to. It is a series of coincidences that cause Leonard Jactefeu to obtain Abel's and Cintia's memoirs and to read the Monk's manuscript. Finally, it is not only a series of coincidental occurrences that lead to the inscription of the message on the slate and to its presence in France. It is also the result of the Roman aristocrat's doctrine of chance, which so disturbs the Monk, causing him to translate the Latin and to doubt his own soul. In a sense, the Monk is right. The Latin writer and Jean-Claude Forêt explore all possible connotations of the terms *fors* and *fortuna* in Latin and *asard* in Occitan. As in French and English, these terms cover the semantic ranges of chance, coincidence, fortune, luck, and hazard. They also touch on the irrational. There is no doubt that they point to a theory of the cosmos whereby, in our world, beneath the moon, no rational, purposive presence (God, providence, reason) can be found. All, without exception, is subject to Fortuna; all that occurs occurs only by chance, according to chaos.

The principal pattern of imagery is lapidary: imagery of stone. The Roman has his slave's poem inscribed on stone. While learning Etruscan and Basque, Abel learns also to speak to the rocks, and they and the

Basque mountains talk to him. The limits to the Roman's doctrine of chance are defined by a lapidary analogy: You let a stone fall from your hand. You do it again and again. Although each time the stone will probably fall, you have no certainty of it, for the act lies beyond your control. Maybe it will fall, maybe it will not, given that the two actions, separate in time and space, are in no way connected. Finally, Cintia is dismayed by the symbolic dislocation which occurs when she removes one rock from an ancient stone wall, for, according to her, both the rock and the wall weep their separation; she also alludes to herself as a rolling stone ('Pèira que gòja'). In this novel of the French mountain country, Forêt revels in the imagery of stone and in the imagery of snow and the cold. We are never allowed to forget that Cintia comes from poor rural folk who live out their lives desperately grasping existence from the soil. Stone evokes, as always, the hard earth of the will, that which can kill, as it evokes the stolid materiality of life, that which endures, as does the Church ('super hanc petram aedificabo ecclesiam meam'). Stone also is part of nature: it lives and speaks. It is therefore ironic and paradoxical that Forêt should choose this imagery of permanence to elaborate his doctrine of impermanence and the irrational.

La Pèira d'asard is a love story. Abel and Cintia lived two years of happiness in their little island in the mountains. Theirs is a torrential passion. Yet it is also riddled with uncertainty, suspicion, and the desperate yearning for separation (obstacle). Courtly love, at its finest, demands jealousy and obstacle, as if love, being human, must contain all of the human condition, including its tragedy and loss. It is, then, the tension between desire and fulfilment and between possession and repudiation which creates much of the interest in this tale. Abel and Cintia are introspective, powerfully lucid erotic entities, with centuries of courtly love and classical passion ingrained in their psyches. One piece of evidence that Forêt undermines as well as exalts in his characters' erotic exaltation is provided by the leprosy motif. The Monk is descended from a family of lepers. As if because of this, he once was a troubadour committed to *fin' amor*. Ever since, he has been haunted by memories of lust from those days. And Cintia, after leaving Abel, ministers to victims of the plague in Ethiopia, where she dies. Forêt is aware of the medieval tradition – in Beroul's *Tristan* and countless other works – which ties Eros to leprosy. It is the medieval belief that leprosy was a venereal disease and that lepers were subject to powerful sex drives. Here, in *La Pèira*, lovers are assimilated to untouchables, to society's rejects, and society's taboo becomes a metaphysical taboo and symbol of guilt.

More important than Eros is the theme of language. That the novel is composed in three distinct registers of Occitan, in three languages almost, forces the implied reader to be aware of language and language problems. Cintia loves her Savoie dialect, and the Monk is fascinated by the Latin manuscript he translates. The Roman author of the manuscript used language variation to illustrate his philosophy of chance. Most of all, however, Abel – in this sense a displaced projection of Jean-Claude Forêt himself – is a linguist and scholar of languages. A Frenchman from Lyon, he learns Cintia's Vivarais speech, and he learns central literary Occitan, the latter well enough to employ it as the medium of his diary and memoirs. He wrote a tourist guide to the Cévennes in the various dialects of the regions. He also completed Chrétien's *Conte du Graal* in the twelfth-century Champenois French, and he knows Egyptian. Then, when Abel comes across the slate, he is so fascinated that he cannot stop until he has deciphered the inscription. To do so, he abandons everything – dropping his work, selling his automobile – to master all that is known about Etruscan and, when that avenue peters out, to learn Basque. He would write literature in Etruscan would somebody agree as to what Etruscan was. Abel is a *fou du langage* and a magnificent one.

On the one hand, Abel and his author Forêt celebrate the high-culture aspects of language, especially the great tongues of the past. This has been a recurring theme in literature since Anatole France's *Le Crime de Sylvestre Bonnard*. Thus, Abel is fascinated by his archaeological find, what a tiny piece of slate can tell. He dreams that he possesses the last text by the last speaker of Etruscan. Then he dreams about having the first text ever in Euskera, in a tongue which was new and open to all possibilities two thousand years ago. He imagines a story to explain how a Basque person might have inscribed a text in Etruscan script in Gaul, and meditates on the fate of the Iberians and the Etruscans. Significantly, he relates the Etruscan situation to that of Occitan. The inscriber of the slate may have been, in the past, the last speaker and writer of Etruscan just as he, Abel, may be the last speaker and writer of Occitan in the present, at least in the Vivarais mountains. The people of Oc, a language without a past as a national tongue, must create that past in the present. Similarly, Cintia meditates on the lost rural past of her Occitan-speaking family and villagers, as compared to the present of capitalist exploitation, symbolized by the bulldozer.

It is clear that language as culture brings Forêt's characters to speculate on the rise and fall of cultures in time: past, present, and future.

Even more, the need to decipher the code and to comprehend the text becomes part of a Balzacian quest for the Absolute, a quest for revelation. Abel undergoes a true ascesis – selling all, embracing poverty – making whatever sacrifices are necessary in order to penetrate the mysteries. Part of the initiation occurs in his dreams on ancient peoples and his new-found capacity to speak directly to the rocks. The Monk also seeks a revelation, demanding truth even if it be heretical and he be damned for his pains. Damned presumably he will be – he commits suicide – but not before having discovered and embraced in its totality the dark doctrine of chaos to which he is so attached.

Forêt's vision is dark indeed. For all three characters the initiation leads to despair; all three perish before their time. According to legend, the Monk commits suicide, leaping off a cliff. The other two also self-destruct, if only symbolically: Abel dies from a fall in the Basque Pyrenees, and Cintia expires while nursing victims of the plague in Ethiopia. All three suffer from the ill working of chance, transmuted into their personal ill fortune, and from the doctrine of chance, which denies a rational explanation of the universe.

Yet this is not all, it is far from being all. Abel is reduced to despair by the inexplicable equivalence of his two documents: the Etruscan slate and Cintia's poem, an equivalence that mocks him with sardonic laughter. Yet he suffers most of all from the failure of his life, not just his scholarly adventures but also the love for Cintia; he despairs because she left him and the slate offers him no answer. Cintia also, who initiates the separation, is destroyed by it. She recognizes that a sort of death occurs to the rock and the wall when one is removed from the other. She commits the fatal act anyway, in part because she also recognizes that separation, obstacle, and loss form part of the amorous life. The Monk knew the bond between *fin' amor* and leprosy; Cintia imposes the bond between her passion and the plague. Eros and Thanatos form a whole, for the one presumes the existence of the other. *La petite mort* is so intimately involved in Big Death; the one substitutes for the other, anticipates the other, and validates the other. Finally, Cintia imposes death on Abel and herself because she endures a despair which transcends the affair with Abel and any other affair she might have. After all, he joys in modern literary Occitan and all other languages. She knows only French and the dialect of her people in the mountains. She loves their children's songs and folk-songs. She makes us relive the harsh lives of her grandmother and uncle. With the arrival of the bulldozers, with the corruption of the local peasantry (an attempted rape of her), with the knowledge that she and Abel are the last to speak the language of this wild frontier of Occitania, she will break free. She will say 'No!' at whatever cost.

Cintia's 'No!,' perhaps a gesture of despair, perhaps an ill-fortuned, irrational embrace of Thanatos, nevertheless gives voice to a sense of brio and élan, a sense of feverish action all too lacking in the bookish reveries of Abel and the Monk. Hers is a gesture of freedom, of daring to sever the rope and break away from the constrictive rural poverty of her family and the comparable constrictions endured in her relationship with Abel. The implied reader discovers (or ought to discover) that, in this novel, nothing is ever what it appears to be.

If such is the case for the love of Abel and Cintia or for the history of the people speaking in Oc, it is also true, I believe, for the greater question of chance. Throughout the novel, from beginning to end, the perceptive implied reader (competent reader or ideal reader) cannot escape the paradox that, whereas presumably expected to marvel at the power of coincidence – as the characters do – he is more likely to relish the implied author's intellectual powers and his command of narrative strategies. Narratology teaches us that in textual reality nothing is left to chance and that Sartre is wrong-headed to expect that a mere literary character, the creature of a human creator, could ever possibly command free will. Jean-Claude Forêt arranges these far-fetched coincidences and then explains them by even more far-fetched causal happenings. All is artifice, in a deliciously artificial, mannered, modernist, *nouveau roman* book. Surely we are meant to be aware of and to marvel at the artifice: when the journalist, Leonard Jactefeu, advises us that we can read the three texts in any order we choose; when, insistently, both Jactefeu and the Monk question whether the ancient Latin text the Monk translates is genuine or a forgery; for that matter when Abel's Roman-Etruscan-Basque inscription does reveal the precise same meaning as Cintia's folk-song. Here Forêt 'proves,' as it were, the Borges paradox: that to rewrite *Don Quixote* in the twentieth century, in Cervantes's own language word for word, would give us a different version and a different book. I suspect that Forêt is also playing with a mannered, modernist version of the surrealist *hasard objectif.* So much that could be coincidental or rational is in fact a performance of disguise, illusion, and deceit, for that matter of direct manipulation. In his book of chance we admire and are taken with the artifice of paradox and ambiguity, created by two masters of deceit, two tricksters: intradiegetically the Roman sceptic, 100 BC, and extradiegetically the author Jean-Claude Forêt who created both the Roman sceptic and all the illusion in this magnificent, bookish, irrational world.

THEATRE

ROBERT LAFONT

The situation of the theatre was and is, for the lands of Occitan, less promising than in Scotland or Brittany. It is true, the South of France enjoyed a tradition of popular drama extending from the Middle Ages up to the Second World War. These works were pastorals and comic, burlesque pieces in the tradition of the carnival. Although the theatrical companies specializing in dialect died out in Bordeaux and Marseille with the twentieth century, semi-amateur troops continued to produce serious and comic plays – *lo teatre paisan* (peasant theater) – for the people. Then, from 1945 on Charles Mouly with Radio Toulouse and Francis Gag with Radio Nice and Radio Montecarlo created the same kind of popular skit as Per Jakez Helias did at Rennes.[46]

Nonetheless, the general sentiment among Occitanists, after the war, was one of failure. Max Rouquette spoke of a sense of hopelessness due to the absence of money to produce plays or even to publish them, the lack of genuine professionals capable of performing in Occitan, and the fact that the new plays were not being printed.[47] He could also have mentioned an increasingly more obvious and painful factor: the lack of a public capable of appreciating or even understanding drama in Occitan. Although many plays were written, a significant percentage exist in manuscript form only, and others are buried in obscure Felibrige publications. Any number were never performed, and many that were are of little value.

A genuine Renaissance in the theatre occurred, as in Brittany, as an outgrowth of 1968. The best-known figure is Claude Alranq, who in 1970 launched Lo Teatre de la Carrièra (Street Theatre). By 1978 he had put on nine original plays, and he would reach some 35,000 spectators in his last year. The three other leaders are André Neyton with Le Centre Dramatique Occitan de Provence, André Benedetto with Le Théâtre des Carmes, and Jean-Claude Scant with Le Théâtre de l'Olivier. Influenced by Brecht, by Ariane Mnouchkine's Théâtre du Soleil, and by the Campesino Chicano from California, the new Occitan theatre was consciously New Left, aiming to have an impact on the urban and, above all, the rural masses. It proved to be powerfully vital, open to the latest currents in European stagecraft, and was led by and oriented to the young. Also, in the face of sociolinguistic reality, all the plays were in French or bilingual – in most cases, largely French with only so much Occitan as would not turn away francophone monolinguals. The Renaissance largely ceased after 1980 with the end of the 1968 mind-set, although a theatre in Oc, derived from it, continues to exist.[48]

A number of the major figures of Occitan modernism were active in writing for the stage. Among these are to be noted Léon Cordes, Max Rouquette, and Robert Lafont. Always at the centre of the Occitan literary world, Lafont was the most prolific and, in my opinion, the most successful dramatist, with seven full-length plays and a number of brief ones. At first Lafont wrote standard comedies and historical dramas, but then, anticipating 1968, he had *Per jòia recomençar* (For Joy to Begin Again) performed at the Fos-Anfos Festival in 1966. This first militant bilingual play, directed against tourism, was closed down by the mayor. Lafont proved to be the only major writer of modernism to join and to write for the new theatre.

La Loba (The She-Wolf), published in 1959, is a historical drama written entirely in Occitan.[49] Directed by André Delcamp, it went on tour in the South. However, as was to be expected, the play enjoyed significantly greater success in a French translation. In that version it was directed by Claude Vernick at the Théâtre Récamier in Paris (1959) and by Bressieux for La Ligue Française de l'Enseignement (1961), and performed at the Festival de Moissac in 1965.

Lafont takes as his immediate source the *vida* of the great satirical troubadour Peire Vidal. According to this thirteenth-century fictional account, Peire Vidal was so enamoured of the Countess Loba that he called himself Lops (Wolf) and, clad in wolf pelts, allowed himself to be hunted down and beaten as a wolf. Overjoyed at this display of courtly wit, Loba and her husband nursed the man back to health.

Lafont builds on this scaffolding a powerful meditation on *fin' amor* – passion – in all its aspects and all its phases. In the play Peire Vidal's love and martyrdom are crucial yet also peripheral to the central love triangle: Loba the wife, Count Ugon the husband, and Rogier the lover. In the last act, Rogier slays Ugon but is then cut down by the lord's serving-men, upon which Loba stabs herself with Rogier's sword, leaving Peire Vidal as the survivor.

La Loba adheres to a relatively traditional kind of theatre, one that some would call bourgeois though I prefer to think of it as classical French. Racine inevitably comes to mind in this text where characters, each standing alone in a unique world, unable to communicate, devour each other, torn by passion, desire, shame, guilt, and the will to conquer. The devouring and the conquering occur through language, discourse that is mannered (courtly) and, for that reason, capable of inflicting deep wounds. Lafont even respects – in his fashion – the three unities. He tells of one action, the desire for Loba of three men: Rogier, Peire, and Ugon. He creates unity of space: the action takes place in various portions of Ugon's castle. He obeys unity of time: the three acts occur at dawn, following three consecutive nights. I envisage two reasons for the Racinian structure. Such a play is new to Occitan, and Lafont demonstrates that Occitan modernism can compete with the French on their own turf, as it were. He also observes that Racinian passion is neither Greek nor Italian. In its origins and essence it is Gallic, and it first came into existence with the troubadours, who wrote not in French but in Occitan.

Throughout, implicitly or explicitly, *fin' amor* is contrasted to the more traditional male feudal ethos of war and knighthood. At one point the Aragonese ambassador praises war over love, confessing that he has a taste for shepherd girls and that he has never loved like Rogier. At one point Rogier is tempted to follow Don Miguel to Barcelona, thus breaking his chains to Loba, to win renown as a warrior. Ugon also urges him to do so. Yet, in the end, 'omnia vincit amor.' *Fin' amor* always carries the day, and the characters, tossed to and fro on the winds of passion, cannot escape their doom.

Lafont offers us the classical triangle of *fin' amor*: a jealous husband, a domineering wife of unearthly beauty, and a bachelor younger than she who explodes with the élan and the commitment to the absolute inherent in *joven*. This nexus is then expanded (and twisted) to include the troubadour. By his extravagant sacrifice of self – allowing himself to be beaten by the peasants in the she-wolf's name – he makes a claim to be worthy of *fin' amor* also. Loba, who remains in love with Rogier, is deeply moved by Peire's gesture, and she gives him a kiss. This kiss conventionally seals the pact of *fin' amor*. Indeed, neither we the implied audience nor Loba herself knows for certain with whom she is in love.

Central to *fin' amor* is the obstacle. The obstacle then gives rise to jealousy and, according to Andreas Capellanus, is a constitutive element of love. Lafont amplifies the traditional motif by making the lover and the husband equally torn by jealousy. In Act I Ugon is tortured by the thought of Loba and Rogier fornicating all night in her chamber: 'E d'aquela pòrta silenciosa qu'ausas pas butar, tota una nuech de tèmps! [...] Femna, Loba, ai que mon revenge, ieu, pèr m'escaufar lo còr a l'auba!' (p. 12) (And that silent door that I dare not push open, all night long! Woman, Wolf, at dawn I have only vengeance to warm my heart!). In Act III Rogier is tortured by not knowing what is going on, and who is doing what, in Loba's chamber. Here Lafont brilliantly makes the classical-bourgeois French stage conventions a central structural and psychological element in his own drama. We observe the jealous male on stage in what is a decentred space, tortured by what goes on or what he thinks goes on (we never know nor does he) directly off stage, behind a closed door, in the metaphorical *hortus conclusus* of Loba's room, bed, and body. Similarly, in temporal terms, the drama whose subtitle is 'la frucha di tres aubas' (the fruit of three dawns), portrays the tension-ridden border between night and day. Three times the characters, after a night of passion or frustrated libido, try to speak, to resolve, to conquer verbally in the light what they could not do physically in the dark. Although they speak at dawn, in the end they grant hegemony to the dark – the world of Eros, the body, the irrational, the female, the 'lunatic' – and to the bird of the dark, the nightingale.

Because of the fierceness of the male lovers, the ferocity of their desire and their jealousy, Loba, for all her courtly mastery – she is the *domna*, the one who dominates – more than once is given over to fear, fear of Rogier's impetuousness, of Peire Vidal's passion, and, since after all she dwells in a Christian universe, fear of sin. Loba has a powerful sense of guilt. In Lafont's vision it may indeed contribute to the power of love, love as transgression. However, even though she and others liken the Eros-filled tension of the castle to Satan's work, Loba, when meditating on a better life in a house of religion, requests instead to be walled up here, in her castle, in her (love) chamber.

It was a truism in courtly doctrine that love is madness, totally opposed to reason yet a secular, erotic *sancta stultitia* justified on its own terms. The troubadour proves his capacity to love and be loved by committing an act of madness – wearing a bear skin he believed to be a gift from Loba and risking his life, hunted down as her beast. Love is madness, and madness is love. As if to prove the point, Lafont has the two other embodiments of male libido – Rogier and Ugon – stirred up by desire (and drink) to the point that they go beyond Peire's courtly game. They become beasts and kill each other for real.

This play and the phenomenon of *fin' amor* itself, while appearing to treat questions of Eros, veil yet also reveal a deeper ideological conflict: between the feudal aristocracy and the clergy, and between the aristocracy and those elements from the outside, such as the troubadours, who would also partake of the courtly world. That the ideology of class impinges upon love and life is evident from the way the gentles react to the troubadour. Even though she fears his passion, Loba treats Peire Vidal with contempt. Even worse, the lover and the husband both employ him as an arm – a decoy – in their private personal war. Rogier lies to Peire, offering him the bear pelt and saying it is a gift from Loba. The aristocrat mocks the low-born poet and also manipulates him, hoping that Ugon will follow the false scent believing that it is the poet who seeks to cuckold him. Ugon, however, is far too shrewd to swallow the bait. Instead, when he perceives Loba giving one kiss to Peire, he denounces his wife and the troubadour in public: 'Venètz vèire lo desonor [...] Remiratz la Dòna qu'oblida son linhatge dins lo liech d'un joglar damnat. La Loba n'a pas pron dis òmes de l'encontrada. Li fau li baugs e li varlets' (p. 122) (Come and behold dishonour. Admire the Lady who forgets about her pedigree in the bed of an accursed juggler. La Loba is no longer satisfied with countrymen. She has to have jesters and varlets). He then orders his loyal vassal – Rogier! – to guard her chamber. By so doing, he prevents Rogier from entering the chamber and pays him back in frustrated desire for frustrated desire. Both ruses threaten Peire's life, concerning which the competing male aristocrats care not a bit. Peire allows himself to be manipulated, utterly lucid as to what is going on. The manipulation and the deceit are thus bound to *fin' amor*, contributing to and emanating from it. This is because passion is so all-pervasive that otherwise chivalrous men will employ any means, however devious, to attain their ends. It is the case also because central to Eros is the will to conquer – mastery as important a goal as *jouissance* – to conquer male rivals while enjoying the female, and to master the female, who, when she is a she-wolf, displays all the competitive traits of a man. Hence the atmosphere of dread which hangs over the play. Hence the recurrence of mockery, one character wounding another verbally – the males mock Peire Vidal and each other, Loba mocks all three – as a means of asserting dominance, as a substitute for and anticipation of eventual physical mastery. The climax occurs when, in Act III (here Lafont corresponds to Corneille in *Rodogune* as much as to Racine), Loba agrees to leave with Rogier only if he slays her husband: 'Partirai amb tu se tuas Ugon. Se lo tuas pas, d'eu totjorn me sovendrai, e lo sovenir totjorn serà entre nosautres' (p. 144) (I will leave with you if you kill Ugon. If you don't kill him, I will always remember him, and the memory will always stand between us). He cannot will himself to do it, so that when Ugon appears on stage he mocks Rogier for that lack of will. Therefore, proclaims Ugon, I have conquered you, and Loba and I, animals of a higher blood line, will remain together. Finally, intimates Lafont, it is only in a highly refined, civilized, quasi-decadent society that people are capable of such games of deceit, mastery, and verbal dexterity. The South of France, insists Lafont, was such a society in the twelfth century, as much so as was Racine's Paris.

This highly refined society is, in addition to being Christian, also feudal-aristocratic, with the nobility grounded in the countryside and in rural doings. Hence, perhaps, one reason for the animal imagery which pervades the text. The title, *La Loba*, names the countess, born and baptized Loba, and reminds us that Loba is the term for she-wolf. Wild beast names, largely absent from modern French and English, are still prevalent in modern Italian (Lupo, Orso) and German (Wolf). The characters allude more than once to the metaphor, intimating that the countess is fierce and untamed, a lone creature savage in her primeval dignity. From this, Rogier draws the stratagem of giving Peire a bear pelt, as a purported offering from the she-wolf. The troubadour accepts the gift and the metaphor, dons the pelt, and allows himself to be torn apart by dogs, as if he were a wolf. Thus, he is convinced, he becomes metaphorically Loba's lover and discovers her love and his own. At the end, Ugon gloats over the fact that he and Loba are both of them wild animals: they are wolves and, fighting like wolves, will grow old together. If these ferocious lovers identify themselves with beasts, they also identify with those who hunt them down. Prior to Act I Rogier had tracked and slain a boar, and Loba loves him for it. Ugon also is a hunter and, at one point, speaks of riding hard a mare, wild with jealousy and desire. Eventually, it is Rogier who chases Ugon and stabs him. The hunt, with its shedding of blood, is a metaphor for the sexual act and for masculine competition in arms and Eros (the topos of *militia et amor*), hence the allusions to boiling wine and flowing blood and to the violence unleashed by desire and the feast. This culminates in Ugon's tale of a husband who, stabbing a lover, makes the blood of truth flow from open mouthlike wounds. His tale, as *mise en abyme*, anticipates the denouement: three creatures of passion who shed each other's blood.

In all this poor Peire Vidal appears to be the outsider, one who would like to be Loba's wolf yet does not belong to the aristocratic world of the feast and chase. He is hunted but never the hunter. Such is the case on one level of imagery yet not on another. For the troubadour is in addition assimilated to the bird of the dark, the nightingale, the singer of Eros, the objective correlative of the poet in love so often evoked in the opening stanza of troubadour and trouvère song. Should these male warriors, or Peire Vidal, hunt birds instead of beasts of the field? Is Peire a genuine rival for Rogier or Ugon? In which case, is the nightingale more dangerous than an exotic, foreign parrot? Rogier, as a *fin' aman,* learns to speak. Thereupon he becomes a nightingale; he becomes like Peire. And, when he dies, Rogier speaks not of wolves or boars. He proclaims that as long as the nightingale can sing, Loba will be his. Is this the ultimate triumph of Peire Vidal and all that he represents? If he cannot become a wolf, at least can Rogier become a nightingale?

The answers to such questions are problematic, if for no other reason than the manner in which Lafont undermines the traditionally assumed connection (assumed by poets) between love and art. In Act I we discover that Peire the troubadour sings like a nightingale. All well and good, except that Rogier maintains courtly discretion (*mezura, celers*); he keeps silent. He is the genuine lover. After the wounding by dogs, now Rogier chatters away, a rhetorician of Eros, a nightingale, whereas it is Peire Vidal, reduced to silence, who has come to know true love. Still worse, as the drama builds to its denouement, during the last of the three nights no one speaks, or sleeps either; the actors and the extras throb with tension and foreboding.

It is clear that Lafont establishes a structure of tension, perhaps even one of antithesis, between speech and action and between poetry and love. This corresponds to the opposition between the troubadours (as learned clerks) and the aristocrats they serve and, ideally, would like to become. On one level, Peire Vidal is not and cannot be a Rogier or a Ugon. This means that, because of his social class but also because he is an artist, he will always stand outside their circle and, because he is an artist, he cannot love as they do. That is one price the artist pays for being what he is. Yet the boundaries between the two social classes and the two states of mind are porous. Rogier crosses the line from one side, and Peire from the other. In the end, when Rogier cries out that Loba will be his as long as the nightingale sings, perhaps he has learned that *fin' amor* is open to all of gentle heart and that he, the *fin' aman,* can be and was a master of speech. Or perhaps he recognizes that he the lover will attain immortality only through the songs of troubadours like Peire Vidal, who, because they are nightingales, can never mate with a wolf.

Ultimately, I believe, *La Loba* is not a play about the countess or about her troubadour. Any of the four principals, and there are four – Loba, Rogier, Ugon, and Peire – can be considered the actant subject, with correspondingly different opposants and adjuvants. However, the donor remains the same – Eros, passion, desire – and the receiver always the subject him/herself. The drama treats of love, explores love, traces love to its tragic end as these magnificent entities destroy each other, each acting alone, encased in a solitary, self-oriented body and consciousness.

La Révolte des 'Cascavèus' is an example of Lafont's new dramatic style, post-1968, under the influence of Brecht and Claude Alranq.[50] This play, in my opinion Lafont's best and the most successful by any writer in the new style, was written for André Neyton's Centre Dramatique Occitan de Provence. Neyton gave it over one hundred performances from October 1977 to January 1981. Then, on 13 August 1985, it was broadcast on television, under the direction of Claude Vernick, who had been responsible for the Parisian run of *La Loba*.

The play commemorates a rebellion of the people of Provence against French centralism and French exploitation in the year 1630. Lafont puts on stage the principals: the upper-class leaders of the rebellion, the Président de Coriolis and his nephew Châteauneuf; and, on the other side, Cardinal Richelieu, his confidant Father Joseph, and his representatives in the province, Forbin and Du Bras. In the spirit of Brecht, Lafont also gives voice to the little people, who, in counterpoint, play as important a role as the principals. These are the peasant rebel Pélican, his girlfriend Marianne, and her bourgeois parents Beneset and Beneseta. The play follows the rebellion from its beginning to a series of preliminary successes and then to defeat at the hands of Louis XIII's army, upon which Coriolis leaves, to die in prison, Pélican is killed, and Beneset is sentenced to be executed.

Lei Cascavèus, a drama of class struggle, depicts a relatively unproblematic world where it is easy to distinguish good from evil. In the year 1630 the people of Provence endure poverty, famine, and the plague. It is winter, and they face cold and hunger. Indeed, Marianne's parents come to accept Pélican as their daughter's suitor because he brings them firewood. It is at this moment that Richelieu imposes new, special taxes to be paid to tax collectors come from the North.

Lafont sketches the opposing forces: North versus South, Paris versus Provence, the king versus his people, exploiters versus the exploited, and the rich versus the poor. Questions of money and social class dominate life in all its registers and categories. Richelieu finds local notables such as Forbin, who, to please the court, accepts his appointment as governor (and tax collector) of Antibes. Coriolis and Châteauneuf are idealists, ready to join the rebellion because the people, not the nobles and clergy, are the future of Provence. However, Châteauneuf is temporarily put off when the masses proceed to rob and pillage, and he temporarily betrays them. Beneset also is caught in the middle. The poor fellow really would like to avoid commitment altogether. Forced to represent the Third Estate, he is incapable of leading or fighting, changes sides like a weathervane, and, in the end, pays the price for others' nobility and others' folly. What might appear to be melodrama (socialist romance) is in fact melodrama and socialist romance, practised by a master who, as he did with *L'Icòna dins l'iscla*, invests in it such passion, integrity, and poetry that it becomes a total work of art.

One pattern of imagery contributing to the totality consists of clothes and clothing, and bells and ringing. As the masses win their first battle and also pillage, they seize pretty raiment, the garb of their 'betters.' Donning these clothes, they start to speak French in place of Occitan. A comic bit of stagecraft anticipates the betrayals of the future. The terms for the rebels and the title-word of the play is 'cascavèus,' which alludes to the bells these men wear on their peasant clothes. But just as the poor can move up in vestimentary terms, the rich can move down. When Châteauneuf and his army bring off a victory, they are not readmitted inside the walls of Aix, and Coriolis is banished. The burghers now also wear bells. They have taken over the rebellion for their purposes. Later, at perhaps the high point of the revolt, the Cascavèus pursue one of the king's officers into the church and up into the steeple and its belfry. His final refuge is on one of the great bells. To dislodge him, the rebels ring it and then ring him. Yet, in the end, bells and clothes with bells will fail. As the royal army from Marseille marches in, their drums drum out the bells as, indeed, symbolically, the instrument of war drowns out the instrument of peace and reform.

La Révolte des 'Cascavèus' is bilingual, in its title and action. As in the Scottish theatre, the bilingualism and its accompanying diglossia contribute to the interpretation of politics and of social class. And, like the Scottish, this is modern theatre, where various linguistic registers can be juxtaposed and will flourish. Richelieu and Père Joseph speak only French. Forbin the governor of Antibes speaks French to his Provençal subjects, who reply in Occitan. Coriolis and Châteauneuf speak French. One of the high points, ideologically and in dramatic terms, occurs when the peasants, monolingual in Occitan, draw up articles for a constitution, and Châteauneuf dilutes and distorts their declaration of independence in his 'official' French translation. Poor Beneset bobs back and forth, speaking Occitan to his family and absurd French when he shows off in public. Led off to be shot, he cries out in tragicomic outrage, 'Ai rèn fach!' (I didn't do a thing!). Thus, as with the peasants who learned French as they wore pretty clothes, language itself reveals and contributes to political power. Lafont's quite subtle variation of register gives the language context credibility while also creating a stage situation where monolingual francophones can follow the action.

The opposition French–Occitan, humorous in itself, is paralleled by another opposition, much older in the history of the stage: the old versus the young. In the tradition of Roman comedy and of Molière, Lafont paints two young lovers, Pélican and Marianne, held back by old Beneset. Pélican is a peasant leader in the Cascavèus movement. Marianne follows him. Beneset, on the contrary, is a burgher, not wanting to be involved, ridiculous in his mechanical shifting back and forth from French to Occitan, from common sense to idiocy, from greed to civic spirit, yet always steadfast in his cowardice.

Pélican and Marianne as a couple, impeded by paternal opposition, a *senex iratus* if there ever was one, embody the class struggle (masses vs. bourgeoisie) and the structure of a Molière comedy, the vital, natural, good Eros of the young seeking to triumph over the sterile, impotent opposition of the old. Eros enters overtly into *Lei Cascavèus* twice. First of all, Lafont indicates that Père Joseph should be played by a woman. In this way he mocks the decadent Parisian court centred around Richelieu. If Père Joseph appears to be a transvestite, then the audience, while laughing at the situation, will not be oblivious to the message that unnatural Eros – transvestism, homosexuality – is prevalent in the Church and among the masters who speak French. On the other hand, at one of the high points in the rebel story, Pélican blesses the Cascavèus in a bilingual (Latin and Occitan) mock Pater Noster. The subsequent festivity assumes the form of carnival, culminating in Pélican making love to Marianne on Richelieu's back. The carnival stands behind much of the old popular theatre in Oc. Here (as in *La Festa*) Lafont presents carnival of the South as desire triumphant, transgression, and the grotesque – positive elements in the rebellion and in the new culture which offer an aesthetic as well as a political alternative to Richelieu's classicist autocracy:

CHÂTEAUNEUF: Ça n'est pas la Fête-Dieu!
MARIANNE: Es la fèsta d'un brave Bòn Dieu de brave diable de pòble! Es la fèsta Dèu tot l'an! (p. 47)
(It's the Good Lord's festival of a devilishly good people! It's Corpus Christi all year long!)

Pélican's mock prayer and his fornication with Marianne constitute one moment of carnival. There are others. The action is disrupted regularly by a medley of song and dance. These medleys give voice to the popular side of rebellion when Forbin, an intendant, and two presidents are literally kicked out of Aix, or when they call for women's liberation. The medleys are the theatrical objective correlative of the people's carnival and the people's revolt. Thus Lafont justifies, in the text of his play and in his ideological vision, a piece of stagecraft typical of Brecht, of the years 1960–80 in France, and of 'living theatre.' The song-and-dance medleys point to the importance of theatricality vis-à-vis the text; they bring to the drama light, sound, movement, and a sense of the body; and they reinforce the aesthetic of the discontinuous and the fragmentary, which also redefine the nature of history.

In addition, the play begins with a company of actors having lost Marianne – the Republic – in their box of props. After a series of jokes on the government and the provinces, Pélican pops out of the box speaking Occitan. The computer made a mistake! And the actors, who would like to do a comedy in French, are condemned to history and a foreign tongue. Here again Lafont incorporates a typically modernist trope of theatre. In Brechtian fashion he creates *Verfremdung* by showing that these are only actors forced to play a role. From the simulacrum comes distancing and the didactic. Because of it we are made to see that Marianne and the others are indeed allegories not people, and that the allegory has a message and can be aesthetically rewarding.

In the end, Pélican is shot and Marianne stuffed back into the prop box. The characters, re-metamorphosed into actors, as actors observe that none of this ever happened in reality. This history is not studied in the schools. It does not exist. For that matter, Provence is not studied in the schools and does not exist. Yet Coriolis returns. He recounts the subsequent Languedoc uprising and his own death in prison. Then he dreams, and ... we are his dream and we are alive! Pélican and Marianne return to life to dance the Carmagnole. They are Coriolis's dream of liberty. The play ends with the realization of that dream – the Revolution and 'Ça ira!'

Lafont uses the modernist defamiliarization of actors' simulacrum to reflect on the denial of history by institutions in power. They determine what is and is not. Similarly, he employs the modernist theatrical convention – also baroque – of the plot which turns out to be the dream-work of one of the characters, also for his own ends. He forces us to acknowledge a problematic sense of time in history where 1630, 1789, and 1977 converge, where past, present, and future fuse, and our collective memory becomes our individual present and future. For Coriolis, Pélican, Marianne, and Lafont, the Cascavèus of 1630, even if denied and forgotten, did not live in vain. They 'prefigured' 1789, and they prefigure progressive desire in our present. We see that Pélican's girlfriend's being named Marianne is no coincidence. She *is* Marianne the Republic in seed, and it is shown that the actors pulled out the right Marianne after all. Neither she nor anyone else will live a life that truly is meaningful without embodying old, blind Coriolis's dream of liberty, a dream which will never die.

La Croisade is Lafont's last completed full-length play.[51] It also was commissioned by André Neyton for the Centre Dramatique Occitan de Provence, where it had a successful run from October 1983 to April 1984. The plot is, in part, that of a chronicle play, following events in the South of France from 1213 to 1229. It focuses on the central event of history (some would say myth) for Occitan militants: the Albigensian Crusade, which, as Lafont perceives it, brought about the crushing of the Catharist religion and the crushing of the South – of the Occitan nation – by French military power.

The protagonist, in one sense, is Raymond VII, Count of Toulouse, who for a time leads the resistance to French and papal rule yet in the end gives way and does penance for the sins of his lands, being whipped on the steps of Notre Dame in Paris. He and the other notables generally speak French. Occitan is spoken for the most part by two women from the people – old Guilhelma and her daughter-in-law Guilhelmeta – later joined by others. Although the women participate in the action, above all they comment on it like a Greek chorus. Theirs is a chorus of resistance. Again, as in *Lei Cascavèus*, we observe the Brechtian principle of history seen through the eyes of the masses, who have a political consciousness absent in the gentles. Their presence underscores the element of social class. It also helps create a structure of fragmentation and discontinuity which underscores the Brechtian aesthetic and Lafont's own vision of history.

The subplot of the little people enables Lafont to interject moments of humour: when Guilhelma and Guilhelmeta decide to go to Rome or when the Anonymous Monk, author of the *Cançon de la Crosada*, reads in medieval literary Occitan and the women don't understand him. Another moment concerns two people from Marseille who join the 'chorus.' We see them first as modern Marseillais in terms of the modern French cliché: lazy, braggart Provençals; then, as they are transported back in time, they speak the old language – not dead inside them – and recover their primal human dignity. Comedy is appropriate to a Baroque tradition of juxtaposition or mixture of styles, with the comic reserved to low-class people in the subplot vis-à-vis tragic heroism for the nobles in the central plot. Lafont insists on the positive role of comedy – as in the *Cascavèus* burlesque – as social protest, in making an aesthetic statement à la Hugo that the sublime contains in it also the grotesque, and because the comedy works on stage and appeals to the public.

Guilhelma and Guilhelmeta are women. Lafont makes a feminist statement and also adheres to a tradition in the literature of protest, which goes back at least to Zola's *Germinal* (and includes Drezen's *Itron Varia Garmez*), whereby women suffer the most in times of socio-economic anarchy, and whereby it is the women, when they enter the fray, who bring off the finest victories. Here Guilhelma and Guilhelmeta embody the women inside Toulouse who, historically, manned the catapult which killed the French leader Simon de Montfort. Among the gentles also, a woman takes pride of place, Esclarmonde, sister to Count Raymond-Roger de Foix; Esclarmonde is a Catharist militant who defends her faith with the purity, idealism, and self-sacrifice that very few of the male figures bring to their concerns.

The question of religion is central to a play entitled *La Croisade* and to historical events by which a crusade brought the entire Languedoc region under Parisian and Vatican hegemony. Opposed to Esclarmonde, in her idealism, stands the French crusader Simon de Montfort, motivated by sectarian extremism and simple greed. The Occitans imagine these invaders as wolves and take as their battle cry 'Al lop!' (Get the wolf!). When the women catapulters slay Simon, they take a wolf skin, toss it on the ground, pierce it with a spike, and then raise it to God in front of his church. In the end, however, Count Raymond, who wishes to bury his father in consecrated ground and is unnerved by his own excommunication, is whipped before Notre Dame, the church militant and triumphant.

Because of religion, the political situation in *La Croisade* is more complex than that in *Lei Cascavèus,* and Lafont treats it in a more complex, subtle, and problematic manner. On the one hand, the Church plays a negative role in this drama of exploitation and subjugation. The *imago* of the crusade is the Holy Cross: its chief intervention in *La Croisade* occurs when Raymond VII and the women argue over a broom taken as the cross, which is the right side and which is the left. Crude but effective sarcasm! Yet the Church and individual churchmen manifest greater Christian charity than Simon de Montfort the layman does. Thus the Church will not grant all power to Simon and urges him to compassion; the pope leaves the land of Toulouse in Simon's hands yet also releases Count Raymond.

The feudal aristocracy also appears in a complex, problematic light. Raymond-Roger of Foix, who compares his secularly radiant sun and spring to Esclarmonde's harsh Catharist winter, goes to Rome. The Cathars are horrified. Raymond-Roger does this as a sort of compromise, yielding to the Church for the sake of his land and secular pleasures, yet in the process he also protects his sister on the pretext of feudal obligation. Now Folquet, bishop of Toulouse, is outraged. On the French side, the rough feudal lord Alain de Roucy counsels prudence to Simon de Montfort and to a bishop, who prefer a fight to the death. Finally, as we saw, Count Raymond VII himself reaches genuine tragic heights. He tried so hard, he really was brave, yet undermined by his own excommunication, having no love for Cathars and wanting to be a good Catholic, as one after another city abandons him; finally, in anguish, he gives up for the sake of his people. After a conversation in Oc with Guilhelma, he decides he can help the masses only by seeming to betray them:

RAYMOND VII: Moi, je ne suis que malheureux. Avez-vous jamais pensé à la vraie solitude du maître de la terre [...]? Avez-vous pensé au sacrifice du seigneur [...]?
L'ANONYME: Qu'allez-vous faire, Raymond, qui ne sera plus réparable?
RAYMOND VII: Vous quitter. Les quitter. Imaginez que ça soit pour les sauver! (p. 78)

Finally, we must not forget the Anonymous Monk, who also comes from the Church and problematizes it still further. Here Lafont dramatizes the genuinely historical if unknown author of a genuine Occitan *chanson de geste, La Cançon de la Crosada,* an engaged history of the time which, more than any other text, buttresses the claim to an Occitan national consciousness in the thirteenth century. The Anoním appears and reads from his book, in the Medieval Occitan or in a modern French translation. He, as much as the women, in a register different from theirs, speaks as a Greek chorus to comment on the events. War is horrid! He cries. How can Christ do this? After Count Raymond seeks his help, the Anoním leaves his monastery to become a fighter – as a fighter, he offers Raymond his book. At the end, when the Count is whipped, the Anoním reads from his book, and his voice drowns out the blows and the chants.

As in Brecht, speech distinct from the plot is directed at the audience. Art intervenes in history to explain. The Anoním's monologues, which create distancing and have a didactic purpose, also serve as action and contribute to it. As in *La Loba*, Lafont raises the issue of the writer as consciousness and as a social force. Here the Monk (or ex-Monk) is engaged in the struggle of the century. As, perhaps, Peire Vidal does with love, he the historian ultimately creates history. With goodwill and the assistance of Robert Lafont, his voice will drown out the lies of the history books. The losers will be heard, and their memory will live on.

POSTMODERN

BREIZH

In France a transformation in aesthetics and in literary production occurred in the late 1960s and the 1970s. The new aesthetic and political consciousness is closely associated with and to some extent derived from the student rebellion of 1968. In Brittany, more so perhaps than in Paris or the South, 1968 heralded an evolution in intellectual circles and also in the popular consciousness – a move in the direction of political militancy, to be found on the Left and acted on in the name of the young. The new, politicized, populist, and youth-oriented current can be designated as the minority culture contribution to postmodernism.

After 1964, and especially after 1968, the Emsav, for the first time in its history, chose to align itself on the Left and to work with French left-wing parties. For the first time, as a movement, it proclaimed that Brittany is a victim of colonialism within France, and it proposed, as relief from the colonialism, socialism as well as national autonomy. The *emsaverien*, especially the young, were moved to action by specific incidents – peasant protests, including the 1972 'guerre du lait,' strikes at Les Forges d'Hennebont and Le Joint Français, and the blowing up of the television antenna at Roc Trédudon (1974) – and by issues of exploitation and national liberation elsewhere: war in Ulster and, above all, in Algeria. In 1964 eleven students founded Unvaniezh Demokratel Breizh (Union Démocratique Bretonne). Their journal was and is *Le Peuple breton*. And the extremist group, Le Front de Libération de la Bretagne, committed acts of violence from 1966 to 1969 and from 1971 on through much of the decade.

Political consciousness was, as always in Brittany, associated with cultural renewal. Since the end of the war the survivors of the Emsav had placed the renewal of folklore, taken in the broadest sense of the term, as their first priority, in part because overt separatist agitation would have been crushed by the state. People in general, and the young in particular, became involved in music – especially the *bagadoù*, marching formations of pipers playing the newly imported Scottish bagpipe (*biniou bras*) – in *gouren* (traditional Breton wrestling), summer festivals, and traditional religious gatherings. In 1955 Loeiz Ropars reintroduced the tradition of *festoù-noz* or evening festivals of song, dance, and satire, concretized in the *Kan ha diskan* (song and refrain). For well over a decade these events were both successful (with the urban and rural masses) and resolutely contestatory on the Left. A popular theatre thrived corresponding to Ariane Mnouchkine's Théâtre du Soleil in Paris. The most interesting and durable troop is Goulc'han Kervella's Strollad ar Vro Bagan (The Company of the Pagan Country), founded in 1974, professionalized in 1978, and running strong today. Whatever the value of Kervella's and the others' plays as literature – as with le Théâtre du Soleil and comparable groups in Occitania, their thrust lies in the direction of spectacle and the didactic rather than the purely literary – Ar Vro Bagan proved and proves the existence of a viable, living Breton public for performances in Breton.

The public was significantly greater for musical performance – in the cadre of the *fest-noz* or in concert, with texts in Breton, in French, or in both. The explosion of Breton music in general, and of the song in particular, marks perhaps the cultural high point of the 1960s and 1970s. Glenmor, Stivell, Servat, and the Tri Yann attained the highest national acclaim and an international audience as well, making their contribution to the revival of Celtic music. It is not just that these composers and performers set to music texts by Yann-Ber Piriou, Youenn Gwernig, and Paol Keineg and thus brought the Sixties Poets into the spotlight. They made their own poems, and Gwernig composed the music for some of his verses. Poets and musicians shared 'la colère bretonne' and gave it expression, together, in symbiosis. In addition, for those ten years (1968–78), any number of amateurs committed to the cause wrote and composed. To understand the Breton revival and the Sixties Poets, Piriou's anthology *Défense de cracher par terre et de parler breton: Poèmes de combat* of 1971 is absolutely essential, and scarcely less so is Durand's anthology *Breizh hiziv* [Brittany Today]: *Anthologie de la chanson en Bretagne* of 1976.[1]

The aesthetic and the texture of the Sixties Poets is comparable to those of literary production throughout Europe and the Americas in that age of protest. The texts come from or are directed to the rebellious and the young. The doctrines are a fusion of Marxism, support for the Third World, and national liberation at home. The stance is one of compassion for the exploited and fierce, visceral hatred of the exploiters. The form is rhetorical, hortatory to the highest degree, relatively simplistic in register, comparable to slogans or tracts, and declamatory in that these texts were often meant to be read, chanted, sung, or shrieked before a crowd of believers. The aesthetic is directed partially against the culture of modernism – considered elitist and excessively recondite. However, this negative modernism was associated with Paris and the French – Mallarmé, Valéry, Char, and Bonnefoy, for example, instead of with Hemon, Abeozen, and Glanndour. On the contrary, poems by Hemon and Glanndour are included in the Piriou anthology. Furthermore, because of the strong oral roots of Breton culture and specifically the oral tradition of satire, and because national liberation has always been a theme of the writers of Emsav, the Sixties Poets were perceived not as cutting their roots but, rather, as a natural and integral current in Breton literature – this perhaps in contrast both to Scotland and Occitania. Finally, even when young poets cut their roots, it means simply that they plant and graft in other fields. Gwernig, Keineg, and Piriou chose their cultural tradition, one, after all, as valid as another – embodied in the oral folklore, Whitman, Rimbaud, Mayakovsky, the Surrealists, and the American Beats, especially Kerouac.

'La colère bretonne' is directed against capitalism and against France. It is stated explicitly that the French are the equivalent of a colonialist foreign power which has colonized Brittany, investing capital, exploiting its resources and people, and removing its produce and profits. The Breton masses are portrayed as the victims of colonialism, weak, oppressed, and subjected to poverty. As a result, the people have, for generations now, been forced off the soil; they have been compelled to emigrate to Paris or elsewhere, exiled from their own country and reduced to manual labour and prostitution. They themselves have been reified, and so has the land, now a patchwork of abandoned farms, its life drained and its beauty tarnished. According to this thematic, in place of the uprooted natives come the colonizers – hated tourists, of course, with their real estate developments and summer houses – but also other manifestations of exploitation such as refineries, nuclear power plants, and military bases. Most serious of all, from the perspective of the Emsav, is the ultimate form of alienation, the deprivation of Breton identity and the suppression and extinction of the Breton language.

In response to this situation the Sixties Poets mock traditional stereotypes, the clichés that Bretons are so very Christian, resigned, self-sacrificing, alcoholic, tubercular, and stupid. They evoke the heroes of past struggles such as Nominoe (ninth century), Charles of Montfort (fourteenth century), and the Bonnets Rouges (seventeenth century). They identify with people from the Third World – Arabs, Blacks, Vietnamese – and from the Celtic world. As with earlier generations of the Emsav, the Irish are taken as a model, along with the Easter Uprising of 1916. The identification with movements of national liberation elsewhere is thus not grounded in nostalgia or pathos. Rather, it is a call to arms and a declaration of war on France and, in passing, on the Great Beast – the United States.

Among the more extreme and more successful examples of this poetry of anger, we can cite in the Piriou anthology An Touseg (Piriou himself) writing 'Itron Varia an Napalm' (Our Lady of Napalm), a text of magnificent sarcasm treating the Los Angeles riots and the American Nazi Lincoln Rockwell, and dedicated to Cardinal Spellman. Per Denez composes a 'Negro Song' for Langston Hughes proclaiming that the Speaker is Breton, a slave, a mercenary, a valet, and a martyr. The Speaker of Erwan Evenou's 'Plouk' (Hick/Rube) proclaims, I am like you, my brother Arab, I am not French. Glanndour's 'Lun Fask' (Easter Monday), alluding to the Dublin uprising, warns us that rabid dogs will bite men and house pets. In the Durand anthology Lama Meur tells his auditor, Don't be an objector, learn to shoot, and aim at the bourgeois. Youenn Gwernig urges the French to send their CRS (the security police) to Algeria; we don't want to have to toss them into the river here and thus poison all the nice fish. P.-M. Mével has his pig squeak that he is dishonoured to be sold for so low a price. Let's all piss together, urges the Speaker, and we'll drown Giscard d'Estaing in his palace!

This poetry of anger displays an engaging passion and wit, and more than a little invention in terms of style and imagery. Yet, inevitably, it has its limits, as did the denunciatory triolets of the Fronde or Voltaire's epigrams. The Piriou anthology also contains verse of a more traditional bent, some of which attains a very high level in terms of the modernist aesthetic itself. The abstruse, Trakl-inspired Abanna/Guy Etienne offers a prayer for Christmas. In Brittany, he writes, we have all that the infant Jesus requires, including wood for the cross and crows to pluck out his eyes. Per Diolier, in 'Ar re drec'het' (The Defeated), evokes the losers, so weak and so afraid to die yet who are already dead. Ronan Huon, the founding editor of *Al Liamm* and a highly successful writer of fiction, has the Speaker describe himself as an old man with grey hair flopping over his ears; such is the result of the struggle and the dream. Is the dam broken and the flood rising? asks the Speaker. No, it is only a dream, and all is calm. Finally, Youenn Gwernig's 'An diri dir' (Steel Stairways) – the book-length version was published in 1976 and his complete opus in 1997 – creates an imaginative world of little people, the poor and the wretched in New York. In verse which recalls both Eliot and Mayakovsky, he writes of the subway station and its trains, crowds on the street, newspaper crime, stories from back home, Tiresias, the cosmic dance, the death of a vagrant bag lady, and the life of a young Puerto Rican beggar, all through the vision of the morally involved and tortured Speaker.[2]

Recognizably the two finest poets of the Sixties group, who rise above the sometimes simplistic rhetoric of protest, are Youenn Gwernig and Paol Keineg. They were both hailed at the time as the new bards of Brittany, embodying a new voice come from the protest movements. Keineg, who has taught French for a number of years in the United States, is best known for his poetry in French.[3] A series of collections from 1969 to the present testify to his presence – a major presence – in contemporary French verse. From an early declamatory style of transgression on politics and love he evolved into a poet of the earth, evoking village and farm life with concrete, everyday imagery, and more recently he has published verse, sometimes powerfully direct and sometimes intertextually complex and arcane, on Celtic cultural figures such as Dahut, Boudica, Taliesen, and the early Welsh poem *Gododdin*. Keineg's oeuvre, still in process, testifies to his command of a number of registers, a multiplicity of voice and stance, and a passionate commitment to the craft of poetry. My own preference goes to the *Dinglichkeit* of *Lieux communs* and the noble idealism in *Dahut*, both of which date from 1974.[4]

Keineg's four collections in Breton extend from 1971 to 1981. In my opinion, the texts in Breton are as good as the ones in French. In the Celtic language Keineg cultivates a register more concentrated than in the French, a plain style which eschews the rhetoric of the early French verse and the intertextual allusiveness of the later.

The 1971 *Barzhonegoù-trakt* (Tract Poems) exemplify the *Défense de cracher par terre* register of protest.[5] Keineg speaks of the workers on a Citroën assembly line herded into little cubes like garbage; the French bosses deprive these people of their rocks, fields, and the birds. You no longer have faces, lips, or mouths, he says. In 'Transocéan, Brest' he contrasts wretched working women in the shipbuilding firm to Mme Couff, wife of the CEO, who is so happy to live in Brittany in the lap of luxury and observe the quaint local mores. In the title poem of the Pi-

riou anthology, in a sequence of surrealist images the Speaker evokes
the Breton pain. Broken bones, sliced fingers, blood cold as a vein of
metal, a child raising his arm to ward off scissors and knives, the sacrifice of children, brains filed down, torture by the screw and by quarter-
ing – all speak to the fact that 'they' forbid both dream and reality and
impose the void on the people of Breizh.

This voice rises to a greater intensity and a more original stance in
Iwerzhon ar C'hreisteiz, Iwerzhon an Hanternoz (Southern Ireland, Northern Ireland), which dates from 1974.[6] It is clear that Keineg takes sides
in the Ulster civil war with the same passion, commitment, and total
gift of self he brought to the Breton protests against France. For him,
the IRA stands for Ireland, the Celtic people, the poor, and the young;
they are rebels seeking to create a just, free, socialist society. From his
perspective, the Ulster authorities and the British army who defend
them are to be identified with England, America, the hated Anglo-Sax-
ons, the rich, and the old; they are oppressors supporting capitalism,
injustice, and scorn for the masses. It is not important whether or not
we agree with Keineg's politics, any more than whether or not we
agree with Hemon's. It is important to recognize that the poet's commitment and rage inspire him to create verse of unusual power on a
little-exploited theme – physical and psychological torture. *Iwerzhon*
describes, portrays, and recounts the reality of torture from the perspective of the tortured, the Irish victims of the occupation army. We
read of kicking and beating by men in boots, of hair and fingernails
yanked out, and of a hand crushed like a cigarette butt. The Speaker
tells us of people pressed into the walls, from which bodily fluids
(urine, tears, sweat, and blood) ooze. Bodies then return from the
walls containing pieces of cement wedged into them, piercing them.
For the tortured, in their delirium, tables, windows, and the ever-
present walls are alive and move, while they themselves, invisibly, also
move in air and water:

> Fiñval a ra an daol
> diskrognal a ra ar prenestr
> traoù gludek a ruilh diouzh ar mogerioù.
>
> Ar boud a zilez an hirgarrezenn
> hag a sav e furmioù all.
>
> [...] an den boureviet a zeu da vezañ treuzwelus

an den boureviet a red en avel hag en dour. (p. 89)

(The table budges the window bares its teeth the walls sweat viscous matter.
Existence forsakes the rectangle and assumes other forms. The tortured
becomes transparent the tortured flows in air and water.)

In the same volume as *Iwerzhon*, Keineg published a second collection
of verse entitled, ironically, *Mojennoù gwir* (True Tales).[7] The irony lies
in the fact that, although these splendid brief little sketches or scenes
may be psychologically true, they cannot have occurred in quotidian
reality; they are products of a demonic dream world, they evoke the terror of the night. Although Galand is surely right to relate these vignettes
to the Breton person suffering at the hands of the French, who have
denied his cultural identity and his language,[8] I believe that *Mojennoù
gwir* also gives voice to a more universal, very twentieth-century sense of
fragmentation and dismemberment, the loss of subjectivity enshrined in
the literature of expressionism and surrealism. The following eight
vignettes are representative of Keineg's intense, understated, and
unique vision. (1) At age five, people carved open the Speaker's head
and implanted a brass hinge. Then, and still today, from time to time
they open him up and massage his brains. (2) Alone in a cell he screams
from electroshock and deprivation of insulin. (3) The Speaker has a
birthmark with a will of its own. It moves and grows. When he sleeps, it
wakes up. Obsessed by the birthmark, the Speaker touches it, reverting
to it again and again, and he will not disrobe in front of people:

Diouzh an noz war va gwele
E goulou al lamp
E sellan outi hag e flouran he ruzder
Ha teuziñ a ran anezhi dindan va allazig
Pa oan bihan ne santen ket anezhi
Met deut war an oad 'deus he kresket
N'en em ziwiskan ket ken dirak an holl (p. 23)

(In the evening in bed in the light of the lamp I look at it and I fondle its
red blotch and I make it melt under my caress. When I was little I didn't
feel it but as I get older it has grown. I never get undressed in front of others anymore.)

(4) As he is taking a stroll, one of the Speaker's limbs falls off. Terrified,

he grasps it. Then, while he is sitting on a park bench, order is restored. (5) The Speaker witnesses a house burning down. A dog howls within, a victim of the flames. People look on, coldly, in indifference. (6) The Speaker is himself the object of others' gaze, a public spectacle so to speak. He recognizes himself to be a mime or the mannequin in a store window. (7) The Speaker has lost his lower jaw, and he can't find it. He is desperate, for without the jaw he is liable to catch germs. (8) Finally, at the home of a young woman he opens the refrigerator door, upon which body parts fall out. Quickly, he closes the door and says nothing.

This verse is derived in part from the postcolonial (or, from Keineg's perspective, the still colonial) situation, that of a Breton or Irishman living under French or English domination. Because of the domination and because of the larger sense of twentieth-century loss of past freedom and certainty including the very language he speaks, Keineg writes poetry of alienation. In his vision of things, the Speaker's loss of subjectivity is expressed in terms of nightmare or insanity. The Speaker loses control of all aspects of his being, including reliance on the physical laws of nature and his own rational thought. He is tortured, dismembered, and violated. He becomes a thing of ooze, rot, and viscous corruption, rendered what he is by the external (other people's) knives, saws, boots, fists, and pieces of cement. In Bachelardian terms, he is soft earth beaten and pummelled by the others' hard earth. In psychoanalytic terms, he himself takes on the sensation of rape and impotence, his self transformed into the passive, masochistic object of others' phallic violence. In every sense he is the victim and they are the torturers, he is the slave and they are the masters. The ultimate loss of self is apparent not only in the dismemberment and the violation of the body but also in the dismemberment and violation of the spirit. The Speaker, no longer a subject even to himself, becomes the object of the gaze of others. Mentally as well as physically, he is reduced to ooze or a concrete wall or a store mannequin. He fails to manifest emotion or compassion in the face of others' suffering, just as the masters fail to react to him. Indeed – in the extreme form of the colonial or the concentration camp situation – he accepts the masters' values and becomes like them. The redeeming feature of the Speaker's situation is that, unlike the Masters, unlike the indifferent others, he is aware of what is happening to him and to them. Whatever else he loses, consciousness remains. And it is this consciousness which allows the Speaker implicitly – and, behind him, the author Paol Keineg explicitly and deliberately – to lay bare this aspect of the human condition, both Breton and universal, in all its tragic horror.

Paol Keineg's Breton poems, in general, manifest greater concentration, intensity, and simplicity than the poetry in French. It is appropriate, then, that in the course of his Breton writings he should strive for still greater condensation and brevity. Keineg's most recent and perhaps his last collection in Breton is *35 haiku*.[9] These texts adhere to the mode of Japanese tanka and haiku in modern European literatures. Composed in brief three-line statements, they reproduce the brevity, simplicity, and allusiveness of the Classical Japanese source-genre. Each poem places a moment in time and a single picture in space. The subject-matter is rural Brittany, the celebration of concrete, physical, daily life. An aura of *Dinglichkeit* emerges with the rendering of a tree, little flowers, lichen, stones, and puddles of water. The verse corresponds to Duval's *Kan an douar* and to Keineg's own *Lieux communs*, except that it has been stripped of all rhetoric, including Duval's personifications, and the author's own residual personal and emotional underscoring. Here, for the first and perhaps only time, Keineg becomes a genuinely impersonal poet, having deleted from his verse the subjectivity of the implied author. We are thus enabled to perceive with the least residual focalization the Speaker's perceptions or, given that these texts were written in America, his memories – a boat, on its side, abandoned on the deserted beach; a fragment of bread lying next to a pair of clogs; a broken plate on the grass; an earthworm severed in half; the cherry trees in spring; the chestnut with its autumn leaves in the field. Or, in classical Japanese style:

Teuziñ a ra ar valafenn
war an dour lano
evel ur bluenn erc'h. (No. 18)

(On tidewater the butterfly melts like a snowflake.)

For this seemingly most rhetorical of poets, one culmination – the culmination of his voice in Breton – is the attaining of absolute simplicity and unadornment, a verse naked and direct, the ultimate in creativity in the plain style and the ultimate in one form of pure poetry.

OCCITANIA

As in Brittany a new force breaks into Occitan culture in the late 1960s and 1970s, which corresponds to and takes its impetus in part from the events of May 1968. Earlier the Decazeville strike of 1961–2 contributed to the politicization (or repoliticization) of the Occitanist movement. Lafont led the fight for a political analysis of 'internal colonialism' and for political action in response to it. With a split in the Institut d'Estudis Occitans in 1964, a number of the older 'culturalists,' including Manciet, left the movement, taking *Oc* with them. Those who remained were committed to a degree of activism and militancy. A number of reviews, including *Viure* (1965), and several study and action groups were founded. With 1968 we observe a bursting forth of new poets and some older poets, gathered around the series '4 vertats' (Four Truths) launched by Jean Larzac. These were present or former students speaking to a new young public of students, with student rebellion and the ideal of revolution central to their consciousness. They and their poems breathe a sense of urgency, of the necessity for action and action now. The dominant figures in the movement were two committed poets and prose writers: Yves Rouquette, the then most recent editor-in-chief of *Oc* and director of the new song and record series 'Ventadorn' (1969), and his brother, the Jean Larzac of '4 vertats.' In 1971, the same year as *Défense de cracher par terre et de parler breton*, P.J. Oswald published *Occitanie 1970: Les poètes de la décolonisation*, an anthology edited by Marie Rouanet, Yves Rouquette's wife. This current remained in the ascendancy well into the 1970s, beginning to taper off only after 1975.[10]

The young poets of decolonization saw themselves as forcing a break with the past. Rouanet, while praising the masters of modernism, also faults them for solitary, individual-only aestheticism and for composing a style of verse which leads to an impasse. She insists that they are simply writing high modernist contemporary French poems in Occitan. There is nothing uniquely Occitan in them, and they have nothing to say to the people. In contrast to their age and to their self-willed ivory tower, we are offered a new group of poets: belonging to a younger generation and committed to political action and to the people. It is true that the poets of decolonization were inspired not by masterpieces from the Occitan past but from contemporary struggles in the world, mass struggles not limited to Toulouse and Marseille. Their poetry was conceived as a political act in the same sense as a tract ('poésie-tract'), meant to be read or sung aloud at gatherings and to be immediately accessible to the masses. Therefore, instead of aesthetic purity and rigour, they sought to break the rules. Poetry would be the shout, the scream, a mural slogan or graffito. It would shock you and itself *be* revolutionary, in form and content. Accordingly, they could identify with a movement of worldwide proportions, joining in a common struggle with the Third World and minorities everywhere, and thus make their minority language speak for all people as a living contemporary medium, both natural and totally up to date.

The themes of the '4 vertats' group and of the Rouanet anthology correspond to the themes of the Sixties Poets in Brittany. This is the case because the writers in both camps knew of each others' existence and were in contact; because they underwent the same 1968 experience; and because, for centuries, they shared the same history in a France, kingdom or republic, governed from Paris.[11] Thus the Occitans, like the Bretons, cultivate the thematics of abandoned villages and young peasants and workers forced into exile to make a living; poverty, unemployment, and the decline of the land; exploitation by capitalist developers come from the North and bringing with them the plague of exploiting and condescending tourists; and, first and always, the decline of the language, treated like a despicable patois, a sign of inferiority and humiliation. Of course, the Poets of Decolonization refuse to accept their fate; they speak out, calling for resistance. The first section of the anthology is given a title from one of Larzac's collections: 'Refús d'entarrar' (Burial Prohibited). Like the Bretons, the Occitans evoke events from the past, earlier persecutions and rebellions in the history of the South: the Albigensian Crusade, the Huguenot Camisard resistance to Louis XIV, the 1907 mutiny, the Decazeville strike, and, of course, 1968. And, like the Bretons, they exalt popular struggles everywhere, identifying with Basques, Greeks, Palestinians, Kurds, Cuba, and Vietnam.

Last but not least, the fourth section of the anthology is devoted to 'Cançons per lo pòple' (Songs for the People). In 1965 Lafont encouraged Guy Broglia to record his musical rendering of the master's poems. Lafont also assured financially the first recordings of Martí and Delbeau (1969). Thus was born the *novèla cançon* (new song). Although Occitan singers never achieved quite the national vogue of Stivell and Glenmor, Martí, Patric, Mans de Breish, Delbeau, and Broglia assumed the same role of encouraging, indeed igniting, a new, populist youth culture and a pride in Oc and Occitania. They composed their own words and also set to music texts by Lafont, Manciet, Boudou, Yves Rouquette, Jean Larzac, and the medieval troubadours.[12]

Some texts by the Poets of Decolonization are only slogans, shouts, screams, and tracts. In this category we can place, for example, Yves Rouquette's obscene and blasphemous 'Messa sens ren pels porcs a vendre' (Mass for the Pigs at Market) or his 'Florida,' which evokes the commercial exploitation of Southern beaches. So too for Jean-Baptiste

Séguy's 'Sirventes' and Bernard Lesfargues's 'Francophonie,' which mocks official Parisian concern for the decline of French in various parts of the world and the infiltration of Franglais at home. Lesfargues cries, 'Mèrda' (Shit), and he laughs.

As with the Bretons, such extremes of slogan and scream have poetic as well as ideological impact and have behind them a tradition in twentieth-century verse: Marinetti, Mayakovsky, and the schools of futurism, not to speak of Kerouac and the American Beats. However, in the Rouanet anthology we also find examples of a more conventionally aesthetic verse which loses none of its power to move. Examples would be Henri Espieux's identification with the sterile, arid land and his desperate, failing attempts to provide (verbal) seed; Serge Bec's passionately lyrical evocation of happiness struggling with the reality of contemporary horror, happiness grounded in flowers and love; Lesfargues, who urges the Rhône river to tell people of the Occitan land or who expresses hatred for cities and a totemic, animist love of animals; and Séguy, who writes movingly of Paris, the poor wretches who dwell there, and the prostitutes, evoked with the ironic counterpoetry of metro stations and allusions to the sacred.

The Christian imagery that radiates from texts by Lesfargues, Séguy, and Yves Rouquette should warn the reader against assuming that the Poets of Decolonization were necessarily dialectical materialists. On the contrary, there is more genuinely Christian thematics at this time than in the generation(s) of modernism. Furthermore, it is my conviction that one poet stands out from the rest who is a major figure and comparable in stature to the giants of modernism. He is Jean Larzac, a militant of the 1960s and of the 1990s, a consciously, overtly Christian poet, and an ordained priest.[13]

Larzac's first collection, *Sola Deitas* (Godhead Only), dating from 1962, shows the poet in his quintessential self.[14] These are meditations on the Stations of the Cross; Larzac's verse, which is powerfully modern and contemporary, in a word ferocious, also partakes of and is grounded in a current of the sacred, of Christian tradition going back to the Middle Ages.

One of Larzac's themes is the suffering of Mary. He evokes the twelve stars which shone at the Annunciation. Yet the twelve blows of love that pierced her breast in ecstasy, and the twelve peals of the bell, are not only her joys but also her sorrows. For each Joy of Our Lady there is a Sorrow. Each joy *is* sorrow. Being loved by God, being the Mother of God, is torture in joy, yes, yet torture. And now she suffers torture in the flesh, 'Mamà paura mamà' (Mother, poor little mother). She can only offer to the Son her arms, like the cross itself. She is Dolores, the Mother of Sorrows ('Maire de las Dolors'). And her cry is the weeping of the vine for the cut grape. Larzac illustrates the suffering of the Mother of God in terms of nature imagery: flowers, plants, and organic growth. Mary is as good and innocent as the green world before the Fall. The Speaker then chooses an image from the green world that relates directly to the symbolism of the mass: the grapes severed from the vine which will be transformed into red wine. The wine is offered in the ritual of the mass, where it becomes Christ's blood, shed on the cross, in order to free mankind from sin and death.

The cross is the dominant image in a sequence devoted to the Stations of the Cross. Larzac insists upon the fusion of Christ and the Holy Rood. Christ is the cross, and the cross is Christ. The Speaker wishes to help Christ bear the cross, to support it in turn, and therefore, in turn, to become the cross. The cross is the Speaker's goal. No longer a tree yet still a tree, it is planted in earth, in heaven, and in the Speaker's heart. Christ and the Speaker endure its pain: pain from the tree, the lance, and the crown of thorns. The Speaker reminds us, implicitly, that the Holy Rood is descended from, and is the typological fulfilment of, the Tree of Life and the Tree of the Knowledge of Good and Evil in the Garden of Eden. A tree had been chosen to seduce Adam and Eve, it had contributed to the Fall. Now the tree of the New Covenant will redeem the old tree. Christ bears on his body the cross that symbolizes our life of sin and our fallen state. By taking it, he takes us in our condition of original sin. He is man and God. He takes unto himself all the pain and the torture of sin – the thorns, lance, nails, and weight of the cross which is the weight of his own flesh – pain and torture which Satan gave to humans disguised by the taste of the fruit. Christ does this as an act of love through death. He loves us by dying for us, and his *Liebestod* is ours. The pain he suffers is fused with the ecstasy of love; it is ecstasy in love and torture, therefore, that the Speaker wants to endure for him. Sacred charity shares so much with the secular love it overcomes and redeems.

The Speaker meditates in church. Typologically, the Church is Christ's body, his human substance; it is also the bodies and souls of all Christians for whom he became incarnate and died. The Speaker alludes to Christ being buried in the cold stone of churches. He laments how cold they are, how empty. This is an allusion to the Holy Sepulchre, where Christ was buried, and to the metaphor of Peter's church, the rock (*petra*) on which it will be built. Yet the Speaker also calls attention to our present, today's church and today's Christians, lacking faith, hope, and love, lacking blood and fire, and to the Speaker's own death, the aridity in his soul. Here and elsewhere the Speaker evokes Christ's gift of self, his personal and divine sacrifice to save us, and, in contrast, our heedless, forgetful, mocking, mediocre routine, our turning away from him then, at Golgotha, and our turning away from him ever since then.

In narratological terms, the function of the Speaker proves to be crucial. This is lyric poetry in the first person, genuinely homodiegetic. As in the sacred verse of the Baroque and as in the verse of Maodez Glanndour, Jean Larzac as implied author assumes an active, obtrusive role, speaking in an active, obtrusive voice. As in the Baroque and in Glanndour, he adopts the stance of the preacher: he urges the implied reader to seek the good and avoid evil, he beseeches the reader to follow Christ. Again exploiting the typological-allegorical tradition, he does so by placing himself in two spatio-temporal frames. On the one hand, he is the twentieth-century witness (and priest), a man who has the right to speak to others of their eternal yet also immediately present concerns. His very humanity permits him to serve as a bridge or conduit from the ancient sacred to the modern secular, from the Unique Godhead of Christ to our human, sin-ridden materiality. On the other hand, he can do this because, prefiguring himself in his sin as implied author and witness and as implied author and prophet, he also exists back then, in Jerusalem, as a spectator of the Stages of the Cross as Christ underwent them. The Speaker is present at the Passion, he personally beholds Mary's suffering, he personally feels the weight of the cross. This is possible because, according to the four levels of allegory with regard to Scripture, the third level – the moral or tropological – is the one by which all Christians, in their daily lives, re-enact the life of Christ and either seek or flee him, either help him bear his cross or hurt him with the lance and the sponge of vinegar. Larzac, so concerned with the misery of the poor and the wretched, makes his own the topos (in Bloy, Bernanos, and others) that each time you help your fellow human being you embrace the Lord, and every time you spurn another, you spit in Christ's face. The Speaker's passion is especially effective given his refusal to assume a stance of superiority or condescension. In partial contrast to the Baroque, he underscores, screaming in agony, his own inadequacy. He screams that he is one of those who killed Christ. He loves and yearns for him yet he also turned away, was absent, or was one of the torturers:

E quand me cercas m'enanavi [...]

Ont èri quand as reviscolat?
Dormissiái sul mont dels Olius
Eri al bordèl èri en viatge (pp. 47, 69, 71)

(And when you came for me I fled. Where was I when you rose from the
dead? I was asleep on the Mount of Olives I was at the whorehouse I was
away travelling.)

For all that, he dares to pray, not because of any merit in himself but
only in the hope of pity, that Christ grant him his face and hand and
voice.

In a number of later collections the Christian thematic is restated. 'La
Boca a la Paraula' (The Mouth That Speaks) (1971) contains speech
directed to God.[15] In vigorous, passionate long lines, the Speaker proclaims his love for Christ. This is sacred erotic poetry à la Teresa of Avila
and Juan de la Cruz. Torn by anguish, he desperately seeks the right
words, desiring Christ's eyes, evoking light and darkness, and the love
which needs not mortal vision. Failing again and again, ever unworthy,
the Speaker desires and will never cease desiring God, for God, who
stands alone, is all.

Inevitably, given his generation, family, and personal temperament,
Jean Larzac also wrote political verse in defence of Occitania and in harmony with 1968 and the poetry of decolonization. After all, it was he
who launched the collection '4 vertats,' and he who published a number of polemical works in prose, the most notable being the two-volume
Descolonisar l'istòria occitana (Decolonizing Occitan History), in which,
like the Breton opponents of Helias, he denounces Lafont and others
for not going far enough in *their* denunciation of France and for not
proclaiming openly the existence of an Occitan nation.[16] Still, Larzac's
most successful committed verse is allied with the sacred and benefits
from the incorporation of sacred imagery and Christian intertextuality.
An example is the 1968 'L'Estrangièr del Dedins' (The Foreigner
Within), a long prose-poem commentary on Psalm 137, 'By the rivers of
Babylon.'[17] Larzac draws all possible similitudes, including the typological, between the situation of the Children of Israel enduring slavery
under Babylonian overlords back then, and the Occitan people enduring allegedly comparable slavery under Parisian French overlords today.
The chief difference between the two events is underscored in the title.

Whereas the Hebrews were forced into exile and led off into Babylonian captivity, because of modern technology and capital the French have no need to be so blatant. They can exert power over the natives, exploiting them in their habitat, transforming them into strangers in their own land. Larzac amplifies water imagery: the weeping of the Daughters of Jerusalem and the suffering of the great rivers of the South – the Rhône and the Garonne – witnesses to and themselves sullied by French developers. As did the Children of Israel, Larzac's Occitans bewail their losses throughout history, and the fact that their artists all left the land. He develops a pattern of prison imagery, the Occitans taken captive in their homes, lied to in school, and victimized by foreign jailors, with the result that their only capital is Babylon (Paris) and they are taught to sing a blasphemous hymn to false gods (the *Marseillaise*). He intersperses satire on folklore and the Felibrige movement, as evidence of cultural slavery and impotence. Yet there is hope. Again following the prophets of Israel, the Speaker denounces the Daughter of Babylon, a harlot on the roads, who will perish, rotting from inside. At the end, lacking Christian charity but revelling in the fanaticism of the Old Testament, the Speaker beholds in a vision Paris burning and, echoing the psalm, approves of Yves Rouquette's wish to squash even the French babies.

A second piece, the 'Refús d'entarrar' from 1969, encompasses a series of meditations on the Occitan corpse.[18] Is it dead? Who killed it? How did it die? Should it be buried? If so, how? With sarcasm he speaks of the body's loneliness and then recounts how it awakens from sleep and devours its own hand or how crows eat away at the corpse, commenting as they do so. The horror and the indignation we receive from these texts is both powerful and deeply moving.

Finally, in his later verse, Larzac develops a pattern of earth imagery. 'En l'Oc' (Nowhere/In Oc) contains a sequence called 'Larzac.'[19] Here the Speaker conflates the heathland evoked in Lafont's *La Festa*, where activists protested against plans for an expanded military base, and his own pen-name, assumed decades before the 1970s confrontation. The Speaker speaks out touchingly on the land, sheep, and shepherds, denounces the occupation of buildings and churches, and also modern life, dominated by plastic and epitomized by toy soldiers and bombs. In an especially moving passage he muses on returning to his beloved earth and taking back his real name (Rouquette); the land cries out with the blood of Abel, it demands justice and, to counter its sterility, children.

Less idealistic, fiercer in its evocation of nightmare modernity, 'Et in Terra' has the bird, tree, and moon lament their existence in a corrupt world, one where the earth is as skin covered with vermin and leprosy (we humans), where we are beasts, and where the suckling baby already has developed a taste for tears and blood.[20] The innocence of nature – the moon pouring milk onto the earth, or the poor poisoned dog that belongs to a weeping child, or the birds and the trees – is contrasted to human degradation. Yet, cries Larzac, let us be what we are, for we are alive! All this in a sequence that alludes to the text of the Gloria: 'and in earth peace, good will towards men.' In his meditation on the human and the divine Jean Larzac reminds us of the sadness of the earth and the waters after Christ left the planet, and their sweetness and joy when some human act reminds them of his presence:

Pasmens de còps
una careça te revèrta e la tèrra arredonís
        sos sèrres e i fa l'èrba doça entre los ròcs
l'èrba doça   l'èrba sauvatja   l'èrba rufa e moissa
e los aubres que pavanejan al gaug de l'aire. (p. 239)

(Yet now and then a caress resembles you and the earth rounds off its peaks and grows sweet grass between the rocks sweet grass wild grass rough and scraggy grass and the trees that strut about to the delight of the air.)

And he tells of those spirits who, adoring the sun, went blind. He also stared at the sun, but then an angel told him to turn around and behold the little things on our earth. So he did and so he does, in a deeply moving corpus of engaged verse, sacred and profane, poetry of paroxysm and of passion, which speaks out in passion on issues and does so in beauty, in texts which stand as a monument to the striving for truth and goodness, and their embodiment in art.

SCOTLAND

Nineteen-sixty-eight is a French phenomenon. The events of 1968 left Scotland largely untouched, where student protests were the mildest in Great Britain and the mildest in most of Western Europe. The late 1960s and the 1970s, therefore, did not witness a revival of cultural nationalism in Scotland and the acceptance of Scottish nationalism in London comparable to the Breton and Occitan resurgence after 1968 and the vogue of 'BZH' and 'OC' bumper stickers among left-wing intellectuals in Paris.

However, Scottish culture was changed decisively by another phenomenon, in its way the Scottish equivalent of the *fest-noz* and *novela cançon*, for that matter the equivalent of the Sixties Poets and the Poets of Decolonization. This is the rise of a new, populist, and Left-oriented literature written not in literary Scots but (more or less faithfully) in the speech of the urban poor, especially the urban poor of Glasgow. This phenomenon, also postmodern as I envisage it, has proved to be more decisive and more long-lasting than the comparable literature of protest in Breizh and Occitania. Similarly, in strictly political terms, the recent partial devolution and the success of the Scottish National party proclaim the extent to which aspirations have had a more serious result in Scotland than in the French regions.

In 1969 *Six Glasgow Poems* brought fame to Tom Leonard, who, in a number of collections, using his personal idiosyncratic orthography, stamped the literary scene with a personal style.[21] Leonard revels in the Glaswegian street patois ('Toonheid Vernacular') as a medium of protest against the high culture that had become a commodity and a means of imposing class distinction. Leonard's wit, sarcasm, and rage give voice to the voiceless; they express the sentiments of the inarticulate and the dispossessed. He now is seen as one among a number of Glaswegian poets, including Stephen Mulrine, Alan Spence, Duncan Glen, Ian Hamilton Finlay, and (in one of his phases) Edwin Morgan, who form one of the central currents in Scottish verse today.[22]

Still more significant, in my opinion, was the flowering, in the 1970s, of a Glaswegian working-class vernacular drama that revolutionized the Scottish stage. These plays – naturalistic in form and socially realistic in content, Hauptmann and Gorky *à l'écossaise* – created excitement at the time because of the novelty and immediacy of their observing proletarian life cast in Scottish working-class speech – a vernacular racy in conversational banter yet also having its own authority and dignity. This current, which was to peter out in the 1980s, has been criticized for non-innovative stage practices and for leftist preaching, or sentimentality, or sensationalism, for contributing to Glasgow Urban Kailyard.[23] I understand the critics yet also agree with those who see in the drama a genuine striving for identity, expression, and human dignity.[24] The political is obtrusive, of course, as it is in McLellan and Campbell. It does not prevent delicious moments of humour, pathos, and the gift of self. Although the movement did peter out, it has had a major impact on the subsequent evolution of the theatre and television with the result that, today, it is the accepted norm that working-class urban and rural Scots are uttered, whenever appropriate, in drama at all levels and in experimental or avant-garde as well as naturalist pieces. Last of all, this proletarian drama is also valid as art on its own terms.[25]

Bill Bryden was associate director of the Lyceum Theatre in Edinburgh, then associate director of the National Theatre in London and director of BBC TV Scotland. As a director and as a practising playwright, he is the man most responsible for the upsurge in urban Scots drama in the 1970s. When his first play, *Willie Rough*, premiered at the Lyceum in February 1972, it caused a sensation.[26]

The plot covers the period from February 1914 to June 1916 at the shipyards in Greenock. Willie Rough, a young riveter, married with two (then three) children, idealistic, shaped by John Maclean and Willie Gallacher, gets a job, becomes shop steward, leads a strike, gives speeches, publishes a seditious article in *The Worker*, is sent to prison for six months, and cannot get his job back. The play depicts Willie's political education and his victories and defeats during the heyday of Red Clydeside. Bryden achieves this end by maintaining the conventions of naturalist drama yet also shaping it in the chronicle tradition, for that matter in the line of the medieval mystery plays, by fragmenting the action and presenting it through eighteen brief scenes, eighteen vignettes in Willie's life over these two and a half years.

What astounded the audience in 1972 and remains meaningful today is the perception of realism – of a low-class urban reality filtered through the medium of low-class urban Scots. But for the employment clerk in the first scene, everyone on stage utters Glaswegian and only Glaswegian. The unique discourse of the play, it soon becomes, for the implied audience or the implied reader, as natural as the air we breathe. The characters discuss politics. They also discuss women, children, and the job. There is much working-class, male, comradely banter. The men play at a little rugby, they walk their dogs, and their wives do the shopping. A number of scenes take place in the pub, where the workers drink and bet on the horses. The bartender, who is also the bookmaker, plays at least as important a role in their lives as the employer or the wife.

Bryden's first play could be characterized as non-Stalinist socialist realism. I say this because the reality or, if you prefer, the perception of reality is shaped by and melded with a strongly left-wing conceptualization of proletarian existence. Willie's life and his education turn around the strike, the war, and his trial and imprisonment. He speaks the truths of class struggle – the exploitation of the Greenock shipbuilders by the capital (London) and by capitalism. He himself embodies the 'positive hero' of socialist realism, accompanied by his friend, Pat, who shares his convictions and is Catholic (this is a class war where sectarian antipathy must be overcome), his supportive wife, and the older man, Hughie, a comic sponger who falls helping the strikers against scabs and the police. Although Jake the foreman sympathizes with the workers and is close to Willie and Pat, in the end we see the foreman's true colours when he accepts the bosses' ban on Willie and refuses to take him back into the yard. All this is a bit facile, even melodramatic. After all, the stage is not the only locus where socialist realism functions as socialist allegory or socialist romance. However, Bryden does also problematize the situation. Willie, all said and done, is a little man, often uncertain, often hesitant, always far from socialist perfection. A riveter he is and a riveter he will remain, in antithesis to Charlie, the communist, a Greenock Ewan Tavendale, who is depicted as an extremist and an opportunist. In contrast to Charlie, Willie loves life; he has a simple, concrete existence with simple, concrete pleasures – something in addition to the class struggle: 'This is the first half-hour's peace I've had in the last fortnight, an' I've come up here tae enjoy it. I want tae be up here lookin doun there. That's my wey o gettin free o't for a wee while. I can see my house, an' the school my laddie goes tae' (p. 67). In perhaps the most powerful scene of the play, Sam returns from the front, embittered, having lost an arm, and Willie and Charlie are so involved in discussing the strike that they fail to notice him.

History takes it toll on all the men, not just Sam. Willie is brokenhearted over his fellow workers turning against him and over the betrayal of the cause by the leaders higher up. At the centre of this historical conjuncture stands the Great War, *the* historical phenomenon, determined by socio-economic forces. Because of the war, workers are seduced by exploitative capitalist propaganda. Because of the war, they become jingoists and displace their wrath harmlessly onto a largely fictitious distant foe, the Germans, instead of onto the concrete class enemy in London or at home; as Willie says: 'Christ, ye've nae sense, the haill lot o' ye. Wan minute they're signin on for the Army, an' the next they're paradin about Cathcart Square lik a shower o bloody clowns, an' nou ye're breakin shop windaes. Hav ye nae sense? Has the war demented the haill toun?' (p. 36). The Great War, which played so decisive a role in the course of Scottish history, especially as the event which made necessary the literary Renaissance, plays an important role in this text, which chronicles two years in the life of one man and also the tragic turning-point in the history of Red Clydeside.

Although *Willie Rough* is, structurally, a linear play that depicts Willie's development, in a sort of *Bildungsdrama*, the play's structure is also cyclical. The *Bildungsdrama* is wedded to the rise and fall of socialist militancy in the shipyards. History does not end, the social combat is not over, and Willie has a life of work and militancy ahead of him. The last scene rejoins the first scene, with the riveter intent upon finding work, supporting his family, and, now, engaged in a struggle which surpasses him and in which he finds his place. Whatever Pat and Jake say or have said, Willie's answer remains the same: 'I will, but. I've got tae' (Yet I will do it, I have to). He loses freedom and job but never his spirit. The drama begins and ends with Willie's determination, which stamps him, us, and the play with the recognition of his decency and integrity, the decency and integrity of mankind.

Roddy McMillan, one of Scotland's leading actors, played the role of Jake the foreman in Bryden's production of *Willie Rough*. In 1973 he played the role of the foreman in his own second and last play, *The Bevellers*, directed and commissioned by Bill Bryden.[27] (McMillan's first play, *All in Good Faith*, dates from 1954).

The Bevellers documents the lives of polishing and bevelling workers in much the same way that *Willie Rough* documents the lives of shipbuilders. They both partake of the relatively new genre – the workplace drama. Also, McMillan's protagonist, Norrie, corresponds to Bryden's Willie as a central focalizing consciousness and as the conscience that grows in the course of the action. The difference between the two is, first of all, one of age. Norrie is much younger than Willie. He is the new boy in the shop, a youth who has just left school and is, for the first time, embarking on learning a trade and making a living. The plot recounts his first and only day on the job. We observe Norrie being jostled, hazed, and, finally, beaten by the other workers. This is his 'initiation,' an ironic counter-initiation to the world of men. Norrie grows up quickly, far more quickly than he would have imagined. In contrast to Willie Rough, Norrie has no political insight and draws no political lessons. He simply quits, bloody and in tears, and the play ends.

The structure becomes, then, more concentrated, more classical in a sense, than Bryden's. The time of the play – three hours, more or less –

is meant to correspond to the time of the plot – a normal workday. All
the action occurs in one place, the little bevelling shop in the basement
of a glass-making firm. The symbolism of the décor is revealed (a trifle
too overtly?) when the workers listen to the academy students marching
off to camp to the music of the pipes. Some people live, move, and
breathe in the fresh, open air above and outside. Down here, in the cellar, in these Gorkian lower depths, the glass-workers are contained
within four walls, with only the foreman allowed to consult with the
manager upstairs. The atmosphere is claustrophobic, and the men inevitably take out their resentments on each other. Symbolism also is drawn
from the trade itself, as Stevenson has observed, for the men not only
polish and bevel mirrors, they also bevel and grind down each other.[28] I
should add that, just as a mirror is occasionally broken, so also Norrie
breaks, to the workers' indifference and management's concern over
the expense.

Just as the play is profoundly naturalist in terms of stagecraft, so again
the material is one of social realism. McMillan goes beyond Bryden by
having his bevellers bevel on stage, so that the implied audience is introduced to the secrets of the trade in roughly the same time span that
Norrie is. The implied audience learns, from Bob the foreman, the history of bevelling and can sense his pride in an old and demanding line
of work which once approximated artistic creation. From Bob and from
Alex, a former employee become an alcoholic and a vagrant, we also discover the extent to which this once prideful trade has come down in the
world, and how it and the conditions of the modern workplace destroy
men's bodies and sap their spirit. Most of all, we follow the banter and
comradely interchange of workers on the job. However, McMillan, in
contrast to Bryden, in no way idealizes male camaraderie. One of
McMillan's strengths is to bring to the fore the viciousness and cruelty
that can and do radiate from these men, ultimately dominating their
lives:

> BOB: Whit ye daein, Rouger, fur Christ's sake, ye want tae kill the boy?
> ROUGER: Jist wettin his heid.
> BOB: Ye couldnae let him go, could ye? You had tae get the needle in. Ye
> might've droont him, ya bliddy eediot.
> ROUGER: Fuck him. He's no wan o us. (p. 69)

The viciousness and cruelty assume the form of something like an
initiation ritual or rite of passage. The older workers join forces against

the newcomer – insiders versus outsider and old versus young. At first it is only a question of jostling and some mild hazing. It must also be said that Norrie is young, inexperienced, not over-bright and not over-dexterous. The older men have reason to be annoyed at his clumsiness, given that their job requires a total team effort. I believe Hutchinson is right when he proposes that the plot attains wider human significance as a metaphor for the struggle between innocence and experience.[29] Such a reading is especially apt in a text where Bob all but declares the bevelling trade to be an allegory of life, and where he speaks of the three categories of men who enter the trade and how each of them turns out.

That the action turns sinister and that Norrie is almost drowned in a trough of water before being beaten tells us much about the men and little about Norrie. He is only a pretext, an instrument if you will, in a rivalry that existed in the plant before his arrival and will continue after his departure. This is the struggle for dominance in a gender-specific, all-male community.

Charlie is the strongest of the workers; he lifts weights and lives for his muscle-building program. He also 'sees' Nancy. Dan the Rouger, who lives for his biker activities on the weekend, fiercely resents Charlie. He competes with Charlie yet fears him. Rivalry in power is then transferred to sexual rivalry. Dan mocks Norrie's mother and sister. He also all but seduces Nancy and would have 'scored' had she not suddenly perceived Norrie overlooking their primal scene. In the end Dan convinces Charlie that Norrie invented the whole thing, and Charlie pummels poor Norrie. Roddy McMillan paints a disturbing picture of cruelty and manipulation in the shop. Brutalized by foul working conditions and brutalized because they are brutes, these men – not all of them, two suffice – degrade each other, fighting over power and sex. Norrie serves as the scapegoat, and he is purged from this vicious society. The initiation hero becomes an initiatory Pharmakos – ironically for his good, we surely hope. And, in the last ironic scene, it is the manager alone who manifests pity for the boy, sending him home to the women – to his mother, a mother who we know died years previously.

Bill Bryden's second play, *Benny Lynch*, was first performed at the Lyceum in 1974.[30] It follows *Willie Rough* (1972) and *The Bevellers* (1973). This work dramatizes the career of Scotland's first world champion in boxing, who topped the flyweight division from 1935 to 1938. The importance of boxing in Glasgow working-class culture as well as the impact of Bryden's play are evidenced by the success of two subsequent pieces on the subject: *The Boxer Benny Lynch* by Peter Arnott (1984) and *Buchanan* by Tom McGrath (1993).

Amplifying the technique of *Willie Rough*, *Benny Lynch* 'covers' twelve years in the fighter's life, concentrating on his rise and then on his fall. Benny has talent, the God-given talent of his body. Otherwise, he is an ordinary lad from the Glasgow slums, incapable of resisting or even comprehending the temptations which dog anyone who becomes a star. Fame, money, power, and the love of his fellows – these flow over him like gifts from a fay. Also flowing over him are women and liquor. The women are portrayed as the reward of fame yet also a temptation that saps his manhood or his purse. Benny's handlers are dismayed when he breaks training before a bout. Not only is 'nookie' bad for a fighter in training; Benny could have contracted venereal disease. Prior to the world championship bout we see the handlers and promoters pay off a pregnant girl and her mother. Fortunately for Benny, Wilma is engaged to a soldier, and her mother asks not much more than the price of an abortion. The alcohol is more immediately destructive, causing Benny to lose a match, to break down, even to make a spectacle of himself at his best friend's funeral. Because of sex and drink, Benny eventually fails to make the flyweight limit, is disqualified, and falls from contention. In one scene he crawls about, lost in a snowstorm, offering snowflakes as gifts to his friends: 'Here's wan for you, an' two for you, an' wan for you. Oh. I forgot about you. You're here. An' wan for me. White. They're a' white. It's the only kind I've got. "Shop's open, come an' buy!"' (p. 87). Tragic irony is generated from the fact that Benny lives for girls and drink, that his boxing prowess grants him both, and that, because his wishes are granted, they destroy him. On an archetypal level, although Mars and Venus love each other and Venus is the reward for Mars's exploits, they compete for a man's loyalty. He must choose between *militia* and *amor*. The greatest of epic heroes – Achilles, Odysseus, Aeneas – renounce or are deprived of pleasure while they undergo a career of prowess. Yet even Aeneas abandoned Dido with regret and only after divine command. Benny lacks will-power and has no divine command, with the result that he is dragged down into lower depths more degrading than any bevellers' shop.

The reality of the slums assumes symbolic weight. We the implied audience are told of the picture shows and of the Blackshirts. We are initiated into the routine of professional fighters. We hear of prostitution and abortions. Ultimately reality concerns the poverty and alienation in which these people live and from which they can never escape, which have shaped their minds so that they will be destroyed no matter what happens, and which follow them wherever they go. This overriding, omnipresent weight of poverty, squalor, and despair helps us to comprehend Glasgow and Glasgow's response to Benny, what he means to the city. A world-champion prizefighter or, later, a world-class footballer shines as a beacon. His is the way out of poverty, squalor, and despair. People live vicariously through him. Also, he stands as an icon not only of material success but also of heroism, something akin to spiritual greatness. Just as Odysseus ennobles Ithaca and Aeneas will found Rome, just as the heroes of *chanson de geste* are assimilated to their city – Guillaume d'Orange, Aimeri de Narbonne, Raoul de Cambrai, Girart de Roussillon, Renaut de Montauban – so here, in this modern, populist, ironic, counter-heroic play, Benny of Glasgow or Benny of the Gorbals casts an aura of greatness on his people, who glow in his reflection, because of him.

Bryden makes this point by having the protagonist appear less on stage than one would imagine. The implied audience views Benny, of course, but, more than Benny, it views the others – the fight crowd, Benny's cronies including trainer, cornerman, second, cutman, physician, manager, and promoter. The action of the play, Benny's story, and Benny the human being are filtered through their consciousness, focalized through their point of view, a novelistic technique common in the theatre. Given Benny's own inarticulateness and absence of self-consciousness, this is the ideal dramatic means for presenting the Benny question without crudely offering a response. We don't know the real Benny, we never apprehend him in his totality, because the cronies never apprehend him and also, perhaps, because there is nothing to apprehend. The tragedy is theirs as much as Benny's, perhaps theirs more than Benny's. They are articulate, chattering all the time, and they reflect a great deal on Benny. He is their life and hope, they are obsessed by him – in part because, without him, they would have to labour like everyone else yet also because they love him. Tragedy is grounded in the fact that, for all their genuinely good intentions and doing the best they can, they cannot help 'the wee man.' In spite of their exertions, he falls. The scene in the snowstorm illustrates this; Benny is lost but so also are the others, who cannot find him. So also does another, magnificent comic scene where they hide the drunken, semi-conscious Benny in a locker to veil his condition from onlookers. Although they succeed, Benny remains inebriated and semi-conscious.

And their exploit re-enacts Benny's trauma as a child when he was shut up in a boiler.

In the end, years later, he perishes of alcoholism and the cold. Times have changed. A new war disturbs Scotland. Icons have changed. And the physician who ministers to the dying vagrant does not recognize the man's name or know who he is.

Tom McGrath has written a number of plays. The 1993 *Buchanan* is the most recent treatment of the Scottish prizefighter theme. His greatest success, however, remains *The Hard Man*, which was produced at the Traverse Theatre in Edinburgh (1973) and has since then been revived at home and in Germany.[31] McGrath wrote this piece in collaboration with Jimmy Boyle, one of Scotland's most wanted criminals and most violent inmates, a legend in his time. The fictional dramatized biography of one Johnnie Byrne alluded, everyone knew, to the notorious historical figure Jimmy Boyle. The play was therefore successful, in part because of its genuine artistic merit and in part because of the sensational subject-matter.

The play treats Johnnie Byrne's life in crime as a free man, and his life in punishment behind bars. The two-act structure moulds us to recognize his evolution as a felon, then his evolution as a prisoner. In Act I the implied audience observes the slum child grow successively into gang member, shoplifter, robber, small enforcer, fence, big enforcer, and major gangster. In Act II the implied audience observes Johnnie respond to violence from the wardens with violence of his own (he causes one warden to lose an eye, he beats the Assistant Governor to a pulp), which leads to the increase of their response to him – beating, a strait-jacket, near-drowning, sleep deprivation, and placing him naked in a cage.

The political message is clear enough. Yes, Johnnie is a criminal and a bad one. Yet he was a slum child with nowhere to go and nothing to do; he and his mates are the children of our society, shaped by it. Behind prison walls, he is all but totally a victim, martyred by sadistic guards, vengeful governors, and indifferent judges. The worst of these guards tells us that he plays the same role in the prison that Johnny plays outside, that he is *our* enforcer just as Johnny was the mob's enforcer:

PAISLEY: So they tolerate me. I'm *their* hard man. And they feel a wee bit guilty about me [...] Just like you should be feeling guilty about us because we're the garbage disposal squad for the social sewage system. [...] The cistern's clanked and you can think you can leave it floating away from you to the depths of the sea. Well, ah've goat news fur you – its pollution. Yir gonnae huv tae look ut it. Because if yae don't, wun day its gonnae destroy yae. (p. 57)

The message is underscored through a number of devices. One is language. The sociology of language and the functioning of language as class marker are made explicit in this play. The gangsters and the wardens speak urban Scots. The lawyers and judges, and the lower-class men when they imitate the speech of lawyers and judges, speak received-pronunciation English. Johnnie, commenting on his own early life, now having had a chance to educate himself, does so in English, though presumably with a Scots accent. The second device is Brechtian stage technique, one example of which is the direction that the two 'screws' be played by the same actors who play Johnnie's cronies. In fact, they don prison officer uniforms on stage. Later, they take on the roles of prosecutor and judge. And, in the Traverse production, other characters in the underworld are played by the same actors as the policemen, lawyers, commandos, and clerks of court.

These effects of symbolism rely upon a more contemporary use of structure than in the dramas by Bryden and McMillan. Johnnie Byrne and a number of the others address the audience, commenting on themselves as characters or on the plot in which they function, creating one level of *Verfremdungseffekt*. In Act I two older women in the slums and in Act II an older trustee inmate function as a Greek chorus, also commenting on the action. A dose of pantomime and near-ballet and the use of percussionist music contribute to the theatrical effect. Indeed, the violence central to the action is represented and, at the same time, stylized by means of percussion and choreography. It functions in the play as percussionist and choreographed violence.

The violence is central to the representation of the 'hard man,' an archetypal figure in modern Scottish culture, a Scottish myth which goes back to Stevenson. McGrath has the implied audience behold Johnnie's acts of violence, beating, cutting, and killing. On the one hand, he assimilates the hard man's violence to the mentally unsound and to the animal, that is, to insanity and bestiality. Early in his career, still as a child, Johnnie impresses the others by his animal ferociousness, which his friends designate as 'lunatic.' Because of it, they are afraid of him. These traits are then amplified in prison. Here Johnnie's enemies take up the old motifs, calling him an animal and locking him naked in a cage, calling him insane and putting him in a strait-jacket.

On the other hand, dissenting voices tell of Johnnie's impossible childhood and, more immediately, cry out that he is not a hard man at all. If he were, he would not lose control of himself and 'act crazy.' In fact, Johnnie is powerfully emotional; it is the emotional side that bursts forth in spasms of uncontainable rage. Similarly, it is not the hard man who, on the outside, impressed his cronies by proposing that they open a bank account (his business sense) and, on the inside, infuriates the wardens by reading books, conducting his own defence, and authoring a 'Prisoner's Charter.'

As with the other plays of proletarian realism, the *Hard Man* has a relatively clear political message on the Left. In his indictment of society and his exaltation of the criminal, McGrath comes closer to Genet than to Gorky. Yet, as with Genet, the message is powerful because the drama is powerful. In the end, the screws have dehumanized Johnnie as much as they can – by locking him, naked, in a cage. They dehumanize him in order to defeat him, to break his spirit:

> PAISLEY: Too late, Byrne. It's too late for you for anything. Your time's up. You've become one of the living dead.
> BYRNE: No. So long as I'm fighting, I know that I'm alive.
> PAISLEY: Aye, well ah've telt yae – we'll be back. And we're gonnae knock the fighting out of your system once and for all. (pp. 67–8)

He then goes one step further. He smears his naked body with his own faeces. Now, he says, the screws will not continue to beat him, now they have to keep away from him. By the ultimate gesture of animality and insanity, by the ultimate in alienation, Johnnie paradoxically proclaims his humanity. The Others may have broken his body and his spirit. Yet, like Campbell's Father Ogilvie, as a proletarian, secularist, criminal anti-Ogilvie, Johnnie proclaims his dignity and his manhood. Thus the human condition prevails.

CONCLUSION

To begin with, this book is not a literary history. For reasons of space and as determined by the economy of presentation, I had to concentrate on a number of representative major figures. Therefore – to cite only the genre of poetry, admittedly the richest – writers of the stature of William Soutar and Alexander Scott, Abeozen and Guy Etienne, and Léon Cordes and Max Rouquette were left out. Guy Etienne / Abanna is, some would claim, the greatest living poet in Breton. I felt it essential to concentrate on Goethe's three *Naturformen* – epic (narrative), lyric, and the drama. And I interpreted *das Epische*, in twentieth-century terms, as extended prose fiction – the novel. Only thus could be substantiated the moderns' claim to have created a modern literature, in all senses of the term, worthy of a modern high-culture language of European scope. To do so, however, meant that I had to neglect non-imaginative prose and also the genre of brief fiction – the *conte* or *nouvelle*. The *nouvelle* is particularly important in the literature of Brittany; Jakez Riou before the Second World War and Ronan Huon, Youenn Olier, and Per Denez more recently have made major contributions. So have Robert McLellan and Sheena Blackhall in Scots. The master of the *nouvelle* in Occitan, Max Rouquette, is justly considered one of the greatest figures in the language. Finally, I concentrated on the writers of modernism, with a foray into the populist, engaged response of the 1960s and 1970s – the equivalent of minority postmodernism. Reasons of space and the economy of presentation prevented my tracing the evolution of the last two decades, which offer a rich, bewildering proliferation of styles and modes, and of writers both young and old.

Nonetheless, given the representative major figures, it is possible to justify the moderns' claim to have created a modern literature. In all three regions, in all three languages, the aims were attained and the results a success. In all three we find writers and books of the very first rank. Scots, Breton, and Occitan cannot hope to compare in quantity with the number of masterpieces that grace our century in French and English. However, their best is very fine indeed, comparable to the best in the languages of wider diffusion and fully equal to the best produced in their tongues in the past (in Breton, far superior to what was produced in the past). The three literatures make a major contribution to the culture of their regions and to the total cultural richness of the United Kingdom and the Republic of France, taken in their totality.

The clearest, most unalloyed triumph, in all three languages, occurs in the domain of poetry. It remains the favourite genre, and the most successful, for a number of reasons. In the brief lyric form, unlike the novel or the drama, poetry is easily published in the reviews, and because it can be composed as well as appear in bits and pieces, as it were, it is a genre which can attain a high level of quality with fewer years of concentrated effort. There is less discrepancy between the small public for verse in French or English and the small public for all literature in minority languages than would be the case for fiction and the theatre. High modernism opted resolutely for a relatively arcane and esoteric mode of writing, especially in verse. High modernism in Scots, Breton, and Occitan, therefore, demands an elite audience, but not necessarily more so than high modernism in French and English. Finally, the minority languages, prior to the moderns, were culturally restricted codes. So much of the preceding cultural tradition, in all three languages, took the form of verse; so that, even when rebelling against that tradition, it appeared more 'natural' for the minority writers to express themselves in *their* accredited literary mode. And, when in search of alternative intertextual roots – Henryson and Dunbar, Bernart de Ventadorn and Godolin, early texts in Irish and Welsh – the moderns would find these roots in old poetry, which would, most appropriately, flower in the form of new poetry.

For the most part, the verse took two forms. There is the ultimate in high modernism, dense, fragmented, contorted, tortured, ripped apart, full of historical and literary allusion – this is the work of Hugh MacDiarmid, Sydney Goodsir Smith, Maodez Glanndour, René Nelli, and Bernard Manciet. This is the tradition of Eliot, Pound, Valéry, St-John Perse, and Char. Then there is another mode, certainly as modern as the first one but closer to the implied reader's horizon of expectations, sometimes sublimely rhetorical and sometimes exploiting the register of *genus medium*. In this category I place Robert Garioch, Tom Scott, Roparz Hemon, Anjela Duval, and Max-Philippe Delavouët. This is the tradition of Yeats, Frost, Aragon, and Eluard. The two registers – three, actually, if we distinguish between the sublime of Hemon and Delavouët and the quotidian of Garioch and Duval – coexist, just as from the 1960s on they coexist together with the *genus humile* of shout and scream. These registers flourish at the same time in the minority literatures just as they do in the literatures of wider currency. Modernism in verse is much more complex, problematic, and polyvocal than most people realize.

In a quite fascinating way the modernist poetry expresses and is grounded in regional concerns and, at the same time, attains the universality of an Eliot or a Valéry. The drunk man and the thistle, the quest on land for the whore in the pubs of Edinburgh, the Breton pilgrim listening to the call from the graves, the sea quest of a Breton for the absolute, the Provençal Adam in search of his Eve, the old *dauna* of Gascony arguing with God – these themes are powerfully local and also as universal as any musings on a waste land or a graveyard by the sea. The poets of Scotland, Brittany, and Occitania attain the universal precisely because of, not in spite of, the local or regional, because they are willing to exploit what they most deeply feel, what most moves them as minority writers working in minority tongues. And also, let us not forget, because they make no compromise with the reader. As writers of modernism and as inhabitants of the twentieth century, they assume the aesthetics of their century with as much passion and as much integrity as they do the issues of their people. The result is – as many have said – that *A Drunk Man Looks at the Thistle* is in no way inferior to *The Waste Land*; and also, and this has not been said, that *Under the Eildon Tree* rivals *Four Quartets*, 'Pirc'hirin ar Mor' and *Imram* rival *Anabase* or *Brocéliande*, *Pouèmo* rivals *Amers*, and *L'Enterrament a Sabres* rivals *Le Fou d'Elsa*.

The novel comes late to the minority writers. Since it never formed part of a generic tradition in the three languages, the writers of modernism created modern novels in their tongues as an act of the will and in defiance of custom. The Breton novel since 1940, the Occitan novel since 1955, and the Scots trilogy by Lewis Grassic Gibbon dating from the 1930s refuse to indulge in gratuitous local colour or any form of nostalgia: no rural idylls, no touching Christian faith, no condescending sentimentality. The genre includes from the beginning, and is grounded in, the tradition in the modern West of realism. The honest, authentic representation of reality – of the lives of little people, in our time, on the farm or in town – dominates Gibbon's *A Scots Quair*, Youenn Drezen's *Itron Varia Garmez*, Roparz Hemon's *Nenn Jani*, Robert Lafont's *Vida de Joan Larsinhac*, and Jean Boudou's *La Grava sul camin*.

These are highly successful and highly finished examples of the genre. Yet the fictional mode veers immediately in other directions, toward romance or allegory or the picaresque. This is the symbolism of Chris Caledonia in a world of rock, cloud, and the passing of time, her Scots Quair, and the symbolic struggle of Drezen's Paol Tirili to create a work of art in stone, dragged down by the sea and the land. These are the allegorical quests of Hemon's mad doctor in *Mari Vorgan* and Boudou's dying intellectual in *Lo Libre dels grands jorns*. This is the fantastic imagination displaced onto the past (Hemon's *Tangi Kerviler*) or the future (Lafont's *L'Icòna dins l'iscla*) or even the present (Boudou's *La Santa Estèla del centenari* and Per Denez's *Diougan Gwenc'hlan*). This is, finally, the mock-epic and mock-quest of the two children in Drezen's *Skol-louarn*.

Why should it be the case? In part, because after two or three centuries of realism (seven centuries if we begin with *La Mort le roi Artu*), writers, in Scots and English as in Breton, Occitan, and French, found that the vein had been mined and only a useless, impure ore ('le petit roman bien fait') remained. Also, the two-, three-, or seven-centuries-old tradition must have appeared powerfully, essentially French and Parisian or English and from London, and therefore not the ideal medium for expressing regional concerns. I suggest that with these strains of quest-romance, symbolism, allegory, mock-epic, and the picaresque, with these elements of the supernatural, the fantastic, and the ludic, the Scots, Breton, and Occitan novel calls to mind another current more closely than it does the stalwarts on the London and Paris publishing scene from the 1920s on, the French examples being Mauriac, Malraux, Sartre, and Camus. This other current, an international current which, in the long run, may well have an impact greater than that of the *nouveau roman*, is found in the fiction of J.S. Alexis, Asturias, Ben Jelloun, Buzzati, Carpentier, García Márquez, S. Germain, Gracq, Grass, J. Green, W. Harris, Jünger, Kroetsch, and Rushdie, among others. It is the current of magical realism.[1] A number of the constituent traits of magical realism are also central to the fiction studied in the preceding chapters. Such are the juxtaposition of the supernatural and the real; periodic eruptions of the uncanny in what would be otherwise standard mimesis; the presence of the marvellous/sacred/uncanny in everyday life; romance archetypes as the cultural manifestation of marginal peoples; a visionary or childlike point of view; displaced structures of space, time, and identity; and, finally, a powerful dose of the carnivalesque and the ludic. One or two theories of postcolonialism posit that magical realism is the natural mode for the postcolonial peoples. I deem such formulations nonsense if they are to be taken ontologically or cosmologically. However, as historical empirical observation they may well be accurate. It should not surprise anyone that novelists in India, Latin America, the Caribbean, Canada, Ireland, North Africa, Scotland, Brittany, and the South of France should find comparable solutions to the same historical problems. In regions of the world formerly or actually subjected to intellectual colonization, modes such as magical realism may well facilitate the defence and illustration of local identity against foreign hegemonic values, especially if the foreign hegemony is associated with empiricism, reason, and the Enlightenment. Magical realism can be thought inherently more 'diverse' than realism and, therefore, capable of voicing local myths and systems of belief. Nor should it surprise anyone (but it probably will) that the less widely used languages and the languages of greater circulation should cultivate the same genres and modes, during the same time in history, responding to the same problems of alienation and identity.

In addition, we must not forget that the realist novel has never been the unique medium for narrative fiction in prose. Realism is a literary doctrine and a conventional way of writing, comparable to other doctrines and conventions, such as *fin' amor* or the Romantic poem of the self. Realism implies only the illusion of reality – the literary perception of mimesis – plus a powerful dose of reaction against the preceding currents of idealism and romance. Prior to the eighteenth century in Europe, prior to the twentieth century in the rest of the world, the dominant modes have been epic, romance, allegory, beast epic, Menippean satire, the picaresque, and the anatomy – not the novel as we know it. It is natural that minority writers, who look for cultural roots in the past, turn from a tradition so recent, so limited in time and space, in order to renew older, more universal medieval and Renaissance forms.

This social and historical context may also help explain the belated yet nonetheless concrete presence of *nouveau roman* in the fiction of Brittany and Occitania. There was no question of *nouveau roman* in the 1940s and 1950s. As a recent Parisian phenomenon, limited to the Parisian avant-garde, Sarraute, Robbe-Grillet, and Butor would have appeared as French as the realism of Balzac. Furthermore, prose fiction, which, in the minority languages as well as in French, was expected to appeal to a broader public than modernist lyrics, could not shock the public with too brusque a shift in the horizon of expectations. However, in time both older and younger writers, Denez, Lafont, and Forêt, among others, saw no reason not to engage in the most recent trends in the exploration of narrative. They did so with resounding success. After all, it was now recognized that the public for minority literature more and more would have to be limited to an intellectual elite. Finally, *nouveau roman* is significantly less innovatory than a Robbe-Grillet would like us to think. Like romance and allegory, like magical realism, it corresponds to registers of narrative which flourished prior to the rise of modern realism or alongside it. The metanarrativity and the ludic in *La Festa*, for example, correspond extremely well to metanarrativity and the ludic in Machaut and Chaucer or in Diderot and Sterne. Theirs also is a rich, vital current in the novel partially occulted by the nineteenth century but now available to us once again.

Although not necessarily one of the earliest concerns of the modernists, the theatre never escaped their attention and always formed part of their program. Problems were posed by the relatively small public to which drama in a minority language could appeal and by the high cost of production or even publication of such plays. The absence of government support, financial as well as cultural, also played a role. As a result, much of the early writing was adapted to a brief format and, among other venues, for the radio. Also, much of it was conservative in form and stagecraft. Furthermore, not all poets eager to write plays possessed a stage instinct comparable to their flights in verse; here, Goodsir Smith would be a good example and not the only one. However, in time the stage was conquered and, with it, especially in Scotland and Brittany, a viable public.

In the long run success in the drama parallels success in poetry and the novel. Per Jakez Helias wrote powerful, totally convincing dramas on Breton rural life situated in the present or the immediate past. These include, among others, *Mevel ar Gosker* and *Katrina Lenn-Zu*. The 1970s, with the works of Bill Bryden, Roddy McMillan, Tom McGrath, and others, gave rise to plays in the Scottish vernacular that treat urban problems and the urban working classes. For the most part, however, the minority writers cultivate a form of historical drama, situating their plays in the past and often, but not exclusively, treating notable figures in history and no less notable historical events. The dramatists turn to the Middle Ages (Helias's *Isild a-heul*, Lafont's *La Loba* and *La Croisade*, and Goodsir Smith's *The Wallace*), the early modern period encompassing the Renaissance and Baroque (Robert McLellan's *Jamie the Saxt*, Donald Campbell's *The Jesuit*, Helias's *Le roi Kado*, and Lafont's *La Révolte des 'Cascavèus'*), and the modern eighteenth and nineteenth centuries

(McLellan's *The Flouers o Edinburgh* and *The Hypocrite* and Campbell's *Somerville the Soldier*).

A number of reasons explain the prevalence of serious historical drama. Conscious of being part of an alienated minority and of existing in a state of cultural dependence – also internal colonialism – vis-à-vis the dominant culture, the dramatists look for cultural roots in the past and for a time when their culture and their political life flourished or when their people rebelled heroically against the oppressor. History plays are written and performed in order to rewrite and re-enact history. For this reason can be placed side by side plays exploring periods or products of high culture (Tristan and Isolt, troubadour courtly love, and the Scottish Enlightenment), plays treating specific historical figures (Count Raymond of Toulouse, William Wallace, King James VI), and plays of opposition or popular rebellion in seventeenth-century Provence or nineteenth-century London.

In addition, by locating the action in the past, when presumably all members of the community spoke the language and spoke it well, the minority dramatist could escape the fetters of the twentieth-century restricted code. On the contrary, he could explore the multiple registers of what was then an expanded code comparable in all ways to French and English.

The prevalence of historical drama and of plays treating the rural present testifies to a constraint which has been discussed in criticism on the theatre in Scots. Although not mentioned in Brittany or the Occitan lands, the same phenomenon is observable there. This is the imposition of a form of mimesis or, if you prefer, sociohistorical verisimilitude concerning the use of language. It is considered appropriate for the minority language to be employed in situations (the historical past, the rural or urban-proletarian present) where, indeed, it would be or would have been uttered. However, it is not considered appropriate to have the professional classes of Edinburgh, Rennes, and Toulouse speak for an entire play their equivalent of the Doric, nor would it be appropriate to have Londoners and Parisians – in the present or the past – speak Scots, Breton, or Occitan. This imposition of decorum is limited to the minority languages. For we can observe, going back to the earliest miracle and mystery plays, that French and English are uttered on stage or in the cinema by all peoples – Greeks, Romans, and the prophets of Israel; Klingons, Vulcans, and those who venture on the planet Dune; and people in France and the United Kingdom who historically would in fact have spoken a minority language (cf. *Braveheart* and *Le Retour de Martin*

Guerre). An exception to this rule would be the case of translation. It is acceptable to put on Liz Lochhead's translation into Scots of a Molière comedy or Roparz Hemon's translation into Breton of a Marlowe tragedy. The writers of modernism have exploited the translation of foreign classics to the full. Yet it remains a fact that, even today, sociohistorical constraint in language provides evidence that the minority languages remain restricted codes, not entirely on the same level as the 'universal' French and English.

The constraint has, at the same time, opened up a creative opportunity for dramatists as well as offering them a means of appealing to an audience not limited to speakers of the language. This is the exploitation of bilingualism, present on the Occitan stage and brilliantly developed in Scotland. One variation has the Scots speak Scots and the English speak English, or Occitanians Occitan and the French, French. In *Jamie the Saxt* everyone speaks Scots but for the English ambassador and his servant; in *Somerville the Soldier* everyone speaks some form of English but for Somerville and his friend. Lafont uses roughly the same convention in *La Croisade* and *Lei Cascavèus*. Scottish plays cast in the eighteenth century elaborate a more subtle strategy. Here McLellan and Robert Kemp explore all the registers possible ranging from pure Scots (spoken to one's estate manager or when one is very angry) to pure English (spoken to the anglophile lady one is courting). The result is not only code-switching but also a range of code-mixing or style-drifting. It gives rise to a glorious panoply of language and a magnificent display of *métissage* – and the public enjoys every minute of it.

The success in achieving the modernist agenda, overall, has to be nuanced by recognition of a relative discrepancy between the three literatures when held up to comparison. The first discrepancy is chronological. The Scottish Renaissance flowered in the 1920s, the period when MacDiarmid was his most creative, and has continued, with inevitable ups and downs, to the present, highlighted by Grassic Gibbon's prose in the 1930s, Goodsir Smith's verse in the 1940s and 1950s, and a flowering of theatre especially in the 1970s. Roparz Hemon founded *Gwalarn* in 1925. However, the period of major literary achievement in Breton begins in the late 1930s and the 1940s, then continues uninterrupted to the present, with the generation of Hemon, the Skol Walarn properly speaking, succeeded by the generation of Denez, itself succeeded by a third generation of young, active, productive figures. Although Nelli, Max Rouquette, and others published in the 1930s and 1940s, the flowering of the Occitan Renaissance has to be located from the 1950s to the present, with the most important works by Lafont and Manciet in the 1980s. Scots, thus, takes the lead (1920s), followed by Breton (1940s) and then Occitan (1950s).

A second discrepancy concerns the shift from a restricted code to an expanded code – in terms of literature, from out-of-date, derivative folklore to modern and universal works of art in their full, assumed textuality. Not all three literatures attained universality in all registers and to the same extent. Here pride of place falls to the Breton. Going back to Meven Mordiern's *Istor ar Bed* (History of the World), modern-oriented Bretons have insisted that the language be cultivated for all possible intellectual and cultural uses. This was Hemon's vision. As a result, Breton is now used as a matter of course for the three major literary modes and also for biography, autobiography, history, literary criticism, the essay, and practical journalism. Occitan has also conquered the three major literary modes, even if the future for the stage (other than *son et lumière* spectacles, where actual use of the language is rare) remains problematic. However, there is nothing in the South of France, in terms of philosophical writing, journalism, and extended literary criticism, quite like what we find in Brittany. The major achievement in Scots poetry and theatre cannot mask the fact that the vernacular has not been employed regularly and systematically in the domain of prose. In spite of excellent short pieces in all the genres, published in *Akros, Lallans*, and elsewhere and now anthologized,[2] *A Scots Quair* as an extended novel remains an isolated masterpiece. This said, in the 1990s, James Kelman, Irvine Welsh, and others have launched a major offshoot of the novel in Scotland, in which the vehicle for discourse is Scots – not the traditional literary High Lallans, but instead the working-class vernacular of Glasgow and Edinburgh. For many, in this area lies the future of Scottish literature and of the language itself as a medium for literature.

In the course of this book I have consistently employed a lexicon and an approach congruent with periodization theory (modernism, postmodernism) and with the theory of postcolonialism. Now is the time to discuss, in a more general way, the validity of such a grid in analysing the minority literatures of Western Europe.

As I see it, periodization does offer insights into the literatures, especially in their historical evolution. Scholars have isolated a number of the constituent characteristics that define the texts of European modernism and the European avant-garde. These include, among others, (1) a rebellion (sometimes conceived as a new classicism) against romanticism, its cult of the personality, its sentimentality, and its roots in populism and folklore; (2) a resolute turning to the reality of urban life and to facing directly – often with disapproval – all aspects of modernity; (3) in terms of form, the creation of fragmented, disjointed, and tormented texts that reflect, as objective correlatives, the fragmentation, disjointedness, and torment of modern life; and (4) a frankly elitist stance vis-à-vis the literary public, resulting in the composition of sometimes difficult and arcane texts yet which also do not hesitate to incorporate, intertextually, vast elements of the preceding European culture, classical, medieval, and modern. In spite of experimentation in form or, rather, congruent with it, we find modern tragic realism, reflecting the political, social, and ecomomic structures of contemporary life and grounded in history, with the lower classes treated seriously and awakening to consciousness. In spite of the fascination with urban centres or, rather, congruent with it, we find local and provincial renascences reacting aginst the hegemonic centre and exploring local and provincial concerns. The rebellion against bourgeois social norms is derived from and also contributes to a cult of youth and to youthful, contestatory *cénacles* of protest. The cultural subversion and critiquing of modern life is derived from and contributes to a sense of apocalypse and alienation, and also artistic self-consciousness (plus a new subjectivity) and aesthetic autonomy. The great modernists – say, Baudelaire, Rimbaud, Valéry, George, Rilke, Yeats, and Pound; Kafka, Mann, Broch, Gide, Proust, Malraux, Mauriac, Joyce, and Faulkner; Ibsen, Strindberg, Pirandello, Lorca, Claudel, and O'Neill – all partake, to a greater or lesser extent, of these traits and work within these parameters.

From this perspective, I think it is clear that MacDiarmid, Hemon, Lafont, their colleagues, and their disciples are modern and modernist, and that their theory and practice fall in line with the dominant currents of twentieth-century literature. With Boudou's and Gibbon's novels of the country; Boudou's, Gibbon's, and Drezen's novels of life in town or city; psychological introspection in fiction by Hemon, Denez, Lafont, and Forêt; poetry of protest and a rebellious subjectivity in MacDiarmid, Goodsir Smith, Scott, Hemon, Duval, and Manciet; poetry of distortion, fragmentation, and rupture in MacDiarmid, Smith, Glanndour, Delavouët, Nelli, and Manciet; the revision and rewriting of history and of historical language in the plays of McLellan, Campbell, Helias, and Lafont, and in the poetry of Garioch, Smith, and Nelli – thus the minority-language modernists partake fully of modernism.

It is important to recognize that the Scots, Breton, and Occitan achievements cannot be accounted for uniquely in regional terms and as a response to regional problems. They are not unique or alien to the total picture. On the contrary, Scots, English, Breton, Occitan, and French (plus German, Italian, etc.) form a European totality and partake together of pan-European modernism. This is true, in part, because the minority writers inevitably adopt themes, motifs, and currents from the contemporary dominant culture. And, for this reason and others, the minority cultures manifest belatedness vis-à-vis the dominant culture. The modern realist novel comes to Breton in the 1940s and to Occitan in the 1950s, two centuries after Marivaux and Prévost, three centuries after *La Princesse de Clèves*. Something roughly comparable occurs with the theatre and stagecraft. Therefore, we find, because of the belatedness, a number of currents or modes coexisting at the same time. Because of the coexistence, for all their advances over the preceding tradition the minority literatures may appear, in strictly formal terms, conservative compared to the literatures of the avant-garde in Paris and London.

Just as the theory of modernism grants insights into the flowering of a modern literature in Scotland, Brittany, and Occitania, so also the evidence brought from minority literatures enriches our conception of modernism and modernity. The hermeneutic process is circular. It has been observed that professors of English (especially in the United States), familiar only with the Anglo-American tradition, make general statements on modernism based on this restricted corpus.[3] Thus, drawing their argument from Eliot, Pound, Lawrence, Yeats, and Joyce, a number have claimed that modernism is inherently reactionary and elitist, indeed 'objectively' fascist. Continental scholars, drawing on Russian futurism and French surrealism, on Mayakovsky, Eluard, and Aragon, plus Brecht, Quasimodo, and Neruda, claim that modernism is inherently avant-garde and emancipatory-revolutionary on the Left. The minority literatures would help to nuance such extreme formulations. Scottish and Occitan modernism is, for the most part, leftist and appears so from the beginnings. Breton modernism has a tradition of leaning to the Right. I suggest that, on the one hand, in all three regions the literature is indeed elitist, in part because the modern movement came into being as a protest against and repudiation of condescending, colonialist populism, and also because, ever since the eighteenth century, with a gigantic increase in the potential literary public and in the modalities of cultural distribution, a greater and greater gap separates the creative artist from his or her public. This said, it must also be recognized that modernism in the regional cultures, whether on the Left or

on the Right, was a literature of authenticity and of protest. The literature was oppositional and, in its essence, emancipatory. One of its major
goals was always the cultural emancipation of the region – the 'nation' –
conceived as all the people dwelling therein.

Because of the weight of Paris in French literature, from Baudelaire
to the surrealists, because of the comparable weight of Berlin with German expressionism and Weimar culture generally, continental scholars
underscore the role of the metropolitan centre in the elaboration of
modernism and modernity. A number of specialists in English, on the
contrary, cite the role of the provincial and/or marginal writer (American, Irish, Scottish, northern English) as the creative focus for a modernism which challenges and stands in a state of tension with the
hegemonic cultural centre that is London. The minority literatures lend
force to the anglicist position, given that minority or regional modernism, even when grounded in an urban cultural centre (Edinburgh,
Rennes, Montpellier), remains nonetheless liminal and contestatory vis-
à-vis Paris and London and the apparatus of the French and British
establishment.[4]

A comparable analysis can be made of what I call minority-literature
postmodernism in the 1960s and 1970s. Postmodernism is a problematic notion, elusive to say the least, with theorists disagreeing as to
whether it represents a crisis within modernism, the conscious rejection
of modernism, an extreme form of modernism, or the necessary and
inevitable outcome of modernism. Furthermore, one person's postmodernism is another person's modernism, and vice versa. Certain traits
associated with postmodernism, such as a crisis in representation, the
primacy of ontology over epistemology, the exalting of pure textuality,
being grounded in signs and simulacra, and the unequivocal rejection
of humanism – these are not relevant to the post-1968 literatures of
Scotland, Brittany, and the South of France. They may not be relevant to
any culture other than that of departments of English on American
campuses.

However, those who define postmodernism as a semi-populist reaction against modernism, with its accompanying left-wing political
engagement and a greater simplicity of form and of intertextual reference, provide a grid for understanding the innovations in literary culture which occurred in the regions. The regional postmodern (the
Sixties Poets, the Poets of Decolonization, the new theatre of Scotland
in the 1970s) is a literature of protest and resistance, of vitalism, and of
mockery and insult. It joys in the picaresque and the ludic; it declares

transgression to be a positive good; and it proclaims the existence and the importance of liminal 'new social movements' (in Jameson's terminology) and class and ethnic minorities. Once again, these cultural events are neither unique to the regions nor to be explained only in postcolonial terms. And, at the same time, they contribute to the worldwide phenomenon of postmodernism and of the immediate contemporary, helping to nuance and to enrich theories based uniquely on the American or Parisian cultural scene.

Postcolonial theory provides an approach to the writings and writers of people formerly colonized, having attained national independence yet where the colonial trace remains and the writers (and the people) undergo a form of cultural hybridity or *métissage*. The 'post' in postcolonial can be read as 'coming after' or 'supplanting' or 'contesting.' This approach has been applied almost exclusively to external colonies where the writers utilize the language of the colonial power – for example, French and English.

One of the purposes of this book is to explore the validity of employing the approach to internal colonies such as Scotland, Brittany, and the Occitan lands and where writers utilize the colonized's native languages, to wit Scots, Breton, and Occitan. The notion can be justified by any number of reasons including the historical fact that, from the 1960s on as a general practice and sporadically for decades previously, writers in the regions themselves used the colonial analogy, and not only as a metaphor but as a slogan. For many among them, their land and their people endure colonization to the same extent and with the same result as India and Nigeria or Senegal and Morocco. In addition, as was stated in the chapter on postmodernism, the post-1968 writers claim identification with and loyalty to the emerging peoples of the Third World. For these reasons – reasons of history – the self-assertion of a neglected culture cannot entirely be separated from the polemic of an oppressed political minority.

Any number of themes that dominate postcolonial literature also find a place in these literatures of Western Europe. The decline of the crofter culture in *Sunset Song* corresponds to the misery of the peasant class in *La Grava sul camin* or *L'Enterrament a Sabres*. The potential and actual (subsequent) enslavement of an urban proletariat and urban tradesmen is developed in *Grey Granite*, *Itron Varia Garmez*, and *La Festa*. Similar conditions thematize rural dramas by Helias and the urban dramas by Bryden, McMillan, and McGrath. In all cases the evils of modernity and the evils of capitalism are massively augmented by the fact that the capitalist harbingers of modernity come from elsewhere – Paris or London – and speak their own tongue. The intellectual or the artist is caught between these competing worlds – the past and the present, the oppressed and the oppressor, the marginal and the centre – and is implacably doomed to alienation. Finally, the alienation is always perceived to be, in part, linguistic and cultural. The language and culture of Scotland, Brittany, and Occitania are themselves degraded by the upper classes or the administrative machinery or the military or simply the spirit of the times, all of which are emanations of the colonist culture emanating from those absent centres, London and Paris. The intellectual's alienation therefore focuses on the language and culture, and on his struggle to retain an identity, which so often ends in failure. This is, straightforwardly or symbolically, the archetypal adventure (Iliad and Odyssey) of the Drunk Man (MacDiarmid), Colquohoun the minister (Gibbon) and Brand the builder (Scott), Hemon's mad doctor and Glanndour's navigator, Delavouët's prince, Lafont's writers, and Forêt's scholar.

Finally, the three languages share in the development of themes which particularize their situation as old cultural and territorial entities included in the all-encompassing (colonialist) French or British state. For all the repudiation of folklore and of sentimental nostalgia, the poets and also the novelists evoke in loving terms the land and the sea, which, poetically, archetypally, symbolize Scotland, Brittany, Provence, and Gascony. Human entities – the farm, the family, and the village – play a similar role even though they are subject to modernist-oriented demystification. The cultural past – the troubadours, Arthurian romance, and Enlightenment Edinburgh – or the political, historical past of resistance exemplified in figures such as Raymond VII, James VI, and Fontanella are the discovery of a quest for cultural roots. Finally, in old Christian lands where the faith of the West has persevered longer than in London and Paris, we find two great Christian poets: Maodez Glanndour and Bernard Manciet. The absence of a comparable luminary in Scotland can perhaps be explained by the fact that the Lallans writers blame Presbyterianism for having unleashed a plague of ills on Scotland and – imported from abroad with its service and scriptures composed in English – having contributed to the decline of the Scottish language and culture.

Minority literatures, even when they cultivate the standard high-culture European genres, arrive at fascinating hybrids which express a postcolonial vision. Such are realist novels treating local concerns and with a local message, romances with their own powerful local reality, utopias and dystopias, a theatre of retrospection/aspiration, and the most dense, abstruse poetry which veils and also reveals mysteries of the new subjectivity and its culture. This is, indeed, territorialization of the imaginary. It is also a fact, as Boehmer argues, that twentieth-century colonized writers (in, say, Africa or India) share fundamental traits with the giants of European modernism.[5] They write texts of exile and alienation, rebel against the establishment, seek identity and new cultural myths, and endure a world-view of fragmentation and distortion. The European minority literatures also testify to the inherent modernity of postcolonial writing and to the shared, global construct of our twentieth-century artistic culture, which proclaims global displacement and transculturation.

One of the dangers of postcolonial theory – actually of most contemporary approaches – is the temptation to reductionism. A number of scholars, using the postcolonial grid, arrive at the same predictable conclusions. These include condemnation of the colonial culture including even the English and French languages, and condemnation of those 'native' writers who, abandoning the local, seek assimilation and become, so to speak, English or French in their writing or in their personal lives. Also, no less categorical is the praise for postcolonial writers torn between the two worlds, more or less aware of their *métissage* and desperately seeking to constitute a viable space in between or partaking of the two worlds. We are told of how, writing in the gaps, they displace, deconstruct, and subvert colonial hegemony by elaborating discursive codes of resistance and abrogate power by negotiating their own identity paradigms.

My conviction is that, with a Haitian or a Breton poet, an Indian or a Scottish novelist, there is no place for judgment based upon whether or not the writer's personal ideology or mode of life adheres to what is currently in fashion on American campuses. Furthermore, although a number of the minority European writers (including some of the greatest, MacDiarmid and Hemon among others) themselves hated the perceived colonial hegemony and, in a sense, genuinely hated England or France, this stance is now largely out of date in the minority cultures. It would be a pity for me or any other outsider to adopt the now surpassed animus of decades ago and to castigate *cum saeva indignatione* England and France, their languages, and their cultures.

A sophisticated postcolonial theory makes us aware of such temptations and also of the phenomenon of nativism among the postcolonial peoples themselves. Nativism occurs when the postcolonial writer or politician, having accepted the binomial opposition between centre and margin, responds to it by simply reversing the value judgment and exalting the margin. The danger is, of course, reverse ethnocentrism, which can be as provincial, exclusionist, and doctrinaire as the original colonial stereotype. As a philosophy of history the problem can be stated thus. The Third-Republic, Jacobin vision of the provinces goes something like this: the provinces had a sort of independent existence prior to union with France, upon which they ceased to exist except in so far as they shared the same unique French identity. This is a good thing. And all efforts at establishing regional identity or semi-autonomy have to be considered nostalgic or reactionary or simply eccentric. The Whig view of British history is remarkably similar. Today, most progressive and reasonably well informed intellectuals understand that the Third-Republic and Whig philosophies of history are inherently flawed. The great modernists in the regions reacted against these flawed doctrines. However, some of them created the mirror-image – a radical, independentist vision from the other side – which is no less flawed. This vision presumes a totally independent Scottish, Breton, or Occitan state(s) or kingdom(s) at some time in the distant past, preferably the Middle Ages, grounded in or emanating from a unified Scottish, Breton, or Occitan nation. This kingdom or nation manifested traits – democracy, civility, tolerance, a lay society – well in advance of the French and the English. It was a good thing. Then, upon invasion and subjugation by the colonial power, all changed for the worse, ending in cultural, even physical genocide, perpetuated up to and including today.

We recognize today that the domination of London and Paris brought benefits as well as ills to the regional cultures, and that the ills themselves were determined more often by factors of history and geography than by the consciously evil, hostile intentions of the enemy. It is false to assume that the minority people in its totality hated the French or the English throughout their history, and that a major concern of intellectuals or the masses throughout the history was to achieve independence from the French or the English. Exploitation there was and is, intolerance there was and is, and the loss of precious languages and cultures there was and is. Yet to displace upon the past an idyllic, prelapsarian vision of wholeness, which then evolves into contemporary decadence, is just as false and just as archetypally mythical as to displace upon the past demonic barbarism, which then evolves into contemporary progress.

Nativism also occurs when the minority writers in languages of less wide diffusion search for literary roots to rival those of the dominant cultures. Scotland is relatively free of such excesses, although Mac-Diarmid, in his later, English-speaking years, claimed the Celtic muse to be the *fons et origo* of just about everything, given that, *dixit* MacDiarmid, the first creators in Central Asia – Georgians and Sumerians – were in fact Celts. In the South of France it was the practice to exaggerate the importance of the troubadours, whereas in Brittany a number of writers, including Helias, assume that medieval Arthurian romance, because it treats Celtic themes and contains Celtic motifs, or because, in French, it is called *le roman breton*, must be Celtic and Breton, and therefore that the works of Marie de France, Beroul, Thomas, and Chrétien are residues from the Breton.

Questions of cultural priority are of more than pedantic interest. It is significant that the minority writers and their colleagues should reclaim their cultural as well as political history and that they should create cultural myths in order to do so.[6] However, from a postcolonial perspective, it is significant that Lafont and others launched the myth that the Middle Ages and the Baroque are quintessentially southern, manifestations of the Occitan spirit, just as Jean Markale, Yann Brekilien, and others launched the myth of a Celtic Middle Ages and the myth that the Middle Ages are quintessentially Breton. They did so in part because the regions did enjoy a rich cultural flowering during those periods and did make a contribution to European culture. They also willed a counterforce to French classicism. Just as with the Romantic predecessors, the very parameters of their discourse were shaped by Paris, in response to Paris. By accepting the Parisian myths of French rationality and French classicism (false myths which fail to account for ten centuries of Frenchness), they then created the mirror shadows of Breton and Occitan poeticity and a Celtic or troubadouresque Middle Ages. A roughly similar cultural phenomenon occurred in Scotland and Ireland vis-à-vis London, and, vis-à-vis the West generally, with the writers of Négritude.

It is important, in studying the minority literature, not to demonize the majority literature and not to ignore it either. In the course of this book I have not had the space to explore the extent to which the minority writing is closely involved in and influenced by immediate contemporary writing in the majority language. Efforts to construct a history of Occitan letters, for example, as a self-contained whole, without referring to the broader French context, are doomed to semi-failure at the very least. Throughout history the minority writers are influenced by, and often consciously imitate, the latest trends in the (foreign) capital. Throughout history, they cultivate, in Occitan terms, the *talvera*, the margins in the field left over from the first ploughing, that is, the margins in the literary space that the central culture neglects.[7] In other terms, the minority writers exist in a situation of literary diglossia vis-à-vis the dominant literature, occupying the vacant stylistic registers and accepting or reacting to the norms set by the dominant literature. Indeed, the terminology of literary history and of periodization, including modernism and postmodernism, is borrowed from the annals of the majority culture. Of course, the minority cultures will seek to combat this dependency – by designating Henryson and Dunbar as the Makars and not as Scottish Chaucerians, or by calling what might have been designated as the Occitan Ronsardians the Baroque of Toulouse.

Scottish criticism has made the most advances in considering the literature(s) of Scotland as a totality, in some form of symbiosis, and in recognizing that all texts by the Scots, writing at home or abroad, in English, Scots, Gaelic, and, for that matter, Latin, comprise that totality.[8] Only in the last twenty years or so has there been recognition of a Breton literature made up of both francophone and celtophone texts, although, up to now, most of the attention has been paid to writing in French.[9] The notion of the literatures in an Occitan domain ('l'espace occitan') has yet to be broached. I am convinced, however, that light can be shed on the majority and minority cultures through a nuanced, problematic comparatism, in this area as in so many others.

To cite just one example, specialists in modern Scottish literature in English, and in modern Breton literature of French expression, comment on the peculiar sense of alienation which characterizes writings in English or French which are, of course, English yet also Scottish and French yet also Breton. Terms such as pluralism, marginality, dissidence, *métissage*, and hybridity are used to characterize such writing. They are also used to characterize the postcolonial literatures of Africa and the Caribbean. To a very real extent, the same situation and the same terminology are apposite for Europeans writing in the minority languages. For them also tension, diglossia, and *métissage* make up the air they breathe and the water they drink. In addition, they live the passion of their language, ever struggling with a tongue which is and is not theirs, is and is not that of their people, is and most definitely is not fully integrated into social existence. For that reason among others, theirs will always be a problematic writing in which, as Gardy has speculated concerning Occitan, they create their own universe, in between chaos and apocalypse, to replace a world no longer there or which, in fact, never was.

For three quarters of a century now in Scotland, for the past three decades in Brittany, writers in the national tongue (English, French) emphasize their Scottishness and their Keltiegezh.[10] Not only do they explore local themes. Theirs is a literature of passion and anguish as they seek out their roots, their psychic loyalties, and their poetic self grounded in the land and the sea. Now, although the writers in the minority languages have exploited the same or comparable thematics, going back to *A Drunk Man Looks at the Thistle*, they do so often with greater reticence and with more than a little self-deprecation, which can take the form of Horatian *urbanitas*. Today we find more and more instances of a minority writer treating subject-matter which has no direct relevance to his land and culture, for instance a plot which could occur anywhere. Such is the case for certain poems by Robert Garioch and Tom Scott, and for novels and *nouvelles* by Robert Lafont and Per Denez. In all three cultures this is a current open to the younger generation. It is as if the act of writing in Scots, Breton, and Occitan suffices to establish one's credentials and one's identity. It is also the case that some minority writers, because the modernist program required a national literature open to all facets of modernity, European in all respects, believe that non-local, non-regional universality has to be their ultimate goal. 'Let the francophones and anglophones embrace the standing stones; we shall write of love and lust, of war and death, of man and God!' One aspect of liberation from the *talvera* would be to write in all genres and on all subjects – all over the field, now their field – as part of a totalized literary structure, an autonomous system no longer dependent on London or Paris, literature as their own institution shaped according to their own will. Therefore, their literature will be most truly itself when freed from the local dialect and from the local colour of the author or his immediate public. They speak from the margins without fetishizing marginality, and they strive for heterogeneity, not a simplified identity or opposition. Theirs will be an authentic cosmopolitan civilization, not ethnicism or provincialism. As Staines writes so tellingly of the literary experience in Canada, a formerly colonial literature attains maturity when it can surpass its own obsession with the here and the there, the marginal and the central, and simply write on anything and everything as part of a global whole.[11]

In modern Lowland Scots, Breton, and Occitan, intellectuals write for other intellectuals, and teachers for other teachers. The modernist reforms, plus the increase of literacy in the national languages, have had one unfortunate though inevitable consequence: that the literature is cut off from the shepherds, artisans, small farmers, and urban labourers who still speak the language (more or less) but cannot or do not read it. The decline in literacy in and daily social use of the vernaculars is the inevitable outcome of a number of socio-economic forces over which the minority writers have no control. It is a fact that, in our modern, industrial, technological, and transnational world, no folk culture can survive except at the level of folklore preservation societies. It is also a fact that the modernity which made a place for and commanded the high culture of modernism, because of its democracy, its mass culture, its media, and its cosmopolitan progress, also threatens modernist high culture in all its domains, including the literature of the lesser-used languages. The present situation – going back a number of decades – offers the paradox of literature flourishing at its greatest as the language itself is in the process of dying or, at least, is at its nadir. This means that more and better writers write while fewer people (including readers) speak, and therefore that as the writers find themselves severed from the living dialect base of the language, they have to rely upon the high-culture tongue – synthetic, plastic, chemical – of their own making, and can also rely upon and incorporate all of world literature available to them. They create their own literary universe to replace the concrete one which is collapsing around them. The pessimists, including some Occitans, almost take pride in the prediction of a *langue d'Oc* uniquely literary in function, freed forever from the triviality of everyday communication,[12] whereas the optimists, including some Bretons, predict that the call for identity among the young and regular, consistent social use of the language by committed circles of intellectuals, including newcomers to the language (the *néo-Bretons*), will succeed in maintaining a residue (say 100,000) for the preservation of the language and its culture.

Whatever the future, which, because it is the future, remains uncertain and problematic, we have now, in the present and in the recent past, the phenomenon of an outpouring of poetry, fictional prose, and theatre of remarkable quality and, all things considered, of remarkable quantity as well. These are beautiful texts that deserve to be known and read, and to join the concert of nations for which they were written. These are great books that make their specific, unique contribution to the three-thousand-year tradition of great books in the West. They are the legacy of individual men and women – creative, artistic, imaginative, idealistic, eccentric, fanatical, stubborn, tortured, neurotic, and eminently lovable human beings who gave their all to the cause and ever fought the good fight. They did so in the face of superhuman obstacles, and they overcame them.

A museum culture, some will say, and a museum culture it is, in some respects – yet not at all in others; and the literatures in classical Chinese, Japanese, Sanskrit, Arabic, and Persian retained aspects of museum culture for centuries and were no worse for it. One trait of a museum culture, and also of postcolonial writing, is the omnipresence of the themes of death and of apocalypse. The metaphor, the allegory actually, is transparent. Many, including a number of writers, are obsessed with the decline and fall of the cultures on which they have staked their life's work. Many believe that the minority tongues will, at some time in the not too distant future, cease to be living languages – that is, no one will have Braid Scots, Brezhoneg, and Occitan as a mother tongue. That this could happen to the languages of the troubadours, and of the Makars, and of Brittany, so rich in history and culture, has, for many of us, a tragic dimension. Fortunately, for them and for us, the writers 'do not go gently into that good night' but 'rage against the dying of the light.' We can hear their rage and their swansong, and behold their Midsummer Night fire with wonder and with love. That also is the human condition.

NOTES

INTRODUCTION

1 See, for example, in the collection *Universitat occitana d'estiu: Actes de l'Université d'été 1994*, ed. Jòrdi Peladan, vol. 1 (Nîmes: M.A.R.P.O.C.-I.E.O., 1995): Helen O'Murchú, 'Les langues de l'Europe,' pp. 7–22; Georg Kremnitz, 'Europa e las lengas minoritarias, cambis recents,' pp. 47–53; and Joëlle Peyriller, 'La Charte des langues régionales et minoritaires,' pp. 54–61.

2 *Barzaz-Breiz: Chants populaires de la Bretagne, par le vicomte Hersart de la Villemarqué*, 1st ed. 1839 (Paris: Librairie Académique Perrin, 1963).

3 William Calin, *In Defense of French Poetry: An Essay in Revaluation* (University Park: Pennsylvania State University Press, 1987), chap. 7. See also Harold Bloom, *The Anxiety of Influence: A Theory of Poetry* (New York: Oxford University Press, 1973), and W. Jackson Bate, *The Burden of the Past and the English Poet* (Cambridge, Mass.: Harvard University, Belknap Press, 1970).

4 One among a number of examples, Pierre Jakez Hélias, *Le Quêteur de mémoire: Quarante ans de recherche sur les mythes et la civilisation bretonne* (Paris: Plon, 1990), p. 289: 'Pas de littérature pour la défendre ni l'illustrer.'

5 I discuss these matters at greater length in 'Suggestions de lecture pour nos textes occitans modernes,' *Bulletins de l'Association Internationale d'Etudes Occitanes* 7 (1991): 40–53.

6 For a selection of items, see the bibliography, pp. 349–51.

SCOTLAND

1 C.M. Grieve, *Albyn, or Scotland and the Future* (London: Kegan Paul, Trench, Trubner, 1927).

2 Hugh MacDiarmid, *At the Sign of the Thistle: A Collection of Essays* (London: Stanley Nott, [1934]).

3 Hugh MacDiarmid, *Burns Today and Tomorrow* (Edinburgh: Castle Wynd, 1959).

4 See Hamish Henderson, 'Flytings Galore: MacDiarmid v. The Folkies,' *Cencrastus* 49 (Autumn 1994): 15–25.

5 See Douglas Young, *'Plastic Scots' and the Scottish Literary Tradition: An Authoritative Introduction to a Controversy* (Glasgow: Maclellan, 1947).

6 [J.K. Annand] 'Editorial,' *Lallans* 1 (Mairtinmas 1973): 2.

7 For example, *Lines Review* 9 (August 1955): 29–31 and *Lallans* 2 (Whitsunday 1974): 4–5.

8 *Lallans* 24 (Whitsuntid 1985): 18–20.

9 David Purves, 'A Scots Orthography,' *Scottish Literary Journal* Supplement 9 (Spring 1979): 62–76; J. Derrick McClure, 'The Spelling of Scots: A Phoneme-Based System,' *Scottish Literary Journal* Supplement 12 (Summer 1980): 25–9. See also McClure, 'The Concept of Standard Scots,' *Chapman* 23–4 (Spring 1979): 90–9.

10 For histories of Scottish literature that discuss the Renaissance and its aftermath, see especially John Speirs, *The Scots Literary Tradition: An Essay in Criticism*, 1940, rev. 2nd ed. (London: Faber and Faber, 1962); Kurt Wittig, *The Scottish Tradition in Literature* (Edinburgh: Oliver and Boyd, 1958); Maurice Lindsay, *History of Scottish Literature*, 1977, rev. ed. (London: Hale, 1992); Alan Bold, *Modern Scottish Literature* (London: Longman, 1983); Roderick Watson, *The Literature of Scotland* (London: Macmillan, 1984); *The History of Scottish Literature*, vol. 4: *Twentieth Century*, ed. Cairns Craig (Aberdeen: Aberdeen University Press, 1987). On the situation of the Scots language, David Murison, *The Guid Scots Tongue* (Edinburgh: Blackwood, 1977); Billy Kay, *Scots: The Mither Tongue*, rev. ed. (Darvel, Ayrshire: Alloway, 1993); Tom McArthur, 'Scots and Southron,' chap. 6 of his *The English Languages* (Cambridge: Cambridge University Press, 1998), pp. 138–59. McArthur observes that Scots is now recognized by the European Bureau of Lesser Used Languages. A number of article collections from the late 1970s to the mid-1980s had a major impact. These include *Languages of Scotland*, ed. A.J. Aitken and Tom McArthur (Edinburgh: Chambers, 1979); and, edited by J. Derrick McClure, *The Scots Language: Planning for Modern Usage* (Edinburgh: Ramsay Head, 1980); *The Scots Language in Education* (Association for Scottish Literary Studies: Occasional Papers No. 3); *Scotland and the Lowland Tongue* (Aberdeen: Aberdeen University Press, 1983).

11 Hugh MacDiarmid, *Complete Poems*, ed. Michael Grieve and W.R. Aitken, vol. 1 (Manchester: Carcanet, 1993), pp. 81–167. The bibliography on MacDiarmid in general, and on *A Drunk Man* in particular, is immense. The reader should consult the selection of items in my Scots bibliography, pp. 351–62.

12 For a feminist demystification of the text, Aileen Christianson, 'Flyting with *A Drunk Man*,' *Scottish Affairs* 5 (Autumn 1993): 126–35; consult also the very

intelligent study by Christopher Whyte, 'Gender and Sexuality in *A Drunk Man*,' ibid., 136–46.

13 On the imagery of the thistle and the moon, among others consult Catherine Kerrigan, *'Whaur Extremes Meet': The Poetry of Hugh MacDiarmid, 1920–1934* (Edinburgh: Thin, Mercat, 1983), chap. 9; Nancy K. Gish, *Hugh MacDiarmid: The Man and His Work* (London: Macmillan, 1984), chap. 3; Harvey Oxenhorn, *Elemental Things: The Poetry of Hugh MacDiarmid* (Edinburgh: Edinburgh University Press, 1984), chap. 3; and John Baglow, *Hugh MacDiarmid: The Poetry of Self* (Kingston and Montreal: McGill-Queen's University Press, 1987), chap. 3.

14 Found in G. Gregory Smith, *Scottish Literature: Character and Influence* (London: Macmillan, 1919), p. 4.

15 As in Roderick Watson, 'The Symbolism of *A Drunk Man Looks at the Thistle*,' in *Hugh MacDiarmid: A Critical Survey*, ed. Duncan Glen (Edinburgh: Scottish Academic Press, 1972), pp. 94–116, and in his subsequent studies; and Gish, *Hugh MacDiarmid*, pp. 73–4.

16 For an excellent study of the problem of meaning in *A Drunk Man*, Christopher Whyte, 'Construction of Meaning in MacDiarmid's "Drunk Man,"' *Studies in Scottish Literature* 23 (1988): 199–238.

17 As in Kenneth Buthlay, *Hugh MacDiarmid*, rev. ed. (Edinburgh: Scottish Academic Press, 1982), chap. 3; Roderick Watson, *MacDiarmid*, rev. ed. (Milton Keynes: Open University Press, 1985); Oxenhorn, *Elemental Things*; and Baglow, *Hugh MacDiarmid*.

18 *Complete Poems*, vol. 1, pp. 179–294.

19 For good readings of *Circumjack*, the books cited above, and John Herdman, 'Hugh MacDiarmid's *To Circumjack Cencrastus*,' *Akros* 34–5 (August 1977): 63–75; Kenneth Buthlay, 'The Scotched Snake,' in *The Age of MacDiarmid: Essays on Hugh MacDiarmid and His Influence on Contemporary Scotland*, ed. P.H. Scott and A.C. Davis (Edinburgh: Mainstream, 1980), pp. 122–56; Margery McCulloch, 'The Undeservedly Broukit Bairn: Hugh MacDiarmid's *To Circumjack Cencrastus*,' *Studies in Scottish Literature* 17 (1982): 165–85; and W.N. Herbert, *To Circumjack MacDiarmid: The Poetry and Prose of Hugh MacDiarmid* (Oxford: Clarendon Press, 1992), chap. 4.

20 Kerrigan, *'Whaur Extremes Meet*,' chap. 11; and Herbert, *To Circumjack MacDiarmid*.

21 *Complete Poems*, vol. 1, pp. 311–14.

22 *Complete Poems*, vol. 2, pp. 735–889, 903–99, 1001–35, 1161–93. For a sympathetic reading of these texts, Alan Bold, *MacDiarmid: Christopher Murray Grieve, A Critical Biography* (Amherst: University of Massachusetts Press, 1988), chap. 14; and Alan Riach, *Hugh MacDiarmid's Epic Poetry* (Edinburgh:

Edinburgh University Press, 1991). For *A Drunk Man* as epic, Christopher Whyte, 'MacDiarmid's *A Drunk Man Looks at the Thistle* as National Epic,' *Coexistence* 29 (1992): 163–75.

23 On this general topic, John MacQueen, 'The Scottish Literary Renaissance and Late Medieval Scottish Poetry,' *Studies in Scottish Literature* 26 (1991): 543–55.

24 Duncan Glen, *Hugh MacDiarmid (Christopher Murray Grieve) and the Scottish Renaissance* (Edinburgh: Chambers, 1964) remains an insightful overview of MacDiarmid and his impact on the Lallans Makars. For excellent surveys, consult Alexander Scott, 'The MacDiarmid Makars,' *Akros* 19 (August 1972): 9–30; the essays on Scottish poetry from the 1920s through to the 1970s in *Akros* 28 (August 1975); Alastair Mackie, 'Change and Continuity in Modern Scots Poetry,' *Akros* 33 (April 1977): 13–40; Alan Bold, 'After the Renaissance – The Reckoning,' *Chapman* 23–4 (Spring 1979): 12–21; Tom Hubbard, 'Reintegrated Scots: The Post-MacDiarmid Makars,' in Craig, *History of Scottish Literature*, pp. 179–93; and Barry Wood, 'Scots, Poets, and the City,' ibid., pp. 337–48.

25 D.M. Black, 'Poets of the Sixties – III: Robert Garioch,' *Lines Review* 23 (Spring 1967): 8–15; Roderick Watson, 'The Speaker in the Gairdens: The Poetry of Robert Garioch,' *Akros* 16 (April 1971): 69–76; Donald Campbell, 'Another Side to Robert Garioch, or, A Glisk of Near-forgotten Hell,' *Akros* 33 (April 1977): 47–52; Bold, 'After the Renaissance'; Raymond J. Ross, 'Edinburgh Grooves: Robert Garioch's Edinburgh,' *Cencrastus* 29 (Spring 1988): 6–8; Mario Relich, 'Scottish Tradition and Robert Garioch's Individual Talent,' *Lines Review* 136 (March 1996): 5–17. On his use of language, Graham Tulloch, 'Robert Garioch's Different Styles of Scots,' *Scottish Literary Journal* 12:1 (May 1985): 53–69, and Douglas Dunn, 'Cantraips and Trauchles: Robert Garioch and Scottish Poetry,' *Cencrastus* 43 (Autumn 1992): 37–43.

26 Robert Garioch, *Complete Poetical Works*, ed. Robin Fulton (Edinburgh: Macdonald, 1983): 'I was fair beat,' p. 85.

27 'And they were richt,' *Complete Poetical Works*, p. 84.

28 'Did ye see me?' *Complete Poetical Works*, p. 83.

29 *Complete Poetical Works*, pp. 6–8.

30 *Complete Poetical Works*, p. 28.

31 *Complete Poetical Works*, pp. 35–7.

32 Henri Bergson, *Le Rire: Essai sur la signification du comique*, 97th ed. (Paris: Presses Universitaires de France, 1950), p. 29.

33 *Complete Poetical Works*, pp. 18–25.

34 *Complete Poetical Works*, pp. 49–53.

35 *Complete Poetical Works*, pp. 54–67. On 'The Wire' and 'The Muir,' consult
    Sydney Tremayne, 'Robert Garioch,' *Akros* 47 (August 1981): 110–13; and
    James B. Caird, 'Robert Garioch – A Personal Appreciation,' *Scottish Literary
    Journal* 10:2 (December 1983): 68–78.

36 Sydney Goodsir Smith, *Collected Poems: 1941–1975* (London: Calder,
    1975).

37 Sydney Goodsir Smith, *The Wallace: A Triumph in Five Acts* (London: Calder,
    1985); *Carotid Cornucopius: Caird of the Cannon Gait and Voyeur of the Outlook
    Touer* (Edinburgh: Macdonald, 1964).

38 *Collected Poems*, pp. 101–4.

39 *Collected Poems*, pp. 217–29.

40 *Collected Poems*, pp. 147–87. Issues of genre and of source are treated exhaus-
    tively in Eric Gold, *Sydney Goodsir Smith's 'Under the Eildon Tree': An Essay* (Pre-
    ston: Akros, 1975).

41 The reader should also consult Alexander Scott, 'Sydney Goodsir Smith: The
    Art of Devilment,' *Akros* 10 (May 1969): 21–8, and 'Goodsir Smith's Master-
    piece: *Under the Eildon Tree*,' in *For Sydney Goodsir Smith* (Edinburgh: Mac-
    donald, 1975), pp. 11–22; Thomas Crawford, 'The Poetry of Sydney Goodsir
    Smith,' *Studies in Scottish Literature* 7 (1969–70): 40–59; Kenneth Buthlay,
    'Sydney Goodsir Smith: Makar Macironical,' *Akros* 31 (August 1976): 46–56;
    James B. Caird, 'Sydney Goodsir Smith,' *Chapman* 26 (Spring 1980): 14–19;
    Thom Nairn, '"A route maist devious": Sydney Goodsir Smith and Edin-
    burgh,' *Cencrastus* 33 (Spring 1989): 6–9; and the pieces collected in *The Auk
    Remembered*, ed. Neil Mathers (Montrose: Corbie, 1995).

42 Among the latter is to be found the poet and academic Alexander Scott. For
    decades Tom Scott and Alexander Scott exchanged hostile reviews, essays,
    and letters to the editor. There is nothing in the annals of Breton and Occi-
    tan comparable to this magnificent, lifelong saga of flyting.

43 *The Collected Shorter Poems of Tom Scott* (London: Agenda and Edinburgh:
    Chapman, 1993), pp. 47–64 and pp. 68–82.

44 *Collected Shorter Poems*, pp. 102–30.

45 Alan Bold, 'Scott the Makar,' *Scotia Review* 13–14 (August–November, 1976):
    3–14.

46 Also, on *Brand the Builder*, Thomas Crawford, 'Tom Scott: From Apocalypse
    to Brand,' *Akros* 31 (August 1976): 57–69; Brian Murdoch, 'Tom Scott's
    "Brand the Builder,"' *Akros* 51 (October 1983): 34–6; Christopher Whyte,
    'Tom Scott: An Imaged World,' *Chapman* 47–8 (Spring 1987): 7–13; William
    Oxley, 'Poetry as the Heightened Vernacular: Tom Scott's *Brand the Builder*,'
    Agenda 30:4 and 31:1 (Winter-Spring 1993): 142–7.

47 *Collected Shorter Poems*, pp. 30–41.

48 John Herdman, 'Towards New Jerusalem: The Poetry of Tom Scott,' *Akros* 16 (April 1971): 43–9, especially 46.

49 See Walter Perrie, 'Tom Scott and the Long Narrative Tradition,' *Scotia Review* 13–14 (August-November 1976): 23–30; Raymond J. Ross, 'The Real Tom Scott,' *Chapman* 47–8 (Spring 1987): 17–23; and in the special Tom Scott issue of *Agenda* 30:4 and 31:1 (Winter-Spring 1993): Thom Nairn, 'Out of Darkness Coming: Some Notes on Tom Scott and Hugh MacDiarmid': 148–64; William Neill, 'Tom Scott and the Scots Tongue': 96–103.

50 Robert McLellan, *Linmill Stories* (Edinburgh: Canongate, 1990); *The New Testament in Scots*, trans. William Laughton Lorimer (Edinburgh: Southside, 1983).

51 James Kelman, *How Late It Was, How Late* (London: Secker and Warburg, 1994); Irvine Welsh, *Trainspotting* (London: Secker and Warburg, 1993).

52 Books on Gibbon include Ian S. Munro, *Leslie Mitchell: Lewis Grassic Gibbon* (Edinburgh: Oliver and Boyd, 1966); Douglas F. Young, *Beyond the Sunset: A Study of James Leslie Mitchell (Lewis Grassic Gibbon)* (Aberdeen: Impulse, 1973); Douglas Gifford, *Neil M. Gunn and Lewis Grassic Gibbon* (Edinburgh: Oliver and Boyd, 1983); William K. Malcolm, *A Blasphemer and Reformer: A Study of James Leslie Mitchell / Lewis Grassic Gibbon* (Aberdeen: Aberdeen University Press, 1984); Ian Campbell, *Lewis Grassic Gibbon* (Edinburgh: Scottish Academic Press, 1985); Uwe Zagratzki, *Libertäre und utopische Tendenzen im Erzählwerk James Leslie Mitchells (Lewis Grassic Gibbons)* (Frankfurt am Main: Peter Lang, 1991); Peter Whitfield, *Grassic Gibbon and His World* (Aberdeen: Aberdeen Journals, 1994). Also, Francis Russell Hart, *The Scottish Novel: A Critical Survey* (London: Murray, 1978), chap. 4.

53 Kurt Wittig, *The Scottish Tradition in Literature*, p. 333; John Burns, 'Lewis Grassic Gibbon and *A Scots Quair*,' *Chapman* 23–4 (Spring 1979): 22–7; Isobel Murray, 'Novelists of the Renaissance,' in Craig, *History of Scottish Literature*, pp. 103–17.

54 Ian Campbell, 'The Grassic Gibbon Style,' in *Studies in Scottish Fiction: Twentieth Century*, ed. Joachim Schwend and Horst W. Drescher (Frankfurt am Main: Peter Lang, 1990), pp. 271–87, especially 272.

55 Lewis Grassic Gibbon, *Sunset Song* (Edinburgh: Canongate, 1988).

56 Graham Trengove, 'Who Is You? Grammar and Grassic Gibbon,' *Scottish Literary Journal* 2:2 (December 1975): 47–62; and Campbell, *Lewis Grassic Gibbon*, pp. 59–63. Also, Isobel Murray, 'Action and Narrative Stance in *A Scots Quair*,' in *Literature of the North*, ed. David Hewitt and Michael Spiller (Aberdeen: Aberdeen University Press, 1983), pp. 109–20; and Glenda Norquay, 'Voices in Time: *A Scots Quair*,' *Scottish Literary Journal* 11:1 (May 1984): 57–68.

57 Lewis Grassic Gibbon, *Cloud Howe* (Edinburgh: Canongate, 1988); Lewis
    Grassic Gibbon, *Grey Granite* (Edinburgh: Canongate, 1990).

58 Among others, Gifford, *Neil M. Gunn*; Malcolm, *A Blasphemer*; Campbell,
    Lewis Grassic Gibbon; Ian [A.] Bell, 'Lewis Grassic Gibbon's Revolutionary
    Romanticism,' in Schwend, *Studies in Scottish Fiction*, pp. 257–70.

59 Cairns Craig, 'The Body in the Kit Bag: History and the Scottish Novel,' *Cen-
    crastus* 1 (Autumn 1979): 18–22, and chap. 2 of his *Out of History: Narrative
    Paradigms in Scottish and English Culture* (Edinburgh: Polygon, 1996). Recent
    studies of Grassic Gibbon's politics include Keith Dixon, 'Letting the Side
    Down: Some Remarks on James Leslie Mitchell's Vision of History,' *Etudes
    écossaises* 1 (1992): 273–81; and John Manson, 'Hugh MacDiarmid and Lewis
    Grassic Gibbon's Politics,' *Cencrastus* 50 (Winter 1994): 39–42.

60 For example, Jack Mitchell, 'The Struggle for the Working-Class Novel in
    Scotland, 1900–1939,' *Zeitschrift für Anglistik und Amerikanistik* 21 (1973):
    384–413; Roy Johnson, 'Lewis Grassic Gibbon and *A Scots Quair*: Politics in
    the Novel,' in *The 1930s: A Challenge to Orthodoxy*, ed. John Lucas (Sussex:
    Harvester, 1978), pp. 42–58; H. Gustav Klaus, 'Socialist Fiction in the 1930s:
    Some Preliminary Observations,' ibid., pp. 13–41; D.M.E. Roskies, 'Lan-
    guage, Class, and Radical Perspective in *A Scots Quair*,' *Zeitschrift für Anglistik
    und Amerikanistik* 29 (1981): 142–53.

61 Among others, Munro, *Leslie Mitchell*; Young, *Beyond the Sunset*; Gifford, *Neil
    M. Gunn*; Patricia J. Wilson, 'Freedom and God: Some Implications of the
    Key Speech in *A Scots Quair*,' *Scottish Literary Journal* 7:2 (December 1980):
    55–79; Deirdre Burton, 'A Feminist Reading of Lewis Grassic Gibbon's *A
    Scots Quair*,' in *The British Working-Class Novel in the Twentieth Century*, ed. Jer-
    emy Hawthorn (London: Arnold, 1984), pp. 35–46; Keith Dixon, 'Rough
    Edges: The Feminist Representation of Women in the Writing of Lewis Gras-
    sic Gibbon,' in Schwend, *Studies in Scottish Fiction*, pp. 289–301; R.F. Clough,
    '*A Scots Quair*: Ewan's Rejection of Ellen,' *Scottish Literary Journal* 20:2
    (November 1993): 41–8.

62 Wittig, *The Scottish Tradition*, pp. 330–1. Also Young, *Beyond the Sunset*; Gif-
    ford, *Neil M. Gunn*; David Macaree, 'Myth and Allegory in Lewis Grassic Gib-
    bon's *A Scots Quair*,' *Studies in Scottish Literature* 2 (1964–65): 45–55.

63 Argued extremely well by Isobel Murray and Bob Tait, *Ten Modern Scottish
    Novels* (Aberdeen: Aberdeen University Press, 1984), pp. 10–31; also, Hart,
    The Scottish Novel; Malcolm, *A Blasphemer*; and Murray, 'Novelists of the
    Renaissance,' in Craig, *History of Scottish Literature*, pp. 103–17.

64 In the *Scottish Chapbook* 1 (August 1922): 27–8.

65 David Hutchison, *The Modern Scottish Theatre* (Glasgow: Molendinar, 1977), a
    most valuable study. Also, Wittig, *The Scottish Tradition*; John Kincaid, 'The

Scottish Dilemma: 50 Years of Prose and Drama,' *Chapman* 23–4 (Spring 1979): 28–31; Bold, *Modern Scottish Literature*; Lindsay, *History of Scottish Literature*.

66 John Thomas Low, 'Mid Twentieth Century Drama in Lowland Scots,' in McLure, *Scotland and the Lowland Tongue*, pp. 170–94; Randall Stevenson, 'Scottish Theatre, 1950–1980,' in Craig, *History of Scottish Literature*, pp. 349–67, and 'Recent Scottish Theatre: Dramatic Developments?' in *Scotland: Literature, Culture, Politics*, ed. Peter Zenzinger (Heidelberg: Winter, 1989), pp. 187–213. Above all, the essays in *Scottish Theatre since the Seventies*, ed. Randall Stevenson and Gavin Wallace (Edinburgh: Edinburgh University Press, 1996).

67 Donald Campbell, 'Robert McLellan: The Playwricht,' *Lallans* 10 (Whitsunday 1978): p. 15 – 'the Faither o the Modren Scots Drama.' See also Allan Leach, 'The High Purposes of Literature: Robert McLellan and His Work,' *Library Review* 23: 1–2 (Spring–Summer 1971): 3–11; Hutchison, *Modern Scottish Theatre*; J.K. Annand, 'Robert McLellan,' *Lallans* 25 (Mairtinmas 1985): 5–8; Donald Campbell, 'A Sense of Community: Robert McLellan, An Appreciation,' *Chapman* 43–4 (Spring 1986): 35–41.

68 Robert McLellan, *Jamie the Saxt: A Historical Comedy*, ed. Ian Campbell and Ronald D.S. Jack (London: Calder and Boyars, 1970); also in his *Collected Plays*, vol. 1 (London: John Calder and New York: Riverrun, 1981), pp. 61–161.

69 Robert McLellan, *The Flouers o Edinburgh: A Comedy of the Eighteenth Century in Three Acts*, in *Collected Plays*, pp. 163–242.

70 Robert McLellan, *The Hypocrite* (London: Calder and Boyars, 1970).

71 Donald Campbell, *The Jesuit: A Play* (Edinburgh: Harris, 1976); *Somerville the Soldier: A Play* (Edinburgh: Harris, 1978); *The Widows of Clyth: A Play* (Edinburgh: Harris, 1979).

72 Campbell also published two studies in the history of the theatre: *Playing for Scotland: A History of the Scottish Stage, 1715–1965* (Edinburgh: Mercat, 1996), and *A Brighter Sunshine: A Hundred Years of the Edinburgh Royal Lyceum Theatre* (Edinburgh: Polygon, 1983).

73 On Campbell as a dramatist, Owen Dudley Edwards, 'The Quest for Ogilvie,' *Chapman* 16 (Summer 1976): 38–48; Lindsay Paterson, 'Donald Campbell: Playwright in Search of a Method,' *Cencrastus* 6 (Autumn 1981): 6–8. Also, in Stevenson, *Scottish Theatre since the Seventies*, Paterson, 'Language and Identity on the Stage,' pp. 75–83, and Ian Brown, 'Plugged into History: The Sense of the Past in Scottish Theatre,' pp. 84–99; and, for a linguistic study, John Corbett, *Language and Scottish Literature: Scottish Language and Literature* (Edinburgh: Edinburgh University Press, 1997), pp. 100–3.

BRITTANY

1 Roparz Hemon, *La Langue bretonne et ses combats* (La Baule: Editions de Bretagne, 1947), pp. 97–8.

2 Roparz Hemon, *Ur Breizhad oc'h adkavout Breizh* (Brest: Al Liamm, 1972). For the first edition of *Eur Breizad* (1931), Roparz Hemon employed the then prevalent KLT orthography. On the rise of a modern literature in Breton, Abeozen / Fañch Elies / Jean-François-Marie Eliès, *Istor Lennegezh Vrezhonek an Amzer-vremañ* (Brest: Al Liamm, 1957); Per Denez, 'Modern Breton Literature,' in *Literature in Celtic Countries*, ed. J.E. Caerwyn Williams (Cardiff: University of Wales Press, 1971), pp. 111–36; Youenn Olier, *Istor hol lennegezh: 'Skol Walarn,'* 2 vols (Rennes: Imbourc'h, 1974–5); Fañch Morvannou and Yann-Ber Piriou, 'La littérature de langue bretonne au XXe siècle,' in *Histoire littéraire et culturelle de la Bretagne*, ed. Jean Balcou and Yves Le Gallo (Paris: Champion, 1987), vol. 3, pp. 175–252; *Roparz Hemon: 1900–1978*, ed. Yves Tymen (Lorient: Dalc'homp Soñj, 1990); René Galand, *Stratégie de la lecture* (New York: Peter Lang, 1990); Francis Favereau, *Littérature et écrivains bretonnants depuis 1945*, *Skol Vreizh* 20 (mars 1991).

3 Yann-Ber Piriou, *Défense de cracher par terre et de parler breton: Poèmes de combat (1950–1970)* (Paris: Oswald, 1971), p. 10.

4 Roparz Hemon and Olivier Mordrel, '*Gwalarn*: Premier et dernier manifeste de *Gwalarn* en langue française,' *Breiz Atao* 74 (février 1925): 524.

5 'Breizh-Uheliz hag ar Brezhoneg,' *Arvor* 3:107 (31 Genver 1943): 2.

6 '*Gwalarn* ... ha goude,' *Al Liamm* 170 (Mae-Mezheven 1975): 164–70, especially 166.

7 '*Gwalarn* ... ha goude': 170.

8 *La Langue bretonne et ses combats*, p. 90.

9 *Breiz Atao* 74 (février 1925): 524.

10 '*Arvor* sera un journal complet,' *Arvor* 1:5 (2 février 1941): 1.

11 'Lutte culturelle,' *Arvor* 1:20 (18 mai 1941): 1.

12 Cited, for example, by Piriou, *Défense de cracher par terre et de parler breton*, pp. 29–30.

13 'Attendrons-nous?' *Arvor* 1:2 (12 janvier 1941): 1.

14 'Kentel an darvoudou,' *Gwalarn* 136–7 (Mae–Mezeven 1941): 341–2.

15 On the history of Roparz Hemon and *Gwalarn* and their impact, consult the essays in Tymen, *Roparz Hemon: 1900–1978*, especially Yann Bouëssel du Bourg, 'Roparz Hemon et le journal *Arvor*,' pp. 43–71 and 'Framm Keltiek Breizh / L'Institut Celtique de Bretagne,' pp. 81–103; also the selection from Hemon's own prose, 'Roparz Hemon s'exprime,' ibid., pp. 133–58. Also Ronan Huon et al., *Gwalarn: Histoire d'un mouvement littéraire; Textes et docu-*

ments, 2 vols (Brest: Bibliothèque Municipale, 1989). Among the many articles on the topic, Per Denez, 'Gwalarn,' *Al Liamm* 20 (Mae–Mezheven 1950):
24–9, 'Kannadig Gwalarn,' *Hor Yezh* 131–2 (miz Meurzh 1980): 51–88, and
'Roparz Hemon ha "Brezhoneg ar Vugale,"' *Hor Yezh* 137 (miz Meurzh
1981): 37–56; Maodez Glanndour, 'Barzhoniezh maread Gwalarn,' *Al Liamm*
124 (Gwengolo–Here 1967): 423–33; Pierrette Kermoal, 'Lennegezh
w*Gwalarn,*' *Preder* 111 (Gwengolo 1968): 21–7, and '*Gwalarn* hag ar vojennouriezh hengeltiek: Youenn Drezen ha Roparz Hemon,' *Al Liamm* 190
(Gwengolo–Here 1978): 378–87; Vefa de Ballaing, 'L'influence de Gwalarn,'
Dalc'homp Soñj 24 (Diskar Amzer 1988): 11–13. See also the collection of
essays by Per Denez, Hemon's most prominent successor, *Yezh ha Bro: Pennadoù ha Studiadennoù* (Lesneven: Mouladurioù Hor Yezh, 1998). Also the negative judgment by Fañch Morvannou, 'Gouestlad gant ar brezhoneg e-pad 50
vloaz,' *Planedenn* 23 (Newez-Amzer 1985): 24–47. On the situation of the language, Jorj Gwegen, *La Langue bretonne face à ses oppresseurs* (Quimper: Nature
et Bretagne, 1975); Fañch Morvannou, *Le Breton: La jeunesse d'une vieille
langue* (Lannion: Presses Populaires de Bretagne, 1980); Per Denez et al.,
Permanence de la langue bretonne: De la linguistique à la psychanalyse (Rennes:
Institut Culturel de Bretagne, 1986); Hervé Abalain, *Destin des langues celtiques* (Paris: Ophrys, 1989); Elmar Ternes, 'The Breton Language,' in *The
Celtic Languages,* ed. Donald MacAulay (Cambridge: Cambridge University
Press, 1992), pp. 371–452; Eva Vetter, *Nicht mehr Bretonisch? Sprachkonflikt in
der ländischen Bretagne* (Frankfurt am Main: Peter Lang, 1997).

16 On Roparz Hemon, Olier, *Istor hol lennegezh,* vol. 1; the issue of *Al Liamm* 190
  (Gwengolo-Here 1978) devoted to Hemon, especially Kenan Kongar,
  'Roparz Hemon, hor mestr': 345–58; and the essays collected in Tymen,
  Roparz Hemon: 1900–1978, and in *Roparz Hemon: Kounioù hag hengoun lennegel
  ar Brezhoneg* (Baile Atha Cliath [Dublin]: Coiscéim, 1990), especially Per
  Denez, 'Roparz Hemon: kounioù,' pp. 8–27. Also, Maodez Glanndour,
  'En ur dreiñ follennoù va eñvor,' *Al Liamm* 191 (Du–Kerzu 1978): 429–37;
  Sylvia Morgan, 'Roparz Hemon: 1900–1978,' *Studia Celtica* 14–15 (1979–80):
  380–7; Lukian Raoul, *Geriadur ar skrivagnerien ha yezhourien vrezhonek, aet da
  anaon a-raok miz Meurzh 1992* (Brest: Al Liamm, 1992), pp. 321–5. For a list
  of Roparz Hemon's works, Per Penneg, 'Roll oberennoù Roparz Hemon,'
  Al Liamm 192–4 (Genver–Mezheven 1979): 34–47, 158–64, 227–37; 251
  (Du–Kerzu 1988): 375–85; 252–6 (Genver–Here 1989): 50–6, 144–7, 222–6,
  299–301.

17 Roparz Hemon, *Barzhonegoù* (Saint-Brieuc: Al Liamm, 1991).

18 *Barzhonegoù,* pp. 10–21.

19 Roparz Hemon adapted into Breton *Sir Gawain and the Green Knight* and used

the pseudonym 'Gawain' for a number of poems published in *Gwalarn* during the war.

20 *Barzhonegoù*, pp. 33–6.

21 *Barzhonegoù*, pp. 37–9.

22 *Barzhonegoù*, p. 124.

23 *Barzhonegoù*, pp. 91–100. On this text and the succeeding one, Galand, *Stratégie de la lecture*, pp. 189–90.

24 *Barzhonegoù*, pp. 101–10.

25 Consult 'Maodez Glanndour gwelet gant skolidi S.A.D.E.D.,' *Al Liamm* 114 (Genver–C'hwevrer 1966): 46–50; Yann Bouëssel du Bourg, 'L'abbé Loeiz ar Floc'h : Maodez Glanndour,' *Dalc'homp Soñj* 18 (Goañv 1987): 36–7, 42; Ronan Huon, 'Maodez Glanndour evel m'am eus e anavezet,' *Al Liamm* 240 (Genver–C'hwevrer 1987): 5–11; Reun ar C'halan, 'Stumm ha ster ar stourm speredel e *Komzoù bev*,' ibid., 12–17 and, in French, his *Stratégie de la lecture*, especially 'Forme et sens dans la poésie de Maodez Glanndour,' pp. 179–85, also 191–3; René Gorvan and Lena an Abad, 'Pennad-kaoz diwar-benn Maodez Glanndour ha *Komzoù bev*,' *Al Liamm* 299 (Du–Kerzu 1996): 453–62; Annaig Renault, 'Maodez Glanndour,' *Al Liamm* 302–3 (Mae-Eost 1997): 316–26.

26 Maodez Glanndour, *Imram*, in his *Komzoù bev* (*Living Speech*) (Brest: Al Liamm, 1985), pp. 143–90.

27 Maodez Glanndour, *Vijelez an deiz diwezhañ* (Brest: Al Liamm, 1978). No pagination.

28 Galand, *Stratégie de la lecture*, p. 192.

29 Anjela Duval, *Kan an douar* (Brest: Al Liamm, 1978).

30 Anjela Duval, *Traoñ an dour* (Brest: Al Liamm, 1982). A second posthumous collection came out quite recently: Anjela Duval, *Stourm a ran war bep tachenn*, kinniget gant Ronan Koadig (Saint-Brieuc: Mignoned Anjela, 1998).

31 On Anjela Duval, Yann-Ber Piriou, 'Kan ar skrilhed e Traoñ-an-Dour,' *Al Liamm* (Meurzh–Ebrel 1967): 168–79; Marsel Klerg, 'Kan an Douar,' *Barr-Heol* 77 (Mezheven 1973): 50–2; Per Mari Mevel, 'Eun oberenn a-bouez braz,' *Brud* 46 (Nevez-Amzer 1974): 26–32; Roger Laouénan, *Anjela Duval* (Quimper: Nature et Bretagne, 1974); the articles in *Al Liamm* 210 (Genver–C'hwevrer 1982), especially Ivona Martin, 'War "hent" Añjela': 19–38; Marsel Klerg, 'Añjela (1905–1981)': 39–54; Yann Talbot, 'Añjela Duval (Doue d'he fardono!): Ur plac'h hag he stourm': 55–69; Soaz an Tieg, 'Añjela a Dreger hag Añjela a Vreizh': 78–83; also Yann Bouëssel du Bourg, 'Across Breton Literature: Three Women. I. Anjela Duval,' *Bro Nevez* 17 (November 1985): 8–10; Annie Pluskelleg, *Anjela Duval: He buhez hag hec'h oberoù* (Lesneven: Mouladurioù Hor Yezh, 1985); Yvette A. Guillemin-Young, 'Anjela Duval: Le

chant de la terre et du combat,' *French Review* 71 (1997–8): 66–73; Janina Cünnen and Hildegard L.C. Tristram, 'Añjela Duval et Sarah Kirsch: Désir du coeur et pour la terre,' in *Breizh ha Pobloù Europa: Pennadoù en enor da bPer Denez*, ed. Herve ar Bihan (Hor Yezh / Klask / Presses Universitaires de Rennes, 1999), pp. 99–126; Lenora A. Timm, *A Modern Breton Political Poet, Anjela Duval: A Biography and an Anthology* (Lewiston: Edwin Mellen, 1990) provides a selection of Duval's verse with very good translations into English and a perceptive introduction.

32 Timm, *A Modern Breton Political Poet*, p. ii.

33 On the question of narrative fiction in Breton, Favereau, *Littérature et écrivains bretonnants*, pp. 21–6.

34 Youenn Drezen, *Itron Varia Garmez* (Brest: Al Liamm, 1977). On Drezen, Olier, *Istor hol lennegezh*, vol. 2, pp. 53–70; in *Al Liamm* 151 (Meurzh–Ebrel 1972), Roparz Hemon, 'Youenn Drezen (14 Gwengolo 1899 – 15 C'hwevrer 1972)': 103–12; Zavier Langleiz, 'E koun Youenn Drezen: Skrivagner ampart ha mignon feal': 117–25; Kenan Kongar, 'Lennadennoù': 128–39; also Per Mari Mevel, 'Eur gwir melezour euz temz-spered Y. Drezen: *Itron Varia Garmez*,' *Brud Nevez* 10 (Kerzu 1977): 23–6; Koulizh Kedez, 'Levrioù,' *Emsav* 125 (1978): 29–48; Annaig Renault, 'Paol Tirili, ur c'hevrinad?' *Al Liamm* 253 (Meurzh-Ebrel 1989): 128–32.

35 For example, Fañch Morvannou, 'La littérature de langue bretonne au XXe siècle,' pp. 230–1.

36 Youenn Drezen, *Skol-louarn Veig Trebern*, 3 vols (Brest: Al Liamm, 1972–4).

37 Per-Jakez Helias, untitled preface to *Skol-louarn*, vol. 1, pp. 7–9.

38 Roparz Hemon, *Mari Vorgan* (Brest: Al Liamm, 1975).

39 In addition, the narrative may have been influenced by the medieval Irish Cycle of Ulster – specifically the triangle of passion (Cú Chulainn, Emer, and Fand) – material that Roparz Hemon developed in his magnificent long poem *Gwarizi vras Emer* (*Barzhonegoù*, pp. 57–87). See Pierrette Kermoal, *Eus 'Gwarizi Vras Emer' da v'Mari Vorgan': Studienn kinniget e sell da zegemerout graz an Drevouriezh, Preder* 91 (Genver 1967); and G.E. Abanna, 'Eil tezenn vrezhonek ar c'hantved: "Eus *Gwarizi Vras Emer* da v*Mari Vorgan*" gant P. Kermoal,' *Al Liamm* 126 (Genver–C'hwevrer 1968): 51–62.

40 However, Olier, *Istor hol lennegezh*, vol. 1, argues convincingly that *Mari Vorgan* is entirely a novel of the imagination.

41 Roparz Hemon, *Tangi Kerviler* (Brest: Al Liamm, 1971).

42 From a different perspective, Olier, *Istor hol lennegezh*, vol. 1, sees Roparz Hemon's work, since 1947, as a flight or escape into his own childhood or Brittany as it might have been. See also Arzel Even, 'Faltazi Roparz Hemon (Tem an dec'hadenn),' *Al Liamm* 142 (Gwengolo–Here 1970): 334–44.

43 Per Denez, *Glas evel daoulagad c'hlas na oant ket ma re* (Brest: Al Liamm, 1979). English trans., J. Ian Press, *Blue like Blue Eyes Which Were Not My Own* (Lesneven: Mouladurioù Hor Yezh, 1993).

44 Franz Stanzel, *Die typischen Erzählsituationen im Roman* (Wien: Braumüller, 1955).

45 Per Denez, *Diougan Gwenc'hlan* (Brest: Al Liamm, 1979).

46 *Barzaz-Breiz: Chants populaires de la Bretagne, par le vicomte Hersart de la Villemarqué*, 1867 ed. (Paris: Librairie Académique Perrin, 1963), pp. 19–24. In 1988 appeared *Barzhaz Breizh*, rakskrid gant Per Denez (Lesneven: Mouladurioù Hor Yezh).

47 Pierre Jakez Hélias, *Le Cheval d'orgueil: Mémoires d'un Breton du pays bigouden* (Paris: Plon, 1975). Recently two books have appeared on Helias the writer, which include sections on his theatre: Pascal Rannou, *Inventaire d'un héritage: Essai sur l'oeuvre littéraire de Pierre-Jakez Hélias* (Relecq-Kerhuon: An Here, 1997), pp. 19–28; and Thierry Glon, *Pierre-Jakez Hélias et la Bretagne perdue* (Rennes: Presses Universitaires de Rennes, 1998), pp. 74–81. See also Anne-Denes Martin, *Itinéraire poétique en Bretagne: De Tristan Corbière à Xavier Grall* (Paris: L'Harmattan, 1995), pp. 225–32; the 'Per-Jakez Helias' issue of *Skol Vreizh* 36 (mars 1997); and Favereau, 'Pierre-Jakez Hélias, maître de l'histoire de vie,' in *Ecrire la Bretagne: 1960–1995*, ed. Bernard Hue and Marc Gontard (Rennes: Presses Universitaires de Rennes, 1995), pp. 93–103; and 'L'évolution du discours bretonnant chez Pierre-Jakez Hélias,' in *L'Ouest et le politique: Mélanges offerts à Michel Denis*, ed. Michel Lagrée and Jacqueline Sainclivier (Rennes: Presses Universitaires de Rennes, 1996), pp. 165–77. Helias was then and is now a figure of controversy. He was attacked by several articles in *Al Liamm* and by Xavier Grall, *Le Cheval couché* (Paris: Hachette, 1977). Rannou, *Inventaire d'un héritage*, offers a relatively severe demystification of the novelist (in French) and the ideologue while avoiding the excesses – grounded in passion and in ignorance – due to Xavier Grall.

48 Pierre-Jakez Hélias, *A-berz eur bed all* (Rennes: Editions Ouest-France, 1991); *Marh al lorh: Envorennou eur Bigouter* (Paris: Plon, 1986).

49 Helias proclaims his attachment to the theatre and early theatrical experiences in *Le Quêteur de mémoire: Quarante ans de recherche sur les mythes et la civilisation bretonne* (Paris: Plon, 1990), pp. 122–37 and 332–6.

50 According to Helias, this was the case for *Le Cheval d'orgueil / Marh al lorh*: see 'Rencontre avec P.J. Hélias,' *Skol Vreizh* 36 (mars 1997): 33–4.

51 Per-Jakez Helias, *Mevel ar Gosker* (Brest: Emgleo Breiz and Brud Nevez, 1985).

52 This question of peasant *verismo* is raised by Rannou, *Inventaire d'un héritage*, and Glon, *Pierre-Jakez Hélias*.

53 Per-Jakez Helias, *Katrina Lenn-Zu* (Brest: Emgleo Breiz, 1994).
54 Per Jakez Helias, *An Isild a-heul* (Brest: Brud Nevez, 1983).
55 Yvette A. Guillemin-Young, 'Hélias's *Yseult Seconde*: The Vindication of Isold of Brittany,' *French Review* 69 (1995–6): 284–90.

OCCITANIA

1 Robert Lafont, *La Révolution régionaliste* (Paris: Gallimard, 1967); *Décoloniser en France: Les régions face à l'Europe* (Paris: Gallimard, 1971); *Sur la France* (Paris: Gallimard, 1968). Just as Xavier Grall attacked Per Jakez Helias for not being sufficiently anti-French, so also Joan/Jean Larzac attacked Lafont in 'Sous la France,' in his *Descolonisar l'istòria occitana, I: Redusèires de caps* (Toulouse: Institut d'Estudis Occitans, 1980), pp. 46–64.
2 Robert Lafont, *Clefs pour l'Occitanie* (Paris: Seghers, 1971).
3 Bernard Manciet and Félix Castan, 'Manifèst neraqués-montalbanés,' *Oc* 204 (abril–mai–junh de 1957): 96.
4 Robert Lafont, *Mistral ou l'illusion* (Paris: Plon, 1954).
5 Max Roqueta, '"OC" ten vint ans (1924–1944),' *Oc* 168 (4me trimèstre de 1945): 38.
6 Renat Nelli, 'Declaración,' *Oc* 165 (ivèrn de 1943): 1.
7 Robert Lafont, 'La langue des poètes occitans contemporains,' *Europe* 669–70 (janvier–février 1985): 96.
8 Loïs Alibert, 'Porguem nostra lenga,' *Oc* 181 (julh de 1951): 34.
9 Loïs Alibert, 'Oc renaissent,' *Oc* 132 (julh–agost de 1931): 3–4.
10 Félix-Marcel Castan, 'Perspective occitane,' *Europe* 669–670 (janvier–février 1985): 16.
11 'Orientacion,' *Oc* 300 (julhet de 1991): 6. Also by Castan, in this line, see 'La direccion de nòstra renaissença poëtica,' *Oc* 208–10 (abril–desembre de 1959): 51–62, and 'Pour l'Institut d'Etudes Occitanes ... 1945–1964,' *Estudis occitans* 18 (2nd semèstre de 1995): 45–59.
12 Carles Camprós, 'Problèma politic?' *Oc* 220–1 (abriu–setembre de 1961): 14.
13 Among the most important studies on the situation of Occitan in recent years, see Brigitte Schlieben-Lange, *Okzitanisch und Katalanisch: Ein Beitrag zur Soziolinguistik zweier romanischer Sprachen* (Tübingen: Narr, 1973), and Georg Kremnitz, *Versuche zur Kodifizierung des Okzitanischen seit dem 19. Jahrhundert und ihre Annahme durch die Sprecher* (Tübingen: Narr, 1974), *Die ethnischen Minderheiten Frankreichs: Bilanz und Möglichkeiten für den Französischunterricht* (Tübingen: Narr, 1975), *Das Okzitanische: Sprachgeschichte und Soziologie* (Tübingen: Niemeyer, 1981), and *Entfremdung, Selbstbefreiung und Norm: Texte aus der okzitanischen Soziolinguistik* (Tübingen: Narr, 1982).

See also *L'Identité occitane: Réflexions théoriques et expériences. Actes du Colloque de Béziers*, ed. François Pic (Montpellier: Section Française de l'Association Internationale d'Etudes Occitanes, 1990). General histories of literature that treat the Occitan modernists include Charles Camproux, *Histoire de la littérature occitane* (Paris: Payot, 1953); Yves Rouquette, *La Littérature d'Oc*, 'Que sais-je?' (Paris: Presses Universitaires de France, 1963); Fritz Peter Kirsch, *Studien zur languedokischen und gaskognischen Literatur der Gegenwart* (Vienna: Braumüller, 1965); Fausta Garavini, *L'Empèri dóu Soulèu: La ragione dialettale nella Francia d'oc* (Milan and Naples: Ricciardi, 1967), and *La letteratura occitanica moderna* (Florence: Sansoni and Milan: Accademia, 1970); Robert Lafont and Christian Anatole, *Nouvelle Histoire de la littérature occitane*, 2 vols (Paris: Presses Universitaires de France, 1970). See also Rosa Anna Greco, 'La nuova generazione di autori nello spazio letterario occitanico contemporaneo,' *Quaderni* (Università degli Studi di Lecce. Facoltà di Magistero. Istituto di Lingue e Letterature Straniere) 5 (1983): 209–77; William Calin and Fritz Peter Kirsch, 'Les tâches de la recherche occitane: Le texte littéraire des XIXe et XXe siècles,' *Bulletins de l'Association Internationale d'Etudes Occitanes* 1 (1985): 21–4; and William Calin, 'Suggestions de lecture pour nos textes occitans modernes,' *Bulletins de l'Association Internationale d'Etudes Occitanes* 7 (1991): 40–53.

14 Mas-Felipe Delavouët, *Pouèmo*, vols 1–3 (Paris: Corti, 1971–7), vols 4–5 (Saint-Remy de Provence: C.R.E.M., 1983–91). On Delavouët, Jean Thunin, *La Présence et le mythe: Lecture de l'oeuvre poétique de Mas-Felipe Delavouët*, 2 vols (Salon-de-Provence: La Destinée, 1984), and articles by Claude Mauron, '*Pouèmo* de Max-Philippe Delavouët,' *Marseille* 91:4 (1972): 79–84 and 92:1 (1973): 62–9; 'Le portail de Saint-Trophime d'Arles chez F. Mistral et M. Ph. Delavouët,' *Lou Prouvençau a l'escolo* 65:2 (1973–4): 12–16; 'Un "Tristan" en provençal moderne: *Ço que Tristan se disié sus la mar*, de Max-Philippe Delavouët,' *Revue des langues romanes* 82 (1977): 181–93; 'Dóu *Rollan a Saragossa*, en ancian prouvençau, a la *Balado d'aquéu que fasié Rouland* en prouvençau moderne, de Mas-Felipe Delavouët,' in *Contacts de langues, de civilisations et intertextualité: Troisième Congrès international de l'Association Internationale d'Etudes Occitanes*, ed. Gérard Gouiran (Montpellier: Centre d'Etudes Occitanes de l'Université de Montpellier, 1992), vol. 2, pp. 505–18; and by William Calin, 'Lecture de *Pouèmo* de Max-Philippe Delavouët,' in *Vingt ans de littérature d'expression occitane, 1968–1988: Actes du Colloque International*, ed. Philippe Gardy and François Pic (Montpellier: Section Française de l'Association Internationale d'Etudes Occitanes, 1990), pp. 88–94, and '*Camin de la Crous*: Max-Philippe Delavouët et le baroque sacré,' in *Contacts de langues*, pp. 417–27. On modern Occitan verse in general, and on the three

poets discussed in this section, see Philippe Gardy, *Une Ecriture en archipel: Cinquante ans de poésie occitane (1940–1990)* (Eglise-Neuve-d'Issac: Fédérop, 1992).

15 Thunin, *La Présence et le mythe*, pp. 97–131.

16 Renat Nelli, *Òbra poëtica occitana (1940–1980)* (Montpellier: Institut d'Estudis Occitans, 1981). For good thematic critical analysis, consult, in *René Nelli (1906–1982): Actes du Colloque de Toulouse (6 et 7 décembre 1985)*, ed. Christian Anatole (Béziers: Centre International de Documentation Occitane, 1986): Gilles Arfi, 'Entre éternité et néant, le temps dans la poésie nellienne,' pp. 21–37; Anne Brenon, 'L'inspiration dualiste dans la poésie de René Nelli,' pp. 57–80; Joan-Frederic Brun, 'Sensualitat e metafisica dins l'òbra poëtica occitana de Renat Nelli,' pp. 81–8; Jacques Gourc, 'Poétique et "Trobar" dans *Arma de Vertat*,' pp. 131–8; Arno Krispin, 'René Nelli: Poésie et folklore, le *monde merveilleux* et le *joi* des troubadours,' pp. 139–54; Robèrt Lafont, 'Lo temps coma arquitectura d'*Arma de Vertat*,' pp. 155–63; Jean-Marie Petit, 'Des mots pour un Bestiaire,' pp. 165–71; Xavier Ravier, 'L'ontologie du paysage dans la poésie de René Nelli,' pp. 233–44. See also Fritz Peter Kirsch, *Studien zur languedokischen und gaskognischen Literatur*, pp. 40–56; and Uta Hahn, 'Réaliser l'invisible – imaginer le réel: La poésie de René Nelli,' *Actes du IVe Congrès International de l'Association Internationale d'Etudes Occitanes*, ed. Ricardo Cierbide (Vitoria-Gasteiz: Universidad del País Vasco, 1994), vol. 2, pp. 469–78, and 'René Nelli – le langage à contre courant,' *Bulletins de l'Association Internationale d'Etudes Occitanes* 14 (avril 1998): 107–13.

17 On tree imagery in Nelli, Jean Arrouye, 'La rumors dels arbres dins l'obra poëtica occitana de Renat Nelli,' in Anatole, *René Nelli (1906–1982)*, pp. 45–56, and Gardy, 'A propos du *temps folzejat*: La veine hésiodique,' ibid., pp. 119–29.

18 René Nelli, *L'Erotique des troubadours* (Toulouse: Privat, 1963). On Nelli's medievalism, Gourc, 'Poétique et "Trobar"'; Krispin, 'René Nelli'; Hahn, 'René Nelli'; and Félix-Marcel Castan, 'La Gaita, Nelli,' *Oc* n.s. 15 (setembre de 1982): 23–33.

19 Emmanuel Le Roy Ladurie, *Montaillou, village occitan, de 1294 à 1324* (Paris: Gallimard, 1975).

20 Excellent brief estimations of Manciet by Guy Latry, 'Bernard Manciet, de B à M,' in Gardy, *Vingt ans de littérature*, pp. 102–7, and Jean-Marie Auzias, 'La place de Bernard Manciet dans la littérature occitane moderne,' in *Bernard Manciet: Le feu est dans la langue. Actes du Colloque de Bordeaux*, ed. Guy Latry (Centre d'Etude de la Littérature Occitane / William Blake, 1996), pp. 157–62. On Manciet's cultural politics, in *Bernard Manciet: Le feu*: Félix-Marcel Castan, 'Manciet et le concept de littérature: Du dialecte à la langue,' pp.

163–7; Christian Coulon, 'La politique de Manciet: Les frontières du vent,' pp. 113–25; and Bernard Traimond, 'Manciet et l'ethnologie,' pp. 127–35.

21 Bernard Manciet, *L'Enterrament a Sabres* (Garein, Landes: Editions Ultreïa, 1989). On Manciet's poetry, Muriel Icard, 'Bernard Manciet: D'une occitanité vers d'autres cultures,' *Garona* 1 (juin 1985): 67–79; and, in Latry, *Bernard Manciet: Le feu*, William Calin, '*L'Enterrament a Sabres* et les structures de l'imaginaire: Bernard Manciet de *R* à *S*,' pp. 13–24; Jean-Yves Casanova, 'Métaphores et images poétiques dans *L'Enterrament a Sabres*: De la parole au style,' pp. 53–61; Robert Lafont, 'Le pli dans l'oeuvre,' pp. 45–51; Jean-Marie Sarpoulet, 'Manciet felibre?' pp. 25–33. Also articles collected in *Aréthuse: Cahiers du Centre de Recherches sur la poésie contemporaine*, Université de Pau 1 (1985), and *Auteurs en scène: Théâtres d'Oc ... et d'ailleurs* 2 (décembre 1997).

22 On Manciet and Mauriac, Philippe Gardy, 'Manciet, Mauriac: L'écrivain au miroir des langues,' *Littérature* 76 (décembre 1989): 24–36. A number of essays in Gardy's *L'Ecriture occitane contemporaine: Une quête des mots* (Paris: L'Harmattan, 1996) treat Manciet's prose writings, including the theme of Gascony and Gascon space.

23 Manciet makes this point repeatedly in *Le Triangle des Landes* (Paris: Arthaud, 1981).

24 Bernard Manciet, *Gesta: Poèmes* (Agen: Cap e Cap, 1972), p. 18.

25 In *Le Triangle des Landes* Manciet devotes a chapter to Sabres, 'Un village dans les marais,' pp. 137–72. He underscores the truculent spirit of resistance in this 'paroisse qui a mauvais caractère' (p. 140).

26 On Boudou, see *Joan Bodon: Documents* (Toulouse: Centre Regional d'Estudis Occitans, 1975); *Jean Boudou (1920–1975): Actes du Colloque de Naucelle (27, 28 et 29 septembre 1985)*, ed. Christian Anatole (Béziers: Centre International de Documentation Occitane, 1987); and Joëlle Ginestet, *Jean Boudou: La force d'aimer* (Vienna: Edition Praesens, 1997).

27 Joan Bodon, *La Grava sul camin* (Rodez: Edicions de Roergue, 1988).

28 On this theme of the little people, Pierre Séguret, 'Jean Boudou, romancier occitan de la pauvreté, héritier des spirituels romans,' in Anatole, *Jean Boudou (1920–1975)*, pp. 131–45; and Jean Arrouye, 'Joan Bodon, romancier de l'exil,' ibid., pp. 173–87.

29 See Robert Lafont, 'Lo mite de la feminitat dins l'òbra romanesca de Bodon,' in Anatole, *Jean Boudou (1920–1975)*, pp. 159–65; also William Calin, '*La Grava sul camin* de J. Bodon: Technique narrative, phénoménologie et les structures du désir,' in *Actes du premier Congrès International de l'Association Internationale d'Etudes Occitanes*, ed. Peter T. Ricketts (London: Westfield College, 1987), pp. 149–56; also William Calin, 'Du réalisme magique dans le roman occitan: Lecture subversive de *La Santa Estèla del centenari* de J. Bou-

dou,' in *Toulouse à la croisée des cultures: Actes du Ve Congrès international de l'Association Internationale d'Etudes Occitanes*, ed. Jacques Gourc and François Pic (Pau: Association Internationale d'Etudes Occitanes, 1998), vol. 2, pp. 477–80.

30 Joan Bodon, *La Santa Estèla del centenari: Conte* (Rodez: Edicions de Roergue, 1990).

31 On the theme of apocalypse, see Jean Salles Loustau, 'Trois écritures de la fin,' in Gardy, *Vingt ans de littérature d'expression occitane*, pp. 74–8.

32 Felip Gardy, 'Entre l'infèrn e lo paradís: L'escriure romanesc de Joan Bodon,' in Anatole, *Jean Boudou (1920–1975)*, pp. 247–58; also Robèrt Marti, 'Lo fantastic dins l'òbra de J. Bodon,' ibid., pp. 243–6.

33 Joan Bodon, *Lo Libre dels Grands Jorns (roman)* (Rodez: Edicions de Roergue, 1996). Ginestet, *Jean Boudou*, devotes a good chapter to this book, pp. 123–57.

34 On religion in this novel and in *Lo Libre de Catòia*, see Jean-Marie Marconot, 'Structure religieuse du livre de Catòia,' in Anatole, *Jean Boudou (1920–1975)*, pp. 146–58, and 'Le thème religieux dans l'oeuvre de Bodon (*Livre des grands jours*),' in *Atti del Secondo Congresso Internazionale della 'Association Internationale d'Etudes Occitanes*,' ed. Giuliano Gasca Queirazza (Turin: Università di Torino, 1993), vol. 1, pp. 479–95.

35 Robert Lafont, *Vida de Joan Larsinhac: Racònte* (Montpellier: Institut d'Estudis Occitans, 1978).

36 Robert Lafont, *L'Icòna dins l'iscla: Faula* (Montpellier: Institut d'Estudis Occitans, 1979). On Lafont as a novelist and on *L'Icòna dins l'iscla*, see Jean Salles Loustau, 'Trois ecritures de la fin'; Fritz Peter Kirsch, 'Temps e istòria dins l'òbra narrativa de Robèrt Lafont,' in Gasca Queirazza, *Atti del Secondo Congresso*, pp. 465–78; Philippe Gardy, 'Tantale romancier? Sur l'oeuvre romantique de Robert Lafont,' in *Universitat occitana d'estiu: Actes de l'Université d'été, 1994*, vol. 2, ed. Jòrdi Peladan (Nîmes: M.A.R.P.O.C./I.E.O., 1995), pp. 65–85; Claire Torreilles, 'La première personne dans l'oeuvre narrative de Robert Lafont,' in *Universitat occitana d'estiu*, pp. 44–64; and Danielle Julien, 'Statuts et fonctions de la langue dans l'oeuvre de Robert Lafont,' in Gourc, *Toulouse à la croisée des cultures*, pp. 527–35.

37 Robert Lafont, *Insularas: Doas faulas* (Institut d'Estudis Occitans, 1996).

38 Robert Lafont, *La Festa*, 2 vols (Lyon/Paris: Obradors / Fédérop / Le Chemin Vert, 1983–4).

39 Danielle Julien, 'Etudes sur *La Festa* de Robert Lafont' (Diss., Université de Montpellier, 1996).

40 For example, Jean-Claude Forêt, 'Cor e racacor, quauquei aspèctes de l'eroi lafontian,' in Peladan, *Universitat occitana d'estiu*, pp. 19–43; see also, in the

same collection, Georg Kremnitz, 'Sartre et Lafont, Lafont et Sartre,' pp. 10–18.

41 On the problematic of language, Philippe Gardy, 'Le roman (1950–1990) comme métaphore de la langue,' in *L'Ecriture occitane contemporaine*, pp. 63–78, and 'Tantale romancier?'; and Fritz Peter Kirsch, 'Temps e istòria.'

42 And Vienna is a centre for the Baroque. See Claire Torreilles, 'Perspectives baroques,' *Impressions du Sud* 23 (automne 1989): 27–33, and 'Références baroques,' in Gardy, *Vingt ans de littérature d'expression occitane*, pp. 34–40.

43 The theme of the characters as 'doubles' is explored by Julien, 'Etudes sur *La Festa*,' and *Per legir 'La Festa' de Robert Lafont* (Montpellier: Centre d'Estudis Occitans de l'Universitat Paul-Valéry, n.d.).

44 Robert Lafont, *La Festa, libre 3: Finisegle* (Eglise-Neuve-d'Issac: Fédérop, 1996).

45 Joan-Claudi Forêt, *La Pèira d'asard* (Institut d'Estudis Occitans / Parlarem en Vivarès / Ostal del Libre, 1990).

46 Excellent documentation is provided by Claude Alranq, *Théâtre d'oc contemporain: Les arts de jouer du Midi de la France* (Pézenas: Editions Domens, 1995).

47 Max Roqueta, 'Rapòrt sul teatre,' *Oc* 185 (julh de 1952): 24–8.

48 The decline of the new Occitan theatre coincides with the waning of post-1968 militancy. See Henri Jeanjean, *De l'utopie au pragmatisme? (Le mouvement occitan, 1976–1990)* (Perpignan: Trabucaire, 1992), pp. 106–8.

49 Robert Lafont, *La Loba, ò la frucha di tres aubas: Peça de tres actes* (Avignon: Aubanel, 1959). For the theatre of this moment, Alranq, *Théâtre d'oc contemporain*, pp. 98–128.

50 Robert Lafont, *La Révolte des 'Cascavèus' / Lei Cascavèus* (Toulon: Centre Dramatique Occitan de Provence, 1977). On the post-1968 theatre, including Lafont, see Alranq, *Théâtre d'oc contemporain*, pp. 129–79.

51 Robert Lafont, *La Croisade* (Aix-en-Provence: Edisud, 1983). For Lafont and this 'génération post-moderne,' Alranq, *Théâtre d'oc contemporain*, pp. 180–241.

POSTMODERN

1 *Défense de cracher par terre et de parler breton: Poèmes de combat (1950–1970)*, ed. Yann-Ber Piriou (Paris: Oswald, 1971); *Breizh hiziv: Anthologie de la chanson en Bretagne*, ed. Philippe Durand (Paris: Oswald, 1976). The bibliography on the Breton revival is immense. The reader should consult Piriou's insightful 'Préface,' pp. 7–46, a *texte de combat* from that period, as was Morvan Lebesque, *Comment peut-on être breton? Essai sur la démocratie française* (Paris: Seuil, 1970); also, from a more recent, scholarly perspective, Francis Favereau,

Bretagne contemporaine: Langue, culture, identité (Morlaix: Skol Vreizh, 1993), and, on the poetry, *Littérature et écrivains bretonnants depuis 1945* (*Skol Vreizh* 20, mars 1991), pp. 14–17. On the music, consult Jacques Vassal, *La Nouvelle Chanson bretonne* (Paris: Michel, 1973), and André-Georges Hamon, *Chantres de toutes les Bretagnes: Vingt ans de chanson bretonne* (Paris: Picollec, 1981).

2 An expanded collection of Gwernig's verse, with translation into English, has recently been published: Youenn Gwernig, *Un Dornad plu / A Handful of Feathers: Brezhoneg ha saozneg* (Brest: Al Liamm, 1997).

3 On Keineg, Jacqueline Hubert, 'L'oeuvre de Paol Keineg,' in Paol Keineg, *Chroniques et croquis des villages verrouillés*, réédition (Paris: Oswald, 1973), pp. 127–60; Charles Dobzynski, 'Paol Keineg: Un barde breton d'aujourd'hui,' *Europe* 625 (mai 1981): 123–6; Marc Gontard, 'Effets de métissage dans la littérature bretonne,' in *Métissage du texte: Bretagne, Maghreb, Québec*, ed. Bernard Hue (Rennes: Presses Universitaires de Rennes, 1993), pp. 27–39, and 'Pour une littérature bretonne de langue française,' in *Ecrire la Bretagne: 1960–1995*, ed. Bernard Hue and Marc Gontard (Rennes: Presses Universitaires de Rennes, 1995), pp. 17–31; Thierry Glon, 'Ecrivains de la "Recouvrance" (de 1960 à 1980),' in *Ecrire la Bretagne*, pp. 33–52; and Anne-Denes Martin, *Itinéraire poétique en Bretagne: De Tristan Corbière à Xavier Grall* (Paris: L'Harmattan, 1995), pp. 233–8.

4 Paol Keineg, *Pibroch de la forêt et de la pluie: Lieux communs*, suivi de *Dahut* (Paris: Gallimard, 1974).

5 Paol Keineg, *Chroniques et croquis des villages verrouillés*, suivi de *Territoire de l'aube, Poèmes-tracts (bilingues), Quelques poèmes d'amour* (Paris: Oswald, 1973), pp. 85–113.

6 Paol Keineg, *Histoires vraies / Mojennoù gwir*, suivi de *Irlande du Sud Irlande du Nord / Iwerzhon ar C'hreisteiz Iwerzhon an Hanternoz: Poèmes traduits du breton par l'auteur avec le texte original* (Paris: Oswald, 1974), pp. 55–117.

7 *Histoires vraies / Mojennoù gwir*, pp. 5–53.

8 René Galand, *Stratégie de la lecture* (New York: Peter Lang, 1990), p. 198.

9 Paol Keineg, *35 haiku* (Morlaix: Editions Bretagne, 1978).

10 *Occitanie 1970: Les poètes de la décolonisation*, ed. Marie Rouanet (Paris: Oswald, 1971). See Rouanet's 'Préface,' pp. 9–32, and Robert Lafont, *Clefs pour l'Occitanie* (Paris: Seghers, 1971), chap. 9, and *La Revendication occitane* (Paris: Flammarion, 1974), pp. 291–302. On the new poetry and its poetics, the insightful Philippe Martel, 'Poésie révolutionnaire en occitan,' in *Vingt ans de littérature d'expression occitane, 1968–1988: Actes du Colloque International*, ed. Philippe Gardy and François Pic (Montpellier: Section Française de l'Association Internationale d'Etudes Occitanes, 1990), pp. 64–73.

11 For an example of Occitan poets writing on Brittany and then being trans-

lated into Breton, see the bilingual volume *Breiz Atao: Poëmas d'Enric Espieut, Joan Larzac e Ives Roqueta, Adaptacion bretona de Youenn Gwernig* (Toulouse: Institut d'Estudis Occitans, 1969).

12 On the *novèla cançon*, Yves Rouquette, *La Nouvelle Chanson occitane* (Toulouse: Privat, 1972); *Antologia de la nòva cançon occitana*, ed. Frederic Bard and Jan-Maria Carlotti (Aix-en-Provence: Edisud, 1982); and Andreas Kisters, *Un pais que vòl cantar: Okzitanische Musik der Gegenwart als Beispiel für Regionalismus in der populären Musikkultur* (Vienna: Edition Praesens, 1997).

13 Joan Larzac, *Òbra poëtica* (Institut d'Estudis Occitans, 1986). Also Ives Roqueta, *L'Escritura, publica o pas: Poèmas (1972–1987)* (Institut d'Estudis Occitans, 1988). On Jean Larzac, Philippe Gardy, *Une Ecriture en archipel: Cinquante ans de poésie occitane (1940–1990)* (Eglise-Neuve-d'Issac: Fédérop, 1992), pp. 82–4; on Yves Rouquette, pp. 70–4.

14 *Òbra poëtica*, pp. 7–71.

15 *Òbra poëtica*, pp. 197–241.

16 Joan Larzac, *Descolonisar l'istòria occitana*, 2 vols (Toulouse: Institut d'Estudis Occitans, 1977–80).

17 *Òbra poëtica*, pp. 145–67.

18 *Òbra poëtica*, pp. 169–95.

19 *Òbra poëtica*, pp. 245–57.

20 *Òbra poëtica*, pp. 287–311.

21 Tom Leonard, *Intimate Voices: Selected Work, 1965–1983* (Newcastle upon Tyne: Galloping Dog, 1984).

22 Among a number of general studies on this group, see (by important cultural figures) Edwin Morgan, 'Glasgow Speech in Recent Scottish Literature,' in *Scotland and the Lowland Tongue: Studies in the Language and Literature of Lowland Scotland in Honour of David D. Murison*, ed. J. Derrick McClure (Aberdeen: Aberdeen University Press, 1983), pp. 195–208; and Philip Hobsbaum, 'Speech Rather Than Lallans: West of Scotland Poetry,' *Lines Review* 113 (June 1990): 5–10.

23 For example, Donald Campbell, 'Whaur's Your Wullie Shakespeare Noo?' *Chapman* 3:1 (1974): 22–6.

24 See Randall Stevenson, 'Recent Scottish Theatre: Dramatic Developments?' in *Scotland: Literature, Culture, Politics*, ed. Peter Zenzinger (Heidelberg: Winter, 1989), pp. 187–213, and the path-breaking collection of essays *Scottish Theatre since the Seventies*, ed. Randall Stevenson and Gavin Wallace (Edinburgh: Edinburgh University Press, 1996), especially Lindsay Paterson, 'Language and Identity on the Stage,' pp. 75–83; and Randall Stevenson, 'Snakes and Ladders, Snakes and Owls: Charting Scottish Theatre,' pp. 1–20, and 'In the Jungle of the Cities,' pp. 100–11.

25 This current must not be confused with John McGrath's perhaps better known 7:84 Theatre Company, which, in 1973, launched a tradition of innovative left-wing stagecraft in the style of Brecht, Piscator, and Fo. The 7:84 is the Scottish equivalent of the Breton Strollad ar Vro Bagan and the Occitan Teatre de la Carrièra. McGrath's plays are almost exclusively in English.

26 Bill Bryden, *Willie Rough: A Play* (Edinburgh: Southside, 1972).

27 Roddy McMillan, *The Bevellers: A Play* (Edinburgh: Southside, 1974).

28 Randall Stevenson, 'Scottish Theatre, 1950–1980,' in *The History of Scottish Literature*, vol. 4, *Twentieth Century*, ed. Cairns Craig (Aberdeen: Aberdeen University Press, 1987), pp. 349–67, especially 358.

29 David Hutchison, 'Roddy McMillan and the Scottish Theatre,' *Cencrastus* 2 (Spring 1980): 5–8. See also the extremely perceptive reading by Adrienne Scullion, 'Feminine Pleasures and Masculine Indignities: Gender and Community in Scottish Drama,' in *Gendering the Nation: Studies in Modern Scottish Literature*, ed. Christopher Whyte (Edinburgh: Edinburgh University Press, 1995), pp. 169–204, especially 179–84.

30 Bill Bryden, *Benny Lynch: Scenes from a Short Life* (Edinburgh: Southside, 1975).

31 Tom McGrath and Jimmy Boyle, *The Hard Man: A Play* (Edinburgh: Canongate, 1977).

CONCLUSION

1 The reader will find a list of works treating magical realism, modernism, postmodernism, and postcolonialism in the first section of the bibliography, entitled 'Literary Theory and Minority Languages.'

2 Two major recent collections are *A Tongue in Yer Heid: A Selection of the Best Contemporary Short Stories in Scots*, ed. James Robertson (Edinburgh: B and W, 1994), and *Mak It New: An Anthology of Twenty-One Years of Writing in 'Lallans,'* ed. Neil R. MacCallum and David Purves (Edinburgh: Mercat, 1995).

3 For two examples of demystification of shoddy scholarship, Astradur Eysteinsson, *The Concept of Modernism* (Ithaca: Cornell University Press, 1990), and Joseph Frank, *The Idea of Spatial Form* (New Brunswick: Rutgers University Press, 1991).

4 For a forthright statement of the anglicist argument, and aware of the role of Scotland as one provincial/marginal generator of modernism, see Robert Crawford, 'Modernism as Provincialism,' chap. 5 of his *Devolving English Literature* (Oxford: Clarendon Press, 1992), pp. 216–70; also, from a theoretical perspective, Hans-Werner Ludwig, 'Province and Metropolis, Centre and Periphery: Some Critical Terms Re-examined,' in *Poetry in the British Isles:*

Non-Metropolitan Perspectives, ed. Hans-Werner Ludwig and Lothar Fietz (Cardiff: University of Wales Press, 1995), pp. 47–69.

5 Elleke Boehmer, *Colonial and Postcolonial Literature: Migrant Metaphors* (Oxford: Oxford University Press, 1995).

6 For Occitan, see William Calin, 'Occitan Literature Today: Cultural Identity and the Sense of the Past,' *Tenso* 11 (1995–6): 64–77.

7 See Alem Surre-Garcia, 'La nocion de talvera,' in *Jean Boudou (1920–1975): Actes du Colloque de Naucelle,* ed. Christian Anatole (Béziers: Centre International de Documentation Occitane, 1987), pp. 219–24, and Philippe Gardy, 'Le roman (1950–1990) comme métaphore de la langue,' in his *L'Ecriture occitane contemporaine: Une quête des mots* (Paris: L'Harmattan, 1996), pp. 63–78.

8 Two outstanding examples: *The History of Scottish Literature,* 4 vols, ed. Cairns Craig (Aberdeen: Aberdeen University Press, 1987–8); and *The Poetry of Scotland,* ed. Roderick Watson (Edinburgh: Edinburgh University Press, 1995).

9 See Yves Chevrel, 'L'université et la culture et la littérature bretonnes: Perspectives offertes par la littérature générale et comparée,' *Skol Vreizh* 45 (avril-juin 1976): 5–8; the collections *Métissage du texte: Bretagne, Maghreb, Québec,* ed. Bernard Hue (Rennes: Presses Universitaires de Rennes, 1993), and *Ecrire la Bretagne: 1960–1995,* ed. Bernard Hue and Marc Gontard (Rennes: Presses Universitaires de Rennes, 1995), especially Marc Gontard, 'Pour une littérature bretonne de langue française,' pp. 17–31, and Thierry Glon, 'Ecrivains de la "Recouvrance" (de 1960 à 1980),' pp. 33–52. Also Anne-Denes Martin, *Itinéraire poétique en Bretagne: De Tristan Corbière à Xavier Grall* (Paris: L'Harmattan, 1995).

10 They also sometimes proclaim their nationalism. The question of Scottish literary nationalism is especially noteworthy. Among the recent studies, consult Susan Manning, 'Scotland and America: National Literatures? National Languages?' *Cencrastus* 32 (New Year 1989): 41–6; Susanne Hagemann, *Die Schottische Renaissance: Literatur und Nation im 20. Jahrhundert* (Frankfurt am Main: Peter Lang, 1992), and '"Bidin Naitural": Identity Questions in Scottish Twentieth-Century Renaissance Literature,' *Scottish Literary Journal* 21:1 (May 1994): 44–55; *Peripheral Visions: Images of Nationhood in Contemporary British Fiction,* ed. Ian A. Bell (Cardiff: University of Wales Press, 1995); and the suggestive remarks in Cairns Craig, *Out of History: Narrative Paradigms in Scottish and English Culture* (Edinburgh: Polygon, 1996).

11 David Staines, *Beyond the Provinces: Literary Canada at Century's End* (Toronto: University of Toronto Press, 1995). Kremnitz tells of his misadventures in trying to place a German translation of Occitan *nouvelles* with editors who found the texts lacking Occitan specificity, that is, not manifesting enough

cultural exoticism: Georg Kremnitz, 'Réflexions sur une politique de la traduction du texte littéraire occitan,' in *Flor enversa: Actes du Colloque International* (Toulouse: Conservatoire Occitan, 1992), pp. 40–6.

12 One example: Joan-Frederic Brun, 'Pòst-occitanisme,' *Oc* 300 (julhet de 1991): 202–10.

SCOTS GLOSSARY

aa all
ablow under
ae one/the same
airn iron
airts directions/ways
awa away
aye always

bairn child/baby
broukit tear-stained
byke swarm of people/hornets' nest

cantraip piece of mischief
chops strikes
cleik link (arms)
coorse course/flow
craws crows
crines shrinks

daur dare
doos doves
douce respectable/comfortable
dree endure

eemis teetering

flegmageerie whim
flichterie flightyness

gey very
gi'e give
gin if
glaur mud/slime
glowered stared intently
goams gazes stupidly
gowp stare open-mouthed
granderie pride/pomp
gree first place
gyte mad

haill/hale whole/sound/healthy
hantle-sicht great deal/considerable number
hauf half
heistit hoisted
howf tavern/pub

ilk each

jalouse guess/suspect
jauggy jagged
jummlin jumbling

laired sunken in mud
laith loath
leid language
leman lover
lift sky

ligg lie
loch lake/pond
loupt sprang
lozen pane of glass
luntan puffing (smoke)

maikless matchless
maisters schoolteachers
maun must
mirk darkness
muir moor

natter nag/grouse
nor than

owre muckle too much

plumm deep pool in a river

quair book/literary work

rale real/genuine
reivers plunderers
repone reply (legal)

sair sore
saxt sixth
scummie with scum

scurl scab
shair sure
siller silver/money
skaith harm
skar take fright
skimmers twinkles
syne afterwards

tae to/too
the day today
tint lost
trauchles drudgery/burden /
  source of anxiety

unkent unknown

virr energy/impetuosity

waas walls
wae woe
watergaw rainbow
whitterick weasel/stoat/ferret/
  thin, small, sharp-featured, inquisitive person
winnock window
wud mad
wudden dream nightmare
wun reach (with difficulty)

BIBLIOGRAPHY

1 LITERARY THEORY AND MINORITY LANGUAGES

Adler, Max K. *Welsh and the Other Dying Languages in Europe: A Sociolinguistic Study.* Hamburg: Buske Verlag, 1977.

Ashcroft, Bill, et al. *The Empire Writes Back: Theory and Practice in Post-Colonial Literatures.* London: Routledge, 1989.

Boehmer, Elleke. *Colonial and Postcolonial Literature: Migrant Metaphors.* Oxford: Oxford University Press, 1995.

Bongie, Chris. *Islands and Exiles: The Creole Identities of Post-Colonial Literature.* Stanford: Stanford University Press, 1998.

Bürger, Peter. *Theorie der Avantgarde.* Frankfurt am Main: Suhrkamp, 1974.

Calinescu, Matei. *Five Faces of Modernity: Modernism, Avant-Garde, Decadence, Kitsch, Postmodernism.* Durham: Duke University Press, 1987.

Calvet, Louis-Jean. *Linguistique et colonialisme: Petit traité de glottophagie.* Paris: Payot, 1974.

Chiti-Batelli, Andrea. *Communication internationale et avenir des langues et des parlers en Europe.* Nice: Presses d'Europe, 1987.

Connor, Steven. *Postmodernist Culture: An Introduction to Theories of the Contemporary.* Oxford: Blackwell, 1989.

Deane, Seamus. Introduction to *Nationalism, Colonialism, and Literature.* Minneapolis: University of Minnesota Press, 1990, pp. 3–19.

DeKoven, Marianne. *Rich and Strange: Gender, History, Modernism.* Princeton: Princeton University Press, 1991.

Deleuze, Gilles, and Félix Guattari. 'Qu'est-ce qu'une littérature mineure?' In their *Kafka: Pour une littérature mineure.* Paris: Editions de Minuit, 1975.

Eysteinsson, Astradur. *The Concept of Modernism.* Ithaca: Cornell University Press, 1990.

Fairlamb, Horace L. *Critical Conditions: Postmodernity and the Question of Foundations.* Cambridge: Cambridge University Press, 1994.

Frank, Joseph. *The Idea of Spatial Form.* New Brunswick: Rutgers University Press, 1991.

Friedrich, Hugo. *Die Struktur der modernen Lyrik: Von Baudelaire bis zur Gegenwart.* Hamburg: Rowohlt, 1956.

Frye, Northrop. *The Modern Century.* Toronto: Oxford University Press, 1967.

García Canclini, Néstor. *Culturas híbridas: Estrategias para entrar y salir de la modernidad.* Mexico, D.F.: Editorial Grijalbo, 1990.

Gellner, Ernest. *Nations and Nationalism.* Ithaca: Cornell University Press, 1983.

Giordan, Henri, ed. *Par les langues de France.* Paris: Centre G. Pompidou, 1984.

Graff, Gerald. 'The Myth of the Postmodern Breakthrough.' In his *Literature against Itself: Literary Ideas in Modern Society.* Chicago: University of Chicago Press, 1979, pp. 31–62.

Grillo, R.D. *Dominant Languages: Language and Hierarchy in Britain and France.* Cambridge: Cambridge University Press, 1989.

Haugen, Einar. *The Ecology of Language: Essays.* Stanford: Stanford University Press, 1972.

Haugen, Einar, et al., eds. *Minority Languages Today.* Edinburgh: Edinburgh University Press, 1981.

Howe, Irving. 'The Culture of Modernism.' In his *Decline of the New.* New York: Harcourt, Brace and World, 1970, pp. 3–33.

Hutcheon, Linda. *A Poetics of Postmodernism: History, Theory, Fiction.* London: Routledge, 1988.

– *The Politics of Postmodernism.* London: Routledge, 1989.

Jameson, Fredric. *Postmodernism, or, The Cultural Logic of Late Capitalism.* Durham: Duke University Press, 1991.

Levin, Harry. 'What Was Modernism?' In his *Refractions: Essays in Comparative Literature.* New York: Oxford University Press, 1966, pp. 271–95.

Lionnet, Françoise, and Ronnie Scharfman, eds. *Post/Colonial Conditions: Exiles, Migrations, and Nomadisms.* 2 vols. *Yale French Studies* 82–3: 1993.

Loomba, Ania. *Colonialism/Postcolonialism.* London: Routledge, 1998.

Lyotard, Jean-François. *La Condition postmoderne: Rapport sur le savoir.* Paris: Editions de Minuit, 1979.

Nicholls, Peter. *Modernisms: A Literary Guide.* Berkeley: University of California Press, 1995.

Petrella, Riccardo. *La Renaissance des cultures régionales en Europe.* Paris: Entente, 1978.

Poggioli, Renato. *Teoria dell'arte d'avanguardia.* Milan: Il Mulino, 1962.

Price, Glanville. *The Languages of Britain.* London: Arnold, 1984.

Roemer, Michael. *Telling Stories: Postmodernism and the Invalidation of Traditional Narrative.* London: Rowman and Littlefield, 1995.

Said, Edward W. *Culture and Imperialism*. New York: Knopf, 1993.

– *Orientalism*. New York: Pantheon, 1978.

Salvi, Sergio. *Le nazioni proibite: Guida a dieci colonie 'interne' dell'Europa occidentale*. Florence: Vallecchi, 1973.

San Juan, Epifanio. *Beyond Postcolonial Theory*. New York: St Martin's Press, 1998.

Schneidau, Herbert N. *Waking Giants: The Presence of the Past in Modernism*. New York: Oxford University Press, 1991.

Simpson, David. *The Academic Postmodern and the Rule of Literature: A Report on Half-Knowledge*. Chicago: University of Chicago Press, 1995.

Staines, David. *Beyond the Provinces: Literary Canada at Century's End*. Toronto: University of Toronto Press, 1995.

Steiner, George. 'In a Post-Culture.' In his *Extraterritorial: Papers on Literature and the Language Revolution*. New York: Atheneum, 1971, pp. 155–71.

Stephens, Meic. *Linguistic Minorities in Western Europe*. Llandysul, Wales: Gomer, 1976.

Tomlinson, John. *Cultural Imperialism: A Critical Introduction*. Baltimore: Johns Hopkins University Press, 1991.

Vermes, Geneviève, ed. *Vingt-cinq communautés linguistiques de la France*. 2 vols. Paris: L'Harmattan, 1988.

Vermes, Geneviève, and Josiane Boutet, eds. *France, pays multilingue*. 2 vols. Paris: L'Harmattan, 1987.

Waugh, Patricia. *Practising Postmodernism, Reading Modernism*. London: Arnold, 1992.

Weisgerber, Jean, ed. *Le Réalisme magique: Roman, peinture et cinéma*. Lausanne: L'Age d'Homme, 1987.

Zamora, Lois Parkinson, and Wendy B. Faris, eds. *Magical Realism: Theory, History, Community*. Durham: Duke University Press, 1995.

2 SCOTS

Aitken, A.J. 'Studies on Scots and Scottish Standard English Today.' In *Languages of Scotland*. Ed. A.J. Aitken and Tom McArthur. Edinburgh: Chambers, 1979, pp. 137–60.

Akros 28 (August 1975). Articles on Scottish poetry from the 1920s through to the 1970s: 6–117.

Annand, J.K. 'Editorial.' *Lallans* 1 (Mairtinmas 1973): 2.

– 'Robert McLellan.' *Lallans* 25 (Mairtinmas 1985): 5–8.

– 'The Vocabulary of Hugh MacDiarmid's Scots Poems.' *Akros* 34–5 (August 1977): 13–19.

Baglow, John. *Hugh MacDiarmid. The Poetry of Self.* Kingston and Montreal: McGill-Queen's University Press, 1987.

Bell, Ian A. 'Lewis Grassic Gibbon's Revolutionary Romanticism.' In Schwend, *Studies in Scottish Fiction,* pp. 257–70.

– ed. *Peripheral Visions: Images of Nationhood in Contemporary British Fiction.* Cardiff: University of Wales Press, 1995.

Black, D.M. [David]. 'In Memoriam: Robert Garioch.' *Chapman* 31 (Winter 1981–2): 1–6.

– 'Poets of the Sixties – III: Robert Garioch.' *Lines Review* 23 (Spring 1967): 8–15.

Bold, Alan. 'After the Renaissance – The Reckoning.' *Chapman* 23–4 (Spring 1979): 12–21.

– *MacDiarmid: Christopher Murray Grieve, A Critical Biography.* Amherst: University of Massachusetts Press, 1988.

– *MacDiarmid: The Terrible Crystal.* London: Routledge and Kegan Paul, 1983.

– *Modern Scottish Literature.* London: Longman, 1983.

– 'Scott the Makar.' *Scotia Review* 13–14 (August–November 1976): 3–14.

Boutelle, Ann Edwards. *Thistle and Rose: A Study of Hugh MacDiarmid's Poetry.* Lewisburg: Bucknell University Press, 1981.

Brown, Ian. 'Plugged into History: The Sense of the Past in Scottish Theatre.' In Stevenson, *Scottish Theatre since the Seventies,* pp. 84–99.

Bryden, Bill. *Benny Lynch: Scenes from a Short Life.* Edinburgh: Southside, 1975.

– 'Bryden Meets Bold.' *Scotia Review* 8 (December 1974): 9–16.

– *Willie Rough: A Play.* Edinburgh: Southside, 1972.

Burns, John. 'Lewis Grassic Gibbon and *A Scots Quair.*' *Chapman* 23–4 (Spring 1979): 22–7.

Burton, Deirdre. 'A Feminist Reading of Lewis Grassic Gibbon's *A Scots Quair.*' In *The British Working-Class Novel in the Twentieth Century.* Ed. Jeremy Hawthorn. London: Arnold, 1984, pp. 35–46.

Buthlay, Kenneth. *Hugh MacDiarmid.* Rev. ed. Edinburgh: Scottish Academic Press, 1982.

– 'The Scotched Snake.' In P.H. Scott, *The Age of MacDiarmid,* pp. 122–56.

– 'Sydney Goodsir Smith: Makar Macironical.' *Akros* 31 (August 1976): 46–56.

Caird, James B. 'Robert Garioch – A Personal Appreciation.' *Scottish Literary Journal* 10:2 (December 1983): 68–78.

– 'Sydney Goodsir Smith.' *Chapman* 26 (Spring 1980): 14–19.

Calder, Angus. 'Scots Language in Transition: Some Thoughts Arising from Hamish Henderson's Essay "Flower and Iron of the Truth."' *Chapman* 82 (1995): 63–70.

Calder, Robert. 'Hear the Values of the Bard.' *Chapman* 69–70 (Autumn 1992): 127–32.

– 'An Overview of Tom Scott's Poetry.' *Chapman* 47–8 (Spring 1987): 28–34.

Campbell, Donald. 'Another Side to Robert Garioch, or, A Glisk of Near-forgotten Hell.' *Akros* 33 (April 1977): 47–52.

– *A Brighter Sunshine: A Hundred Years of the Edinburgh Royal Lyceum Theatre.* Edinburgh: Polygon, 1983.

– *The Jesuit: A Play.* Edinburgh: Harris, 1976.

– *Playing for Scotland: A History of the Scottish Stage, 1715–1965.* Edinburgh: Mercat, 1996.

– 'Plays in Print: A Personal Statement on the Publication of Scots Drama.' *Chapman* 23–4 (Spring 1979): 32–3.

– 'Robert McLellan: The Playwricht.' *Lallans* 10 (Whitsunday 1978): 13–15.

– 'A Sense of Community: Robert McLellan, An Appreciation.' *Chapman* 43–4 (Spring 1986): 35–41.

– *Somerville the Soldier: A Play.* Edinburgh: Harris, 1978.

– 'Whaur's Your Wullie Shakespeare Noo?' *Chapman* 3:1 (1974): 22–6.

– *The Widows of Clyth: A Play.* Edinburgh: Harris, 1979.

Campbell, Ian. 'Chris Caledonia: The Search for an Identity.' *Scottish Literary Journal* 1:2 (December 1974): 45–57.

– 'The Grassic Gibbon Style.' In Schwend, *Studies in Scottish Fiction*, pp. 271–87.

– *Lewis Grassic Gibbon.* Edinburgh: Scottish Academic Press, 1985.

– 'Lewis Grassic Gibbon and the Mearns.' In *A Sense of Place: Studies in Scottish Local History.* Ed. Graeme Cruickshank. Edinburgh: Scotland's Cultural Heritage, 1988, pp. 15–26.

Christianson, Aileen. 'Flyting with *A Drunk Man.*' *Scottish Affairs* 5 (Autumn 1993): 126–35.

Clough, R.F. '*A Scots Quair*: Ewan's Rejection of Ellen.' *Scottish Literary Journal* 20:2 (November 1993): 41–8.

Corbett, John. *Language and Scottish Literature: Scottish Language and Literature.* Edinburgh: Edinburgh University Press, 1997.

Craig, Cairns. 'The Body in the Kit Bag: History and the Scottish Novel.' *Cencrastus* 1 (Autumn 1979): 18–22.

– 'Fearful Selves: Character, Community, and the Scottish Imagination.' *Cencrastus* 4 (Winter 1980–1): 29–32.

– ed. *The History of Scottish Literature.* Vol. 4, *Twentieth Century.* Aberdeen: Aberdeen University Press, 1987.

– *Out of History: Narrative Paradigms in Scottish and English Culture.* Edinburgh: Polygon, 1996.

– 'Twentieth Century Scottish Literature: An Introduction.' In his *History of Scottish Literature*, pp. 1–9.

Craig, David. 'MacDiarmid the Marxist Poet.' In Duval, *Hugh MacDiarmid*, pp. 87–99.

Crawford, Robert. 'A Drunk Man Looks at the Waste Land.' *Scottish Literary Journal* 14:2 (November 1987): 62–78.

– 'Modernism as Provincialism.' Chap. 5 of his *Devolving English Literature*. Oxford: Clarendon Press, 1992, pp. 216–70.

Crawford, Thomas. 'The Poetry of Sydney Goodsir Smith.' *Studies in Scottish Literature* 7 (1969–70): 40–59.

– 'Tom Scott: From Apocalypse to Brand.' *Akros* 31 (August 1976): 57–69.

Cuthbertson, Iain. 'Sydney and the Plays.' In *For Sydney Goodsir Smith*, pp. 65–71.

Daiches, David. 'Hugh MacDiarmid and Scottish Poetry.' *Poetry* 72 (1948): 202–18.

– 'Hugh MacDiarmid and the Scottish Literary Tradition.' In P.H. Scott, *The Age of MacDiarmid*, pp. 59–82.

Dixon, Keith. 'Letting the Side Down: Some Remarks on James Leslie Mitchell's Vision of History.' *Etudes écossaises* 1 (1992): 273–81.

– 'Rough Edges: The Feminist Representation of Women in the Writing of Lewis Grassic Gibbon.' In Schwend, *Studies in Scottish Fiction*, pp. 289–301.

Dunn, Douglas. 'Cantraips and Trauchles: Robert Garioch and Scottish Poetry.' *Cencrastus* 43 (Autumn 1992): 37–43.

Duval, K.D., and Sydney Goodsir Smith, eds. *Hugh MacDiarmid: A Festschrift.* Edinburgh: Duval, 1962.

Edwards, Owen Dudley. 'The Quest for Ogilvie.' *Chapman* 16 (Summer 1976): 38–48.

Findlay, William. 'Diaskeuasts of the Omnific Word.' *Cencrastus* 23 (June–August 1986): 48–52.

For Sydney Goodsir Smith. Edinburgh: Macdonald, 1975.

Fournier, Jean-Marie. 'Hugh MacDiarmid lecteur de Joyce.' In *De Joyce à Stoppard: Ecritures de la modernité*. Ed. Adolphe Haberer. Lyon: Presses Universitaires de Lyon, 1991, pp. 45–58.

Freedman, Carl. 'Possibilities of a Political Aesthetic: The Case of Hugh MacDiarmid.' *Minnesota Review* n.s. 23 (Fall 1984): 41–57.

Fulton, Robin. *Contemporary Scottish Poetry: Individuals and Contexts*. Loanhead, Midlothian: Macdonald, 1974.

Garioch, Robert. '*Carotid Cornucopius*.' In *For Sydney Goodsir Smith*, pp. 47–54.

– *Complete Poetical Works*. Ed. Robin Fulton. Edinburgh: Macdonald, 1983.

– 'Under the Eildon Tree.' *Akros* 10 (May 1969): 41–7.

Gibbon, Lewis Grassic. *Cloud Howe*. Edinburgh: Canongate, 1988.

- *Grey Granite*. Edinburgh: Canongate, 1990.
- *Sunset Song*. Edinburgh: Canongate, 1988.
Gifford, Douglas. *Neil M. Gunn and Lewis Grassic Gibbon*. Edinburgh: Oliver and Boyd, 1983.
Gish, Nancy K., ed. *Hugh MacDiarmid: Man and Poet*. Edinburgh: Edinburgh University Press, 1992.
- *Hugh MacDiarmid: The Man and His Work*. London: Macmillan, 1984.
- 'MacDiarmid Reading *The Waste Land*: The Politics of Quotation.' In Gish, *Hugh MacDiarmid* (1992), pp. 207–29.
Glen, Duncan. 'Editorial: A Curly Snake.' *Akros* 14 (April 1970): 2–4.
- ed. *Hugh MacDiarmid, A Critical Survey*. Edinburgh: Scottish Academic Press, 1972.
- *Hugh MacDiarmid (Christopher Murray Grieve) and the Scottish Renaissance*. Edinburgh: Chambers, 1964.
Gold, Eric. *Sydney Goodsir Smith's 'Under the Eildon Tree': An Essay*. Preston: Akros, 1975.
Hagemann, Susanne. ' "Bidin naitural": Identity Questions in Scottish Twentieth-Century Renaissance Literature.' *Scottish Literary Journal* 21:1 (May 1994): 44–55.
- *Die Schottische Renaissance: Literatur und Nation im 20. Jahrhundert*. Frankfurt am Main: Peter Lang, 1992.
Hart, Francis Russell. *The Scottish Novel: A Critical Survey*. London: Murray, 1978.
Henderson, Hamish. 'Flytings Galore: MacDiarmid v. The Folkies.' *Cencrastus* 49 (Autumn 1994): 15–25.
- 'Zeus as Curly Snake: The Chthonian Image.' *Cencrastus* 52 (Summer 1995): 7–9.
Herbert, W.N. 'MacDiarmid: Mature Art.' *Scottish Literary Journal* 15:2 (November 1988): 24–38.
- *To Circumjack MacDiarmid: The Poetry and Prose of Hugh MacDiarmid*. Oxford: Clarendon Press, 1992.
Herdman, John. 'Hugh MacDiarmid's *To Circumjack Cencrastus*.' *Akros* 34–5 (August 1977): 63–75.
- 'Tom Scott's Translations from the French.' *Scotia Review* 13–14 (August–November 1976): 38–40.
- 'Towards New Jerusalem: The Poetry of Tom Scott.' *Akros* 16 (April 1971): 43–9.
Hobsbaum, Philip. 'Speech Rather Than Lallans: West of Scotland Poetry.' *Lines Review* 113 (June 1990): 5–10.
Hubbard, Tom. 'Reintegrated Scots: The Post-MacDiarmid Makars.' In Cairns Craig, *History*, pp. 179–93.

Hutchison, David. *The Modern Scottish Theatre.* Glasgow: Molendinar, 1977.

– 'Roddy McMillan and the Scottish Theatre.' *Cencrastus* 2 (Spring 1980): 5–8.

Jackson, Alan. 'The Knitted Claymore: An Essay on Culture and Nationalism.' *Lines Review* 37 (June 1971): 3–38.

Johnson, Roy. 'Lewis Grassic Gibbon and *A Scots Quair.* Politics in the Novel.' In Lucas, *The 1930s,* pp. 42–58.

Kay, Billy. *Scots: The Mither Tongue.* Rev. ed. Darvel, Ayrshire: Alloway, 1993.

Kelman, James. *How Late It Was, How Late.* London: Secker and Warburg, 1994.

Kemp, Robert. 'Conflicting Influences in the Scottish Theatre.' *Saltire Review* 1:1 (April 1954): 8–11.

Kerrigan, Catherine. 'Underground Men: Dostoevsky in the Work of Hugh Mac-Diarmid.' *Journal of Narrative Technique* 17 (1987): 45–50.

– *'Whaur Extremes Meet': The Poetry of Hugh MacDiarmid, 1920–1934.* Edinburgh: Thin, Mercat, 1983.

Kincaid, John. 'The Scottish Dilemma: 50 Years of Prose and Drama.' *Chapman* 23–4 (Spring 1979): 28–31.

Klaus, H. Gustav. 'Socialist Fiction in the 1930s: Some Preliminary Observations.' In Lucas, *The 1930s,* pp. 13–41.

Leach, Allan. 'The High Purposes of Literature: Robert McLellan and His Work.' *Library Review* 23: 1–2 (Spring–Summer 1971): 3–11.

Lindsay, Maurice. *History of Scottish Literature.* Rev. ed. London: Hale, 1992.

Lorimer, William Laughton, trans. *The New Testament in Scots.* Edinburgh: Southside, 1983.

Low, John Thomas. 'Mid Twentieth Century Drama in Lowland Scots.' In McClure, *Scotland and the Lowland Tongue,* pp. 170–94.

Lucas, John, ed. *The 1930s: A Challenge to Orthodoxy.* Sussex: Harvester, 1978.

Ludwig, Hans-Werner. 'Province and Metropolis, Centre and Periphery: Some Critical Terms Re-examined.' In *Poetry in the British Isles: Non-Metropolitan Perspectives.* Ed. Hans-Werner Ludwig and Lothar Fietz. Cardiff: University of Wales Press, 1995, pp. 47–69.

Macaree, David. 'Myth and Allegory in Lewis Grassic Gibbon's *A Scots Quair.*' *Studies in Scottish Literature* 2 (1964–5): 45–55.

MacCallum, Neil R., and David Purves, ed. *Mak It New: An Anthology of Twenty-One Years of Writing in 'Lallans.'* Edinburgh: Mercat, 1995.

MacDiarmid, Hugh [C.M. Grieve]. *Albyn, or Scotland and the Future.* London: Kegan Paul, Trench, Trubner, 1927.

– *At the Sign of the Thistle: A Collection of Essays.* London: Stanley Nott, 1934.

– *Burns Today and Tomorrow.* Edinburgh: Castle Wynd, 1959.

– *Complete Poems.* Ed. Michael Grieve and W.R. Aitken. 2 vols. Manchester: Carcanet, 1993.

– 'Sydney Goodsir Smith: A Redeeming Feature.' *Akros* 10 (May 1969): 17–20.

Mackie, Alastair. 'Change and Continuity in Modern Scots Poetry.' *Akros* 33 (April 1977): 13–40.

Maclean, Sorley. *'Figs and Thistles.'* In *For Sydney Goodsir Smith,* pp. 73–8.

MacQueen, John. 'The Scottish Literary Renaissance and Late Medieval Scottish Poetry.' *Studies in Scottish Literature* 26 (1991): 543–55.

Malcolm, William K. *A Blasphemer and Reformer: A Study of James Leslie Mitchell / Lewis Grassic Gibbon.* Aberdeen: Aberdeen University Press, 1984.

Malzahn, Manfred. 'The Industrial Novel.' In Cairns Craig, *History,* pp. 229–42.

Manning, Susan. 'Scotland and America: National Literatures? National Languages?' *Cencrastus* 32 (New Year 1989): 41–6.

Manson, John. 'Hugh MacDiarmid and Lewis Grassic Gibbon's Politics.' *Cencrastus* 50 (Winter 1994): 39–42.

Mason, Leonard. *Two Younger Poets: Duncan Glen and Donald Campbell, A Study of Their Scots Poetry.* Preston: Akros, 1976.

Mathers, Neil, ed. *The Auk Remembered.* Montrose: Corbie, 1995.

Maynard, Katherine K. 'Hugh MacDiarmid and Thomas Hardy: Local Realities and the "Revolt against All Accepted Things."' *Studies in Scottish Literature* 27 (1992): 189–202.

McArthur, Tom. 'Scots and Southron.' Chap. 6 of his *The English Languages.* Cambridge: Cambridge University Press, 1998, pp. 138–59.

McCaig, Norman. 'The Poetry of Sydney Goodsir Smith.' *Saltire Review* 1:1 (April 1954): 14–19.

McCarey, Peter. *Hugh MacDiarmid and the Russians.* Edinburgh: Scottish Academic Press, 1987.

McClure, J. Derrick. 'The Concept of Standard Scots.' *Chapman* 23–4 (Spring 1979): 90–9.

– 'Developing Scots as a National Language.' In *The Scots Language: Planning for Modern Usage.* Edinburgh: Ramsay Head, 1980, pp. 11–14.

– 'Modern Scots Prose Writing.' In his ed. *The Scots Language in Education.* Association for Scottish Literary Studies: Occasional Papers No. 3, pp. 54–67.

– ed. *Scotland and the Lowland Tongue: Studies in the Language and Literature of Lowland Scotland in Honour of David D. Murison.* Aberdeen: Aberdeen University Press, 1983.

– 'Scots in Dialogue: Some Uses and Implications.' In his *Scotland and the Lowland Tongue,* pp. 129–48.

– 'Scots: Its Range of Uses.' In *Languages of Scotland.* Ed. A.J. Aitken and Tom McArthur. Edinburgh: Chambers, 1979, pp. 26–48.

– 'The Spelling of Scots: A Phoneme-Based System.' *Scottish Literary Journal* Supplement 12 (Summer 1980): 25–9.

– 'The Synthesisers of Scots.' In *Minority Languages Today*. Ed. Einar Haugen et al. Edinburgh: Edinburgh University Press, 1981, pp. 91–9.

McCulloch, Margery. 'Modernism and the Scottish Tradition: The Duality of *A Drunk Man Looks at the Thistle*.' *Chapman* 25 (August 1979): 50–6.

– 'The Undeservedly Broukit Bairn: Hugh MacDiarmid's *To Circumjack Cencrastus*.' *Studies in Scottish Literature* 17 (1982): 165–85.

McGrath, Tom, and Jimmy Boyle. *The Hard Man: A Play*. Edinburgh: Canongate, 1977.

McLellan, Robert. *The Flouers o Edinburgh: A Comedy of the Eighteenth Century in Three Acts*. In his *Collected Plays*. Vol. 1. London: Calder and New York: Riverrun, 1981, pp. 163–242.

– *The Hypocrite*. London: Calder and Boyars, 1970.

– *Jamie the Saxt: A Historical Comedy*. Ed. Ian Campbell and Ronald D.S. Jack. London: Calder and Boyars, 1970.

– *Linmill Stories*. Edinburgh: Canongate, 1990.

McMillan, Roddy. *The Bevellers: A Play*. Edinburgh: Southside, 1974.

Meldon d'Arcy, Julian. 'Chris Guthrie, Ellen Johns, and the Two Ewan Tavendales: Significant Parallels in *A Scots Quair*.' *Scottish Literary Journal* 23:1 (May 1996): 42–9.

Mitchell, Jack. 'The Struggle for the Working-Class Novel in Scotland, 1900–1939.' *Zeitschrift für Anglistik und Amerikanistik* 21 (1973): 384–413.

Morgan, Edwin. 'Glasgow Speech in Recent Scottish Literature.' In McClure, *Scotland and the Lowland Tongue*, pp. 195–208.

– *Hugh MacDiarmid*. Harlow: Longman, 1976.

– 'Hugh MacDiarmid's Later Poetry against an International Background.' *Scottish Literary Journal* 5:2 (December 1978): 20–35.

Munro, Ian S. *Leslie Mitchell: Lewis Grassic Gibbon*. Edinburgh: Oliver and Boyd, 1966.

Murdoch, Brian. 'Tom Scott's "Brand the Builder."' *Akros* 51 (October 1983): 34–6.

Murison, David. *The Guid Scots Tongue*. Edinburgh: Blackwood, 1977.

– 'The Language of Sydney Goodsir Smith.' In *For Sydney Goodsir Smith*, pp. 23–9.

Murray, Isobel. 'Action and Narrative Stance in *A Scots Quair*.' In *Literature of the North*. Ed. David Hewitt and Michael Spiller. Aberdeen: Aberdeen University Press, 1983, pp. 109–20.

– 'Novelists of the Renaissance.' In Cairns Craig, *History*, pp. 103–17.

Murray, Isobel, and Bob Tait. *Ten Modern Scottish Novels*. Aberdeen: Aberdeen University Press, 1984.

Nairn, Thom. 'Out of Darkness Coming: Some Notes on Tom Scott and Hugh MacDiarmid.' *Agenda* 30:4 and 31:1 (Winter–Spring 1993): 148–64.

- '"A route maist devious": Sydney Goodsir Smith and Edinburgh.' *Cencrastus* 33 (Spring 1989): 6–9.

Neill, William. 'Tom Scott and the Scots Tongue.' *Agenda* 30:4 and 31:1 (Winter–Spring 1993): 96–103.

Nichol, Don W. 'Belli Up to Date: Scots and English Sonnet Translations by Robert Garioch and Anthony Burgess.' *Chapman* 39 (Autumn 1984): 34–41.

Norquay, Glenda. 'Voices in Time: *A Scots Quair*.' *Scottish Literary Journal* 11:1 (May 1984): 57–68.

Oxenhorn, Harvey. *Elemental Things: The Poetry of Hugh MacDiarmid.* Edinburgh: Edinburgh University Press, 1984.

Oxley, William. 'Poetry as the Heightened Vernacular: Tom Scott's *Brand the Builder*.' *Agenda* 30:4 and 31:1 (Winter–Spring 1993): 142–7.

Paterson, Lindsay. 'Donald Campbell: Playwright in Search of a Method.' *Cencrastus* 6 (Autumn 1981): 6–8.

- 'Language and Identity on the Stage.' In Stevenson, *Scottish Theatre since the Seventies*, pp. 75–83.

Perrie, Walter. 'Nietzsche and the Drunk Man.' *Cencrastus* 2 (Spring 1980): 9–12.

- 'Tom Scott and the Long Narrative Tradition.' *Scotia Review* 13–14 (August–November 1976): 23–30.

Purves, David. 'A Scots Orthography.' *Scottish Literary Journal* Supplement 9 (Spring 1979): 62–76.

Reid, Charlotte. *List of Plays in Scots.* Glasgow: Glasgow City Council, Libraries Department, 1991.

Relich, Mario. 'Scottish Tradition and Robert Garioch's Individual Talent.' *Lines Review* 136 (March 1996): 5–17.

Riach, Alan. 'Hugh MacDiarmid and Charles Olson.' In Gish, *Hugh MacDiarmid* (1992), pp. 123–44.

- *Hugh MacDiarmid's Epic Poetry.* Edinburgh: Edinburgh University Press, 1991.

- 'The Mortal Memory.' *Lines Review* 125 (June 1993): 5–10.

- '"The Present Is Prologue": Postmodernist Scotland.' *Vesse* 4:2 (June 1987): 47–50.

Robertson, James, ed. *A Tongue in Yer Heid: A Selection of the Best Contemporary Short Stories in Scots.* Edinburgh: B and W, 1994.

Roskies, D.M.E. 'Language, Class, and Radical Perspective in *A Scots Quair*.' *Zeitschrift für Anglistik und Amerikanistik* 29 (1981): 142–53.

Ross, Raymond J. 'Edinburgh Grooves: Robert Garioch's Edinburgh.' *Cencrastus* 29 (Spring 1988): 6–8.

- 'The Real Tom Scott.' *Chapman* 47–8 (Spring 1987): 17–23.

Schwend, Joachim, and Horst W. Drescher, eds. *Studies in Scottish Fiction: Twentieth Century.* Frankfurt am Main: Peter Lang, 1990.

Scott, Alexander. 'Daylight and the Dark: Edinburgh in the Poetry of Robert Fergusson and Sydney Goodsir Smith.' *Lines Review* 3 (Summer 1953): 9–13.

– 'Goodsir Smith's Masterpiece: *Under the Eildon Tree.*' In *For Sydney Goodsir Smith,* pp. 11–22.

– 'The MacDiarmid Makars.' *Akros* 19 (August 1972): 9–30.

– 'Sydney Goodsir Smith: The Art of Devilment.' *Akros* 10 (May 1969): 21–8.

Scott, P.H., and A.C. Davis, eds. *The Age of MacDiarmid: Essays on Hugh MacDiarmid and His Influence on Contemporary Scotland.* Edinburgh: Mainstream, 1980.

Scott, Tom. *The Collected Shorter Poems of Tom Scott.* London: Agenda; Edinburgh: Chapman, 1993.

Scullion, Adrienne. 'Feminine Pleasures and Masculine Indignities: Gender and Community in Scottish Drama.' In *Gendering the Nation: Studies in Modern Scottish Literature.* Ed. Christopher Whyte. Edinburgh: Edinburgh University Press, 1995, pp. 169–204.

Smith, G. Gregory. *Scottish Literature: Character and Influence.* London, Macmillan, 1919.

Smith, Iain Crichton. 'The Golden Lyric: An Essay on the Poetry of Hugh MacDiarmid.' In Glen, *Hugh MacDiarmid* (1972), pp. 124–40.

Smith, Stephen P. 'Invitations to a Voyage: Scott's Translations of Baudelaire and Villon in *The Ship and Ither Poems.*' *Agenda* 30:4 and 31:1 (Winter-Spring 1993): 126–34.

Smith, Sydney Goodsir. *Carotid Cornucopius: Caird of the Cannon Gait and Voyeur of the Outlook Touer.* Edinburgh: Macdonald, 1964.

– *Collected Poems, 1941–1975.* London: Calder, 1975.

– 'MacDiarmid's Three Hymns to Lenin.' In Duval, *Hugh MacDiarmid,* pp. 73–86.

– 'Trahison des Clercs or the Anti-Scottish Lobby in Scottish Letters.' *Studies in Scottish Literature* 2 (1964–5): 71–86.

– *The Wallace: A Triumph in Five Acts.* London: Calder, 1985.

Speirs, John. *The Scots Literary Tradition: An Essay in Criticism.* Rev. 2nd ed. London: Faber and Faber, 1962.

Stephens, Charles. 'The Poet and the Revolution: MacDiarmid and Blok.' *Cencrastus* 32 (New Year 1989): 26–8.

Stevenson, Randall. 'In the Jungle of the Cities.' In his *Scottish Theatre since the Seventies,* pp. 100–11.

– 'Recent Scottish Theatre: Dramatic Developments?' In *Scotland: Literature, Culture, Politics.* Ed. Peter Zenzinger. Heidelberg: Winter, 1989, pp. 187–213.

- 'Scottish Theatre, 1950–1980.' In Cairns Craig, *History*, pp. 349–67.
- 'Snakes and Ladders, Snakes and Owls: Charting Scottish Theatre.' In his *Scottish Theatre since the Seventies*, pp. 1–20.

Stevenson, Randall, and Gavin Wallace, eds. *Scottish Theatre since the Seventies*. Edinburgh: Edinburgh University Press, 1996.

Thomaneck, J.K.A. '*A Scots Quair* in East Germany.' *Scottish Literary Journal* 3:1 (July 1976): 62–6.

Tremayne, Sydney. 'Robert Garioch.' *Akros* 47 (August 1981): 110–13.

Trengove, Graham. 'Who Is You? Grammar and Grassic Gibbon.' *Scottish Literary Journal* 2:2 (December 1975): 47–62.

Tulloch, Graham. 'Robert Garioch's Different Styles of Scots.' *Scottish Literary Journal* 12:1 (May 1985): 53–69.

Wagner, Geoffrey. '"The Greatest since Galt": Lewis Grassic Gibbon.' *Essays in Criticism* 2 (1952): 295–310.

- 'The Use of Lallans for Prose.' *Journal of English and Germanic Philology* 51 (1952): 212–25.

Wallace, Gavin, and Randall Stevenson, eds. *The Scottish Novel since the Seventies*. Edinburgh: Edinburgh University Press, 1993.

Watson, Roderick. *The Literature of Scotland*. London: Macmillan, 1984.

- *MacDiarmid*. Rev. ed. Milton Keynes: Open University Press, 1985.
- ed. *The Poetry of Scotland*. Edinburgh: Edinburgh University Press, 1995.
- 'The Speaker in the Gairdens: The Poetry of Robert Garioch.' *Akros* 16 (April 1971): 69–76.
- 'The Symbolism of *A Drunk Man Looks at the Thistle*.' In Glen, *Hugh MacDiarmid* (1972), pp. 94–116.

Welsh, Irvine. *Trainspotting*. London: Secker and Warburg, 1993.

Whitfield, Peter. *Grassic Gibbon and His World*. Aberdeen: Aberdeen Journals, 1994.

Whyte, Christopher. 'Construction of Meaning in MacDiarmid's "Drunk Man."' *Studies in Scottish Literature* 23 (1988): 199–238.

- 'Gender and Sexuality in *A Drunk Man*.' *Scottish Affairs* 5 (Autumn 1993): 136–46.
- 'MacDiarmid's *A Drunk Man Looks at the Thistle* as National Epic.' *Coexistence* 29 (1992): 163–75.
- 'Tom Scott: An Imaged World.' *Chapman* 47–8 (Spring 1987): 7–13.

Wilson, Norman, ed. *Scottish Writing and Writers*. Edinburgh: Ramsay Head, 1977.

Wilson, Patricia J. 'Freedom and God: Some Implications of the Key Speech in *A Scots Quair*.' *Scottish Literary Journal* 7:2 (December 1980): 55–79.

Wittig, Kurt. *The Scottish Tradition in Literature*. Edinburgh: Oliver and Boyd, 1958.

Wolmark, Jenny. 'Problems of Tone in *A Scots Quair.' Red Letters* 11 (1981): 15–23.

Wood, Barry. 'Scots, Poets, and the City.' In Cairns Craig, *History*, pp. 337–48.

Young, Douglas. *'Plastic Scots' and the Scottish Literary Tradition: An Authoritative Introduction to a Controversy.* Glasgow: Maclellan, 1947.

Young, Douglas F. *Beyond the Sunset: A Study of James Leslie Mitchell (Lewis Grassic Gibbon).* Aberdeen: Impulse, 1973.

Zagratzki, Uwe. *Libertäre und utopische Tendenzen im Erzählwerk James Leslie Mitchells (Lewis Grassic Gibbons).* Frankfurt am Main: Peter Lang, 1991.

Zenzinger, Peter. 'Contemporary Scottish Fiction.' In his ed. *Scotland: Literature, Culture, Politics.* Heidelberg: Winter, 1989, pp. 215–42.

3   BRETON

Abalain, Hervé. *Destin des langues celtiques.* Paris: Ophrys, 1989.

Abanna, G.E. [Guy Etienne]. 'Eil tezenn vrezhonek ar c'hantved: "Eus *Gwarizi Vras Emer* da v*Mari Vorgan*" gant P. Kermoal.' *Al Liamm* 126 (Genver–C'hwevrer 1968): 51–62.

Abeozen [Fañch Elies]. *Istor Lennegezh Vrezhonek an Amzer-vremañ.* Brest: Al Liamm, 1957.

Andouard, Loeiz. 'Ar c'hoariva brezhonek.' *Skrid* 17 (miz Kerzu 1978): 27–57.

– 'Ar c'hoariva brezhonek e Paris.' *Al Liamm* 151 (Meurzh–Ebrel 1972): 163–71.

An Tieg, Soaz. 'Añjela a Dreger hag Añjela a Vreizh.' *Al Liamm* 210 (Genver–C'hwevrer 1982): 78–83.

Barzaz-Breiz: Chants populaires de la Bretagne, par le vicomte Hersart de la Villemarqué. 1867 ed. Paris: Librairie Académique Perrin, 1963.

Barzhaz Breizh. Rakskrid gant Per Denez. Lesneven: Mouladurioù Hor Yezh, 1988.

Barzhaz, kant barzhoneg berr (1350–1953). Al Liamm 41 (Du–Kerzu 1953).

Benead [Madalen St Gal de Pons]. '"Mari Vorgan" romant gant Roparz Hemon.' *Al Liamm* 174 (Genver–C'hwevrer 1976): 59–60.

Bouëssel du Bourg, Yann. 'L'abbé Loeiz ar Floc'h : Maodez Glanndour.' *Dalc'homp Soñj* 18 (Goañv 1987): 36–37, 42.

– 'Across Breton Literature: Three Women. I. Anjela Duval.' *Bro Nevez* 17 (November 1985): 8–10.

– 'Framm Keltiek Breizh / L'Institut Celtique de Bretagne.' In Tymen, *Roparz Hemon*, pp. 81–103.

– 'Roparz Hemon et le journal *Arvor.*' In Tymen, *Roparz Hemon*, pp. 43–71.

Calin, William. 'The Modern Novel in Breton and the Quest for a European Literature.' *French Forum* 22 (1997): 235–42.

Caoussin, Herry. 'Roparz Hemon et l'art dramatique breton.' In Tymen, *Roparz Hemon*, pp. 170–4.

Chevrel, Yves. 'L'université et la culture et la littérature bretonnes: Perspectives offertes par la littérature générale et comparée.' *Skol Vreizh* 45 (avril–juin 1976): 5–8.

Cünnen, Janina, and Hildegard L.C. Tristram. 'Añjela Duval et Sarah Kirsch: Désir du coeur et pour la terre.' In *Breizh ha Pobloù Europa: Pennadoù en enor da bPer Denez*. Ed. Herve ar Bihan. Hor Yezh / Klask / Presses Universitaires de Rennes, 1999, pp. 99–126.

Danno, Fañch. 'Kenlabour gand Anjela Duval.' *Brud Nevez* 47 (miz Eost ha miz Gwengolo 1981): 33–6.

De Ballaing, Vefa. 'L'influence de Gwalarn.' *Dalc'homp Soñj* 24 (Diskar Amzer 1988): 11–13.

Denez, Per. *Blue like Blue Eyes Which Were Not My Own*. Trans. J. Ian Press. Lesneven: Mouladurioù Hor Yezh, 1993.

– *Diougan Gwenc'hlan*. Brest: Al Liamm, 1979.

– *Glas evel daoulagad c'hlas na oant ket ma re*. Brest: Al Liamm, 1979.

– 'Gwalarn.' *Al Liamm* 20 (Mae–Mezheven 1950): 24–9.

– 'Kannadig Gwalarn.' *Hor Yezh* 131–2 (miz Meurzh 1980): 51–88.

– 'Modern Breton Literature.' In *Literature in Celtic Countries*. Ed. J.E. Caerwyn Williams. Cardiff: University of Wales Press, 1971, pp. 111–36.

– 'Roparz Hemon ha "Brezhoneg ar Vugale."' *Hor Yezh* 137 (miz Meurzh 1981): 37–56.

– 'Roparz Hemon: Kounioù.' In *Roparz Hemon: Kouniwhere hag hengoun lennegel ar Brezhoneg*. Dublin: Coiscéim, 1990, pp. 8–27.

– 'Roparz Hemon (1900–1978).' *Dalc'homp Soñj* 24 (Diskar Amzer 1988): 6–10.

– 'Ar skrivagner en ur vro drevadennet.' *Al Liamm* 141 (Gouere–Eost 1970): 290–8.

– *Yezh ha Bro: Pennadoù ha Studiadennoù*. Lesneven: Mouladurioù Hor Yezh, 1998.

Denez, Per, et al. *Permanence de la langue bretonne: De la linguistique à la psychanalyse*. Rennes: Institut Culturel de Bretagne, 1986.

Dobzynski, Charles. 'Paol Keineg: Un barde breton d'aujourd'hui.' *Europe* 625 (mai 1981): 123–6.

Drezen, Youenn. *Itron Varia Garmez*. Brest: Al Liamm, 1977.

– *Skol-louarn Veig Trebern*. 3 vols. Brest: Al Liamm, 1972–4.

Durand, Philippe, ed. *Breizh hiziv: Anthologie de la chanson en Bretagne*. Paris: Oswald, 1976.

Duval, Anjela. *Kan an douar*. Brest: Al Liamm, 1978.

– *Stourm a ran war bep tachenn.* Kinniget gant Ronan Koadig. Saint-Brieuc: Mignoned Anjela, 1998.

– *Traoñ an dour.* Brest: Al Liamm, 1982.

Elegoët, Fañch. 'Bilinguisme ou domination linguistique?' *Les Temps Modernes* 324–6 (août–septembre 1973): 213–22.

Even, Arzel. 'Faltazi Roparz Hemon (Tem an dec'hadenn).' *Al Liamm* 142 (Gwengolo–Here 1970): 334–44.

Favereau, Francis [Frañsez]. *Bretagne contemporaine: Langue, culture, identité.* Morlaix: Skol Vreizh, 1993.

– 'L'évolution du discours bretonnant chez Pierre-Jakez Hélias.' In *L'Ouest et le politique: Mélanges offerts à Michel Denis.* Ed. Michel Lagrée and Jacqueline Sainclivier. Rennes: Presses Universitaires de Rennes, 1996, pp. 165–77.

– *Littérature et écrivains bretonnants depuis 1945. Skol Vreizh* 20 (mars 1991).

– 'Pierre-Jakez Hélias, maître de l'histoire de vie.' In Hue, *Ecrire la Bretagne,* pp. 93–103.

– 'P.J. Helias, evel am eus e anavezet (un tamm bennak).' *Al Liamm* 292 (Gwengolo–Here 1995): 363–70.

Fournel, Gilles. *Le Théâtre en Bretagne.* Rennes: Maison de la Culture de Rennes, 1981.

Galand, René [Reun ar C'halan]. *Stratégie de la lecture.* New York: Peter Lang, 1990.

– 'Stumm ha ster ar stourm speredel e *Komzoù bev.*' *Al Liamm* 240 (Genver–C'hwevrer 1987): 12–17.

Glanndour, Maodez. 'Barzhoniezh maread Gwalarn.' *Al Liamm* 124 (Gwengolo–Here 1967): 423–33.

– 'En ur dreiñ follennoù va eñvor.' *Al Liamm* 191 (Du–Kerzu 1978): 429–37.

– *Imram.* In his *Komzoù bev.* Brest: Al Liamm, 1985, pp. 143–90.

– 'Lennegezh evit ar bobl?' *Al Liamm* 76 (Gwengolo–Here 1959): 355–64.

– 'Al Lennegezh vrezhonek a-vremañ.' *Al Liamm* 94 (Gwengolo–Here 1962): 357–63.

– *Vijelez an deiz diwezhañ.* Brest: Al Liamm, 1978.

Glon, Thierry. 'Ecrivains de la "Recouvrance" (de 1960 à 1980).' In Hue, *Ecrire la Bretagne,* pp. 33–52.

– *Pierre-Jakez Hélias et la Bretagne perdue.* Rennes: Presses Universitaires de Rennes, 1998.

Gontard, Marc. 'Effets de métissage dans la littérature bretonne.' In *Métissage du texte: Bretagne, Maghreb, Québec.* Ed. Bernard Hue. Rennes: Presses Universitaires de Rennes, 1993, pp. 27–39.

– 'Pour une littérature bretonne de langue française.' In Hue, *Ecrire la Bretagne,* pp. 17–31.

Gorvan, René, and Lena an Abad. 'Pennad-kaoz diwar-benn Maodez Glanndour ha *Komzoù bev.*' *Al Liamm* 299 (Du–Kerzu 1996): 453–62.

Grall, Xavier. *Le Cheval couché.* Paris: Hachette, 1977.

Guillemin-Young, Yvette A. 'Anjela Duval: Le chant de la terre et du combat.' *French Review* 71 (1997–8): 66–73.

– 'Hélias's *Yseult Seconde:* The Vindication of Isold of Brittany.' *French Review* 69 (1995–6): 284–90.

Gwegen, Jorj. *La Langue bretonne face à ses oppresseurs.* Quimper: Nature et Bretagne, 1975.

Gwernig, Youenn. *Un Dornad plu / A Handful of Feathers: Brezhoneg ha saozneg.* Brest: Al Liamm, 1997.

Hamon, André-Georges. *Chantres de toutes les Bretagnes: Vingt ans de chanson bretonne.* Paris: Picollec, 1981.

Helias, Per Jakez [Pierre-Jakez Hélias]. *A-berz eur bed all.* Rennes: Editions Ouest-France, 1991.

– *Le Cheval d'orgueil: Mémoires d'un Breton du pays bigouden.* Paris: Plon, 1975.

– *An Isild a-heul.* Brest: Brud Nevez, 1983.

– *Katrina Lenn-Zu.* Brest: Emgleo Breiz, 1994.

– *Lettres de Bretagne: Langue, culture et civilisations bretonnes.* Paris: Editions Galilée, 1978.

– *Marh al lorh: Envorennou eur Bigouter.* Paris: Plon, 1986.

– *Mevel ar Gosker.* Brest: Emgleo Breiz and Brud Nevez, 1985.

– *Le Quêteur de mémoire: Quarante ans de recherche sur les mythes et la civilisation bretonne.* Paris: Plon, 1990.

– 'Rencontre avec P.J. Hélias.' *Skol Vreizh* 36 (mars 1997): 25–41.

Hemon, Roparz [Pendaran]. 'Arvor sera un journal complet.' *Arvor* 1:5 (2 février 1941): 1.

– 'Attendrons-nous?' *Arvor* 1:2 (12 janvier 1941): 1.

– *Barzhonegoù.* Saint-Brieuc: Al Liamm, 1991.

– *Ur Breizhad oc'h adkavout Breizh.* Brest: Al Liamm, 1972.

– 'Breizh-Uheliz hag ar Brezhoneg.' *Arvor* 3:107 (31 Genver 1943): 1–2.

– '*Gwalarn* ... ha goude.' *Al Liamm* 170 (Mae–Mezheven 1975): 164–70.

– 'Kentel an darvoudou.' *Gwalarn* 136–7 (Mae–Mezheven 1941): 341–2.

– *La Langue bretonne et ses combats.* La Baule: Editions de Bretagne, 1947.

– 'Lutte culturelle.' *Arvor* 1:20 (18 mai 1941): 1.

– *Mari Vorgan.* Brest: Al Liamm, 1975.

– 'Roparz Hemon s'exprime.' In Tymen, *Roparz Hemon*, pp. 133–58.

– *Tangi Kerviler.* Brest: Al Liamm, 1971.

– 'Youenn Drezen (14 Gwengolo 1899–15 C'hwevrer 1972).' *Al Liamm* 151 (Meurzh–Ebrel 1972): 103–12.

Hemon, Roparz, and Olivier Mordrel. '*Gwalarn:* Premier et dernier manifeste de *Gwalarn* en langue française.' *Breiz Atao* 74 (février 1925): 524.

Hubert, Jacqueline. 'L'oeuvre de Paol Keineg.' In Keineg, *Chroniques et croquis,* pp. 127–60.

Hue, Bernard, and Marc Gontard, eds. *Ecrire la Bretagne: 1960–1995.* Rennes: Presses Universitaires de Rennes, 1995.

Huon, Ronan. 'Maodez Glanndour evel m'am eus e anavezet.' *Al Liamm* 240 (Genver–C'hwevrer 1987): 5–11.

– 'Pezhioù-c'hoari.' *Al Liamm* 105 (Gouere–Eost 1964): 306–9.

Huon, Ronan, et al. *Gwalarn: Histoire d'un mouvement littéraire; Textes et documents.* 2 vols. Brest: Bibliothèque Municipale, 1989.

Huon, Tudual. 'Ar romant dre-wall-biv.' *Al Liamm* 248–9 (Mae–Eost 1988): 173–84.

Kandji, Mamadou. 'Du "Rameau d'or" à "L'Herbe d'or": Etude herméneutique et interprétation d'un signe.' *Bridges* 3 (1991): 47–54.

Kedez, Koulizh. 'Melezour Youenn Drezen.' *Emsav* 125 (1978): 29–48.

Keineg, Paol. *Chroniques et croquis des villages verrouillés,* suivi de *Territoire de l'aube, Poèmes-tracts (bilingues), Quelques poèmes d'amour.* Paris: Oswald, 1973.

– *Histoires vraies / Mojennoù gwir,* suivi de *Irlande du Sud Irlande du Nord / Iwerzhon ar C'hreisteiz Iwerzhon an Hanternoz: Poèmes traduits du breton par l'auteur avec le texte original.* Paris: Oswald, 1974.

– *Pibroch de la forêt et de la pluie: Lieux communs,* suivi de *Dahut.* Paris: Gallimard, 1974.

– *35 haiku.* Morlaix: Editions Bretagne, 1978.

Kermoal, Pierrette. *Eus 'Gwarizi Vras Emer' da v'Mari Vorgan': Studienn kinniget e sell da zegemerout graz an Drevouriezh. Preder* 91 (Genver 1967).

– '*Gwalarn* hag ar vojennouriezh hengeltiek: Youenn Drezen ha Roparz Hemon.' *Al Liamm* 190 (Gwengolo–Here 1978): 378–87.

– 'Lennegezh w*Gwalarn.*' *Preder* 111 (Gwengolo 1968): 21–7.

Kervella, Frañsez [Kenan Kongar]. 'Diazezoù ar sevel gwerzioù.' *Al Liamm* 108–12 (1965): 40–53, 101–18, 183–93, 261–74, 322–32.

Kervella, Goulc'han. 'Un nebeut evezhiadennoù diwar-benn ar c'hoariva brezhonek pe Reflexionoù profitabl war-bropos an teatr brezhonek.' *Al Liamm* 193 (Meurzh–Ebrel 1979): 136–57.

Kervella, Rivanon. 'Ar romantoù polis.' *Al Liamm* 131 (Du–Kerzu 1968): 424–31.

Klerg, Marsel. 'Añjela (1905–1981).' *Al Liamm* 210 (Genver–C'hwevrer 1982): 39–54.

– 'Kan an Douar.' *Barr-Heol* 77 (Mezheven 1973): 50–2.

Kongar, Kenan [Frañsez Kervella]. 'Lennadennoù.' *Al Liamm* 151 (Meurzh–Ebrel 1972): 128–39.

- 'Roparz Hemon, hor mestr.' *Al Liamm* 190 (Gwengolo–Here 1978): 345–58.
Langleiz, Zavier. 'E koun Youenn Drezen: Skrivagner ampart ha mignon feal.' *Al Liamm* 151 (Meurzh–Ebrel 1972): 117–25.
Laouénan, Roger. *Anjela Duval.* Quimper: Nature et Bretagne, 1974.
Lebesque, Morvan. *Comment peut-on être breton? Essai sur la démocratie française.* Paris: Seuil, 1970.
Madeg, Mikael. 'Al lennegez testeni e brezoneg.' *Brud Nevez* 115 (miz Mae 1988): 29–38.
- 'Al lennegezh vrezhoneg e Bro-Leon.' *Ar Falz* n.s. 56 (1986): 21–39.
'Maodez Glanndour gwelet gant skolidi S.A.D.E.D.' *Al Liamm* 114 (Genver–C'hwevrer 1966): 46–50.
Martin, Anne-Denes. *Itinéraire poétique en Bretagne: De Tristan Corbière à Xavier Grall.* Paris: L'Harmattan, 1995.
Martin, Ivona. 'War "hent" Añjela.' *Al Liamm* 210 (Genver–C'hwevrer 1982): 19–38.
Mevel, Per Mari. 'Eur gwir melezour euz temz-spered Y. Drezen: *Itron Varia Garmez.' Brud Nevez* 10 (Kerzu 1977): 23–6.
- 'Eun oberenn a-bouez braz.' *Brud* 46 (Nevez-Amzer 1974): 26–32.
Morgan, Sylvia. 'Roparz Hemon: 1900–1978.' *Studia Celtica* 14–15 (1979–80): 380–87.
Morvannou, Fañch. *Le Breton: La jeunesse d'une vieille langue.* Lannion: Presses Populaires de Bretagne, 1980.
- 'Gouestlad gant ar brezhoneg e-pad 50 vloaz.' *Planedenn* 23 (Newez-Amzer 1985): 24–47.
Morvannou, Fañch, and Yann-Ber Piriou. 'La littérature de langue bretonne au XXe siècle.' In *Histoire littéraire et culturelle de la Bretagne.* Ed. Jean Balcou and Yves Le Gallo. Paris: Champion, 1987, vol. 3, pp. 175–252.
Olier, Youenn. *Istor hol lennegezh: 'Skol Walarn.'* 2 vols. Rennes: Imbourc'h, 1974–5.
- *Istor hol lennegezh: 'Skol Walarn.'* Vol. 1, *Roparz Hemon.* Rennes: Imbourc'h, 1974.
- 'Prederiadennoù diwar-benn un nebeut skrivagnerion vrezhonek: Notennoù diwar-benn dremmoù 'zo eus oberenn Maodez Glanndour.' *Al Liamm* 23 (Du–Kerzu 1950): 52–68.
– 'Prederiadennoù e sigur un nebeut skrivagnerion vrezhonek: Notennoù diwar-benn oberenn Youenn Drezen.' *Al Liamm* 28 (Gwengolo–Here 1951): 54–63.
Pennaod, Goulven. 'Situation et structure du breton.' *Kannadig Ker Vreizh* 52 (Gwengolo 1973): 25–52.
Penneg, Per. 'Roll oberennoù Roparz Hemon.' *Al Liamm* 192–4 (Genver–

Mezheven 1979): 34–47, 158–64, 227–37; 251 (Du–Kerzu 1988): 375–85; 252–6 (Genver–Here 1989): 50–6, 144–7, 222–6, 299–301.

Per-Jakez Helias. Skol Vreizh 36 (mars 1997).

Piriou, Yann-Ber, ed. *Défense de cracher par terre et de parler breton: Poèmes de combat (1950–1970).* Paris: Oswald, 1971.

– 'Kan ar skrilhed e Traoñ-an-Dour.' *Al Liamm* 121 (Meurzh–Ebrel 1967): 168–79.

– 'Préface' to his *Défense de cracher par terre,* pp. 7–46.

– 'Usage spontané et usage littéraire du breton.' *Les Temps Modernes* 324–6 (août–septembre 1973): 195–212.

Pluskelleg, Annie. *Anjela Duval: He buhez hag hec'h oberoù.* Lesneven: Mouladurioù Hor Yezh, 1985.

Rannou, Pascal. *Inventaire d'un héritage: Essai sur l'oeuvre littéraire de Pierre-Jakez Hélias.* Relecq-Kerhuon: An Here, 1997.

Raoul, Lukian. *Geriadur ar skrivagnerien ha yezhourien vrezhonek, aet da anaon a-raok miz Meurzh 1992.* Brest: Al Liamm, 1992.

Reed-Danahay, Deborah E. 'Leaving Home: Schooling Stories and the Ethnography of Auto-Ethnography in Rural France.' In her ed. *Auto-Ethnography: Rewriting the Self and the Social.* Oxford: Berg, 1997, pp. 123–43.

Renault, Annaig. 'Maodez Glanndour.' *Al Liamm* 302–3 (Mae–Eost 1997): 316–26.

– 'Paol Tirili, ur c'hevrinad?' *Al Liamm* 253 (Meurzh–Ebrel 1989): 128–32.

Rudel, Yves-Marie. *Panorama de la littérature bretonne, des origines à nos jours: Ecrivains de langue bretonne et de langue française.* Rennes: Imprimerie Bretonne, 1950.

Stéphan, Andrée. 'Pouldreuzic et Péribonka: Les communautés rurales du *Cheval d'orgueil* et de *Maria Chapdelaine.' Etudes canadiennes* 12 (1986): 227–34.

Talbot, Yann. 'Añjela Duval (Doue d'he fardono!): Ur plac'h hag he stourm.' *Al Liamm* 210 (Genver–C'hwevrer 1982): 55–69.

Ternes, Elmar. 'The Breton Language.' In *The Celtic Languages.* Ed. Donald MacAulay. Cambridge: Cambridge University Press, 1992, pp. 371–452.

Timm, Lenora A. 'Añjela Duval: Breton Poet, Peasant, and Militant.' *Women's Studies International Forum* 9 (1986): 481–90.

– *A Modern Breton Political Poet, Anjela Duval: A Biography and an Anthology.* Lewiston: Edwin Mellen, 1990.

– 'The Shifting Linguistic Frontier in Brittany.' In *Essays in Honor of Charles F. Hockett.* Ed. Frederick B. Agard et al. Leiden: Brill, 1983, pp. 443–57.

Tymen, Yves, ed. *Roparz Hemon: 1900–1978.* Lorient: Dalc'homp Soñj, 1990.

Vassal, Jacques. *La Nouvelle Chanson bretonne.* Paris: Michel, 1973.

Vetter, Eva. *Nicht mehr Bretonisch? Sprachkonflikt in der ländischen Bretagne.* Frankfurt am Main: Peter Lang, 1997.

4 OCCITAN

Alibert, Loïs. 'Oc renaissent.' *Oc* 132 (julh–agost de 1931): 1–4.
– 'Porguem nostra lenga.' *Oc* 181 (julh de 1951): 34–7.
Alranq, Claude. *Théâtre d'oc contemporain: Les arts de jouer du Midi de la France.* Pézenas: Editions Domens, 1995.
Anatole, Christian, ed. *Jean Boudou (1920–1975): Actes du Colloque de Naucelle (27, 28 et 29 septembre 1985).* Béziers: Centre International de Documentation Occitane, 1987.
– ed. *René Nelli (1906–1982): Actes du Colloque de Toulouse (6 et 7 décembre 1985).* Béziers: Centre International de Documentation Occitane, 1986.
Aréthuse: Cahiers du Centre de Recherches sur la poésie contemporaine, Université de Pau 1 (1985).
Arfi, Gilles. 'Entre éternité et néant, le temps dans la poésie nellienne.' In Anatole, *René Nelli,* pp. 21–37.
Arrouye, Jean. 'Joan Bodon, romancier de l'exil.' In Anatole, *Jean Boudou,* pp. 173–87.
– 'La rumors dels arbres dins l'obra poètica occitana de Renat Nelli.' In Anatole, *René Nelli,* pp. 45–56.
Auteurs en scène: Théâtres d'Oc … et d'ailleurs 2 (décembre 1997): *Bernard Manciet: La voix d'une oeuvre.*
Auzias, Jean-Marie. 'Le local et le global, le proche et le lointain dans la littérature occitane actuelle.' In Gardy, *Vingt ans,* pp. 26–31.
– 'La place de Bernard Manciet dans la littérature occitane moderne.' In Latry, *Bernard Manciet,* pp. 157–62.
Bard, Frederic, and Jan-Maria Carlotti, eds. *Antologia de la nòva cançon occitana.* Aix-en-Provence: Edisud, 1982.
Blasco Ferrer, Eduardo. 'Réflexions autour de l'identification: conscience linguistique = communauté minoritaire. Parallélismes et divergences entre les cas sarde, catalan, dolomitique et occitan.' In Pic, *L'Identité occitane,* pp. 7–19.
Bodon, Joan [Jean Boudou]. *La Grava sul camin.* Rodez: Edicions de Roergue, 1988.
– *Lo Libre dels Grands Jorns (roman).* Rodez: Edicions de Roergue, 1996.
– *La Santa Estèla del centenari: Conte.* Rodez: Edicions de Roergue, 1990.
Bosc, Zefir. 'J. Bodon e lo Felibrige.' In Anatole, *Jean Boudou,* pp. 37–45.
Brenon, Anne. 'L'inspiration dualiste dans la poésie de René Nelli.' In Anatole, *René Nelli,* pp. 57–80.

Brun, Joan-Frederic. 'Pòst-occitanisme.' *Oc* 300 (julhet de 1991): 202–10.
– 'Sensualitat e metafisica dins l'òbra poëtica occitana de Renat Nelli.' In Anatole, *René Nelli*, pp. 81–8.
Calin, William. '*Camin de la Crous*: Max-Philippe Delavouët et le baroque sacré.' In Gouiran, *Contacts de langues*, vol. 2, pp. 417–27.
– 'Du réalisme magique dans le roman occitan: Lecture subversive de *La Santa Estèla del centenari* de J. Boudou.' In Gourc, *Toulouse*, pp. 477–80.
– '*L'Enterrament a Sabres* et les structures de l'imaginaire: Bernard Manciet de *R* à *S*.' In Latry, *Bernard Manciet*, pp. 13–24.
– '*La Grava sul camin* de J. Bodon: Technique narrative, phénoménologie et les structures du désir.' In *Actes du premier Congrès International de l'Association Internationale d'Etudes Occitanes*. Ed. Peter T. Ricketts. London: Westfield College, 1987, pp. 149–56.
– 'Lecture de *Pouèmo* de Max-Philippe Delavouët.' In Gardy, *Vingt ans*, pp. 88–94.
– 'La littérature occitane contemporaine: Un témoignage.' *Garona* 10 (1993): 131–8.
– 'Occitan Literature Today: Cultural Identity and the Sense of the Past.' *Tenso* 11 (1995–6): 64–77.
– 'Suggestions de lecture pour nos textes occitans modernes.' *Bulletins de l'Association Internationale d'Etudes Occitanes* 7 (1991): 40–53.
Calin, William, and Fritz Peter Kirsch. 'Les tâches de la recherche occitane: Le texte littéraire des XIXe et XXe siècles.' *Bulletins de l'Association Internationale d'Etudes Occitanes* 1 (1985): 21–4.
Camproux, Charles [Carles Camprós]. *Histoire de la littérature occitane*. Paris: Payot, 1953.
– 'Problèma politic?' *Oc* 220–1 (abriu–setembre de 1961): 14.
Casanova, Jean-Yves [Joan-Ives]. 'Métaphores et images poétiques dans l'*Enterrament a Sabres*: De la parole au style.' In Latry, *Bernard Manciet*, pp. 53–61.
– 'Renat Nelli e la filosofia catara.' *Jorn* 7–8 (1982): 24–5.
Castan, Félix-Marcel. 'La direccion de nòstra renaissença poëtica.' *Oc* 208–10 (abril-desembre de 1959): 51–62.
– 'La Gaita, Nelli.' *Oc* n.s. 15 (setembre de 1982): 23–33.
– 'Manciet et le concept de littérature: Du dialecte à la langue.' In Latry, *Bernard Manciet*, pp. 163–7.
– 'Perspective occitane.' *Europe* 669–70 (janvier–février 1985): 12–18.
– 'Pour l'Institut d'Etudes Occitanes ... 1945–1964.' *Estudis occitans* 18 (2nd semèstre de 1995): 45–59.
– 'René Nelli, Jean Boudou: Deux écrivains, une seule littérature.' *Europe* 669–70 (janvier–février 1985): 29–34.

Cierbide, Ricardo, ed. *Actes du IVe Congrès International de l'Association Internationale d'Etudes Occitanes: Vitoria-Gasteiz, 22–28 août 1993.* 2 vols. Vitoria-Gasteiz: Universidad del País Vasco, 1994.

Colloque international sur la recherche en domaine occitan: 28, 29, 30 août 1974, Béziers. Montpellier: Centre d'Estudis Occitans, Universitat de Montpelhièr III, 1975.

Coulon, Christian. 'La politique de Manciet: Les frontières du vent.' In Latry, *Bernard Manciet,* pp. 113–25.

Delavouët, Mas-Felipe [Max-Philippe]. *Pouèmo.* Vols 1–3. Paris: Corti, 1971–7. Vols 4–5. Saint-Remy de Provence: C.R.E.M., 1983–91.

Enseigner l'occitan: Le tableau est-il si noir? Amiras/Repères 21 (1990).

Eucher, René. 'Le balancement dialectique dans les pièces tardives: Les *Òdas* et le *Temps folzejat.*' In Anatole, *René Nelli,* pp. 107–18.

Forêt, Jean-Claude [Joan-Claudi]. 'Cor e racacor, quauquei aspèctes de l'eroi lafontian.' In Peladan, *Universitat occitana,* pp. 19–43.

– *La Pèira d'asard.* Institut d'Estudis Occitans / Parlarem en Vivarès / Ostal del Libre, 1990.

Garavini, Fausta. *L'Empèri dóu Soulèu: La ragione dialettale nella Francia d'oc.* Milan and Naples: Ricciardi, 1967.

– *La letteratura occitanica moderna.* Florence: Sansoni; Milan: Accademia, 1970.

Gardy, Philippe [Felip]. 'A propos du *temps folzejat*: La veine hésiodique.' In Anatole, *René Nelli,* pp. 119–29.

– 'Dans les bourrasques du siècle: La littérature occitane.' In Gardy, *Vingt ans,* pp. 10–14.

– 'Une écriture de l'ambiguïté? Le "lien à la langue" dans l'écriture occitane, 1965–1994.' In his *L'Ecriture occitane contemporaine,* pp. 79–97.

– *Une Ecriture en archipel: Cinquante ans de poésie occitane (1940–1990).* Eglise-Neuve-d'Issac: Fédérop, 1992.

– *L'Ecriture occitane contemporaine: Une quête des mots.* Paris: L'Harmattan, 1996.

– 'Entre l'infèrn e lo paradís: L'escriure romanesc de Joan Bodon.' In Anatole, *Jean Boudou,* pp. 247–58.

– 'La langue comme étiquette ou les dégelées du sense.' In Pic, *L'Identité occitane,* pp. 99–116.

– 'Legir la "literatura" occitana.' *Obradors* n.s. 1 (1973): 49–63.

– 'OC, ò lei camins d'una originalitat literària.' *Oc* 300 (julhet de 1991): 60–5.

– 'Los païsatges mitologics dins lo roman occitan (1950–1986): Assag d'aproximacion preliminara.' In Gasca Queirazza, *Atti,* pp. 441–54.

– 'Le roman (1950–1990) comme métaphore de la langue.' In his *L'Ecriture occitane contemporaine,* pp. 63–78.

- 'Tantale romancier? Sur l'oeuvre romantique de Robert Lafont.' In Peladan, *Universitat occitana*, pp. 65–85.
- 'Lo temps que se revira: Renat Nelli, Joë Bousquet.' *Jorn* 7–8 (1982): 17–19.

Gardy, Philippe, and François Pic, eds. *Vingt ans de littérature d'expression occitane, 1968–1988: Actes du Colloque International (Château de Castries, 25, 26, 27 et 28 octobre 1989)*. Montpellier: Section Française de l'Association Internationale d'Etudes Occitanes, 1990.

Gasca Queirazza, Giuliano, ed. *Atti del Secondo Congresso Internazionale della 'Association Internationale d'Etudes Occitanes': Torino, 31 agosto–5 settembre 1987*. 2 vols. Turin: Dipartimento di Scienze Letterarie, Università di Torino, 1993.

Ginestet, Joëlle. *Jean Boudou: La force d'aimer*. Vienna: Edition Praesens, 1997.
- 'Negre e blanc: Una dinamica de l'òbra de Joan Bodon.' In Gourc, *Toulouse*, vol. 2, pp. 481–91.

Gouiran, Gérard, ed. *Contacts de langues, de civilisations et intertextualité: Troisième Congrès international de l'Association Internationale d'Etudes Occitanes, Montpellier, 20–26 septembre 1990*. 3 vols. Montpellier: Centre d'Etudes Occitanes de l'Université de Montpellier, 1992.

Gourc, Jacques. 'Poétique et "Trobar" dans *Arma de Vertat*.' In Anatole, *René Nelli*, pp. 131–8.

Gourc, Jacques, and François Pic, eds. *Toulouse à la croisée des cultures: Actes du Ve Congrès international de l'Association Internationale d'Etudes Occitanes, Toulouse, 19–24 août 1996*. 2 vols. Pau: Association Internationale d'Etudes Occitanes, 1998.

Greco, Rosa Anna. 'Chemins de la poésie occitane contemporaine.' In Gardy, *Vingt ans*, pp. 58–62.
- 'La nuova generazione di autori nello spazio letterario occitanico contemporaneo.' *Quaderni* (Università degli Studi di Lecce. Facoltà di Magistero. Istituto di Lingue e Letterature Straniere.) 5 (1983): 209–77.

Hahn, Uta. 'Jean Boudou: Le double pays.' In Gourc, *Toulouse*, vol. 2, pp. 493–8.
- 'Réaliser l'invisible'– imaginer le réel: La poésie de René Nelli.' In Cierbide, *Actes*, vol. 2, pp. 469–78.
- 'René Nelli – le langage à contre courant.' *Bulletins de l'Association Internationale d'Etudes Occitanes* 14 (avril 1998): 107–13.

Icard, Muriel. 'Bernard Manciet: D'une occitanité vers d'autres cultures.' *Garona* 1 (juin 1985): 67–79.

L'I.E.O. e l'occitanisme dempuèi 1945. *Estudis occitans* 18 (2nd semèstre de 1995).

Jeanjean, Henri. *De l'utopie au pragmatisme? (Le mouvement occitan, 1976–1990)*. Perpignan: Trabucaire, 1992.

Joan Bodon: Documents. Toulouse: Centre regional d'Estudis Occitans, 1975.

Julien, Danielle [Danièla]. *Per legir 'La Festa' de Robert Lafont.* Montpellier: Centre d'Estudis Occitans de l'Universitat Paul-Valéry, n.d.

– 'Etudes sur *La Festa* de Robert Lafont.' Diss., Université de Montpellier, 1996.

– 'Statuts et fonctions de la langue dans l'oeuvre de Robert Lafont.' In Gourc, *Toulouse,* vol. 2, pp. 527–35.

Kirsch, Fritz Peter. 'La Natura en çò de Joan Bodon.' In Gardy, *Vingt ans,* pp. 80–6.

– 'Pier Paolo Pasolini et la littérature d'oc.' In Gouiran, *Contacts de langues,* pp. 473–84.

– *Studien zur languedokischen und gaskognischen Literatur der Gegenwart.* Vienna: Braumüller, 1965.

– 'Temps e istòria dins l'òbra narrativa de Robèrt Lafont.' In Gasca Queirazza, *Atti,* vol. 1, pp. 465–78.

Kisters, Andreas. *Un païs que vòl cantar: Okzitanische Musik der Gegenwart als Beispiel für Regionalismus in der populären Musikkultur.* Vienna: Edition Praesens, 1997.

Kremnitz, Georg [Jòrdi]. 'Bodon e Alemanha.' In Anatole, *Jean Boudou,* pp. 207–18.

– 'Conditions psycholinguistiques et sociolinguistiques de l'écriture occitane actuelle.' In Gardy, *Vingt ans,* pp. 16–25.

– ed. *Entfremdung, Selbstbefreiung und Norm: Texte aus der okzitanischen Soziolinguistik.* Tübingen: Narr, 1982.

– *Die ethnischen Minderheiten Frankreichs: Bilanz und Möglichkeiten für den Französischunterricht.* Tübingen: Narr, 1975.

– *Das Okzitanische: Sprachgeschichte und Soziologie.* Tübingen: Niemeyer, 1981.

– 'Réflexions sur une politique de la traduction du texte littéraire occitan.' In *Flor enversa: Actes du Colloque International.* Toulouse: Conservatoire Occitan, 1992, pp. 40–6.

– 'Sartre et Lafont, Lafont et Sartre.' In Peladan, *Universitat occitana,* pp. 10–18.

– *Versuche zur Kodifizierung des Okzitanischen seit dem 19. Jahrhundert und ihre Annahme durch die Sprecher.* Tübingen: Narr, 1974.

Krispin, Arno. 'René Nelli: Poésie et folklore, le *monde merveilleux* et le *joi* des troubadours.' In Anatole, *René Nelli,* pp. 139–54.

Lafont, Robert. *Clefs pour l'Occitanie.* Paris: Seghers, 1971.

– *La Croisade.* Aix-en-Provence: Edisud, 1983.

– *Décoloniser en France: Les régions face à l'Europe.* Paris: Gallimard, 1971.

– *La Festa.* 2 vols. Lyon/Paris: Obradors / Fédérop / Le Chemin Vert, 1983–4.

– *L'Icòna dins l'iscla: Faula.* Montpellier: Institut d'Estudis Occitans, 1979.

– 'La langue des poètes occitans contemporains.' *Europe* 669–70 (janvier–février 1985): 96–7.

– *La Loba, ò la frucha di tres aubas: Peça de tres actes.* Avignon: Aubanel, 1959.
– *Mistral ou l'illusion.* Paris: Plon, 1954.
– 'Lo mite de la feminitat dins l'òbra romanesca de Bodon.' In Anatole, *Jean Boudou,* pp. 159–65.
– 'Nivèls de lenga e de lengatges dins l'escrich occitan: Introduccion a una estilistica d'oc.' *Obradors* 1 (1969): 7–21 and 2 (1969): 5–19.
– 'Le pli dans l'oeuvre.' In Latry, *Bernard Manciet,* pp. 45–51.
– *La Revendication occitane.* Paris: Flammarion, 1974.
– *La Révolte des 'Cascavèus' / Lei Cascavèus.* Toulon: Centre Dramatique Occitan de Provence, 1977.
– *La Révolution régionaliste.* Paris: Gallimard, 1967.
– *Sur la France.* Paris: Gallimard, 1968.
– 'Lo temps coma arquitectura d'*Arma de Vertat.*' In Anatole, *René Nelli,* pp. 155–63.
– *Vida de Joan Larsinhac: Racònte.* Montpellier: Institut d'Estudis Occitans, 1978.
Lafont, Robert, and Christian Anatole. *Nouvelle Histoire de la littérature occitane.* 2 vols. Paris: Presses Universitaires de France, 1970.
Lapassade, Roger. 'La pensada de J. Bodon: Après leger *Lo Libre dels grands jorns.*' In Anatole, *Jean Boudou,* pp. 189–92.
Larzac, Jean [Joan]. *Descolonisar l'istòria occitana.* 2 vols. Toulouse: Institut d'Estudis Occitans, 1977–80.
– *Òbra poëtica.* Institut d'Estudis Occitans, 1986.
– 'Santat o fin dels temps?' *Viure* 5 (prima de 1966): 2–6.
– 'Trois poètes d'oc et la conscience occitane.' *Esprit* n.s. 5 (1962): 756–67.
Latry, Guy. 'Bernard Manciet, de B à M.' In Gardy, *Vingt ans,* pp. 102–7.
– ed. *Bernard Manciet: Le feu est dans la langue. Actes du Colloque de Bordeaux (20 et 21 novembre 1992.)* Centre d'Etude de la Littérature Occitane / William Blake, 1996.
Le Roy Ladurie, Emmanuel. *Montaillou, village occitan, de 1294 à 1324.* Paris: Gallimard, 1975.
Manciet, Bernard. *L'Enterrament a Sabres.* Garein, Landes: Editions Ultreïa, 1989. 2nd ed. Bordeaux: Mollat, 1996.
– *Gesta: Poèmes.* Agen: Cap e Cap, 1972.
– *Le Triangle des Landes.* Paris: Arthaud, 1981.
Manciet, Bernard, and Félix Castan. 'Manifèst neraqués-montalbanés.' *Oc* 204 (abril-mai-junh de 1957): 95–6.
Marconot, Jean-Marie. 'Structure religieuse du livre de Catòia.' In Anatole, *Jean Boudou,* pp. 146–58.
– 'Le thème religieux dans l'oeuvre de Bodon (*Livre des grands jours*).' In Gasca Queirazza, *Atti,* vol. 1, pp. 479–95.

Martel, Philippe. 'Poésie révolutionnaire en occitan.' In Gardy, *Vingt ans*, pp. 64–73.

Marti, Robèrt. 'Lo fantastic dins l'òbra de J. Bodon.' In Anatole, *Jean Boudou*, pp. 243–6.

Mauron, Claude. *Bibliographie de Mas-Felipe Delavouët*. Nîmes: Barnier, 1992.

– 'Dóu *Rollan a Saragosssa*, en ancian prouvençau, a la *Balado d'aquéu que fasié Rouland* en prouvençau moderne, de Mas-Felipe Delavouët.' In Gouiran, *Contacts de langues*, vol. 2, pp. 505–18.

– 'Le portail de Saint-Trophime d'Arles chez F. Mistral et M. Ph. Delavouët.' *Lou Prouvençau a l'escolo* 65:2 (1973–4): 12–16.

– '*Pouèmo* de Max-Philippe Delavouët.' *Marseille* 91:4 (1972): 79–84; 92:1 (1973): 62–9.

– 'Un "Tristan" en provençal moderne: *Ço que Tristan se disié sus la mar*, de Max-Philippe Delavouët.' *Revue des langues romanes* 82 (1977): 181–93.

Nelli, René [Renat]. 'Declaración.' *Oc* 165 (ivèrn de 1943): 1–3.

– *L'Erotique des troubadours*. Toulouse: Privat, 1963.

– *Òbra poëtica occitana (1940–1980)*. Montpellier: Institut d'Estudis Occitans, 1981.

'Orientacion.' *Oc* 300 (julhet de 1991): 5–7.

Peladan, Jòrdi, ed. *Universitat occitana d'estiu: Actes de l'Université d'été, 1994*. Vol. 2. Nîmes: M.A.R.P.O.C./I.E.O., 1995.

Petit, Jean-Marie. 'Des mots pour un Bestiaire.' In Anatole, *René Nelli*, pp. 165–71.

– 'Jean Boudou et la tradition orale du conte occitan.' In Anatole, *Jean Boudou*, pp. 121–30.

Pic, François. 'Essai de bibliographie de l'oeuvre publiée et inédite de Bernard Manciet.' In Latry, *Bernard Manciet*, pp. 203–41.

– 'Essai de bibliographie de l'oeuvre publiée et inédite de René Nelli.' In Anatole, *René Nelli*, pp. 173–232.

– ed. *L'Identité occitane: Réflexions théoriques et expériences. Actes du Colloque de Béziers (4, 5 et 6 septembre 1986)*. Montpellier: Section Française de l'Association Internationale d'Etudes Occitanes, 1990.

Ravier, Xavier. 'L'ontologie du paysage dans la poésie de René Nelli.' In Anatole, *René Nelli*, pp. 233–44.

Rouanet, Marie, ed. *Occitanie 1970: Les poètes de la décolonisation*. Paris: Oswald, 1971.

Rouquette, Max [Max Roqueta]. '"OC" ten vint ans (1924–1944).' *Oc* 168 (4me trimèstre de 1945): 38–40.

– 'Per saludar Nelli.' *Oc* n.s. 14 (junh de 1982): 17–21.

– 'Rapòrt sul teatre.' *Oc* 185 (julh de 1952): 24–8.

Rouquette, Yves [Ives Roqueta]. *L'Escritura, publica o pas: Poèmas (1972–1987)*. Institut d'Estudis Occitans, 1988.

– *La Littérature d'Oc.* 'Que sais-je?' Paris: Presses Universitaires de France, 1963.

– *La Nouvelle Chanson occitane.* Toulouse: Privat, 1972.

Salles Loustau, Jean. 'Trois écritures de la fin.' In Gardy, *Vingt ans*, pp. 74–8.

Sarpoulet, Jean-Marie. 'Manciet felibre?' In Latry, *Bernard Manciet*, pp. 25–33.

Schlieben-Lange, Brigitte. *Okzitanisch und Katalanisch: Ein Beitrag zur Soziolinguistik zweier romanischer Sprachen.* Tübingen: Narr, 1973.

Séguret, Pierre. 'Jean Boudou, romancier occitan de la pauvreté, héritier des spirituels romans.' In Anatole, *Jean Boudou*, pp. 131–45.

Séguy, Jean-Baptiste. 'De l'aliénation au fantastique: Problèmes de la prose littéraire d'oc.' *Esprit* (décembre 1968): 669–83.

Souyris, Augustin, and Jean-Denis Souyris. 'La violence dans l'oeuvre de J. Boudou.' In Anatole, *Jean Boudou*, pp. 193–205.

Surre-Garcia, Alem. 'La nocion de talvera.' In Anatole, *Jean Boudou*, pp. 219–24.

Thunin, Jean. *La Présence et le mythe: Lecture de l'oeuvre poétique de Mas-Felipe Delavouët.* 2 vols. Salon-de-Provence: La Destinée, 1984.

Torreilles, Claire. 'Bodon, Jaurès et les lycéens.' *Lengas* 16 (1984): 23–32.

– 'Perspectives baroques.' *Impressions du Sud* 23 (automne 1989): 27–33.

– 'La première personne dans l'oeuvre narrative de Robert Lafont.' In Peladan, *Universitat occitana*, pp. 44–64.

– 'Références baroques.' In Gardy, *Vingt ans*, pp. 34–40.

Traimond, Bernard. 'Manciet et l'ethnologie.' In Latry, *Bernard Manciet*, pp. 127–35.

Viaut, Alain. 'L'Espagne dans l'oeuvre de Bernard Manciet.' In Latry, *Bernard Manciet*, pp. 137–49.

Viguièr, Joan-Loïs. 'La revista *OC* e la Catalonha de las annadas trenta o detz ans d'illusion lirica.' *Oc* 300 (julhet de 1991): 88–106.

INDEX